MW00666926

50% OFF Online HESI A2 Prep Course!

Dear Customer,

We consider it an honor and a privilege that you chose our HESI A2 Study Guide. As a way of showing our appreciation and to help us better serve you, we have partnered with Mometrix Test Preparation to offer **50% off our online HESI A2 Prep Course.** Many HESI A2 courses are needlessly expensive and don't deliver enough value. With their course, you get access to the best HESI A2 prep material, and **you only pay half price**.

Mometrix has structured their online course to perfectly complement your printed study guide. The HESI A2 Prep Course contains **in-depth lessons** that cover all the most important topics, **180+ video reviews** that explain difficult concepts, **over 3,350 practice questions** to ensure you feel prepared, and **550+ digital flashcards** so you can fit some studying in while you're on the go.

Online HESI A2 Prep Course

Topics Covered:

- Mathematics
- Reading Comprehension
- Vocabulary and General Knowledge
- Grammar
- Biology
- Chemistry
- Anatomy and Physiology
- And more!

Course Features:

- HESI A2 Study Guide
  - Get content that complements our best-selling study guide.
- 9 Full-Length Practice Tests
  - With over 3,350 practice questions, you can test yourself again and again.
- Mobile Friendly
  - If you need to study on-the-go, the course is easily accessible from your mobile device.
- HESI A2 Flashcards
  - The course includes a flashcard mode consisting of over 550 content cards to help you study.

To receive this discount, simply head to their website: mometrix.com/university/hesi or simply scan this QR code with your smartphone. At the checkout page, enter the discount code: **TPBHESI50**

If you have any questions or concerns, please contact Mometrix at support@mometrix.com.

Sincerely,

Test Prep Books in partnership with Mometrix TEST PREPARATION

SCAN HERE

FREE Test Taking Tips Video/DVD Offer

To better serve you, we created videos covering test taking tips that we want to give you for FREE. **These videos cover world-class tips that will help you succeed on your test.**

We just ask that you send us feedback about this product. Please let us know what you thought about it—whether good, bad, or indifferent.

To get your **FREE videos**, you can use the QR code below or email freevideos@studyguideteam.com with "Free Videos" in the subject line and the following information in the body of the email:

a. The title of your product

b. Your product rating on a scale of 1-5, with 5 being the highest

c. Your feedback about the product

If you have any questions or concerns, please don't hesitate to contact us at info@studyguideteam.com.

Thank you!

SCAN HERE

HESI A2 Study Guide 2024-2025 for Nursing

2,000+ Questions (6 Practice Tests) and Review Prep Book for the HESI Admission Assessment Exam [11th Edition]

Lydia Morrison

Written and edited by TPB Publishing.

ISBN 13: 9781637753965

Table of Contents

Welcome

Dear Reader,

Welcome to your new Test Prep Books study guide! We are pleased that you chose us to help you prepare for your exam. There are many study options to choose from, and we appreciate you choosing us. Studying can be a daunting task, but we have designed a smart, effective study guide to help prepare you for what lies ahead.

Whether you're a parent helping your child learn and grow, a high school student working hard to get into your dream college, or a nursing student studying for a complex exam, we want to help give you the tools you need to succeed. We hope this study guide gives you the skills and the confidence to thrive, and we can't thank you enough for allowing us to be part of your journey.

In an effort to continue to improve our products, we welcome feedback from our customers. We look forward to hearing from you. Suggestions, success stories, and criticisms can all be communicated by emailing us at info@studyguideteam.com.

Sincerely,
Test Prep Books Team

FREE Videos/DVD OFFER

Doing well on your exam requires both knowing the test content and understanding how to use that knowledge to do well on the test. We offer completely FREE test taking tip videos. **These videos cover world-class tips that you can use to succeed on your test.**

To get your **FREE videos**, you can use the QR code below or email freevideos@studyguideteam.com with "Free Videos" in the subject line and the following information in the body of the email:

a. The title of your product
b. Your product rating on a scale of 1-5, with 5 being the highest
c. Your feedback about the product

If you have any questions or concerns, please don't hesitate to contact us at info@studyguideteam.com.

SCAN HERE

Quick Overview

As you draw closer to taking your exam, effective preparation becomes more and more important. Thankfully, you have this study guide to help you get ready. Use this guide to help keep your studying on track and refer to it often.

This study guide contains several key sections that will help you be successful on your exam. The guide contains tips for what you should do the night before and the day of the test. Also included are test-taking tips. Knowing the right information is not always enough. Many well-prepared test takers struggle with exams. These tips will help equip you to accurately read, assess, and answer test questions.

A large part of the guide is devoted to showing you what content to expect on the exam and to helping you better understand that content. In this guide are practice test questions so that you can see how well you have grasped the content. Then, answer explanations are provided so that you can understand why you missed certain questions.

Don't try to cram the night before you take your exam. This is not a wise strategy for a few reasons. First, your retention of the information will be low. Your time would be better used by reviewing information you already know rather than trying to learn a lot of new information. Second, you will likely become stressed as you try to gain a large amount of knowledge in a short amount of time. Third, you will be depriving yourself of sleep. So be sure to go to bed at a reasonable time the night before. Being well-rested helps you focus and remain calm.

Be sure to eat a substantial breakfast the morning of the exam. If you are taking the exam in the afternoon, be sure to have a good lunch as well. Being hungry is distracting and can make it difficult to focus. You have hopefully spent lots of time preparing for the exam. Don't let an empty stomach get in the way of success!

When travelling to the testing center, leave earlier than needed. That way, you have a buffer in case you experience any delays. This will help you remain calm and will keep you from missing your appointment time at the testing center.

Be sure to pace yourself during the exam. Don't try to rush through the exam. There is no need to risk performing poorly on the exam just so you can leave the testing center early. Allow yourself to use all of the allotted time if needed.

Remain positive while taking the exam even if you feel like you are performing poorly. Thinking about the content you should have mastered will not help you perform better on the exam.

Once the exam is complete, take some time to relax. Even if you feel that you need to take the exam again, you will be well served by some down time before you begin studying again. It's often easier to convince yourself to study if you know that it will come with a reward!

Test-Taking Strategies

1. Predicting the Answer

When you feel confident in your preparation for a multiple-choice test, try predicting the answer before reading the answer choices. This is especially useful on questions that test objective factual knowledge. By predicting the answer before reading the available choices, you eliminate the possibility that you will be distracted or led astray by an incorrect answer choice. You will feel more confident in your selection if you read the question, predict the answer, and then find your prediction among the answer choices. After using this strategy, be sure to still read all of the answer choices carefully and completely. If you feel unprepared, you should not attempt to predict the answers. This would be a waste of time and an opportunity for your mind to wander in the wrong direction.

2. Reading the Whole Question

Too often, test takers scan a multiple-choice question, recognize a few familiar words, and immediately jump to the answer choices. Test authors are aware of this common impatience, and they will sometimes prey upon it. For instance, a test author might subtly turn the question into a negative, or he or she might redirect the focus of the question right at the end. The only way to avoid falling into these traps is to read the entirety of the question carefully before reading the answer choices.

3. Looking for Wrong Answers

Long and complicated multiple-choice questions can be intimidating. One way to simplify a difficult multiple-choice question is to eliminate all of the answer choices that are clearly wrong. In most sets of answers, there will be at least one selection that can be dismissed right away. If the test is administered on paper, the test taker could draw a line through it to indicate that it may be ignored; otherwise, the test taker will have to perform this operation mentally or on scratch paper. In either case, once the obviously incorrect answers have been eliminated, the remaining choices may be considered. Sometimes identifying the clearly wrong answers will give the test taker some information about the correct answer. For instance, if one of the remaining answer choices is a direct opposite of one of the eliminated answer choices, it may well be the correct answer. The opposite of obviously wrong is obviously right! Of course, this is not always the case. Some answers are obviously incorrect simply because they are irrelevant to the question being asked. Still, identifying and eliminating some incorrect answer choices is a good way to simplify a multiple-choice question.

4. Don't Overanalyze

Anxious test takers often overanalyze questions. When you are nervous, your brain will often run wild, causing you to make associations and discover clues that don't actually exist. If you feel that this may be a problem for you, do whatever you can to slow down during the test. Try taking a deep breath or counting to ten. As you read and consider the question, restrict yourself to the particular words used by the author. Avoid thought tangents about what the author *really* meant, or what he or she was *trying* to say. The only things that matter on a multiple-choice test are the words that are actually in the question. You must avoid reading too much into a multiple-choice question, or supposing that the writer meant something other than what he or she wrote.

5. No Need for Panic

It is wise to learn as many strategies as possible before taking a multiple-choice test, but it is likely that you will come across a few questions for which you simply don't know the answer. In this situation, avoid panicking. Because most multiple-choice tests include dozens of questions, the relative value of a single wrong answer is small. As much as possible, you should compartmentalize each question on a multiple-choice test. In other words, you should not allow your feelings about one question to affect your success on the others. When you find a question that you either don't understand or don't know how to answer, just take a deep breath and do your best. Read the entire question slowly and carefully. Try rephrasing the question a couple of different ways. Then, read all of the answer choices carefully. After eliminating obviously wrong answers, make a selection and move on to the next question.

6. Confusing Answer Choices

When working on a difficult multiple-choice question, there may be a tendency to focus on the answer choices that are the easiest to understand. Many people, whether consciously or not, gravitate to the answer choices that require the least concentration, knowledge, and memory. This is a mistake. When you come across an answer choice that is confusing, you should give it extra attention. A question might be confusing because you do not know the subject matter to which it refers. If this is the case, don't eliminate the answer before you have affirmatively settled on another. When you come across an answer choice of this type, set it aside as you look at the remaining choices. If you can confidently assert that one of the other choices is correct, you can leave the confusing answer aside. Otherwise, you will need to take a moment to try to better understand the confusing answer choice. Rephrasing is one way to tease out the sense of a confusing answer choice.

7. Your First Instinct

Many people struggle with multiple-choice tests because they overthink the questions. If you have studied sufficiently for the test, you should be prepared to trust your first instinct once you have carefully and completely read the question and all of the answer choices. There is a great deal of research suggesting that the mind can come to the correct conclusion very quickly once it has obtained all of the relevant information. At times, it may seem to you as if your intuition is working faster even than your reasoning mind. This may in fact be true. The knowledge you obtain while studying may be retrieved from your subconscious before you have a chance to work out the associations that support it. Verify your instinct by working out the reasons that it should be trusted.

8. Key Words

Many test takers struggle with multiple-choice questions because they have poor reading comprehension skills. Quickly reading and understanding a multiple-choice question requires a mixture of skill and experience. To help with this, try jotting down a few key words and phrases on a piece of scrap paper. Doing this concentrates the process of reading and forces the mind to weigh the relative importance of the question's parts. In selecting words and phrases to write down, the test taker thinks about the question more deeply and carefully. This is especially true for multiple-choice questions that are preceded by a long prompt.

9. Subtle Negatives

One of the oldest tricks in the multiple-choice test writer's book is to subtly reverse the meaning of a question with a word like *not* or *except*. If you are not paying attention to each word in the question, you can easily be led astray by this trick. For instance, a common question format is, "Which of the following is...?" Obviously, if the question instead is, "Which of the following is not...?," then the answer will be quite different. Even worse, the test makers are aware of the potential for this mistake and will include one answer choice that would be correct if the question were not negated or reversed. A test taker who misses the reversal will find what he or she believes to be a correct answer and will be so confident that he or she will fail to reread the question and discover the original error. The only way to avoid this is to practice a wide variety of multiple-choice questions and to pay close attention to each and every word.

10. Reading Every Answer Choice

It may seem obvious, but you should always read every one of the answer choices! Too many test takers fall into the habit of scanning the question and assuming that they understand the question because they recognize a few key words. From there, they pick the first answer choice that answers the question they believe they have read. Test takers who read all of the answer choices might discover that one of the latter answer choices is actually *more* correct. Moreover, reading all of the answer choices can remind you of facts related to the question that can help you arrive at the correct answer. Sometimes, a misstatement or incorrect detail in one of the latter answer choices will trigger your memory of the subject and will enable you to find the right answer. Failing to read all of the answer choices is like not reading all of the items on a restaurant menu: you might miss out on the perfect choice.

11. Spot the Hedges

One of the keys to success on multiple-choice tests is paying close attention to every word. This is never truer than with words like *almost*, *most*, *some*, and *sometimes*. These words are called "hedges" because they indicate that a statement is not totally true or not true in every place and time. An absolute statement will contain no hedges, but in many subjects, the answers are not always straightforward or absolute. There are always exceptions to the rules

in these subjects. For this reason, you should favor those multiple-choice questions that contain hedging language. The presence of qualifying words indicates that the author is taking special care with his or her words, which is certainly important when composing the right answer. After all, there are many ways to be wrong, but there is only one way to be right! For this reason, it is wise to avoid answers that are absolute when taking a multiple-choice test. An absolute answer is one that says things are either all one way or all another. They often include words like *every*, *always*, *best*, and *never*. If you are taking a multiple-choice test in a subject that doesn't lend itself to absolute answers, be on your guard if you see any of these words.

12. Long Answers

In many subject areas, the answers are not simple. As already mentioned, the right answer often requires hedges. Another common feature of the answers to a complex or subjective question are qualifying clauses, which are groups of words that subtly modify the meaning of the sentence. If the question or answer choice describes a rule to which there are exceptions or the subject matter is complicated, ambiguous, or confusing, the correct answer will require many words in order to be expressed clearly and accurately. In essence, you should not be deterred by answer choices that seem excessively long. Oftentimes, the author of the text will not be able to write the correct answer without offering some qualifications and modifications. Your job is to read the answer choices thoroughly and completely and to select the one that most accurately and precisely answers the question.

13. Restating to Understand

Sometimes, a question on a multiple-choice test is difficult not because of what it asks but because of how it is written. If this is the case, restate the question or answer choice in different words. This process serves a couple of important purposes. First, it forces you to concentrate on the core of the question. In order to rephrase the question accurately, you have to understand it well. Rephrasing the question will concentrate your mind on the key words and ideas. Second, it will present the information to your mind in a fresh way. This process may trigger your memory and render some useful scrap of information picked up while studying.

14. True Statements

Sometimes an answer choice will be true in itself, but it does not answer the question. This is one of the main reasons why it is essential to read the question carefully and completely before proceeding to the answer choices. Too often, test takers skip ahead to the answer choices and look for true statements. Having found one of these, they are content to select it without reference to the question above. The savvy test taker will always read the entire question before turning to the answer choices. Then, having settled on a correct answer choice, he or she will refer to the original question and ensure that the selected answer is relevant. The mistake of choosing a correct-but-irrelevant answer choice is especially common on questions related to specific pieces of objective knowledge.

15. No Patterns

One of the more dangerous ideas that circulates about multiple-choice tests is that the correct answers tend to fall into patterns. These erroneous ideas range from a belief that B and C are the most common right answers, to the idea that an unprepared test-taker should answer "A-B-A-C-A-D-A-B-A." It cannot be emphasized enough that pattern-seeking of this type is exactly the WRONG way to approach a multiple-choice test. To begin with, it is highly unlikely that the test maker will plot the correct answers according to some predetermined pattern. The questions are scrambled and delivered in a random order. Furthermore, even if the test maker was following a pattern in the assignation of correct answers, there is no reason why the test taker would know which pattern he or she was using. Any attempt to discern a pattern in the answer choices is a waste of time and a distraction from the real work of taking the test. A test taker would be much better served by extra preparation before the test than by reliance on a pattern in the answers.

Bonus Content

We host multiple bonus items online, including all six practice tests in digital format. Scan the QR code or go to this link to access this content:

testprepbooks.com/bonus/hesi

The first time you access the page, you will need to register as a "new user" and verify your email address.

If you have any issues, please email support@testprepbooks.com.

Introduction to the HESI Admission Assessment

Function of the Test

The Health Education Systems, Inc. (HESI) Admission Assessment (A2) Exam is an entrance exam intended for high school graduates seeking admission to post-secondary health programs such as nursing schools. Test-takers have typically not received any training in specific medical subjects. The test is offered nationwide by the colleges and universities that require it as part of an applicant's admission package.

Test Administration

Many of the specifics of the process of HESI administration are determined at the discretion of the testing institution. For instance, each school may choose to administer the entire HESI exam or any portion thereof. Accordingly, there is no set process or schedule for taking the exam; instead, the schedule is determined on a case-by-case basis by the institution administering the exam. Likewise, the cost of the HESI is set by the administering institution. The typical cost is usually around $40-$70.

Find out ahead of time which sections you will be required to take so that you can focus your studying those areas.

Retesting is generally permitted by HESI, but individual schools may have their own rules on the subject. Likewise, individual schools may set their own policies on whether section scores from different sessions of the HESI can be combined to get one score, or whether a score must come from one coherent session. Students with disabilities may seek accommodations from the schools administering the exam.

Test Format

The exam can include up to eight academic sections with the following distribution of questions:

Section	# of Questions
Mathematics	55
Reading Comprehension	55
Vocabulary	55
Grammar	55
Biology	30
Chemistry	30
Anatomy & Physiology	30
Physics	30

Each academic section contains five unscored pilot questions that are only used to gather data on their effectiveness before potentially including them as scored questions on future exams. Additionally, there is a Personality Profile and Learning Style Assessment that may be included. Like the academic sections, schools can pick and choose whether to include one, both, or neither of these assessments. Each takes about 15 minutes, and you do not need to study for them.

Scoring

Prospective students and their educational institutions both receive detailed score reports after a prospective applicant completes the exam. Individual student reports include scoring explanations and breakdowns by topic for incorrect answers. The test taker's results can also include study tips based on the individual's Learning Style assessment and identification of the test taker's dominant personality type, strengths, weaknesses, and suggested learning techniques, based on the Personality Profile.1

There is no set passing score for the HESI. Instead, individual schools set their own requirements and processes for incorporating scores into admissions decisions. However, HESI recommends that RN and HP programs require a 75% score to pass, and that LPN/LVN programs require a 70% score to pass

Study Prep Plan

1 **Schedule** - Develop a study schedule based on the sections of the exam that you will be taking.

2 **Relax** - Test anxiety can hurt event the best students. There are many ways to reduce stress. Find the one that works best for you.

3 **Execute** - Once you have a good plan in place, be sure to stick to it

Sample Study Plans

One Week Study Schedule

Day 1	
Day 2	
Day 3	
Day 4	
Day 5	
Day 6	
Day 7	Take Your Exam!

Two Week Study Schedule

Day 1		Day 8	
Day 2		Day 9	
Day 3		Day 10	
Day 4		Day 11	
Day 5		Day 12	
Day 6		Day 13	
Day 7		Day 14	Take Your Exam!

One Month Study Schedule

Day 1		Day 11		Day 21	
Day 2		Day 12		Day 22	
Day 3		Day 13		Day 23	
Day 4		Day 14		Day 24	
Day 5		Day 15		Day 25	
Day 6		Day 16		Day 26	
Day 7		Day 17		Day 27	
Day 8		Day 18		Day 28	
Day 9		Day 19		Day 29	
Day 10		Day 20		Day 30	Take Your Exam!

Build your prep plan online by visiting:
testprepbooks.com/prep

As you study for your test, we'd like to take the opportunity to remind you that you are capable of great things! With the right tools and dedication, you truly can do anything you set your mind to. The fact that you are holding this book right now shows how committed you are. In case no one has told you lately, you've got this! Our intention behind including this coloring page is to give you the chance to take some time to engage your creative side when you need a little brain-break from studying. As a company, we want to encourage people like you to achieve their dreams by providing good quality study materials for the tests and certifications that improve careers and change lives. As individuals, many of us have taken such tests in our careers, and we know how challenging this process can be. While we can't come alongside you and cheer you on personally, we can offer you the space to recall your purpose, reconnect with your passion, and refresh your brain through an artistic practice. We wish you every success, and happy studying!

Mathematics

Numbers usually serve as an adjective representing a quantity of objects. They function as placeholders for a value. Numbers can be better understood by their type and related characteristics.

Definitions

A few definitions:

Whole numbers: describes a set of numbers that does not contain any fractions or decimals. The set of whole numbers includes zero.

Example: 0, 1, 2, 3, 4, 189, 293 are all whole numbers.

Integers: describes whole numbers and their negative counterparts. (Zero does not have a negative counterpart here. Instead, zero is its own negative.)

Example: -1, -2, -3, -4, -5, 0, 1, 2, 3, 4, 5 are all integers.

-1, -2, -3, -4, -5 are considered negative integers, and 1, 2, 3, 4, 5 are considered positive integers.

Absolute value: describes the value of a number regardless of its sign. The symbol for absolute value is | |.

Example: The absolute value of 24 is 24 or $|24|=24$.

The absolute value of -693 is 693 or $|-693|=693$.

Even numbers: describes any number that can be divided by 2 evenly, meaning the answer has no decimal or remainder portion.

Example: 2, 4, 9082, -2, -16, -504 are all considered even numbers, because they can be divided by 2, without leaving a remainder or forming a decimal. It does not matter whether the number is positive or negative.

Odd numbers: describes any number that does not divide evenly by 2.

Example: 1, 21, 541, 3003, -9, -63, -1257 are all considered odd numbers, because they cannot be divided by 2 without a remainder or a decimal.

Prime numbers: describes a number that is only evenly divisible, resulting in no remainder or decimal, by 1 and itself.

Example: 2, 3, 7, 13, 113 are all considered prime numbers because each can only be evenly divided by 1 and itself.

Composite numbers: describes a positive integer that is formed by multiplying two smaller integers together. Composite numbers can be divided evenly by numbers other than 1 or itself.

Example: 8, 24, 66, 2348, 10002 are all considered composite numbers because they are the result of multiplying two smaller integers together. In particular, these are all divisible by 2.

Decimals: designated by a decimal point which indicates that what follows the point is a value that is less than 1 and is added to the integer number preceding the decimal point. The digit immediately following the decimal point is in the tenths place, the digit following the tenths place is in the hundredths place, and so on.

For example, the decimal number 1.735 has a value greater than 1 but less than 2. The 7 represents seven tenths of the unit 1 (0.7 or $\frac{7}{10}$); the 3 represents three hundredths of 1 (0.03 or $\frac{3}{100}$); and the 5 represents five thousandths of 1 (0.005 or $\frac{5}{1000}$).

Real numbers: describes rational numbers and irrational numbers.

Rational numbers: describes any number that can be expressed as a fraction, with a non-zero denominator. Since any integer can be written with 1 in the denominator without changing its value, all integers are considered rational numbers. Every rational number has a decimal expression that terminates or repeats. That is, any rational number either will have a countable number of nonzero digits or will end with an ellipsis or a bar (3.6666... or $3.\bar{6}$) to depict repeating decimal digits. Some examples of rational numbers include 12, -3.54, $110.\overline{256}$, $\frac{-35}{10}$, and $4.\bar{7}$.

Irrational numbers: describes numbers that cannot be written as a finite or repeating decimal. Pi (π) is considered to be an irrational number because its decimal portion is unending or a non-repeating decimal. Pi (π) is the most common irrational number, but there are other well-known irrational numbers like e and $\sqrt{2}$.

Basic Addition and Subtraction

Addition

Addition is the combination of two numbers so their quantities are added together cumulatively. The sign for an addition operation is the+symbol. For example, $9 + 6 = 15$. The 9 and 6 combine to achieve a cumulative value, called a **sum**.

Addition holds the **commutative property**, which means that the order of the numbers in an addition equation can be switched without altering the result. The formula for the commutative property is $a + b = b + a$. Let's look at a few examples to see how the commutative property works:

$$7 = 3 + 4 = 4 + 3 = 7$$

$$20 = 12 + 8 = 8 + 12 = 20$$

Addition also holds the **associative property**, which means that the grouping of numbers doesn't matter in an addition problem. In other words, the presence or absence of parentheses is irrelevant. The formula for the associative property is $(a + b) + c = a + (b + c)$. Here are some examples of the associative property at work:

$$30 = (6 + 14) + 10 = 6 + (14 + 10) = 30$$

$$35 = 8 + (2 + 25) = (8 + 2) + 25 = 35$$

There are set columns for addition: ones, tens, hundreds, thousands, ten-thousands, hundred-thousands, millions, and so on. To add how many units there are total, each column needs to be combined, starting from the right, or the ones column.

THOUSANDS	HUNDREDS	TENS	ONES

Every 10 units in the ones column equals one in the tens column, and every 10 units in the tens column equals one in the hundreds column, and so on.

Example: The number 5,432 has 2 ones, 3 tens, 4 hundreds, and 5 thousands. The number 371 has 3 hundreds, 7 tens and 1 one. To combine, or add, these two numbers, simply add up how many units of each column exist. The best way to do this is by lining up the columns:

$$\begin{array}{r} 5\,4\,3\,2 \\ +\quad 3\,7\,1 \\ \hline \end{array}$$

The ones column adds $2 + 1$ for a total (sum) of 3.

The tens column adds $3 + 7$ for a total of 10; since 10 of that unit was collected, add 1 to the hundreds column to denote the total in the next column:

$$\begin{array}{r} 1 \\ 5\,4\,3\,2 \\ +\quad 3\,7\,1 \\ \hline 0\,3 \end{array}$$

When adding the hundreds column, this extra 1 needs to be combined, so it would be the sum of 4, 3, and 1.

$$4 + 3 + 1 = 8$$

The last, or thousands, column listed would be the sum of 5. Since there are no other numbers in this column, that is the final total.

The answer would look as follows:

$$\begin{array}{r} 5\,4\,3\,2 \\ +\quad 3\,7\,1 \\ \hline 5\,8\,0\,3 \end{array}$$

Example

Find the sum of 9,734 and 895.

Set up the problem:

$$\begin{array}{r} 9\,7\,3\,4 \\ +\quad 8\,9\,5 \\ \hline \end{array}$$

Total the columns:

$$\begin{array}{r} 9\,7\,3\,4 \\ +\quad 8\,9\,5 \\ \hline 1\,0\,6\,2\,9 \end{array}$$

In this example, another column (ten-thousands) is added to the left of the thousands column, to denote a carryover of 10 units in the thousands column. The final sum is 10,629.

When adding using all negative integers, the total is negative. The integers are simply added together and the negative symbol is tacked on.

$$(-12) + (-435) = -447$$

Subtraction

Subtraction is taking away one number from another, so their quantities are reduced. The sign designating a subtraction operation is the – symbol, and the result is called the **difference**. For example, $9 - 6 = 3$. The number *6* detracts from the number *9* to reach the difference *3*.

Unlike addition, subtraction follows neither the commutative nor associative properties. The order and grouping in subtraction impact the result.

$$15 = 22 - 7 \neq 7 - 22 = -15$$

$$3 = (10 - 5) - 2 \neq 10 - (5 - 2) = 7$$

When working through subtraction problems involving larger numbers, it's necessary to regroup the numbers. Let's work through a practice problem using regrouping:

$$\begin{array}{r} 3\,2\,5 \\ -\ 7\,7 \\ \hline \end{array}$$

Here, it is clear that the ones and tens columns for 77 are greater than the ones and tens columns for 325. To subtract this number, borrow from the tens and hundreds columns. When borrowing from a column, subtracting 1 from the lender column will add 10 to the borrower column:

$$\begin{array}{cccc} & 3-1 & 10+2-1 & 10+5 \\ - & & 7 & 7 \\ \hline \end{array} = \begin{array}{cccc} & 2 & 11 & 15 \\ - & & 7 & 7 \\ \hline & 2 & 4 & 8 \end{array}$$

After ensuring that each digit in the top row is greater than the digit in the corresponding bottom row, subtraction can proceed as normal, and the answer is found to be 248.

Addition and Subtraction with Negative Integers

When adding mixed-sign integers, determine which integer has the larger absolute value. Absolute value is the distance of a number from zero on the number line. Absolute value is indicated by these symbols: ||.

Take this equation for example:

$$12 + (-435)$$

The absolute value of each of the numbers is as follows:

$$|12| = 12$$

$$|-435| = 435$$

Since -435 is the larger integer, the final number will have its sign. In this case, that sign is negative. Now, subtract the smaller integer from the larger one. If this equation is worked out, it will look like this:

$$12 + (-435) = -423$$

Mathematically, the equation looks like the one above, but practically speaking it will be done it like this:

$$435 - 12 = 423$$

(then add the negative sign)

When subtracting with negative integers, every unmarked integer is assumed to have a positive sign. Subtracting an integer is the same as adding a negative integer.

Example:
$-3 - 4$
$-3 + (-4)$
$-3 + (-4) = -7$

Subtracting a negative integer is the same as adding a positive integer.

Example
$-3 - (-4)$
$-3 + 4$
$-3 + 4 = 1$

Multiplication of Whole Numbers

Multiplication involves adding together multiple copies of a number. It is indicated by an $\times$ symbol or a number immediately outside of a parenthesis. For example:

$$5(8 - 2)$$

The two numbers being multiplied together are called **factors**, and their result is called a **product**. For example, $9 \times 6 = 54$. This can be shown alternatively by expansion of either the 9 or the 6:

$$9 \times 6 = 9 + 9 + 9 + 9 + 9 + 9 = 54$$

$$9 \times 6 = 6 + 6 + 6 + 6 + 6 + 6 + 6 + 6 + 6 = 54$$

Like addition, multiplication holds the commutative and associative properties:

$$115 = 23 \times 5 = 5 \times 23 = 115$$

$$84 = 3 \times (7 \times 4) = (3 \times 7) \times 4 = 84$$

Multiplication also follows the **distributive property**, which allows the multiplication to be distributed through parentheses. The formula for distribution is $a \times (b + c) = ab + ac$. This is clear after the examples:

$$45 = 5 \times 9 = 5(3 + 6) = (5 \times 3) + (5 \times 6) = 15 + 30 = 45$$

$$20 = 4 \times 5 = 4(10 - 5) = (4 \times 10) - (4 \times 5) = 40 - 20 = 20$$

For larger-number multiplication, the way the numbers are lined up can make it easier to obtain the product. It is simplest to put the number with the most digits on top and the number with fewer digits on the bottom. If they have the same number of digits, select one for the top and one for the bottom. Line up the problem, and begin by multiplying the far-right column on the top and the far-right column on the bottom. If the answer to a column is more than 9, the ones place digit will be written below that column and the tens place digit will carry to the top of the next column to be added after those digits are multiplied. Write the answer below that column. Move to the next column to the left on the top, and multiply it by the same far-right column on the bottom. Keep moving to the left one column at a time on the top number until the end.

Example

Multiply 37×8

Line up the numbers, placing the one with the most digits on top.

$$\begin{array}{r} 3\ 7 \\ \times\ \ \ 8 \\ \hline \end{array}$$

Multiply the far-right column on the top with the far-right column on the bottom (7×8). Write the answer, 56, as below: The ones value, 6, gets recorded, the tens value, 5, is carried.

$$\begin{array}{r} {\scriptstyle +5}\ \ \ \\ 3\ 7 \\ \times\ \ \ 8 \\ \hline 6 \end{array}$$

Move to the next column left on the top number and multiply with the far-right bottom (3×8). Remember to add any carry over after multiplying: $3 \times 8 = 24$, $24 + 5 = 29$. Since there are no more digits on top, write the entire number below.

$$\begin{array}{r} {\scriptstyle +5}\ \ \ \\ 3\ 7 \\ \times\ \ \ 8 \\ \hline 2\ 9\ 6 \end{array}$$

The solution is 296.

If there is more than one column to the bottom number, move to the row below the first strand of answers, mark a zero in the far-right column, and then begin the multiplication process again with the far-right column on top and the second column from the right on the bottom. For each digit in the bottom number, there will be a row of answers, each padded with the respective number of zeros on the right. Finally, add up all of the answer rows for one total number.

Example: Multiply 512×36.

Line up the numbers (the one with the most digits on top) to multiply.

Begin with the right column on top and the right column on bottom (2×6).

$$\begin{array}{r} 5\ 1\ 2 \\ \times \quad 3\ 6 \\ \hline \end{array}$$

Move one column left on top and multiply by the far-right column on the bottom (1×6). Add the carry over after multiplying: $1 \times 6 = 6, 6 + 1 = 7$.

$$\begin{array}{r} {}^{+1}\ \ \ \\ 5\ 1\ 2 \\ \times \quad 3\ 6 \\ \hline 7\ 2 \end{array}$$

Move one column left on top and multiply by the far-right column on the bottom (5×6). Since this is the last digit on top, write the whole answer below.

$$\begin{array}{r} 5\ 1\ 2 \\ \times \quad 3\ 6 \\ \hline 3\ 0\ 7\ 2 \end{array}$$

Now move on to the second column on the bottom number. Starting on the far-right column on the top, repeat this pattern for the next number left on the bottom (2×3). Write the answers below the first line of answers; remember to begin with a zero placeholder on the far right.

$$\begin{array}{r} 5\ 1\ 2 \\ \times \quad 3\ 6 \\ \hline 3\ 0\ 7\ 2 \\ 6\ 0 \end{array}$$

Continue the pattern (1×3).

$$\begin{array}{r} 5\ 1\ 2 \\ \times \quad 3\ 6 \\ \hline 3\ 0\ 7\ 2 \\ 3\ 6\ 0 \end{array}$$

Since this is the last digit on top, write the whole answer below.

$$\begin{array}{r} 5\ 1\ 2 \\ \times \quad 3\ 6 \\ \hline 3\ 0\ 7\ 2 \\ 1\ 5\ 3\ 6\ 0 \end{array}$$

Now add the answer rows together. Pay attention to ensure they are aligned correctly.

$$\begin{array}{r} 512 \\ \times \quad 36 \\ \hline 3072 \\ 15360 \\ \hline 18432 \end{array}$$

The solution is 18,432.

Division of Whole Numbers

Division and multiplication are inverses of each other in the same way that addition and subtraction are opposites. The signs designating a division operation are the ÷ and / symbols. In division, the second number divides into the first.

The number before the division sign is called the **dividend** or, if expressed as a fraction, the **numerator**. For example, in $a \div b$, a is the dividend, while in $\frac{a}{b}$, a is the numerator.

The number after the division sign is called the **divisor** or, if expressed as a fraction, the **denominator.** For example, in $a \div b$, b is the divisor, while in $\frac{a}{b}$, b is the denominator.

Like subtraction, division doesn't follow the commutative property, as it matters which number comes before the division sign, and division doesn't follow the associative or distributive properties for the same reason. For example:

$$\frac{3}{2} = 9 \div 6 \neq 6 \div 9 = \frac{2}{3}$$

$$2 = 10 \div 5 = (30 \div 3) \div 5 \neq 30 \div (3 \div 5) = 30 \div \frac{3}{5} = 50$$

$$25 = 20 + 5 = (40 \div 2) + (40 \div 8) \neq 40 \div (2 + 8) = 40 \div 10 = 4$$

The answer to a division problem is called the **quotient.** If a divisor doesn't divide into a dividend evenly, whatever is left over is termed the **remainder**. The remainder can be further divided out into decimal form by using long division; however, this doesn't always give a quotient with a finite number of decimal places, so the remainder can also be expressed as a fraction over the original divisor.

Example

Solve $\frac{1,050}{42}$ or $1,050 \div 42$.

Set up the problem with the denominator being divided into the numerator.

$$42 \overline{)1050}$$

Check for divisibility into the first unit of the numerator, 1.

42 cannot go into 1, so add on the next unit in the denominator, 0.

42 cannot go into 10, so add on the next unit in the denominator, 5.

42 can be divided into 105 two times. Write the 2 over the 5 in 105 and multiply 42 x 2. Write the 84 under 105 for subtraction and note the remainder, 21 is less than 42.

$$\begin{array}{r} 2 \\ 42\overline{)1050} \\ -84 \\ \hline 21 \end{array}$$

Drop the next digit in the numerator down to the remainder (making 21 into 210) to create a number 42 can divide into. 42 divides into 210 five times. Write the 5 over the 0 and multiply 42×5.

$$\begin{array}{r} 25 \\ 42\overline{)1050} \\ -84 \\ \hline 210 \end{array}$$

Write the 210 under 210 for subtraction. The remainder is 0.

$$\begin{array}{r} 25 \\ 42\overline{)1050} \\ -84 \\ \hline 210 \\ -210 \\ \hline 0 \end{array}$$

The solution is 25.

Example

Divide $375/4$ or $375 \div 4$.

Set up the problem.

$$4\overline{)375}$$

4 cannot divide into 3, so add the next unit from the numerator, 7. 4 divides into 37 nine times, so write the 9 above the 7. Multiply $4 \times 9 = 36$. Write the 36 under the 37 for subtraction. The remainder is 1 (1 is less than 4).

$$\begin{array}{r} 9 \\ 4\overline{)375} \\ -36 \\ \hline 1 \end{array}$$

Drop the next digit in the numerator, 5, making the remainder 15. 4 divides into 15, three times, so write the 3 above the 5. Multiply 4×3. Write the 12 under the 15 for subtraction, remainder is 3 (3 is less than 4).

```
     9 3
  4|3 7 5
   - 3 6
   -----
     1 5
   - 1 2
   -----
       3
```

The solution is 93 remainder 3 or 93 ¾ (the remainder can be written over the original denominator).

Decimals

Decimals mark the separation between the whole portion and the fractional (or decimal) portion of a number. For example, 3.15 has 3 in the whole portion and 15 in the fractional or decimal portion. A number such as 645 is all whole, but there is still a decimal place. The decimal place in 645 is to the right of the 5, but usually not written, since there is no fractional or decimal portion to this number. The same number can be written as 645.0 or 645.00 or 645.000, etc. The position of the decimal place can change the entire value of a number, and impact a calculation. In the United States, the decimal place is used when representing money. You'll often be asked to round to a certain decimal place. Here is a review of some basic decimal **place value** names:

thousands	hundreds	tens	ones	tenths	hundredths	thousandths

↑ Decimal (between ones and tenths)

The number 12,302.2 would be read as "twelve thousand, three hundred two and two-tenths."

In the United States, a period denotes the decimal place; however, some countries use a comma. The comma is used in the United States to separate thousands, millions, and so on.

To round to the nearest whole number (eliminating the decimal portion), the example would become 12,302. For rounding, go to the number that is one place to the right of what you are rounding to. If the number is 0 through 4, there will be no change. For numbers 5 through 9, round up to the next whole number.

Example

Round 6,423.7 to the ones place.

Since the tenths place is the position to the right of the ones place, we use that number to determine if we round up or not. In this case, the 3 is in the ones place and the 7 is in the tenths place. (6,423.7)

The 7 in the tenths place means we round the 3 up, so the final number will be 6,424.0

Example

Round 542.88 to the nearest tens

Since the ones place is the position to the right of the tens, we use that number to determine if we round up or not. In this case, the 4 is in the tens place and the 2 is in the ones place (542.88).

The 2 in the ones place means we do not round the 4 up, so the final number will be 540.00

Note: Everything to the right of the rounded position goes to 0 as a placeholder.

Example: Say you wanted to post an advertisement to sell a used vehicle for $2000.00. However, when typing the price, you accidentally moved the decimal over one place to the left. Now the asking price appears as $200.00. This difference of a factor of 10 is dramatic. As numbers get bigger or smaller, the impact of this mistake becomes more pronounced. If you were looking to sell a condo for $1,000,000.00, but made an error and moved the decimal place to the left one position, the price posts at $100,000.00. A mistake of a factor of 10 cost $900,000.00.

In dividing by 10, you move the decimal one position to the left, making a smaller number than the original. If multiplying by 10, move the decimal one position to the right, making a larger number than the original.

Example

Divide 100 by 10 or $100 \div 10$.

Move the decimal one place to the left, so the result is a smaller number than the original.

$$100 \div 10 = 10$$

Example

Divide 1.0 by 10 or $1.0 \div 10$.

Move the decimal one place to the left, so the result is a smaller number than the original.

$$1.0 \div 10 = 0.1$$

Example

Multiply 100 by 10 or 100×10.

Move the decimal one place to the right, so the result is a larger number than the original.

$$100 \times 10 = 1{,}000$$

Example

Multiply 0.1 by 10 or 0.1×10.

Move the decimal one place to the right, so the result is a larger number than the original.

$$0.1 \times 10 = 1.0$$

Prefixes

Moving the decimal place to the left or to the right illustrates multiplying or dividing by factors of 10. The metric system of units for measurement utilizes factors of 10 as displayed in the following table:

kilo	1,000 units
hecto	100 units
deca	10 units
base unit	
deci	0.1 units
centi	0.01 units
milli	0.001 units

It is important to have the ability to quickly manipulate by 10 according to prefixes for units.

Example: How many milliliters are in 5 liters of saline solution?

There are 1,000 milliliters for every 1 liter. If we have 5 liters, it would be $5 \times 1{,}000 = 5{,}000$ mL

You may also count the zeros and which side of the decimal place they are on: 1,000 has three zeroes to the left of the decimal, so insert three zeroes between the 5 and the decimal, or move the decimal place over three places to the right, for your answer of 5,000 mL.

Example

How many kilograms are in 4.8 grams?

There is 1 gram for every 0.001 kilograms. Since there is one-thousandth of a kilogram for each gram, that means divide by 1,000, or move the decimal to the left by 3 places – 1 place for each 0. So, the result would be 0.0048 kg.

For quick conversions, move the decimal place the set number of spaces left or right to match the column/slot, as depicted below.

To convert from one prefix to another to the left or right of the base unit (follow the arrow to the left or right), move the decimal place the number of columns/slots as counted.

mega 1,000,000	100,000	10,000	kilo 1,000	hecto 100	deca 10	base unit	deci .1	centi .01	milli .001	.0001	.00001	micro .000001

move decimal to the left   move decimal to the right

Example

How many centiliters are in 4.7 kiloliters?

To convert a number with a unit prefixed as kilo into a unit prefixed as centi, move across five columns to the right, meaning move the decimal place five places to the right.

$$4.7 \text{ kL} = 470{,}000 \text{ cL}$$

Example

How many liters are in 30 microliters?

Start with the unit marked micro and count the columns moving to the left until you reach the base unit for liters. Be sure to count the blank columns, as they are important placeholders. There are six columns from micro to the base unit moving to the left, so move the decimal place six places to the left.

$$30 \text{ mL} = 0.000030 \text{ L}$$

Decimal Addition

Addition with decimals is done the same way as regular addition. All numbers could have decimals, but are often removed if the numbers to the right of the decimal are zeros. Line up numbers at the decimal place.

Example: Add $345.89 + 23.54$

Line the numbers up at the decimal place and add.

$$\begin{array}{r} 345.89 \\ +\quad 23.54 \\ \hline 369.43 \end{array}$$

Decimal Subtraction

Subtraction with decimals is done the same way as regular subtraction.

Example: Subtract $345.89 - 23.54$

Line the numbers up at the decimal place and subtract.

$$\begin{array}{r} 345.89 \\ -\quad 23.54 \\ \hline 322.35 \end{array}$$

Decimal Multiplication

The simplest way to handle multiplication with decimals is to calculate the multiplication problem pretending the decimals are not there, then count how many decimal places there are in the original problem. Use that total to place the decimal the same number of places over, counting from right to left.

Example: Multiply 42.33×3.3

Line the numbers up and multiply, pretending there are no decimals.

$$\begin{array}{r} 4233 \\ \times\quad 33 \\ \hline 12699 \\ 126990 \\ \hline 139689 \end{array}$$

Now look at the original problem and count how many decimal places were removed. Two decimal places were removed from 42.33 to get 4,233, and one decimal place from 3.3 to get 33. Removed were $2 + 1 = 3$ decimal places. Place the decimal three places from the right of the number 139,689. The answer is 139.689.

Another way to think of this is that when you move the decimal in the original numbers, it is like multiplying by 10. To put the decimals back, you need to divide the number by 10 the same amount of times you multiplied. It would still be three times for the above solution.

Example: Multiply 0.03×1.22

Line the numbers up and multiply, pretending there are no decimals. The zeroes in front of the 3 are unnecessary, so take them out for now.

$$\begin{array}{r} 1\ 2\ 2 \\ \times \quad\quad 3 \\ \hline 3\ 6\ 6 \end{array}$$

Look at the original problem and count how many decimals places were removed, or how many times each number was multiplied by 10. The 1.22 moved two places (or multiplied by 10 twice), as did 0.03. That is $2 + 2 = 4$ decimal places removed. Count that number, from right to left of the number 366, and place the decimal. The result is 0.0366.

Decimal Division

Division with decimals is simplest when you eliminate some of the decimal places. Since you divide the bottom number of a fraction into the top, or divide the denominator into the numerator, the bottom number dictates the movement of the decimals. The goal is to remove the decimals from the denominator and mirror that movement in the numerator. You do not need the numerator to be decimal free, however. Divide as you would normally.

Example

Divide $\frac{4.21}{0.2}$ or $4.21 \div 0.2$

Move the decimal over one place to the right in the denominator, making 0.2 simply 2. Move the decimal in the numerator, 4.21, over the same amount, so it is now 42.1.

$$0.2\overline{)4.21}$$

Becomes:

$$2\overline{)42.1}$$

Divide:

$$\begin{array}{r} 21.05 \\ 2\overline{)42.10} \end{array}$$

The answer is 21.05 with the correct decimal placement. In decimal division, move the decimal the same amount for both numerator and denominator. There is no need to adjust anything after the problem is completed.

Fractions

A fraction is an equation that represents a part of a whole but can also be used to present ratios or division problems. An example of a fraction is $\frac{x}{y}$. In this example, x is called the **numerator**, while y is the **denominator**. The numerator represents the number of parts, and the denominator is the total number of parts. They are separated by a line or slash, known as a **fraction bar**. In simple fractions, the numerator and denominator can be nearly any integer. However, the denominator of a fraction can never be zero because dividing by zero is a function that is undefined.

Imagine that an apple pie has been baked for a holiday party, and the full pie has eight slices. After the party, there are five slices left. How could the amount of the pie that remains be expressed as a fraction? The numerator is 5 since there are 5 pieces left, and the denominator is 8 since there were eight total slices in the whole pie. Thus, expressed as a fraction, the leftover pie totals $\frac{5}{8}$ of the original amount.

Fractions come in three different varieties: proper fractions, improper fractions, and mixed numbers. **Proper fractions** have a numerator less than the denominator, such as $\frac{3}{8}$, but **improper fractions** have a numerator greater than the denominator, such as $\frac{7}{2}$. **Mixed numbers** combine a whole number with a proper fraction, such as $3\frac{1}{2}$. Any mixed number can be written as an improper fraction by multiplying the integer by the denominator, adding the product to the value of the numerator, and dividing the sum by the original denominator. For example:

$$3\frac{1}{2} = \frac{3 \times 2 + 1}{2} = \frac{7}{2}$$

Whole numbers can also be converted into fractions by placing the whole number as the numerator and making the denominator 1. For example, $3 = \frac{3}{1}$.

One of the most fundamental concepts of fractions is their ability to be manipulated by multiplication or division. This is possible since $\frac{\text{n}}{\text{n}} = 1$ for any non-zero integer. As a result, multiplying or dividing by $\frac{\text{n}}{\text{n}}$ will not alter the original fraction since any number multiplied or divided by 1 doesn't change the value of that number. Fractions of the same value are known as equivalent fractions. For example, $\frac{2}{4}, \frac{4}{8}, \frac{50}{100}$, and $\frac{75}{150}$ are equivalent, as they all equal $\frac{1}{2}$.

Although many equivalent fractions exist, they are easier to compare and interpret when reduced or simplified. The numerator and denominator of a simple fraction will have no factors in common other than 1. When reducing or simplifying fractions, divide the numerator and denominator by the **greatest common factor**. A simple strategy is to divide the numerator and denominator by low numbers, like 2, 3, or 5 until arriving at a simple fraction, but the same thing could be achieved by determining the greatest common factor for both the numerator and denominator and dividing each by it. Using the first method is preferable when both the numerator and denominator are even, end in 5, or are obviously a multiple of another number. However, if no numbers seem to work, it will be necessary to factor the numerator and denominator to find the GCF. For example:

1) Simplify the fraction $\frac{6}{8}$:

Dividing the numerator and denominator by 2 results in $\frac{3}{4}$, which is a simple fraction.

2) Simplify the fraction $\frac{12}{36}$:

Dividing the numerator and denominator by 2 leaves $\frac{6}{18}$. This isn't a simple fraction, as both the numerator and denominator have factors in common. Dividing each by 3 results in $\frac{2}{6}$, but this can be further simplified by dividing by 2 to get $\frac{1}{3}$. This is the simplest fraction, as the numerator is 1. In cases like this, multiple division operations can be avoided by determining the greatest common factor between the numerator and denominator.

3) Simplify the fraction $\frac{18}{54}$ by dividing by the greatest common factor:

First, determine the factors for the numerator and denominator. The factors of 18 are 1, 2, 3, 6, 9, and 18. The factors of 54 are 1, 2, 3, 6, 9, 18, 27, and 54. Thus, the greatest common factor is 18. Dividing both the numerator and denominator by 18 leaves $\frac{1}{3}$, which is the simplest fraction. This method takes slightly more work, but it definitively arrives at the simplest fraction.

Operations with Fractions

Multiplication of Fractions

Of the four basic operations that can be performed on fractions, the one that involves the least amount of work is multiplication. To multiply two fractions, simply multiply the numerators together, multiply the denominators together, and place the products of each as a fraction. Whole numbers and mixed numbers can also be expressed as a fraction, as described above, to multiply with a fraction. Here are a few examples:

1) $\frac{2}{5} \times \frac{3}{4} = \frac{6}{20} = \frac{3}{10}$

2) $\frac{4}{9} \times \frac{7}{11} = \frac{28}{99}$

Division of Fractions

Dividing fractions is similar to multiplication with one key difference. To divide fractions, flip the numerator and denominator of the second fraction, and then proceed as if it were a multiplication problem:

1) $\frac{7}{8} \div \frac{4}{5} = \frac{7}{8} \times \frac{5}{4} = \frac{35}{32}$

2) $\frac{5}{9} \div \frac{1}{3} = \frac{5}{9} \times \frac{3}{1} = \frac{15}{9} = \frac{5}{3}$

Addition and Subtraction of Fractions

Addition and subtraction require more steps than multiplication and division, as these operations require the fractions to have the same denominator, also called a **common denominator**. It is always possible to find a common denominator by multiplying the denominators. However, when the denominators are large numbers, this method is unwieldy, especially if the answer must be provided in its simplest form. Thus, it's beneficial to find the **least common denominator** of the fractions—the least common denominator is incidentally also the least common multiple.

Once equivalent fractions have been found with common denominators, simply add or subtract the numerators to arrive at the answer:

1) $\frac{1}{2}+\frac{3}{4}=\frac{2}{4}+\frac{3}{4}=\frac{5}{4}$

2) $\frac{3}{12}+\frac{11}{20}=\frac{15}{60}+\frac{33}{60}=\frac{48}{60}=\frac{4}{5}$

3) $\frac{7}{9}-\frac{4}{15}=\frac{35}{45}-\frac{12}{45}=\frac{23}{45}$

4) $\frac{5}{6}-\frac{7}{18}=\frac{15}{18}-\frac{7}{18}=\frac{8}{18}=\frac{4}{9}$

Changing Fractions to Decimals

To change a fraction into a decimal, divide the denominator into the numerator until there are no remainders. There may be repeating decimals, so rounding is often acceptable. A straight line above the repeating portion denotes that the decimal repeats.

Example

Express $\frac{4}{5}$ as a decimal.

Set up the division problem.

$$5\overline{)4}$$

5 does not go into 4, so place the decimal and add a zero.

$$5\overline{)4.0}$$

5 goes into 40 eight times. There is no remainder.

$$\begin{array}{r} 0.8 \\ 5\overline{)4.0} \\ -\underline{4.0} \\ 0 \end{array}$$

The solution is 0.8.

Example

Express $33\frac{1}{3}$ as a decimal.

Since the whole portion of the number is known, set it aside to calculate the decimal from the fraction portion.

Set up the division problem.

$$3\overline{)1}$$

3 does not go into 1, so place the decimal and add zeros. 3 goes into 10 three times.

$$3\overline{)1.0}\quad 0.3$$

This will repeat with a remainder of 1.

```
   0.333
3|1.000
  -9
   10
   -9
    10
```

So, we will place a line over the 3 to denote the repetition. The solution is written $33.\overline{3}$.

Changing Decimals to Fractions

To change decimals to fractions, place the decimal portion of the number, the numerator, over the respective place value, the denominator, then reduce, if possible.

Example

Express 0.25 as a fraction.

This is read as twenty-five hundredths, so put 25 over 100. Then reduce to find the solution.

$$\frac{25}{100} = \frac{1}{4}$$

Example

Express 0.455 as a fraction

This is read as four hundred fifty-five thousandths, so put 455 over 1,000. Then reduce to find the solution.

$$\frac{455}{1000} = \frac{91}{200}$$

There are two types of problems that commonly involve percentages. The first is to calculate some percentage of a given quantity, where you convert the percentage to a decimal, and multiply the quantity by that decimal. Secondly, you are given a quantity and told it is a fixed percent of an unknown quantity. In this case, convert to a decimal, then divide the given quantity by that decimal.

Example

What is 30% of 760?

Convert the percent into a useable number. "Of" means to multiply.

$$30\% = 0.30$$

Set up the problem based on the givens, and solve.

$$0.30 \times 760 = 228$$

Example

8.4 is 20% of what number?

Convert the percent into a useable number.

$$20\% = 0.20$$

The given number is a percent of the answer needed, so divide the given number by this decimal rather than multiplying it.

$$\frac{8.4}{0.20} = 42$$

Ratios and Proportions

Ratios

Ratios are used to show the relationship between two quantities. The ratio of oranges to apples in the grocery store may be 3 to 2. That means that for every 3 oranges, there are 2 apples. This comparison can be expanded to represent the actual number of oranges and apples, such as 36 oranges to 24 apples. Another example may be the number of boys to girls in a math class. If the ratio of boys to girls is given as 2 to 5, that means there are 2 boys to every 5 girls in the class. Ratios can also be compared if the units in each ratio are the same. The ratio of boys to girls in the math class can be compared to the ratio of boys to girls in a science class by stating which ratio is higher and which is lower.

Rates are used to compare two quantities with different units. *Unit rates* are the simplest form of rate. With **unit rates**, the denominator in the comparison of two units is one. For example, if someone can type at a rate of 1,000 words in 5 minutes, then their unit rate for typing is $\frac{1{,}000}{5} = 200$ words in one minute or 200 words per minute. Any rate can be converted into a unit rate by dividing to make the denominator one. 1,000 words in 5 minutes has been converted into the unit rate of 200 words per minute.

Ratios and rates can be used together to convert rates into different units. For example, if someone is driving 50 kilometers per hour, that rate can be converted into miles per hour by using a ratio known as the **conversion factor.** Since the given value contains kilometers and the final answer needs to be in miles, the ratio relating miles to kilometers needs to be used. There are 0.62 miles in 1 kilometer. This, written as a ratio and in fraction form, is $\frac{0.62 \text{ miles}}{1 \text{ km}}$. To convert 50 km/hour into miles per hour, the following conversion needs to be set up:

$$\frac{50 \text{ km}}{\text{hour}} \times \frac{0.62 \text{ miles}}{1 \text{ km}} = 31 \text{ miles per hour}$$

The ratio between two similar geometric figures is called the **scale factor**. For example, a problem may depict two similar triangles, A and B. The scale factor from the smaller triangle A to the larger triangle B is given as 2 because the length of the corresponding side of the larger triangle, 16, is twice the corresponding side on the smaller triangle, 8. This scale factor can also be used to find the value of a missing side, x, in triangle A. Since the scale factor from the smaller triangle (A) to larger one (B) is 2, the larger corresponding side in triangle B (given as 25) can be divided by 2 to find the missing side in A ($x = 12.5$). The scale factor can also be represented in the equation $2A = B$ because two times the lengths of A gives the corresponding lengths of B. This is the idea behind similar triangles.

Proportions

Much like a scale factor can be written using an equation like $2A = B$, a **relationship** is represented by the equation $Y = kX$. X and Y are proportional because as values of X increase, the values of Y also increase. A relationship that is inversely proportional can be represented by the equation $Y = \frac{k}{X}$, where the value of Y decreases as the value of X increases and vice versa.

Proportional reasoning can be used to solve problems involving ratios, percentages, and averages. Ratios can be used in setting up proportions and solving them to find unknowns. For example, if a student completes an average of 10 pages of math homework in 3 nights, how long would it take the student to complete 22 pages? Both ratios can be written as fractions. The second ratio would contain the unknown.

The following proportion represents this problem, where x is the unknown number of nights:

$$\frac{10 \text{ pages}}{3 \text{ nights}} = \frac{22 \text{ pages}}{x \text{ nights}}$$

Solving this proportion entails cross-multiplying (multiplying both sets of numbers that are diagonally across and setting them equal to each other) and results in the following equation: $10x = 22 \times 3$. Simplifying and solving for x results in the exact solution: $x = 6.6$ nights. The result would be rounded up to 7 because the homework would actually be completed on the 7th night.

The following problem uses ratios involving percentages:

If 20% of the class is girls and 30 students are in the class, how many girls are in the class?

To set up this problem, it is helpful to use the common proportion: $\frac{\%}{100} = \frac{is}{of}$. Within the proportion, % is the percentage of girls, 100 is the total percentage of the class, *is* is the number of girls, and *of* is the total number of students in the class. Most percentage problems can be written using this language. To solve this problem, the proportion should be set up as $\frac{20}{100} = \frac{x}{30}$ and then solved for x. Cross-multiplying results in the equation $20 \times 30 = 100x$, which results in the solution $x = 6$. There are 6 girls in the class.

Ratios can be used to solve problems that concern length, volume, and other units. For example, A problem may ask for the volume of a cone that has a radius, $r = 7$ m and a height, $h = 16$ m. Referring to the formulas provided on the test, the volume of a cone is given as: $V = \pi r^2 \frac{h}{3}$, where r is the radius, and h is the height. Plugging $r = 7$ and $h = 16$ into the formula, the following is obtained:

$$V = \pi(7^2)\frac{16}{3}$$

Therefore, the volume of the cone is found to be approximately 821 m^3. Sometimes, answers in different units are sought. If this problem wanted the answer in liters, 821 m^3 would need to be converted.

Using the equivalence statement $1 \text{ m}^3 = 1{,}000 \text{ L}$, the following ratio would be used to solve for liters:

$$821 \text{ m}^3 \times \frac{1{,}000 \text{ L}}{1 \text{ m}^3}$$

Cubic meters in the numerator and denominator cancel each other out, and the answer is converted to 821,000 liters, or 8.21×10^5 L.

Other conversions can also be made between different given and final units. If the temperature in a pool is 30°C, what is the temperature of the pool in degrees Fahrenheit? To convert these units, an equation is used relating Celsius to Fahrenheit. The following equation is used:

$$T_{°F} = 1.8T_{°C} + 32$$

Plugging in the given temperature and solving the equation for T yields the result:

$$T_{°F} = 1.8(30) + 32 = 86°\text{F}$$

Both units in the metric system and U.S. customary system are widely used.

Here are some more examples of how to solve for proportions:

1) $\frac{75\%}{90\%} = \frac{25\%}{x}$

To solve for x, the fractions must be cross multiplied: $(75\%x = 90\% \times 25\%)$. To make things easier, let's convert the percentages to decimals: $(0.9 \times 0.25 = 0.225 = 0.75x)$. To get rid of x's coefficient, each side must be divided by that same coefficient to get the answer $x = 0.3$. The question could ask for the answer as a percentage or fraction in lowest terms, which are 30% and $\frac{3}{10}$, respectively.

2) $\frac{x}{12} = \frac{30}{96}$

Cross-multiply: $96x = 30 \times 12$

Multiply: $96x = 360$

Divide: $x = 360 \div 96$

Answer: $x = 3.75$

3) $\frac{0.5}{3} = \frac{x}{6}$

Cross-multiply: $3x = 0.5 \times 6$

Multiply: $3x = 3$

Divide: $x = 3 \div 3$

Answer: $x = 1$

You may have noticed there's a faster way to arrive at the answer. If there is an obvious operation being performed on the proportion, the same operation can be used on the other side of the proportion to solve for x. For example, in the first practice problem, 75% became 25% when divided by 3, and upon doing the same to 90%, the correct answer of 30% would have been found with much less legwork. However, these questions aren't always so intuitive, so it's a good idea to work through the steps, even if the answer seems apparent from the outset.

Percentages

Think of percentages as fractions with a denominator of 100. In fact, **percentage** means "per hundred." Problems often require converting numbers from percentages, fractions, and decimals. The following explains how to work through those conversions.

Conversions

Decimals and Percentages: Since a percentage is based on "per hundred," decimals and percentages can be converted by multiplying or dividing by 100. Practically speaking, this always amounts to moving the decimal point two places to the right or left, depending on the conversion. To convert a percentage to a decimal, move the decimal point two places to the left and remove the % sign. To convert a decimal to a percentage, move the decimal point two places to the right and add a % sign. Here are some examples:

$65\% = 0.65$
$0.33 = 33\%$
$0.215 = 21.5\%$
$99.99\% = 0.9999$
$500\% = 5.00$
$7.55 = 755\%$

Fractions and Percentages: Remember that a percentage is a number per one hundred. So, a percentage can be converted to a fraction by making the number in the percentage the numerator and putting 100 as the denominator:

$$43\% = \frac{43}{100}$$

$$97\% = \frac{97}{100}$$

$$4.7\% = \frac{47}{1000}$$

Note in the last example, that the decimal can be removed by going from 100 to 1,000, because it's accomplished by multiplying the numerator and denominator by 10.

Note that the percent symbol (%) kind of looks like a 0, a 1, and another 0. So, think of a percentage like 54% as 54 over 100. Note that it's often good to simplify a fraction into the smallest possible numbers. So, $\frac{54}{100}$ would then become $\frac{27}{50}$:

$$\frac{54}{100} \div \frac{2}{2} = \frac{27}{50}$$

To convert a fraction to a percent, follow the same logic. If the fraction happens to have 100 in the denominator, you're in luck. Just take the numerator and add a percent symbol:

$$\frac{28}{100} = 28\%$$

Another option is to make the denominator equal to 100. Be sure to multiply the numerator and the denominator by the same number. For example:

$$\frac{3}{20} \times \frac{5}{5} = \frac{15}{100}$$

$$\frac{15}{100} = 15\%$$

If neither of those strategies work, divide the numerator by the denominator to get a decimal:

$$\frac{9}{12} = 0.75$$

Then convert the decimal to a percentage:

$$0.75 = 75\%$$

Percent Formula

The percent formula looks like this:

$$\frac{\boldsymbol{part}}{\boldsymbol{whole}} = \frac{\%}{\mathbf{100}}$$

After numbers are plugged in, multiply the diagonal numbers and then divide by the remaining one. It works every time.

So, when a question asks what percent 5 is of 10, plug the numbers in like this:

$$\frac{\mathbf{5}}{\mathbf{10}} = \frac{\%}{\mathbf{100}}$$

Multiply the diagonal numbers:

$$5 \times 100 \ = 500$$

Divide by the remaining number:

$$\frac{500}{10} = 50\%$$

The percent formula can be applied in a number of different circumstances by plugging in the numbers appropriately.

Regular Time vs. Military Time

When telling time with a regular or 12-hour clock, start counting at 12 a.m., or midnight, increasing each hour by whole numbers: 1 a.m., 2 a.m., 3 a.m., and so on. Once the count reaches 12 again, it becomes 12 p.m., or noon, and the count goes from 1 p.m., 2 p.m., 3 p.m., and so on. This switching of a.m. to p.m. and back continues in a cycle. A colon is used to separate the hours from the minutes and the minutes from the seconds.

Military time uses a 24-hour clock. Military time also begins at midnight and continues on to 1, 2, 3, and so on. It does not use a.m. or p.m. Midnight is the 24th hour in the count. What regular time considers 1 a.m. is called 0100, pronounced "zero one hundred hours" or "oh one hundred hours," in military time. This continues for the entire count – 0200, 0300, 0400, etc. – until, what regular time calls ,12 p.m. or 1200, pronounced "twelve hundred hours," and then continues the count to 1300, 1400, 1500, and so on. See the following page for a comparison chart.

Regular	Military
12 a.m. Midnight	2400 Midnight/Twenty-four hundred hours
1 a.m. One o'clock	0100 Zero one hundred hours
2 a.m. Two o'clock	0200 Zero two hundred hours
3 a.m. Three o'clock	0300 Zero three hundred hours
4 a.m. Four o'clock	0400 Zero four hundred hours
5 a.m. Five o'clock	0500 Zero five hundred hours
6 a.m. Six o'clock	0600 Zero six hundred hours
7 a.m. Seven o'clock	0700 Zero seven hundred hours
8 a.m. Eight o'clock	0800 Zero eight hundred hours
9 a.m. Nine o'clock	0900 Zero nine hundred hours
10 a.m. Ten o'clock	1000 Ten hundred hours
11 a.m. Eleven o'clock	1100 Eleven hundred hours
12 p.m. Noon	1200 Noon/Twelve hundred hours
1 p.m. One o'clock	1300 Thirteen hundred hours
2 p.m. Two o'clock	1400 Fourteen hundred hours
3 p.m. Three o'clock	1500 Fifteen hundred hours
4 p.m. Four o'clock	1600 Sixteen hundred hours
5 p.m. Five o'clock	1700 Seventeen hundred hours
6 p.m. Six o'clock	1800 Eighteen hundred hours
7 p.m. Seven o'clock	1900 Nineteen hundred hours
8 p.m. Eight o'clock	2000 Twenty hundred hours
9 p.m. Nine o'clock	2100 Twenty-one hundred hours
10 p.m. Ten o'clock	2200 Twenty-two hundred hours
11 p.m. Eleven o'clock	2300 Twenty-three hundred hours

A trick for converting from military to regular time is if the time is twelve hundred hours or less, it is equivalent to the a.m. version in regular time. If the time is thirteen hundred hours or more, subtract twelve and add p.m. to convert it to regular time.

Example

You are to meet someone at fourteen hundred hours. Note that the military time is more than thirteen hundred, so subtract twelve from the time.

$$14 - 12 = 2 \text{ p.m.}$$

Example

A person needs his medicine at twenty-three hundred hours. Note the military time is more than thirteen hundred, so subtract twelve from the time.

$$23 - 12 = 11 \text{ p.m.}$$

Properties of Exponents

Exponents are used in mathematics to express a number or variable multiplied by itself a certain number of times. For example, x^3 means x is multiplied by itself three times. In this expression, x is called the **base**, and 3 is the exponent. Exponents can be used in more complex problems when they contain fractions and negative numbers.

Order of Operations

When solving equations with multiple operations, special rules apply. These rules are known as the **Order of Operations**. The order is as follows: Parentheses, Exponents, Multiplication and Division from left to right, and Addition and Subtraction from left to right. A popular mnemonic device to help remember the order is Please Excuse My Dear Aunt Sally (PEMDAS).

Evaluate the following two problems to understand the Order of Operations:

1) $4 + (3 \times 2)^2 \div 4$

First, solve the operation within the parentheses: $4 + 6^2 \div 4$.
Second, solve the exponent: $4 + 36 \div 4$.
Third, solve the division operation: $4 + 9$.
Fourth, finish the operation with addition for the answer, 13.

2) $2 \times (6 + 3) \div (2 + 1)^2$

$2 \times 9 \div (3)^2$
$2 \times 9 \div 9$
$18 \div 9$
2

Algebra

Algebra is used to describe things in mathematics that have differing or changeable variables. It is easily applied to real-world situations, due to its versatility. Algebra often uses **variables**, which represent unknown quantities or values. Variables are usually represented by a letter, such as X or Y. These are helpful when attempting to solve story problems. In algebra, letters are sometimes used to symbolize fixed values. In this case, the letters are called constants.

Below are some basic tips for navigating algebra.

To ensure multiplication signs (x) and unknown variables (X) are not confused, parentheses are placed around an object in an equation to signify multiplication.

Example
6×5 is the same as writing $6\ (5)$.

Eliminate the multiplication sign between numbers and variables. It is understood they are multiplied.

Example
$3\ (X)$ and $3 \times X$ and $3X$ all signify the same thing.

The multiplication symbol is sometimes replaced by a dot.

Example
$6\ \times\ 5$ can be written as $6 \cdot 5$.

Solving Equations in One Variable
Solving equations with one variable is the process of isolating a variable on one side of the equation. For example, in $3x - 7 = 20$, the variable is $3x$, and it needs to be isolated. The numbers (also called **constants**) are -7 and 20. That means $3x$ needs to be on one side of the equals sign (either side is fine), and all the numbers need to be on the other side of the equals sign.

To accomplish this, the equation must be manipulated by performing opposite operations of what already exists. Remember that addition and subtraction are opposites and that multiplication and division are opposites. Any action taken to one side of the equation must be taken on the other side to maintain equality.

So, since the 7 is being subtracted, it can be moved to the right side of the equation by adding seven to both sides:

$$3x - 7 = 20$$

$$3x - 7 + 7 = 20 + 7$$

$$3x = 27$$

Now that the variable $3x$ is on one side and the constants (now combined into one constant) are on the other side, the 3 needs to be moved to the right side. 3 and x are being multiplied together, so 3 then needs to be divided from each side.

$$\frac{3x}{3} = \frac{27}{3}$$

$$x = 9$$

Now that x has been completely isolated, we know its value.

The solution is found to be $x = 9$. This solution can be checked for accuracy by plugging $x = 9$ in the original equation. After simplifying the equation, $20 = 20$ is found, which is a true statement:

$$3 \times 9 - 7 = 20$$

$$27 - 7 = 20$$

$$20 = 20$$

Equations that require solving for a variable (**algebraic equations**) come in many forms. Here are some more examples:

No coefficient attached to the variable:

$$x + 8 = 20$$

$$x + 8 - 8 = 20 - 8$$

$$x = 12$$

A fractional coefficient:

$$\frac{1}{2}z + 24 = 36$$

$$\frac{1}{2}z + 24 - 24 = 36 - 24$$

$$\frac{1}{2}z = 12$$

Now we multiply the fraction by its inverse:

$$\frac{2}{1} \times \frac{1}{2}z = 12 \times \frac{2}{1}$$

$$z = 24$$

Multiple instances of x:

$$14x + x - 4 = 3x + 2$$

All instances of x can be combined.

$$15x - 4 = 3x + 2$$

$$15x - 4 + 4 = 3x + 2 + 4$$

$$15x = 3x + 6$$

$$15x - 3x = 3x + 6 - 3x$$

$$12x = 6$$

$$\frac{12x}{12} = \frac{6}{12}$$

$$x = \frac{1}{2}$$

Evaluating Expressions

Sometimes expressions have multiple variables. For example:

$$5x + y - z$$

If you know what the variable equals, you can plug those numbers in for the variables and then solve the problem.

$$x = 3$$
$$y = 2$$
$$z = -3$$

$5(3) + 2 - (-3)$	Plug in the numbers for the variables
$15 + 2 - (-3)$	Follow the order of operations and perform multiplication first.
$15 + 2 + 3$	Subtraction of a negative can be changed to addition of a positive.
20	Add the terms

Algebraic **expressions** are built out of monomials. A monomial is a variable raised to some power multiplied by a constant: ax^n, where a is any constant and n is a whole number. A constant is also a monomial.

A polynomial is a sum of monomials. An example of a polynomial includes $3x^4 + 2x^2 - x - 3$.

Roman Numerals

Another form of denoting number value is through **Roman numerals**, which utilizes a finite set of letters from the alphabet to represent numbers. This numbering system doesn't account for 0, decimal, or negative numbers.

See the tables below:

Arabic Numeral	Roman Numeral
1	I
5	V
10	X
50	L
100	C
500	D
1,000	M

Arabic Numeral	Roman Numeral	Arabic Numeral	Roman Numeral
1	I	6	VI
2	II	7	VII
3	III	8	VIII
4	IV	9	IX
5	V	10	X

There are two important steps to accurately read and write Roman numerals. First, any smaller number immediately preceding a larger number is deducted from the larger number. Second, any smaller numbers after the largest ones are added.

Here's an example: XLIII equals 43. In the first step, X is smaller than L, so its value is deducted from that of L, leaving 40. But the III to the right of the L is now added to the remaining 40, giving a result of 43.

Here are some more examples:

Example
XXX is what number?

Since it is the same number next to itself, add the values together.

$$10 + 10 + 10 = 30$$

Example
XL is what number?

Since X is smaller than L, and X is in front of L, it means $\mathrm{L} - \mathrm{X}$.

$$50 - 10 = 40$$

Example
ML is what number?

Since L is smaller than M, and L is after M, it means $\mathrm{M} + \mathrm{L}$.

$$1{,}000 + 50 = 1{,}050$$

Example
XXIX is what number?

There are two identical numbers next to each other (XX), so add them: $10 + 10 = 20$. Next, there is a smaller number (I) in front of a larger number (X), so subtract those: $10 - 1 = 9$. Finally, combine all portions to get the total $20 + 9 = 29$.

Example

What is 1988 in Roman numerals?

Break down the number into columns; $1000 + 900 + 80 + 8 = 1988$

$1000 = \text{M}, 900 = \text{CM}, 80 = \text{LXXX}, 8 = \text{VIII}$

Combine them from left to right to get the final solution: MCMLXXXVIII

Identifying Relative Sizes of Measurement Units

The United States customary system and the metric system each consist of distinct units to measure lengths and volume of liquids. The U.S. customary units for length, from smallest to largest, are: inch (in), foot (ft), yard (yd), and mile (mi). The metric units for length, from smallest to largest, are: millimeter (mm), centimeter (cm), decimeter (dm), meter (m), and kilometer (km). The relative size of each unit of length is shown below.

U.S. Customary	Metric	Conversion
$12 \text{ in} = 1 \text{ ft}$	$10 \text{ mm} = 1 \text{ cm}$	$1 \text{ in} = 2.54 \text{ cm}$
$36 \text{ in} = 3 \text{ ft} = 1 \text{ yd}$	$10 \text{ cm} = 1 \text{ dm(decimeter)}$	$1 \text{ m} \approx 3.28 \text{ ft} \approx 1.09 \text{ yd}$
$5{,}280 \text{ ft} = 1{,}760 \text{ yd} = 1 \text{ mi}$	$100 \text{ cm} = 10 \text{ dm} = 1 \text{ m}$	$1 \text{ mi} \approx 1.6 \text{ km}$
	$1{,}000 \text{ m} = 1 \text{ km}$	

The U.S. customary units for volume of liquids, from smallest to largest, are: fluid ounces (fl oz), cup (c), pint (pt), quart (qt), and gallon (gal). The metric units for volume of liquids, from smallest to largest, are: milliliter (mL), centiliter (cL), deciliter (dL), liter (L), and kiloliter (kL). The relative size of each unit of liquid volume is shown below.

U.S. Customary	Metric	Conversion
$8 \text{ fl oz} = 1 \text{ c}$	$10 \text{ mL} = 1 \text{ cL}$	$1 \text{ pt} \approx 0.473 \text{ L}$
$2 \text{ c} = 1 \text{ pt}$	$10 \text{ cL} = 1 \text{ dL}$	$1 \text{ L} \approx 1.057 \text{ qt}$
$4 \text{ c} = 2 \text{ pt} = 1 \text{ qt}$	$1{,}000 \text{ mL} = 100 \text{ cL} = 10 \text{ dL} = 1\text{L}$	$1 \text{ gal} \approx 3.785 \text{ L}$
$4 \text{ qt} = 1 \text{ gal}$	$1{,}000 \text{ L} = 1 \text{ kL}$	

The U.S. customary system measures weight (how strongly Earth is pulling on an object) in the following units, from least to greatest: ounce (oz), pound (lb), and ton. The metric system measures mass (the quantity of matter within an object) in the following units, from least to greatest: milligram (mg), centigram (cg), gram (g), kilogram (kg), and metric ton (MT).

The relative sizes of each unit of weight and mass are shown below.

U.S. Measures of Weight	Metric Measures of Mass
$16 \text{ oz} = 1 \text{ lb}$	$10 \text{ mg} = 1 \text{ cg}$
$2{,}000 \text{ lb} = 1 \text{ ton}$	$100 \text{ cg} = 1 \text{ g}$
	$1{,}000 \text{ g} = 1 \text{ kg}$
	$1{,}000 \text{ kg} = 1 \text{ MT}$

Please keep in mind that all word problems on the actual test may be hospital-related.

Practice Quiz

1. After a 20% sale discount, Frank purchased a new refrigerator for $850. How much did he save compared to the original price?
   a. $170
   b. $212.50
   c. $105.75
   d. $200

2. A construction company is building a new housing development with the property of each house measuring 30 feet wide. If the length of the street is zoned off at 345 feet, how many houses can be built on the street?
   a. 11
   b. 115
   c. 11.5
   d. 12

3. Mo needs to buy enough material to cover the walls around the stage for a theater performance. If he needs 79 feet of wall covering, what is the minimum number of yards of material he should purchase if the material is sold only by whole yards?
   a. 23 yards
   b. 25 yards
   c. 26 yards
   d. 27 yards

4. You measure the width of your door to be 36 inches. The true width of the door is 35.75 inches. What is the relative error in your measurement?
   a. 0.7%
   b. 0.007%
   c. 0.99%
   d. 0.1%

5. A couple buys a house for $150,000. They sell it for $165,000. By what percentage did the house's value increase?
   a. 10%
   b. 13%
   c. 15%
   d. 17%

See answers on the next page.

Answer Explanations

1. B: Since \$850 is the price *after* a 20% discount, \$850 represents 80% of the original price. To determine the original price, set up a proportion with the ratio of the sale price (850) to original price (unknown) equal to the ratio of the sale percentage (where x represents the unknown original price):

$$\frac{850}{x} = \frac{80}{100}$$

To solve a proportion, cross multiply and set the products equal to each other:

$$(850)(100) = (80)(x)$$

Multiplying each side results in the equation:

$$85{,}000 = 80x$$

To solve for x, divide both sides by 80:

$$\frac{85{,}000}{80} = \frac{80x}{80}$$

$$x = 1{,}062.5$$

Remember that x represents the original price. Subtracting the sale price from the original price (\$1,062.50 – \$850) indicates that Frank saved \$212.50.

2. A: To determine the number of houses that can fit on the street, we can divide the length of the street by the width of each house's property:

$$345 \div 30 = 11.5.$$

However, the construction company is not going to build half a house, so they will need to build either 11 or 12 houses. Since the width of 12 houses (360 feet) would extend past the length of the street, only 11 houses can be built.

3. D: A yard is 3 feet. The equation to calculate the minimum number of yards is $79 \div 3 = 26\frac{1}{3}$.

If the material is sold only by whole yards, then Mo would need to round up to the next whole yard in order to cover the extra $\frac{1}{3}$ yard. Therefore, the answer is 27 yards. None of the other choices meets the minimum whole yard requirement.

4. A: The relative error can be found by finding the absolute error and making it a percent of the true value. The absolute error is $36 - 35.75 = 0.25$. This error is then divided by 35.75 — the true value — to find 0.7%.

5. A: The value went up by $\$165{,}000 - \$150{,}000 = \$15{,}000$. Out of \$150,000, this is $\frac{15{,}000}{150{,}000} = \frac{1}{10}$. If we multiply the top and bottom by 10 to give us a denominator of 100, the result is $\frac{10}{100}$, or 10%.

Reading Comprehension

Identifying the Main Idea

Topics and main ideas are critical parts of any writing. The **topic** is the subject matter of the piece, and it is a broader, more general term. The **main idea** is what the writer wants to say about that topic. The topic can be expressed in a word or two, but the main idea should be a complete thought.

The topic and main idea are usually easy to recognize in nonfiction writing. An author will likely identify the topic immediately in the first sentence of a passage or essay. The main idea is also typically presented in the introductory paragraph of an essay. In a single passage, the main idea may be identified in the first or the last sentence, but will likely be directly stated and easily recognized by the reader. Because it is not always stated immediately in a passage, it's important to carefully read the entire passage to identify the main idea.

Also remember that when most authors write, they want to make a point or send a message. This point or message of a text is known as the theme. Authors may state themes explicitly, like in *Aesop's Fables*. More often, especially in modern literature, readers must infer the theme based on text details. Usually after carefully reading and analyzing an entire text, the reader can identify the theme. Typically, the longer the piece, the more themes you will encounter, though often one theme dominates the rest, as evidenced by the author's purposeful revisiting of it throughout the passage.

The main idea should not be confused with the thesis statement. A thesis statement is a clear statement of the writer's specific stance, and can often be found in the introduction of a nonfiction piece. The main idea is more of an overview of the entire piece, while the thesis is a specific sentence found in that piece.

In order to illustrate the main idea, a writer will use **supporting details** in a passage. These details can provide evidence or examples to help make a point. Supporting details are most commonly found in nonfiction pieces that seek to inform or persuade the reader.

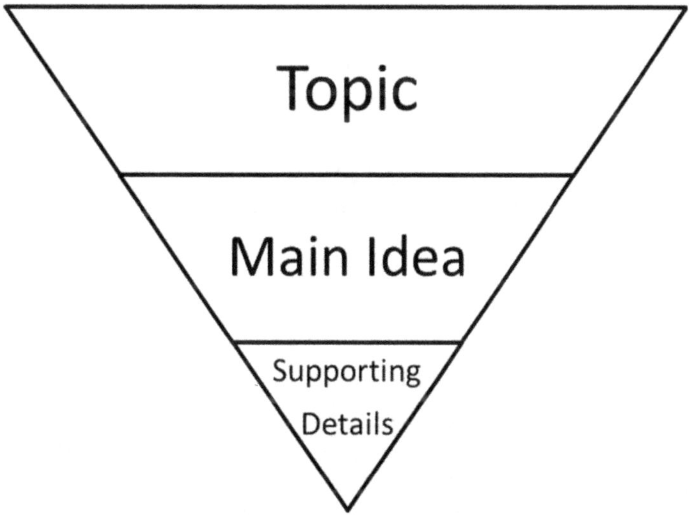

As a reader, you will want to carefully examine the author's supporting details to be sure they are credible. Consider whether they provide evidence of the author's point and whether they directly support the main idea. You might find that an author has used a shocking statistic to grab your attention, but that the statistic doesn't really support the main idea, so it isn't being effectively used in the piece.

Identifying Supporting Details

Supporting details help readers better develop and understand the main idea. Supporting details answer questions like *who, what, where, when, why,* and *how*. Different types of supporting details include examples, facts and statistics, anecdotes, and sensory details.

Persuasive and informative texts often use supporting details. In persuasive texts, authors attempt to make readers agree with their points of view, and supporting details are often used as "selling points." If authors make a statement, they need to support the statement with evidence in order to adequately persuade readers. Informative texts use supporting details such as examples and facts to inform readers. Review the previous "Cheetahs" passage to find examples of supporting details.

Cheetahs

> *Cheetahs are one of the fastest mammals on the land, reaching up to 70 miles an hour over short distances. Even though cheetahs can run as fast as 70 miles an hour, they usually only have to run half that speed to catch up with their choice of prey. Cheetahs cannot maintain a fast pace over long periods of time because their bodies will overheat. After a chase, cheetahs need to rest for approximately 30 minutes prior to eating or returning to any other activity.*

In the example, supporting details include:

- Cheetahs reach up to 70 miles per hour over short distances.
- They usually only have to run half that speed to catch up with their prey.
- Cheetahs will overheat if they exert a high speed over longer distances.
- Cheetahs need to rest for 30 minutes after a chase.

Look at the diagram below (applying the cheetah example) to help determine the hierarchy of topic, main idea, and supporting details.

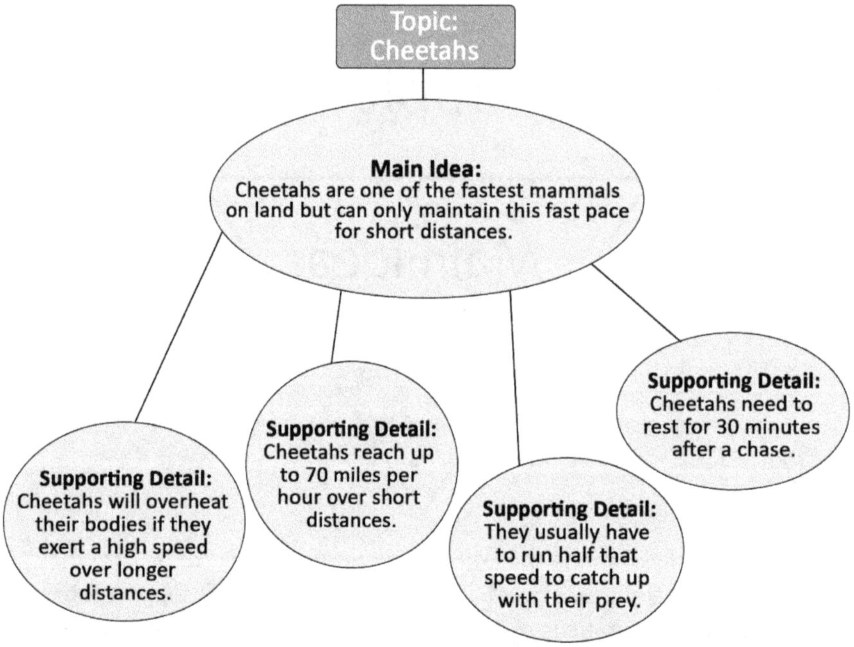

Finding the Meaning of Words and Phrases in Context

There will be many occasions in one's reading career in which an unknown word or a word with multiple meanings will pop up. There are ways of determining what these words or phrases mean that do not require the use of the dictionary, which is especially helpful during a test where one may not be available. Even outside of the exam, knowing how to derive an understanding of a word via **context clues** will be a critical skill in the real world. The context is the circumstances in which a story or a passage is happening, and can usually be found in the series of words directly before or directly after the word or phrase in question. The clues are the words that hint towards the meaning of the unknown word or phrase. The author may use synonyms or antonyms that you can use. **Synonyms** refer to words that have the same meaning as another word (e.g., instructor/teacher/educator, canine/dog, feline/cat, herbivore/vegetarian). **Antonyms** refer to words that have the opposite meaning as another word (e.g., true/false, up/down, in/out, right/wrong).

There may be questions that ask about the meaning of a particular word or phrase within a passage. There are a couple ways to approach these kinds of questions:

- Define the word or phrase in a way that is easy to comprehend (using context clues).
- Try out each answer choice in place of the word.

To demonstrate, here's an example from *Alice in Wonderland*:

> Alice was beginning to get very tired of sitting by her sister on the bank, and of having nothing to do: once or twice she <u>peeped</u> into the book her sister was reading, but it had no pictures or conversations in it, "and what is the use of a book," thought Alice, "without pictures or conversations?"

Q: As it is used in the selection, the word <u>peeped</u> means:

Using the first technique, before looking at the answers, define the word *peeped* using context clues and then find the matching answer. Then, analyze the entire passage in order to determine the meaning, not just the surrounding words.

To begin, imagine a blank where the word should be and put a synonym or definition there: "once or twice she ___ into the book her sister was reading." The context clue here is the book. It may be tempting to put *read* where the blank is, but notice the preposition word, *into*. One does not read *into* a book, one simply reads a book, and since reading a book requires that it is seen with a pair of eyes, then *look* would make the most sense to put into the blank: "once or twice she <u>looked</u> into the book her sister was reading."

Once an easy-to-understand word or synonym has been supplanted, check to make sure it makes sense with the rest of the passage. What happened after she looked into the book? She thought to herself how a book without pictures or conversations is useless. This situation in its entirety makes sense.

Now check the answer choices for a match:

a. To make a high-pitched cry
b. To smack
c. To look curiously
d. To pout

Since the word was already defined, answer choice (c) is the best option.

Using the second technique, replace the figurative blank with each of the answer choices and determine which one is the most appropriate. Remember to look further into the passage to clarify that they work, because they could still make sense out of context.

Once or twice, she made a high pitched cry into the book her sister was reading.

Once or twice, she smacked the book her sister was reading.

Once or twice, she looked curiously into the book her sister was reading.

Once or twice, she pouted into the book her sister was reading.

For Choice *A,* it does not make much sense in any context for a person to cry into a book, unless maybe something terrible has happened in the story. Given that afterward Alice thinks to herself how useless a book without pictures is, this option does not make sense within context.

For Choice *B,* smacking a book someone is reading may make sense if the rest of the passage indicates there a reason for doing so. If Alice was angry or her sister had shoved it in her face, then maybe smacking the book would make sense within context. However, since whatever she does with the book causes her to think, "what is the use of a book without pictures or conversations?" then answer Choice *B* is not an appropriate answer.

Answer Choice *C* fits well within context, given her subsequent thoughts on the matter.

Answer Choice *D* does not make sense in context or grammatically, as people do not pout into things.

This is a simple example to illustrate the techniques outlined above. There may, however, be a question in which all of the definitions are correct and also make sense out of context, in which the appropriate context clues will really need to be honed in on in order to determine the correct answer. For example, here is another passage from *Alice in Wonderland*:

> ...but when the Rabbit actually took a watch out of its waistcoat pocket, and looked at it, and then hurried on, Alice started to her feet, for it flashed across her mind that she had never before seen a rabbit with either a waistcoat-pocket or a watch to take out of it, and burning with curiosity, she ran across the field after it, and was just in time to see it pop down a large rabbit-hole under the hedge.

Q: As it is used in the passage, the word started means:

a. To turn on
b. To begin
c. To move quickly
d. To be surprised

All of these words qualify as a definition of start, but using context clues, the correct answer can be identified using one of the two techniques above. It's easy to see that one does not turn on, begin, or be surprised to one's feet. The selection also states that she "ran across the field after it," indicating that she was in a hurry. Therefore, to move quickly would make the most sense in this context.

The same strategies can be applied to vocabulary that may be completely unfamiliar. In this case, focus on the words before or after the unknown word in order to determine its definition. Take this sentence, for example:

"Sam was such a miser that he forced Andrew to pay him twelve cents for the candy, even though he had a large inheritance and he knew his friend was poor."

Unlike with assertion questions, for vocabulary questions, it may be necessary to apply some critical thinking skills when something isn't explicitly stated within the passage. Think about the implications of the passage, or what the text is trying to say. With this example, it is important to realize that it is considered unusually stingy for a person to demand so little money from someone instead of just letting their friend have the candy, especially if this person is already wealthy. Hence, a miser is a greedy or stingy individual.

Questions about complex vocabulary may not be explicitly asked, but this is a useful skill to know. If there is an unfamiliar word while reading a passage and its definition goes unknown, it is possible to miss out on a critical message that could inhibit the ability to appropriately answer the questions. Practicing this technique in daily life will sharpen this ability to derive meanings from context clues with ease.

Identifying a Writer's Purpose and Tone

Purpose

Writing can be classified under four passage types: narrative, expository, descriptive (sometimes called technical), and persuasive. Though these types are not mutually exclusive, one form tends to dominate the rest. By recognizing the *type* of passage you're reading, you gain insight into *how* you should read. If you're reading a narrative, you can assume the author intends to entertain, which means you may skim the text without losing meaning. A technical document might require a close read because skimming the passage might cause the reader to miss salient details.

1. **Narrative writing**, at its core, is the art of storytelling. For a narrative to exist, certain elements must be present. First, it must have characters. While many characters are human, characters could be defined as anything that thinks, acts, and talks like a human. For example, many recent movies, such as *Lord of the Rings* and *The Chronicles of Narnia*, include animals, fantastical creatures, and even trees that behave like humans. Second, it must have a plot or sequence of events. Typically, those events follow a standard plot diagram, but recent trends start *in medias res* or in the middle (near the climax). In this instance, foreshadowing and flashbacks often fill in plot details. Finally, along with characters and a plot, there must also be conflict. Conflict is usually divided into two types: internal and external. Internal conflict indicates the character is in turmoil and is presented through the character's thoughts. External conflicts are visible. Types of external conflict include a person versus nature, another person, or society.

2. **Expository writing** is detached and to the point. Since expository writing is designed to instruct or inform, it usually involves directions and steps written in second person ("you" voice) and lacks any persuasive or narrative elements. Sequence words such as *first*, *second*, and *third*, or *in the first place*, *secondly*, and *lastly* are often given to add fluency and cohesion. Common examples of expository writing include instructor's lessons, cookbook recipes, and repair manuals.

3. Due to its empirical nature, **technical writing** is filled with steps, charts, graphs, data, and statistics. The goal of technical writing is to advance understanding in a field through the scientific method. Experts such as teachers, doctors, or mechanics use words unique to the profession in which they operate. These words, which often incorporate acronyms, are called *jargon*. Technical writing is a type of expository writing but is not meant to be understood by the general public. Instead, technical writers assume readers have received a formal education in a particular field of study and need no explanation as to what the jargon means. Imagine a doctor trying to understand a diagnostic reading for a car or a mechanic trying to interpret lab results. Only professionals with proper training will fully comprehend the text.

4. **Persuasive writing** is designed to change opinions and attitudes. The topic, stance, and arguments are found in the thesis, positioned near the end of the introduction. Later supporting paragraphs offer relevant quotations, paraphrases, and summaries from primary or secondary sources, which are then interpreted, analyzed, and evaluated. The goal of persuasive writers is not to stack quotes but to develop original ideas by using sources as a starting point. Good persuasive writing makes powerful arguments with valid sources and thoughtful analysis. Poor

persuasive writing is riddled with bias and logical fallacies. Sometimes logical and illogical arguments are sandwiched together in the same piece. Therefore, readers should display skepticism when reading persuasive arguments.

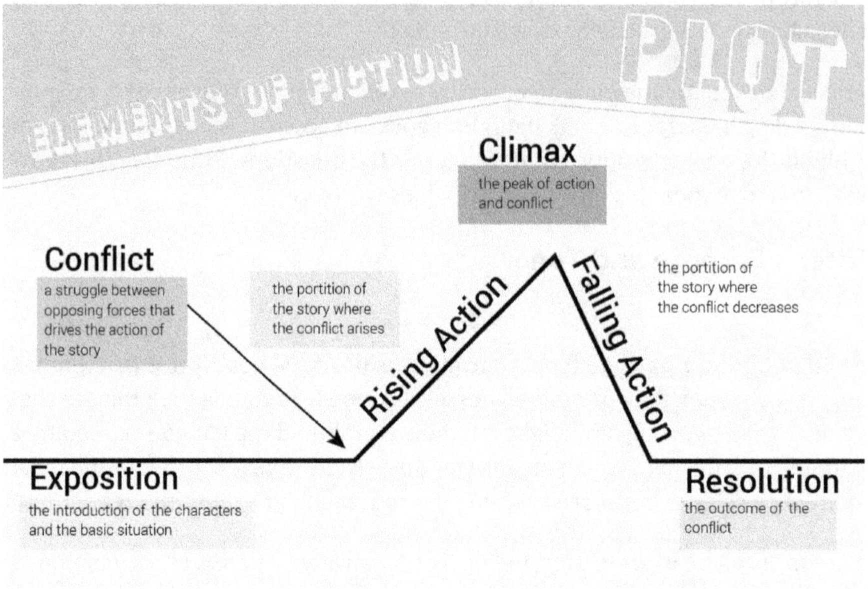

Tone

Tone refers to the writer's attitude toward the subject matter. Tone conveys how the writer feels about characters, situations, events, ideas, etc.

A lot of nonfiction writing has a neutral tone, which is an important one for the writer to use. A **neutral tone** demonstrates that the writer is presenting a topic impartially and letting the information speak for itself. On the other hand, nonfiction writing can be just as effective and appropriate if the tone isn't neutral. The following short passage provides an example of tone in nonfiction writing:

> Seat belts save more lives than any other automobile safety feature. Many studies show that airbags save lives as well; however, not all cars have airbags. For instance, some older cars don't. Furthermore, air bags aren't entirely reliable. For example, studies show that in 15% of accidents airbags don't deploy as designed, but, on the other hand, seat belt malfunctions are extremely rare. The number of highway fatalities has plummeted since laws requiring seat belt usage were enacted.

In this passage, the writer mostly chooses to retain a neutral tone when presenting information. If instead, the author chose to include their own personal experience of losing a friend or family member in a car accident, the tone would change dramatically. Or, if the author used words and phrases such as, "Ever since the government required individuals to wear seat belts, the amount of hard-working American lives that have been saved is extraordinary! Such a small task to undertake has changed the entire country." The tone would no longer be neutral and would show the reader the seriousness, joy, sadness, etc. of the situation. When analyzing tone, the reader should consider what the writer is trying to achieve in the text and how they *create* the tone using style.

The following two poems and the essay concern the theme of death and are presented to demonstrate how to evaluate tone:

"Queen Mab," Percy Bysshe Shelley

How wonderful is Death,

Death, and his brother Sleep!

One, pale as yonder waning moon

With lips of lurid blue;

The other, rosy as the morn

When throned on ocean's wave

It blushes o'er the world;

Yet both so passing wonderful!

"After Great Pain, A Formal Feeling Comes," Emily Dickinson

After great pain, a formal feeling comes –

The Nerves sit ceremonious, like Tombs –

The stiff Heart questions 'was it He, that bore,'

And 'Yesterday, or Centuries before'?

The Feet, mechanical, go round –

A Wooden way

Of Ground, or Air, or Ought –

Regardless grown,

A Quartz contentment, like a stone –

This is the Hour of Lead –

Remembered, if outlived,

As Freezing persons, recollect the Snow –

First – Chill – then Stupor – then the letting go –

The Process of Dying

Death occurs in several stages. The first stage is the pre-active stage, which occurs a few days to weeks before death, in which the desire to eat and drink decreases, and the person may feel restless, irritable, and anxious. The second stage is the active stage, where the skin begins to cool, breathing becomes difficult as the lungs become congested (known as the "death rattle"), and the person loses control of their bodily fluids.

Once death occurs, there are also two stages. The first is clinical death, when the heart stops pumping blood and breathing ceases. This stage lasts approximately 4-6 minutes, and during this time, it is possible for a victim to be resuscitated via CPR or a defibrillator. After 6 minutes however, the oxygen stores within the brain begin to deplete, and the victim enters biological death. This is the point of no return, as the cells of the brain and vital organs begin to die, a process that is irreversible.

Readers should notice the differences in the word choices between the two poems. Percy Shelley's word choices—"wonderful," "rosy," "blushes," "ocean"—surrounding death indicates that he views death in a welcoming manner as his words carry positive charges. However, Dickinson's word choices—"pain," "wooden," "stone," "lead," "chill," "tombs"—carry negative connotations, which indicates an aversion to death. **Connotation** refers to the implied meaning of a word or phrase. Connotations are the ideas or feelings that words or phrases invoke other than their literal meaning. In contrast, the expository passage has no emotionally-charged words of any kind, and seems to view death simply as a process that happens, neither welcoming nor fearing it. The tone in this passage, therefore, is neutral.

Distinguishing between Fact and Opinion

It is important to distinguish between fact and opinion when reading a piece of writing. Readers should check the validity and accuracy of the facts that an author presents. When authors use opinion, they are sharing their own thoughts and feelings about the subject. You can recognize a piece that relies on opinion when the author uses words like *think, feel, believe,* or *in my opinion,* though these words won't always appear in an opinion piece, especially if it is formally written. An author's opinion may be backed up by facts, which gives it more credibility, but it should not be taken as fact. A critical reader should be wary of an author's opinion, especially if it is only supported by other opinions. Here are some examples of facts versus opinions:

Facts	Opinions
There are 9 innings in a game of baseball.	Baseball games run too long.
Eisenhower expanded Social Security.	This action was helpful for the country.
McDonalds has stores in 118 countries.	McDonalds has the best hamburgers.

As a critical reader, you must examine the facts that are used to support the author's argument. You can check the facts against other sources to be sure they are correct. You can also check the validity of the sources used to be sure they are credible, academic, and peer reviewed sources. Consider that when an author uses another person's opinion to support the argument, even if it is an expert's opinion, it is still only an opinion, and should not be taken as fact. A strong argument uses valid, measurable facts to support ideas. Even then, the reader may disagree with the argument, as it is rooted in the author's **assumptions**, which are the author's personal beliefs.

Making Logical Inferences

Critical readers should be able to make inferences. Making an **inference** requires the reader to read between the lines and look for what is implied rather than what is explicitly stated. That is, using information that *is* known from the text, the reader is able to make a logical assumption about information that is not explicitly stated but is probably true. Read the following passage:

"Hey, do you wanna meet my new puppy?" Jonathan asked.

"Oh, I'm sorry but please don't—" Jacinta began to protest, but before she could finish Jonathan had already opened the passenger side door of his car and a perfect white ball of fur came bouncing towards Jacinta.

"Isn't he the cutest?" beamed Jonathan.

"Yes—achoo!—he's pretty—aaaachooo!!—adora—aaa—aaaachoo!" Jacinta managed to say in between sneezes. "But if you don't mind, I—I—achoo!—need to go inside."

Which of the following can be inferred from Jacinta's reaction to the puppy?

a. She hates animals.
b. She is allergic to dogs.
c. She prefers cats to dogs.
d. She is angry at Jonathan.

An inference requires the reader to consider the information presented and then form their own idea about what is probably true. Based on the details in the passage, what is the best answer to the question? Important details to pay attention to include the tone of Jacinta's dialogue, which is overall polite and apologetic, as well as her reaction itself, which is a long string of sneezes. Choices *A* and *D* both express strong emotions ("hates" and "angry") that are not evident in Jacinta's speech or actions. Choice *C* mentions cats, but there is nothing in the passage to indicate Jacinta's feelings about cats. Choice *B,* "she is allergic to dogs," is the most logical choice. Based on the fact that she began sneezing as soon as a fluffy dog approached her, it makes sense to guess that Jacinta might be allergic to dogs. Using the clues in the passage, it is reasonable to guess that this is true even though Jacinta never directly states, "Sorry, I'm allergic to dogs!"

Making inferences is crucial for readers of literature because literary texts often avoid presenting complete and direct information to readers about characters' thoughts or feelings, or they present this information in an unclear way, leaving it up to the reader to interpret clues given in the text. In order to make inferences while reading, readers should ask themselves:

- What details are being presented in the text?
- Is there any important information that seems to be missing?
- Based on the information that the author *does* include, what else is probably true?
- Is this inference reasonable based on what is already known?

Summarizing

A **summary** is a shortened version of the original text. It focuses on the main points of the original text and includes only the relevant details. Since summaries are generally significantly shorter than the text they are about, summaries need to get straight to the point. It's important that a summary retain the original meaning of the text. Generally, a summary should follow the flow of the passage by explaining the points in the same order as the original passage; however, this is not a necessity.

Please keep in mind that passages found in the actual exam may be hospital-related.

Practice Quiz

The next five questions are based on the following passage:

As long ago as 1860 it was the proper thing to be born at home. At present, so I am told, the high gods of medicine have decreed that the first cries of the young shall be uttered upon the anesthetic air of a hospital, preferably a fashionable one. So young Mr. and Mrs. Roger Button were fifty years ahead of style when they decided, one day in the summer of 1860, that their first baby should be born in a hospital. Whether this anachronism had any bearing upon the astonishing history I am about to set down will never be known.

I shall tell you what occurred, and let you judge for yourself.

The Roger Buttons held an enviable position, both social and financial, in ante-bellum Baltimore. They were related to the This Family and the That Family, which, as every Southerner knew, entitled them to membership in that enormous peerage which largely populated the Confederacy. This was their first experience with the charming old custom of having babies—Mr. Button was naturally nervous. He hoped it would be a boy so that he could be sent to Yale College in Connecticut, at which institution Mr. Button himself had been known for four years by the somewhat obvious nickname of "Cuff."

On the September morning consecrated to the enormous event he arose nervously at six o'clock, dressed himself, adjusted an impeccable stock, and hurried forth through the streets of Baltimore to the hospital, to determine whether the darkness of the night had borne in new life upon its bosom.

When he was approximately a hundred yards from the Maryland Private Hospital for Ladies and Gentlemen he saw Doctor Keene, the family physician, descending the front steps, rubbing his hands together with a washing movement—as all doctors are required to do by the unwritten ethics of their profession.

Mr. Roger Button, the president of Roger Button & Co., Wholesale Hardware, began to run toward Doctor Keene with much less dignity than was expected from a Southern gentleman of that picturesque period. "Doctor Keene!" he called. "Oh, Doctor Keene!"

The doctor heard him, faced around, and stood waiting, a curious expression settling on his harsh, medicinal face as Mr. Button drew near.

"What happened?" demanded Mr. Button, as he came up in a gasping rush. "What was it? How is she? A boy? Who is it? What—"

"Talk sense!" said Doctor Keene sharply. He appeared somewhat irritated.

"Is the child born?" begged Mr. Button.

Doctor Keene frowned. "Why, yes, I suppose so—after a fashion." Again he threw a curious glance at Mr. Button.

The Curious Case of Benjamin Button, F. S. Fitzgerald, 1922

1. What major event is about to happen in this story?
    a. Mr. Button is about to go to a funeral.
    b. Mr. Button's wife is about to have a baby.
    c. Mr. Button is getting ready to go to the doctor's office.
    d. Mr. Button is about to go shopping for new clothes.

2. What kind of tone does the above passage have?
    a. Nervous and excited
    b. Sad and angry
    c. Shameful and confused
    d. Grateful and joyous

3. What is the meaning of the word "consecrated" in paragraph 4?
    a. Numbed
    b. Chained
    c. Dedicated
    d. Moved

4. What does the author mean to suggest by adding the following statement?

"rubbing his hands together with a washing movement—as all doctors are required to do by the unwritten ethics of their profession."

    a. Suggest that Mr. Button is tired of the doctor.
    b. Try to explain the detail of the doctor's profession.
    c. Hint to readers that the doctor is an unethical man.
    d. Give readers a visual picture of what the doctor is doing.

5. Which of the following best describes the development of this passage?
    a. It starts in the middle of a narrative in order to transition smoothly to a conclusion.
    b. It is a chronological narrative from beginning to end.
    c. The sequence of events is backwards—we go from future events to past events.
    d. To introduce the setting of the story and its characters

See answers on the next page.

Answer Explanations

1. B: The passage begins by giving the reader information about traditional birthing situations. Then, we are told that Mr. and Mrs. Button decide to go against tradition to have their baby in a hospital. The next few passages are dedicated to letting the reader know how Mr. Button dresses and goes to the hospital to welcome his new baby. There is a doctor in this excerpt, as Choice *C* indicates, and clothes are discussed, as Choice *D* indicates. However, Mr. Button is not going to the doctor's office, nor is he about to go shopping for new clothes.

2. A: We are told in the fourth paragraph that Mr. Button "arose nervously." We also see him running without caution to the doctor to find out about his wife and baby—this indicates his excitement. We also see him stuttering in a nervous yet excited fashion as he asks the doctor if it's a boy or girl. Though the doctor may seem a bit abrupt at the end, indicating a bit of anger or shame, neither of these choices is the overwhelming tone of the entire passage. Despite the circumstances, joy and gratitude are not the main tone in the passage.

3. C: Mr. Button is dedicated to the task before him. Choice *A*, *numbed*, Choice *B*, *chained*, and Choice *D*, *moved*, all could grammatically fit in the sentence. However, they do not match the excerpt's use of *consecrated* the way *dedicated* does.

4. D: The author describes a visual image—the doctor rubbing his hands together—first and foremost. The author may be trying to make a comment about the profession; however, the author does not "explain the detail of the doctor's profession" as Choice *B* suggests.

5. D: We know we are being introduced to the setting because we are given the year in the very first paragraph along with the season: "one day in the summer of 1860." This is a classic structure for an introduction of the setting. In the third paragraph we also get a long explanation of Mr. Button, who is related to him, and what his life is like.

Vocabulary

Identifying Roots

By analyzing and understanding Latin, Greek, and Anglo-Saxon word roots and structure, authors better convey the thoughts they want to express to the readers of their words and help them to determine their meanings within the flow and without missing a beat. For instance, **context**—how words are used in sentences—is from the Latin for *contextus*, which means "together"+"to weave," and gives readers a graphic for the minds' eyes to see the coming together of their usage. Like every other topic discussed herein, context is needed for understanding. This element actually has a second, crucial meaning. Context is not only the *how*, but the revealed moment of the *why* a writing has been composed; it is the "Aha" moment.

The way *how* words are used in sentences is important because it also gives meaning and cohesion from sentence to sentence, paragraph to paragraph, and page after page. In other words, it gives the document continuity.

Another upside of the how side is that readers have opportunities to understand new words with which they are unfamiliar. Of course, people can always look words up if a dictionary or thesaurus, if available, but meaning might be gleaned on the spot in a piece that is well-written. **Synonyms** (words or phrases that mean about the same) and **antonyms** (words or phrases that mean the opposite of the specific word) in context give clues to meanings, and sometimes reiteration of a word might add clarification. Repetition, wisely used, can also serve as a part of how a piece flows.

The revealed moment of the *why* is important because context, up to that moment, has determined the shape of the text. This is, essentially, to bring out what it is all about.

Prefixes

A **prefix** is a word, letter, or number that is placed before another. It adjusts or qualifies the original word's meaning.

Four prefixes represent 97 percent of English words with prefixes. They are:

- *dis-* means "not" or "opposite of"; *dis*abled
- in-, im-, il-, ir- mean "not"; illiterate
- *re-* means "again"; *re*turn
- *un-* means "not"; *un*predictable

Other commons prefixes include:

- *anti-* means "against"; antibacterial
- *fore-* means "before"; forefront
- *mis-* means "wrongly"; misunderstand
- *non-* means "not"; nonsense
- *over-* means "over"; overabundance
- *pre-* means "before"; preheat
- *super-* means "above"; superman

Suffixes

The official definition of a **suffix** is "a morpheme added at the end of a word to form a derivative." In simpler terms, that means a suffix is a letter or group of letters added at the end of a word to form another word. The word created with the addition is either a different tense of the same word (*help+ed=helped)* or a new word (*help+ful=helpful).*

Some common suffixes include:

- *-ed* is used to make present tense verbs into past tense verbs; wash*ed*
- *-ing* is used to make a present tense verb into a present participle verb; wash*ing*
- *-ly* is used to make characteristic of; love*ly*
- *-s* or *–es* are used to make more than one; chairs or box*es*
- *-able* means can be done; deplor*able*
- *-al* means having characteristics of; comic*al*
- *-est* means comparative; great*est*
- *-ful* means full of; wonder*ful*
- *-ism* means belief in; commun*ism*
- *-less* means without; faith*less*
- *-ment* means action or process; accomplish*ment*
- *-ness* means state of; happi*ness*
- *-ize* means to render, to make; terror*ize,* steril*ize*
- *-ise* is primarily the British variant of *–ize;* surpr*ise,* advert*ise*
- *-ced* means go; spelling variations include -cede (concede, recede); -ceed (only three: proceed, exceed, succeed); -sede (the only one: supersede)

(Note: In some of the examples above, the *e* has been deleted.)

Word Origins

The study of the origin of a particular word, as well as how its meaning has changed over time, is called **etymology.** As an example, one might research the word *cool* and learn when that word took on a meaning other than in relation to *cold.*

Here are some common terms both in general usage as well as some common in medical usage:

Abstain (v.): Decline or refuse to do something; to refrain or hold back. *Example:* The doctor abstained from giving the patient another prescription of medication, because he had concerns that the patient was exaggerating their symptoms.

Accountable (adj.): Required to justify one's decisions to another individual, organization, or institution. *Example:* Nurses need to be held accountable for their actions when mistakes are made.

Acute (adj.): Severe or intense degree. *Example:* The doctor gave specific instructions to the patient after prescribing them a medication for their acute pain.

Adhere (v.): Listen or comply. *Example:* In order to adhere to the patient's request, the nurses and doctors only allowed family members in the room.

Adverse (adj.): Preventing success; a negative outcome. *Example:* Because of the patients' adverse reaction to the anesthesia, the surgeon had to reevaluate her treatment plan.

Ambivalent (adj.): Having contradictory ideas or a doubtful disposition. *Example:* After doing extensive research on a patient's case, the surgeon was ambivalent to performing surgery, knowing there was a lot of risk involved.

Ambulate (v.): To move around by walking. *Example:* The woman began to ambulate approximately one week after her surgery.

Apply (v.): To put on; to spread. *Example:* The doctor applied padding all the way around the patient's broken arm before applying the casting.

Assent (n.): The expression to approve or agree. *Example:* The doctor wanted the patient's assent before giving them the anesthesia.

Audible (adj.): The ability to be heard. *Example:* The patient's voice could be heard audibly throughout the hall when their shoulder was put back into its place.

Bacteria (n.): Single-celled living organisms; some can cause disease while others are essential to life. *Example:* Studies show that bacteria can live on surfaces for days; that's why it's so important for hospitals to sterilize equipment between patients.

Bilateral (adj.): Relating or affecting both sides of something. *Example:* After completing the MRI, it was discovered that the patient had bilateral tumors on both lungs.

Cardiac (adj.): Relating or referring to the heart. *Example:* Cardiac stimulants may be essential to prevent heart failure in some patients.

Cavity (n.): A hole or empty space within a solid object, specifically the human body. *Example:* The thoracic cavity, also known as the chest cavity, contains the lungs and the heart.

Cease (v.): To bring to an end, or cause to stop. *Example:* They had to cease drawing the patient's blood due to verbal discomfort and nausea expressed by the patient.

Chronic (adj.): A specification that indicates a disease is long-lasting. *Example:* The patient was diagnosed with a chronic illness; the specialist suggested the importance of learning about the illness and how to mitigate its harsher symptoms.

Chronology (n.): The arranging of events according to the ascending or descending order of dates. *Example:* the nurses referred to the patients' chart regularly in order to know the chronology of the daily medication.

Compensatory (adj.): Adjusting in order to make up for something. *Example:* A compensatory payment was put in place to make up for psychological damages.

Concave (adj.): Having a surface that curves inward. *Example:* The top of a new born baby's head is slightly concaved after birth, due to the pressure in the vaginal canal.

Concise (adj.): Giving information clearly in a comprehensive, but brief way. *Example:* The doctor needed a concise run through of all the patient's symptoms so they could treat them immediately.

Congenital (adj.): The presentation of a disease that is inherited or persistent from birth. *Example:* The symptoms in the new infant were consistent with those of congenital heart disease.

Consistency (n.): The thickness in a liquid; how a liquid holds together. *Example:* The consistency of certain foods caused the patient to present an intense gag reflex.

Constrict (v.): To become narrow, specifically by the encircling of pressure. *Example:* Smoking can cause blood vessels to constrict, which can cause circulation in extremities to be cut off.

Contingent (adj.): Occurring only under specific circumstances; dependent on. *Example:* After testing, the doctor concluded that the patient's allergic reaction was contingent on gluten consumption.

Contraindication (n.): When a medical procedure is discouraged because of a certain condition. *Example:* The surgery was contraindicated with the current medication the patient was taking.

Convulsive (adj.): Producing uncontrolled movements or spasms. *Example:* The patient explained they were experiencing multiple convulsive episodes, so the doctor prescribed them a new medication.

Cursory (adj.): Hasty; not thorough. *Example:* Because of the cursory assessment, they missed doing a full body x-ray and failed to diagnose the rib break the patient had.

Defecate (v.): To discharge feces from the body. *Example:* The patient had an abnormally difficult time defecating daily, even with medication to help, so the doctor had them stay for observation.

Deficit (n.): A lack in something. *Example:* The doctor told the teen patient that if they kept listening to their music at extreme volumes, they would risk having a hearing deficit.

Depress (v.): The motion of going downward. *Example:* The doctor used a tongue depressor to move the tongue and look down the patient's throat.

Depth (n.): The distance from the surface downward. *Example:* The depth of the glass in the patient's foot was farther than the doctors thought.

Deteriorating (adj.): Falling apart or declining in health. *Example:* After blunt trauma to the head, the patient's lucidness was deteriorating quickly.

Diagnosis (n.): An identification of the nature of an illness by the examination of a problem or of the symptoms. *Example:* After having the patient undergo multiple blood tests, the doctor diagnosed the patient with anemia.

Diffuse (v.): To spread throughout the body; not localized in a specific area. *Example:* The pain diffused from his shoulder to fingers.

Dilate (v.): To become wider, larger, or more open. *Example:* The patient's cervix was dilated 8 cm; only 2 cm more until the doctor will instruct the patient to push.

Dilute (v.): To be made thinner or weaker. *Example:* The liquid medicine was diluted in order to make the bitter taste easier to consume.

Discrete (adj.): Distinct; separate. Not joined with another. *Example:* The doctor would describe the patient's tumor as discrete from the tissues around it.

Distal (adj.): Situated away from something; specifically, the body. *Example:* The thumb is distal from the hand.

Distended (adj.): Swollen due to pressure. *Example*: The doctors were concerned because of the patient's distended stomach, which didn't seem to be caused by anything obvious.

Dysfunction (n.): Impairment or abnormality in functioning. *Example:* After various tests, the doctor concluded that the patient had a bowel dysfunction.

Empathy (n.): The ability to understand the feelings of another individual. *Example:* The nurse had empathy for this patient, because, due to inconclusive results, some very uncomfortable tests had to be repeated.

Equilibrium (n.): A chemical balance in the body. *Example:* When they took the pain meds, the patient felt a difference in their equilibrium.

Etiology (n.): The set of causes in a disease. *Example:* Even though the diagnosis was accurate and confirmed, the doctor could not find the etiology of this sickness.

Exacerbate (v.): To make a problem or bad situation worse. *Example:* In students, it's common that the stress of worrying about school exacerbates any health conditions.

Expand(v.): To enlarge or stretch. *Example:* Throughout pregnancy, the skin in the torso continues to expand.

Exposure (n.): The state of being subjected to something which may have a harmful effect. *Example:* During flu season, nurses are often exposed to the flu.

Extension (n.): Returning a limb to its original position by straightening or stretching. *Example:* The doctor asked the patient for a leg extension in order to analyze the severity of the injury before an x-ray.

Fatal (adj.): Emphasizes inevitability; unable to prevent death. *Example:* The blunt force trauma to the patient was fatal, causing the heart to immediately stop.

Fatigue (n.): The vague feeling of being weak, exhausted, or tired. *Example:* The patient disclosed that her constant fatigue had been present ever since the death of her husband.

Febrile (adj.): A state of high fever. *Example:* Since the child had a febrile response to the medication, the doctor switched to something else and marked the reaction in the patient's chart.

Flexion (n.): The capacity of a limb to flex or bend. *Example:* The flexion of fingers results in a fist.

Flushed (adj.): A redness typically over the cheeks and neck. *Example:* Some people get flushed when embarrassed or nervous.

Gastrointestinal (adj.): Referring to the stomach and intestines. *Example:* The investigation of choice is endoscopy of the upper gastrointestinal tract.

Hematologic (adj.): Relating or referring to blood. *Example:* They were studying hematologic cancers in class that week.

Hydration (n.): The process of introducing additional fluid into the body. *Example:* Hydration is extremely important, especially for athletes who lose a lot of body fluid due to sweat.

Hygiene (n.): The preventative measures taken to maintain health and prevent disease. *Example:* Studies show that students who keep up proper handwashing and nail hygiene prevent the spread of sickness by approximately 20%.

Impaired (adj.): Weakened or damaged; a specific disability. *Example:* The patient explained to the doctor that they were experiencing episodes of impaired vision along with slight nausea and dizziness.

Impending (adj.): Something that is about to happen; forthcoming. *Example:* The doctor was worried about the impending necessity for insulin if the patient didn't change their diet and exercise habits.

Impervious (adj.): Not allowing the passage of any liquids or fluids through. *Example:* This blanket will keep you dry, as it's impervious to water.

Imply (v.): To insinuate or suggest something. *Example:* The patient had a distended area around the stomach and expressed discomfort; it was implied that they had an inguinal hernia.

Incidence (n.): The occurrence of something. *Example:* Incidents of nausea are common after going under general anesthesia.

Infection (n.): When pathogenic organisms such as viruses and bacteria invade the body that normally are not present. *Example:* The patient's infection was prominent because a surface wound wasn't properly treated.

Infer (v.): To make a conclusion based upon facts or events that have previously occurred. *Example:* After the patient disclosed some eating habits, and discomfort in her chest, the doctor was able to infer that the patient was experiencing mild heartburn.

Inflamed (adj.): When a part of the body is swollen or red. *Example:* Due to an allergic reaction, the patient's eyes and face were severely inflamed.

Ingest (v.): To consume, or to put in the body through absorbing or swallowing. *Example:* What you consume affects your body and how you feel throughout the day.

Initiate (v.): The action or processing of beginning something. *Example:* The nurse had to initiate CPR.

Insidious (adj.): Harmful effects, but on a gradual timeline. *Example:* According to studies, most STD's are insidious and often come with little to no symptoms.

Intact (adj.): Undamaged; completely whole. *Example:* Although there was bruising in the ribs, all of them were intact.

Intubate (v.): The act of inserting a tube into a person, usually to help with breathing. *Example:* They decided to intubate the patient after learning that their airway was not working properly.

Invasive (adj.): Something that infiltrates areas of the body. *Example:* Surgery is invasive.

Kinetic (adj.): Referring to motion or movement. *Example:* Some practices use kinetic therapy, which utilizes movement to provide a more holistic form of healing.

Labile (adj.): Changed or altered. *Example:* The man came into the ER with labile behavior and seemed very confused as to who he was.

Laceration (n.): A cut. *Example:* The young patient has a deep laceration because he played with one of the kitchen knives.

Latent (adj.): To be hidden, or lying dormant; concealed. *Example:* Oftentimes, after the initial attack of the virus that causes chicken pox, it will remain latent. Many years later, if it becomes reactivated, it will cause shingles.

Lateral (adj.): From or toward the side. *Example:* The arms are lateral to the torso.

Lethargic (adj.): Characterized by fatigue or sluggishness. *Example:* The patient explained they were feeling lethargic due to the intense lack of sleep and poor diet.

Manifestation (n.): The symptom or appearance of an ailment. *Example:* With the symptoms showing headache, a stiff neck, and a fever, the doctor concluded this was a manifestation of meningitis.

Musculoskeletal (adj.): Involving both the muscular and skeletal parts of the body. *Example:* A treatment for musculoskeletal back pain is a low intensity laser irradiation that is controlled and randomized throughout the needed areas.

Neurologic (adj.): Involving the functions of the nervous system. *Example:* A common neurologic disorder is Alzheimer's Disease.

Neurovascular (adj.): Involving or relating to blood vessels and nerves. *Example:* Migraines are described as a neurovascular condition by headache specialists.

Nutrient (adj.): Essential for the maintenance of life and provides nourishment. *Example:* Having a nutrient-rich diet is important to maintain a healthy body and lifestyle.

Occluded (v.): To obstruct or clog up. *Example:* Nurses must look out for blood clots in patients, since they can occlude the flow of oxygen through the veins.

Ongoing (adj.): Being in progress, continuing. *Example:* Some diseases, like Type I diabetes, are continuous and require ongoing treatment throughout the patient's life.

Oral (adj.): Relating to the mouth. *Example:* Oral hygiene is essential to keeping your gums and teeth healthy.

Otic (adj.): Relating to the ear. *Example:* Oftentimes, otic solutions are prescribed to treat ear infections.

Parameter (n.): A set of factors that are used to measure or express something. *Example:* Certain parameters have been set in place to decrease the spread of sickness in hospitals.

Patent (adj.): Referring to being open. *Example:* Patent surgeries typically have a higher risk because they are more invasive.

Pathogenic (adj.): An organism capable of producing disease. *Example:* Most organisms are harmless and not pathogenic.

Pathology (n.): The study of behaviors and manifestation of a disease. *Example:* She was interested in studying pathology at university.

Posterior (adj.): Situated behind in the body. *Example:* The hamstrings are located on the posterior side of the body.

Potent (adj.): Having a great influence or effect. *Example:* The doctor explained to take the directed amount of dosage since the medication was extremely potent.

Potential (adj.): The capacity or ability to develop something in the future. *Example:* The patient had a high potential to get Type II diabetes due to a poor diet and lack of exercise.

Precaution (n.): A measure taken to prevent a future occurrence. *Example:* Many precautions are taken in an operating room to prevent infection as much as possible.

Precipitous (adj.): Done suddenly or to happen without control. *Example:* The doctor explained that the condition was precipitous and would've been almost impossible to catch early.

Predispose (v.): To be inclined or prone to a specific condition. *Example:* Certain individuals can be predisposed to having heart attacks if it's common in family medical history.

Preexisting (adj.): A condition existing prior to a specific time. *Example:* The condition was preexisting, even though symptoms didn't show for several months after birth.

Primary (adj.): Referring to the first or earliest of something. *Example:* Primary care is the first point of contact between an individual and the healthcare system.

Priority (n.): Being regarded or placed as more important. *Example:* The paramedic's first priority was to make sure the patient didn't have an obstructed airway.

Prognosis (n.): The forecast or course of a disease. *Example:* The family received a good prognosis from the doctor regarding their son's illness.

Rationale (n.): The logical reason for a course of action. *Example:* The rationale for the treatment was based on years of scientific studies.

Recur (v.): Occur again repeatedly. *Example:* After the patient left the hospital, the nurse told him to call back should the rash recur.

Renal (adj.): Involving the kidneys. *Example:* Fatigue, blood in urine, swollen feet, and cramping muscles are symptoms consistent with renal disease.

Residual (n.): A substance or thing that continues or is left over from an event. *Example:* The residual cancer would need to be monitored yearly to avoid a relapse.

Respiration (n.): The act of breathing. *Example:* The patient was given artificial respiration along with cardiopulmonary resuscitation.

Retain (v.): To hold or keep in one place. *Example:* Her team noticed that she began to retain the fluids and her feet began to swell, so they immediately checked her for congestive heart failure.

Status (adj.): The description of an individual's state of being. *Example:* Before transporting the patient to a separate unit, they needed to first check his status.

Subcutaneous (adj.): Applied or lying underneath the skin. *Example:* A subcutaneous injection of insulin was given to the diabetic patient.

Sublingual (adj.): Applied underneath the tongue. *Example:* This is a sublingual medication, so place it in the mouth and let it dissolve underneath the tongue.

Supplement (n.): A substance or thing that adds to something else to make it whole. *Example:* The nurse said a vitamin supplement of B12 is necessary for individuals partaking in a plant-based diet.

Suppress (v.): To lower or inhibit the activity of something. *Example:* Since that medication suppresses the immune system, we suggest the flu vaccination as well as caution among crowded places.

Symmetric (symmetrical) (adj.): Equally distributed parts in relation to a center. *Example:* The attendant looked to see if the limbs were symmetric in order to rule out a fractured hip.

Symptom (n.): A manifestation in the body caused by an underlying illness or disease. *Example:* Her symptoms of headache, fever, and body aches were consistent with symptoms of the flu.

Syndrome (n.): Collective symptoms within a person that indicate a certain condition. *Example:* She was thought to have dry eye syndrome due to her various symptoms of dryness, irritation, and discharge in the eye.

Therapeutic (adj.): Healing, curing, or restorative. *Example:* Our therapeutic interventions include medication along with holistic treatment such as exercise and meditation.

Toxic (adj.): A substance that is poisonous or harmful to the human body. *Example:* A high dose of this medication may be toxic.

Transdermal (adj.): Absorbed through the skin. *Example:* A transdermal patch may be more comfortable for patients who are afraid of an injection.

Transmission (n.): The act of passing a thing from one place to another. *Example:* We'd like to lessen transmission of the virus through resources such as vaccination, hygiene, and public knowledge.

Trauma (n.): An experience that is distressing or damaging to an individual in a physical or emotional way. *Example:* The individual who was brought in from the car accident sustained multiple traumas, especially to the head and chest.

Triage (n.): The assignment of order of treatment determined by severity of trauma or illness. *Example:* I told the pregnant patient to call triage if she had any more concerns with the contractions.

Ubiquitous (adj.): Present or existing everywhere at once. *Example:* Bacteria is considered ubiquitous, as it can thrive anywhere in the human body.

Urinate (v.): Discharge water through the body. *Example:* After the epidural, the patient needed a catheter in order to urinate, since she could not move from the bed.

Vascular (adj.): Relating to blood vessels. *Example:* The vascular system delivers oxygen and nutrients to tissues in the human body.

Virulent (adj.): Extremely harmful or noxious. *Example:* A virulent strain of the virus has been circulating throughout the U.S., wreaking havoc on unprepared communities.

Virus (n.): An infectious microorganism that inhabits and reproduces within a human body, plant, or animal. *Example:* Cases of the flu virus have dwindled this year due to the population wearing masks, sanitizing their hands, and social distancing.

Vital (n): Essential or necessary. *Example:* The pharmacist told her it was vital that she avoid aspirin with her prescription, as the two medications were contraindicated.

Volume (n.): The space that a liquid takes up in a container. *Example:* Her low blood volume indicated that she may have hypovolemia.

Practice Quiz

1. Select the correct meaning of the italicized word in the following sentence:

    The nurse measured her *sublingual* temperature against her axillary temperature.

    a. In the ear
    b. In the rectum
    c. Under the armpit
    d. Under the tongue

2. What is the best definition of the word *dysfunction*?
    a. Exacerbate
    b. Abnormality
    c. Dilate
    d. Lethargic

3. What does *abstain* mean?
    a. To regurgitate
    b. To imbibe
    c. To refrain from something
    d. To prolong

4. Select the correct meaning of the underlined word in the following sentence:

    The surgeon was concerned about the patient's <u>prognosis</u>.

    a. Outlook
    b. Etiology
    c. Mechanism of transmission
    d. Incidence in the population

5. What word meaning "to widen or expand" best fits in the following sentence:

    The nitrous oxide was administered to _______ his blood vessels.

    a. dilute
    b. dilate
    c. occlude
    d. distill

6. What is the best definition of the word *transdermal*?
    a. Beyond the body
    b. Through the skin
    c. To go beyond
    d. Not the skin

7. Select the correct meaning of the word in brackets in the following sentence

The doctor was baffled by the patient's unusual [manifestation] of the disease.

a. Explanation
b. Articulation
c. Understanding
d. Appearance

8. Which word meaning *hasty* best fits in the sentence?

Even with just a __________ look, the life-threatening nature of the injuries was apparent.

a. Cursory
b. Personal
c. Meticulous
d. Comprehensive

9. Select the meaning of the word in brackets in the sentence.

Two drops of the medicine were administered to the patient in a [sublingual] manner.

a. In the eye
b. Under the tongue
c. While unconscious
d. Slow and steady

10. Which word meaning "to occur again" best fits in the sentence?

He thought his condition was well-managed until the symptoms began to __________.

a. Appear
b. Curate
c. Recur
d. Occlude

11. What is the best definition of the word *exacerbate*?
a. To remove tubes
b. To carefully remove
c. To make a problem worse
d. To be outside the body

12. Select the meaning of the word in brackets in the following sentence:

Even a tiny amount of the medicine would be incredibly [potent].

a. Having a large effect
b. Expensive
c. Illegal
d. Having a small impact

13. Which word meaning "to spread" best fits in the sentence?

The numbness seemed to __________ up his leg from the location of the bite.

a. Retain
b. Diffuse
c. Envelop
d. Adverse

14. Select the meaning of the word in brackets in the following sentence:

The first beaker did not have sufficient [volume] to hold the sample.

a. Level of noise
b. Thickness
c. Antibacterial cleanliness
d. Space for a liquid

15. What is the best definition of the word *intubate*?
a. To remove bandages
b. To enhance comfort
c. To place into storage
d. To insert a tube

See answers on the next page.

Answer Explanations

1. D: The correct answer Choice is *D*, under the tongue. The root word of *sublingual* is *lingual*, which means tongue. The prefix is *sub*, which means under. Therefore, if we pay attention the prefix and how it relates to the root word, we get "under the tongue." Choice *A*, *in the ear*, would be the word *tympanic*. Choice *B*, in the rectum, would be the word *rectal*. Choice *C*, under the armpit, would be the word *axillary*.

2. B: In the word *dysfunction*, we have the root word *function* and the prefix *dys*. *Function* means to work or operate in a particular way. The prefix *dys* denotes bad or difficult. Therefore, the word *dysfunction* would mean functioning with difficulty; the word closest to this is *abnormality*, which means the quality or state of being abnormal or defected, which is Choice *B*. Choice *A*, *exacerbate*, means something that becomes more intense in nature. Choice *C*, *dilate*, means to enlarge or extend. Choice *D*, *lethargic*, means sluggish or apathetic.

3. C: *Abstain* means to refrain from something. For example, someone who chooses to *abstain* from alcohol does not drink alcohol.

4. A: The *prognosis* is the expected likely course of an illness or injury.

5. B: To *dilute* is to make a solution less concentrated, *occlude* means to block or obstruct, and *distill* means to purify a liquid or to extract the most important aspects or meaning of something.

6. A: *Transdermal* refers to something absorbed through the skin. The prefix *trans-* means through, and *dermal* refers to the skin.

7. D: In the context of this sentence, the best definition of *manifestation* is the appearance or symptoms of the ailment.

8. A: Of the answers provided, only *cursory* means hasty. *Meticulous* and *comprehensive* convey the opposite effect because they both imply a precise, thorough investigation.

9. B: *Sublingual* means under the tongue; the prefix *sub-* means under, and *lingual* refers to the tongue.

10. C: Of the presented options, only *recur* means to occur again. While symptoms could begin to *appear*, and would in this scenario, that word does indicate repetition or occurring again.

11. C: *Exacerbate* means to make a problem or bad situation worse. While the beginning of the word may be confused with the prefix *exo-*, meaning outside or external, the meanings are unrelated.

12. A: *Potent* is an adjective that describes something with great influence or effect. The sentence is saying that a small amount of the medicine would still be very powerful.

13. B: *Diffuse* means to spread. In this sentence, numbness is spreading throughout the body from a wound site.

14. D: As used in this sentence, *volume* refers to the space that a liquid takes up in a container. While *volume* can also refer to a level of noise, that definition does not make sense in this context.

15. D: *Intubate* is a verb that refers to inserting a tube into a person.

Grammar

Why is grammar important? Why should we study, teach, and use proper grammar? The English language, a uniquely human achievement, deserves our consideration and examination. Language is arguably the most important tool we have for creating an impact on the world around us. Without proper grammar, language loses its efficacy for communicating well with others. Reading, writing, listening, and speaking all have a greater effect when grammar is used proficiently.

Let's begin with the basic conventions, or the **eight parts of speech:** nouns, adjectives, adverbs, pronouns, prepositions, interjections, verbs, and conjunctions.

Parts of Speech

Nouns

A **common noun** is a word that identifies any of a class of people, places, or things. Examples include numbers, objects, animals, feelings, concepts, qualities, and actions. *A, an,* or *the* usually precedes the common noun. These parts of speech are called *articles*. Here are some examples of sentences using nouns preceded by articles.

> *A* building is under construction.
>
> *The* girl would like to move to *the* city.

An **abstract noun** is an idea, state, or quality. It is something that can't be touched, such as happiness, courage, evil, or humor.

A **proper noun** (also called a **proper name**) is used for the specific name of an individual person, place, or organization. The first letter in a proper noun is capitalized. "My name is *Mary*." "I work for *Walmart*."

Nouns sometimes serve as adjectives (which themselves describe nouns), such as "hockey player" and "state government."

Pronouns

A word used in place of a noun is known as a **pronoun**. Pronouns are words like *I, mine, hers,* and *us*.

Pronouns can be split into different classifications (as shown below) which make them easier to learn; however, it's not important to memorize the classifications.

- **Personal pronouns:** refer to people, places, things, etc.
- **First person pronouns:** we, I, our, mine
- **Second person pronouns:** you, yours
- **Third person pronouns:** he, she, they, them, it
- **Possessive pronouns:** demonstrate ownership (mine, my, his, yours)
- **Interrogative pronouns:** ask questions (what, which, who, whom, whose)
- **Relative pronouns:** include the five interrogative pronouns and others that are relative (whoever, whomever, that, when, where)

- **Demonstrative pronouns:** replace something specific (this, that, those, these)
- **Reciprocal pronouns:** indicate something was done or given in return (each other, one another)
- **Indefinite pronouns:** have a nonspecific status (anybody, whoever, someone, everybody, somebody)

Indefinite pronouns such as *anybody, whoever, someone, everybody,* and *somebody* command a singular verb form, but others such as *all, none,* and *some* could require a singular or plural verb form.

Antecedents

An **antecedent** is the noun to which a pronoun refers; it needs to be written or spoken before the pronoun is used. For many pronouns, antecedents are imperative for clarity. In particular, a lot of the personal, possessive, and demonstrative pronouns need antecedents. Otherwise, it would be unclear who or what someone is referring to when they use a pronoun like *he* or *this*.

Pronoun reference means that the pronoun should refer clearly to one, clear, unmistakable noun (the antecedent).

Pronoun-antecedent agreement refers to the need for the antecedent and the corresponding pronoun to agree in gender, person, and number. Here are some examples:

> The *kidneys* (plural antecedent) are part of the urinary system. *They* (plural pronoun) serve several roles.
>
> The kidneys are part of the *urinary system* (singular antecedent). *It* (singular pronoun) is also known as the renal system.

Pronoun Cases

The **subjective pronouns** —*I, you, he/she/it, we, they,* and *who*—are the subjects of the sentence.

> Example: *They* have a new house.

The **objective pronouns**—*me, you* (*singular*), *him/her, us, them,* and *whom*—are used when something is being done for or given to someone; they are objects of the action.

> Example: The teacher has an apple for *us*.

The **possessive pronouns**—*mine, my, your, yours, his, hers, its, their, theirs, our,* and *ours*—are used to denote that something (or someone) belongs to someone (or something).

> Example: It's *their* chocolate cake.
>
> Even Better Example: It's *my* chocolate cake!

One of the greatest challenges and worst abuses of pronouns concerns *who* and *whom*. Just knowing the following rule can eliminate confusion. *Who* is a subjective-case pronoun used only as a subject or subject complement. *Whom* is only objective-case and, therefore, the object of the verb or preposition.

> *Who* is going to the concert?
>
> You are going to the concert with *whom*?

Hint: When using *who* or *whom*, think of whether someone would say *he* or *him*. If the answer is *he*, use *who*. If the answer is *him*, use *whom*. This trick is easy to remember because *he* and *who* both end in vowels, and *him* and *whom* both end in the letter *M*.

Many possessive pronouns sound like contractions. For example, many people get *it's* and *its* confused. The word *it's* is the contraction for *it is*. The word *its* without an apostrophe is the possessive form of *it*.

> I love that wooden desk. It's beautiful. (contraction)

> I love that wooden desk. Its glossy finish is beautiful. (possessive)

If you are not sure which version to use, replace *it's/its* with *it is* and see if that sounds correct. If so, use the contraction (*it's*). That trick also works for *who's/whose, you're/your*, and *they're/their*.

Adjectives

"The *extraordinary* brain is the *main* organ of the central nervous system." The adjective *extraordinary* describes the brain in a way that causes one to realize it is more exceptional than some of the other organs while the adjective *main* defines the brain's importance in its system.

An **adjective** is a word or phrase that names an attribute that describes or clarifies a noun or pronoun. This helps the reader visualize and understand the characteristics—size, shape, age, color, origin, etc.—of a person, place, or thing that otherwise might not be known. Adjectives breathe life, color, and depth into the subjects they define. Life would be *drab* and *colorless* without adjectives!

Adjectives often precede the nouns they describe.

> *She drove her new car.*

However, adjectives can also come later in the sentence.

> *Her car is new.*

Adjectives using the prefix *a*– can only be used after a verb.

> Correct: The dog was alive until the car ran up on the curb and hit him.

> Incorrect: The alive dog was hit by a car that ran up on the curb.

Other examples of this rule include *awake, ablaze, ajar, alike,* and *asleep*.

Other adjectives used after verbs concern states of health.

> The girl was finally *well* after a long bout of pneumonia.

> The boy was *fine* after the accident.

An adjective phrase is not a bunch of adjectives strung together, but a group of words that describes a noun or pronoun and, thus, functions as an adjective. Very happy is an adjective phrase; so are way too hungry and passionate about traveling.

Possessives

In grammar, *possessive nouns* and *possessive pronouns* show ownership.

Singular nouns are generally made possessive with an apostrophe and an *s* (*'s*).

My *uncle's* new car is silver.

The *dog's* bowl is empty.

James's ties are becoming outdated.

Plural nouns ending in *s* are generally made possessive by just adding an apostrophe ('):

The pistachio nuts' saltiness is added during roasting. (The saltiness of pistachio nuts is added during roasting.)

The students' achievement tests are difficult. (The achievement tests of the students are difficult.)

If the plural noun does not end in an *s* such as *women,* then it is made possessive by adding an *apostrophe s* (*'s*)—*women's.*

Possessive pronouns can be first person (mine), second person (yours), or third person (theirs).

Indefinite possessive pronouns such as nobody or someone become possessive by adding an apostrophe s to become nobody's or someone's.

Verbs

A **verb** is the part of speech that describes an action, state of being, or occurrence.

A verb forms the main part of a predicate of a sentence. This means that the verb explains what the noun is doing. A simple example is *time flies*. The verb *flies* explains what the action of the noun, *time*, is doing. This example is a *main* verb.

Helping (auxiliary) verbs are words like *have, do, be, can, may, should, must,* and *will.* "I *should* go to the store." Helping verbs assist main verbs in expressing tense, ability, possibility, permission, or obligation.

Particles are minor function words like *not, in, out, up,* or *down* that become part of the verb itself. "I might *not.*"

Participles are words formed from verbs that are often used to modify a noun, noun phrase, verb, or verb phrase.

The *running* teenager collided with the cyclist.

Participles can also create compound verb forms.

He is *speaking.*

Participial phrases are made up of the participle and modifiers, complements, or objects.

Crying for most of an hour, the baby didn't seem to want to nap.

Having already taken this course, the student was bored during class.

Verbs have five basic forms: the **base** form, the ***-s*** form, the ***-ing*** form, the **past** form, and the **past participle** form.

The past forms are either **regular** (*love/loved; hate/hated*) or **irregular** because they don't end by adding the common past tense suffix "-ed" (*go/went; fall/fell; set/set*).

Adverbs

Adverbs have more functions than adjectives because they modify or qualify verbs, adjectives, or other adverbs as well as word groups that express a relation of place, time, circumstance, or cause. Therefore, adverbs answer any of the following questions: *How, when, where, why, in what way, how often, how much, in what condition,* and/or *to what degree. How good looking is he? He is very handsome.*

Here are some examples of adverbs for different situations:

- how: quickly
- when: daily
- where: there
- in what way: easily
- how often: often
- how much: much
- in what condition: badly
- what degree: hardly

As one can see, for some reason, many adverbs end in *-ly.*

Adverbs do things like emphasize (*really, simply,* and *so*), amplify (*heartily, completely,* and *positively*), and tone down (*almost, somewhat,* and *mildly*).

Adverbs also come in phrases.

The dog ran as though his life depended on it.

Prepositions

Prepositions are connecting words and, while there are only about 150 of them, they are used more often than any other individual groups of words. They describe relationships between other words. They are placed before a noun or pronoun, forming a phrase that modifies another word in the sentence. **Prepositional phrases** begin with a preposition and end with a noun or pronoun, the **object of the preposition.** *A pristine lake is near the store and behind the bank.*

Some commonly used prepositions are *about, after, anti, around, as, at, behind, beside, by, for, from, in, into, of, off, on, to,* and *with.*

Complex prepositions, which also come before a noun or pronoun, consist of two or three words such as *according to, in regards to,* and *because of.*

Interjections

Interjections are words used to express emotion. Examples include *wow*, *ouch*, and *hooray*. Interjections are often separate from sentences; in those cases, the interjection is directly followed by an exclamation point. In other cases, the interjection is included in a sentence and followed by a comma. The punctuation plays a big role in the intensity of the emotion that the interjection is expressing. Using a comma or semicolon indicates less excitement than using an exclamation mark.

Conjunctions

Conjunctions are vital words that connect words, phrases, thoughts, and ideas. Conjunctions show relationships between components. There are two types:

Coordinating conjunctions are the primary class of conjunctions placed between words, phrases, clauses, and sentences that are of equal grammatical rank; the coordinating conjunctions are *for, and, nor, but, or, yet*, and *so.* A useful memorization trick is to remember that all the first letters of these conjunctions collectively spell the word fanboys.

> I need to go shopping, *but* I must be careful to leave enough money in the bank.
>
> She wore a black, red, *and* white shirt.

Subordinating conjunctions are the secondary class of conjunctions. They connect two unequal parts, one **main** (or **independent**) and the other **subordinate** (or **dependent**). I must go to the store *even though* I do not have enough money in the bank.

> *Because* I read the review, I do not want to go to the movie.

Notice that the presence of subordinating conjunctions makes clauses dependent. *I read the review* is an independent clause, but *because* makes the clause dependent. Thus, it needs an independent clause to complete the sentence.

Sentences

First, let's review the basic elements of sentences.

A **sentence** is a set of words that make up a grammatical unit. The words must have certain elements and be spoken or written in a specific order to constitute a complete sentence that makes sense.

1. A sentence must have a **subject** (a noun or noun phrase). The subject tells whom or what the sentence is addressing (i.e., what it is about).

2. A sentence must have an **action** or **state of being** (*a* verb). To reiterate: A verb forms the main part of the predicate of a sentence. This means that it explains what the noun is doing.

3. A sentence must convey a complete thought.

When examining writing, be mindful of grammar, structure, spelling, and patterns. Sentences can come in varying sizes and shapes; so, the point of grammatical correctness is not to stamp out creativity or diversity in writing. Rather, grammatical correctness ensures that writing will be enjoyable and clear. One of the most common methods for catching errors is to mouth the words as you read them. Many typos are fixed automatically by our brain, but mouthing the words often circumvents this instinct and helps one read what's actually on the page. Often, grammar errors are caught not by memorization of grammar rules but by the training of one's mind to know whether something *sounds* right or not.

Types of Sentences

There isn't an overabundance of absolutes in grammar, but here is one: every sentence in the English language falls into one of four categories.

- Declarative: a simple statement that ends with a period

  The price of milk per gallon is the same as the price of gasoline.

- Imperative: a command, instruction, or request that ends with a period

  Buy milk when you stop to fill up your car with gas.

- Interrogative: a question that ends with a question mark

  Will you buy the milk?

- Exclamatory: a statement or command that expresses emotions like anger, urgency, or surprise and ends with an exclamation mark

  Buy the milk now!

Declarative sentences are the most common type, probably because they are comprised of the most general content, without any of the bells and whistles that the other three types contain. They are, simply, declarations or statements of any degree of seriousness, importance, or information.

Imperative sentences often seem to be missing a subject. The subject is there, though; it is just not visible or audible because it is *implied*. Look at the imperative example sentence.

> Buy the milk when you fill up your car with gas.

You is the implied subject, the one to whom the command is issued. This is sometimes called *the understood you* because it is understood that *you* is the subject of the sentence.

Interrogative sentences—those that ask questions—are defined as such from the idea of the word *interrogation*, the action of questions being asked of suspects by investigators. Although that is serious business, interrogative sentences apply to all kinds of questions.

To exclaim is at the root of **exclamatory sentences**. These are made with strong emotions behind them. The only technical difference between a declarative or imperative sentence and an exclamatory one is the exclamation mark at the end. The example declarative and imperative sentences can both become an exclamatory one simply by putting an exclamation mark at the end of the sentences.

> The price of milk per gallon is the same as the price of gasoline!
> Buy milk when you stop to fill up your car with gas!

After all, someone might be really excited by the price of gas or milk, or they could be mad at the person that will be buying the milk! However, as stated before, exclamation marks in abundance defeat their own purpose! After a while, they begin to cause fatigue! When used only for their intended purpose, they can have their expected and desired effect.

Independent and Dependent Clauses

Independent and dependent clauses are strings of words that contain both a subject and a verb. An **independent clause** *can* stand alone as complete thought, but a **dependent clause** *cannot*. A dependent clause relies on other words to be a complete sentence.

Independent clause: The keys are on the counter.
Dependent clause: If the keys are on the counter

Notice that both clauses have a subject (*keys*) and a verb (*are*). The independent clause expresses a complete thought, but the word *if* at the beginning of the dependent clause makes it *dependent* on other words to be a complete thought.

Independent clause: If the keys are on the counter, please give them to me.

This example constitutes a complete sentence since it includes at least one verb and one subject and is a complete thought. In this case, the independent clause has two subjects (*keys* & an implied *you*) and two verbs (*are* & *give*).

Independent clause: I went to the store.
Dependent clause: Because we are out of milk,

Complete Sentence: Because we are out of milk, I went to the store.
Complete Sentence: I went to the store because we are out of milk.

Sentence Structures

A **simple sentence** has one independent clause.

I am going to win.

A **compound sentence** has two independent clauses. A comma and a conjunction—*for, and, nor, but, or, yet, so*—links them together. Note that each of the independent clauses has a subject and a verb.

I am going to win, but the odds are against me.

A **complex sentence** has one independent clause and one or more dependent clauses.

I am going to win, even though I don't deserve it.

Even though I don't deserve it is a dependent clause. It does not stand on its own. Some conjunctions that link an independent and a dependent clause are *although, because, before, after, that, when, which,* and *while.*

A **compound-complex sentence** has at least three clauses, two of which are independent and at least one that is a dependent clause.

While trying to dance, I tripped over my partner's feet, but I regained my balance quickly.

The dependent clause is *While trying to dance*.

Run-Ons and Fragments

Run-Ons

A common mistake in writing is the run-on sentence. A **run-on** is created when two or more independent clauses are joined without the use of a conjunction, a semicolon, a colon, or a dash. We don't want to use commas where periods belong. Here is an example of a run-on sentence:

> Making wedding cakes can take many hours I am very impatient, I want to see them completed right away.

There are a variety of ways to correct a run-on sentence. The method you choose will depend on the context of the sentence and how it fits with neighboring sentences:

> Making wedding cakes can take many hours. I am very impatient. I want to see them completed right away. (Use periods to create more than one sentence.)

> Making wedding cakes can take many hours; I am very impatient—I want to see them completed right away. (Correct the sentence using a semicolon, colon, or dash.)

> Making wedding cakes can take many hours, and I am very impatient and want to see them completed right away. (Correct the sentence using coordinating conjunctions.)

> I am very impatient because I would rather see completed wedding cakes right away than wait for it to take many hours. (Correct the sentence by revising.)

Fragments

Remember that a complete sentence must have both a subject and a verb. Complete sentences consist of at least one independent clause. Incomplete sentences are called **sentence fragments**. A sentence fragment is a common error in writing. Sentence fragments can be independent clauses that start with subordinating words, such as *but, as, so that,* or *because,* or they could simply be missing a subject or verb.

A fragment error can be corrected by adding the fragment to a nearby sentence or by adding or removing words to make it an independent clause. For example:

> Dogs are my favorite animals. Because cats are too lazy. (Incorrect; the word because creates a sentence fragment)

> Dogs are my favorite animals because cats are too lazy. (Correct; this is a dependent clause.)

> Dogs are my favorite animals. Cats are too lazy. (Correct; this is a simple sentence.)

Subject and Predicate

Every complete sentence can be divided into two parts: the subject and the predicate.

Subjects: Subjects are needed in sentences to tell the reader who or what the sentence describes. Subjects can be simple or complete, and they can be direct or indirect. There can also be compound subjects.

Simple subjects are the noun or pronouns the sentence describes, without modifiers. The simple subject can come before or after the verb in the sentence:

The big brown dog is the calmest one.

Complete subjects are the subject together with all of its describing words or modifiers.

The big brown dog is the calmest one. (The complete subject is big brown dog.)

Direct subjects are subjects that appear in the text of the sentence, as in the example above. **Indirect subjects** are implied. The subject is "you," but the word *you* does not appear.

Indirect subjects are usually in imperative sentences that issue a command or order:

Feed the short skinny dog first. (The understood you is the subject.)

Watch out—he's really hungry! (The sentence warns you to watch out.)

Compound subjects occur when two or more nouns join together to form a plural subject.

Carson and Emily make a great couple.

Predicates: Once we have identified the subject of the sentence, the rest of the sentence becomes the predicate. Predicates are formed by the verb, the direct object, and all words related to it.

We went to see the Cirque du' Soleil performance.

The gigantic green character was funnier than all the rest.

A **predicate nominative** renames the subject:

John is a carpenter.

A **predicate adjective** describes the subject:

Margaret is beautiful.

Direct objects are the nouns in the sentence that are receiving the action. Sentences don't necessarily need objects. Sentences only need a subject and a verb.

The clown brought the acrobat the hula-hoop. (What is being brought? the hula-hoop)

Then he gave the trick pony a soapy bath. (What is being given? a soapy bath)

Indirect objects are words that tell us to or for whom or what the action is being done. For there to be an indirect object, there first must always be a direct object.

The clown brought the acrobat the hula-hoop. (Who is getting the direct object? the acrobate)

Then he gave the trick pony a soapy bath. (What is getting the bath? the trick pony)

Phrases

A **phrase** is a group of words that go together but do not include both a subject and a verb. They are used to add information, explain something, or make the sentence easier for the reader to understand. Unlike clauses, phrases can never stand alone as their own sentence. They do not form complete thoughts. There are noun phrases, prepositional phrases, verbal phrases, appositive phrases, and absolute phrases. Here are some examples of phrases:

I know <u>all the shortest routes</u>.

<u>Before the sequel</u>, we wanted to watch the first movie. (introductory phrase)

The jumpers have hot cocoa<u> to drink right away</u>.

Subject-Verb Agreement

The subject of a sentence and its verb must agree. The cornerstone rule of subject-verb agreement is that subject and verb must agree in number. Whether the subject is singular or plural, the verb must follow suit.

Incorrect: The houses is new.

Correct: The houses are new.

Also Correct: The house is new.

In other words, a singular subject requires a singular verb; a plural subject requires a plural verb.

The words or phrases that come between the subject and verb do not alter this rule.

Incorrect: The houses built of brick is new.

Correct: The houses built of brick are new.

Incorrect: The houses with the sturdy porches is new.

Correct: The houses with the sturdy porches are new.

The subject will always follow the verb when a sentence begins with *here* or *there.* Identify these with care.

Incorrect: Here *is* the *houses* with sturdy porches.

Correct: Here *are* the *houses* with sturdy porches.

The subject in the sentences above is not *here*, it is *houses*. Remember, *here* and *there* are never subjects. Be careful that contractions such as *here's* or *there're* do not cause confusion!

Two subjects joined by *and* require a plural verb form, except when the two combine to make one thing:

Incorrect: Garrett and Jonathan is over there.

Correct: Garrett and Jonathan are over there.

Incorrect: Spaghetti and meatballs are a delicious meal!

Correct: Spaghetti and meatballs is a delicious meal!

In the example above, *spaghetti and meatballs* is a compound noun. However, *Garrett and Jonathan* is not a compound noun.

Two singular subjects joined by *or, either/or,* or *neither/nor* call for a singular verb form.

Incorrect: Butter or syrup are acceptable.

Correct: Butter or syrup is acceptable.

Plural subjects joined by *or, either/or,* or *neither/nor* are, indeed, plural.

The chairs or the boxes are being moved next.

If one subject is singular and the other is plural, the verb should agree with the closest noun.

Correct: The chair or the boxes are being moved next.

Correct: The chairs or the box is being moved next.

Some plurals of money, distance, and time call for a singular verb.

Incorrect: Three dollars *are* enough to buy that.

Correct: Three dollars *is* enough to buy that.

For words declaring degrees of quantity such as *many of, some of,* or *most of,* let the noun that follows *of* be the guide:

Incorrect: Many of the books is in the shelf.

Correct: Many of the books are in the shelf.

Incorrect: Most of the pie *are* on the table.

Correct: Most of the pie *is* on the table.

For indefinite pronouns like anybody or everybody, use singular verbs.

Everybody *is* going to the store.

However, the pronouns *few, many, several, all, some,* and *both* have their own rules and use plural forms.

Some *are* ready.

Some nouns like *crowd* and *congress* are called *collective nouns* and they require a singular verb form.

Congress *is* in session.

The news *is* over.

Books and movie titles, though, including plural nouns such as *Great Expectations*, also require a singular verb. Remember that only the subject affects the verb. While writing tricky subject-verb arrangements, say them aloud. Listen to them. Once the rules have been learned, one's ear will become sensitive to them, making it easier to pick out what's right and what's wrong.

Dangling and Misplaced Modifiers

A **modifier** is a word or phrase meant to describe or clarify another word in the sentence. When a sentence has a modifier but is missing the word it describes or clarifies, it's an error called a **dangling modifier**. We can fix the sentence by revising to include the word that is being modified.

Consider the following examples with the modifier underlined:

> Incorrect: Having walked five miles, this bench will be the place to rest. (This implies that the bench walked the miles, not the person.)
>
> Correct: Having walked five miles, Matt will rest on this bench. (*Having walked five miles* correctly modifies *Matt*, who did the walking.)
>
> Incorrect: Since midnight, my dreams have been pleasant and comforting. (The adverb clause *since midnight* cannot modify the noun *dreams*.)
>
> Correct: Since midnight, I have had pleasant and comforting dreams. (*Since midnight* modifies the verb have had, telling us when the dreams occurred.)

Sometimes the modifier is not located close enough to the word it modifies for the sentence to be clearly understood. In this case, we call the error a **misplaced modifier**. Here is an example with the modifier underlined.

> Incorrect: We gave the hot cocoa to the children that was filled with marshmallows. (This sentence implies that the children are what are filled with marshmallows.)
>
> Correct: We gave the hot cocoa that was filled with marshmallows to the children. (The cocoa is filled with marshmallows. The modifier is near the word it modifies.)

Parallel Structure in a Sentence

Parallel structure, also known as **parallelism**, refers to using the same grammatical form within a sentence. This is important in lists and for other components of sentences.

> Incorrect: At the recital, the boys and girls were dancing, singing, and played musical instruments.
> Correct: At the recital, the boys and girls were dancing, singing, and playing musical instruments.

Notice that in the second example, *played* is not in the same verb tense as the other verbs, nor is it compatible with the helping verb *were*. To test for parallel structure in lists, try reading each item as if it were the only item in the list.

> The boys and girls were dancing.
> The boys and girls were singing.
> The boys and girls were played musical instruments.

Suddenly, the error in the sentence becomes very clear. Here's another example:

Incorrect: After the accident, I informed the police *that Mrs. Holmes backed* into my car, *that Mrs. Holmes got out* of her car to look at the damage, and *she was driving* off without leaving a note.

Correct: After the accident, I informed the police *that Mrs. Holmes backed* into my car, *that Mrs. Holmes got out* of her car to look at the damage, and *that Mrs. Holmes drove off* without leaving a note.

Correct: After the accident, I informed the police that Mrs. Holmes *backed* into my car, *got out* of her car to look at the damage, and *drove off* without leaving a note.

Note that there are two ways to fix the nonparallel structure of the first sentence. The key to parallelism is consistent structure.

Punctuation

Commas

A **comma** (,) is the punctuation mark that signifies a pause—breath—between parts of a sentence. It denotes a break of flow. As with so many aspects of writing structure, authors will benefit by memorizing all of the different ways in which commas can be used so as not to abuse them.

In a complex sentence—one that contains a subordinate (dependent) clause or clauses—the use of a comma is dictated by where the subordinate clause is located. If the subordinate clause is located before the main clause, a comma is needed between the two clauses.

I will not pay for the steak, *because I don't have that much money.*

Generally, if the subordinate clause is placed after the main clause, no punctuation is needed. I did well on my exam because I studied two hours the night before. Notice how the last clause is dependent because it requires the earlier independent clauses to make sense.

Use a comma on both sides of an interrupting phrase.

I will pay for the ice cream, chocolate and vanilla, and then will eat it all myself.

The words forming the phrase in italics are nonessential (extra) information. To determine if a phrase is nonessential, try reading the sentence without the phrase and see if it's still coherent.

A comma is not necessary in this next sentence because no interruption—nonessential or extra information—has occurred. Read sentences aloud when uncertain.

I will pay for his chocolate and vanilla ice cream and then will eat it all myself.

If the nonessential phrase comes at the beginning of a sentence, a comma should only go at the end of the phrase. If the phrase comes at the end of a sentence, a comma should only go at the beginning of the phrase.

Other types of interruptions include the following:

- interjections: Oh no, I am not going.
- abbreviations: Barry Potter, M.D., specializes in heart disorders.
- direct addresses: Yes, Claudia, I am tired and going to bed.

- parenthetical phrases: His wife, lovely as she was, was not helpful.
- transitional phrases: Also, it is not possible.

The second comma in the following sentence is called an Oxford comma.

> I will pay for ice cream, syrup, and pop.

It is a comma used after the second-to-last item in a series of three or more items. It comes before the word *or* or *and*. Not everyone uses the Oxford comma; it is optional, but many believe it is needed. The comma functions as a tool to reduce confusion in writing. So, if omitting the Oxford comma would cause confusion, then it's best to include it.

Commas are used in math to mark the place of thousands in numerals, breaking them up so they are easier to read. Other uses for commas are in dates (*March 19, 2016*), letter greetings (*Dear Sally,*), and in between cities and states (*Louisville, KY*).

Apostrophes

This punctuation mark, the apostrophe ('), is a versatile little mark. It has a few different functions:

- Quotes: Apostrophes are used when a second quote is needed within a quote.
- In my letter to my friend, I wrote, "The girl had to get a new purse, and guess what Mary did? She said, 'I'd like to go with you to the store.' I knew Mary would buy it for her."
- Contractions: Another use for an apostrophe in the quote above is a contraction. *I'd* is used for *I would.*

  The basic rule for making *contractions* is one area of spelling that is pretty straightforward: combine the two words by inserting an apostrophe (') in the space where a letter is omitted. For example, to combine *you* and *are*, drop the *a* and put the apostrophe in its place: *you're*.

  > he+is=he's
  >
  > you+all=y'all (informal but often misspelled)

- Possession: An apostrophe followed by the letter *s* shows possession (*Mary's* purse). If the possessive word is plural, the apostrophe generally just follows the word.
- The trees' leaves are all over the ground.

Ellipses

An **ellipsis** (…) is used to show that there is more to the quoted text than is necessary for the current discussion. Writers use them in place of words, lines, phrases, list content, or paragraphs that might just as easily have been omitted from a passage of writing. This can be done to save space or to focus only on the specifically relevant material.

> Exercise is good for some unexpected reasons. Watkins writes, "Exercise has many benefits such as…reducing cancer risk."

In the example above, the ellipsis takes the place of the other benefits of exercise that are more expected.

The ellipsis may also be used to show a pause in sentence flow.

> "I'm wondering... how this could happen," Dylan said in a soft voice.

Semicolons

The **semicolon** (;) might be described as a heavy-handed comma. Take a look at these two examples:

> I will pay for the ice cream, but I will not pay for the steak.
> I will pay for the ice cream; I will not pay for the steak.

What's the difference? The first example has a comma and a conjunction separating the two independent clauses. The second example does not have a conjunction, but there are two independent clauses in the sentence, so something more than a comma is required. In this case, a semicolon is used.

Two independent clauses can only be joined in a sentence by either a comma and conjunction or a semicolon. If one of those tools is not used, the sentence will be a run-on. Remember that while the clauses are independent, they need to be closely related in order to be contained in one sentence.

Another use for the semicolon is to separate items in a list when the items themselves require commas.

> The family lived in Phoenix, Arizona; Oklahoma City, Oklahoma; and Raleigh, North Carolina.

Colons

Colons (:) have many miscellaneous functions. Colons can be used preceding further information or a list. In these cases, a colon should only follow an independent clause.

> Humans take in sensory information through five basic senses: sight, hearing, smell, touch, and taste.

The meal includes the following components:

- Caesar salad
- spaghetti
- garlic bread
- cake

Colons can also be used to introduce an appositive.

> The family got what they needed: a reliable vehicle.

While a comma is more common, a colon can also precede a formal quotation.

> He said to the crowd: "Let's begin!"

The colon is used after the greeting in a formal letter.

> Dear Sir:
> To Whom It May Concern:

In the writing of time, the colon separates the minutes from the hour (*4:45 p.m.*). The colon can also be used to indicate a ratio between two numbers (*50:1*).

Hyphens

The **hyphen** (-) is a little hash mark that can be used to join words to show that they are linked.

Hyphens can connect two words that work together as a single adjective (a compound adjective).

honey-covered biscuits

Some words always require hyphens even if not serving as an adjective.

merry-go-round

Hyphens always go after certain prefixes like *anti-* & *all-*.

Hyphens should also be used when the absence of the hyphen would cause a strange vowel combination (*semi-engineer*) or confusion. For example, *re-collect* should be used to describe something being gathered twice rather than being written as *recollect*, which means to remember.

Parentheses and Dashes

Parentheses are half-round brackets that look like this: *( )*. They set off a word, phrase, or sentence that is an afterthought, explanation, or side note relevant to the surrounding text but not essential. A pair of commas is often used to set off this sort of information, but parentheses are generally used for information that would not fit well within a sentence or that the writer deems not important enough to be structurally part of the sentence.

The picture of the heart (see above) shows the major parts you should memorize.
Mount Everest is one of three mountains in the world that are over 28,000 feet high (K2 and Kanchenjunga are the other two).

See how the sentences above are complete without the parenthetical statements? In the first example, *see above* would not have fit well within the flow of the sentence. The second parenthetical statement could have been a separate sentence, but the writer deemed the information not pertinent to the topic.

The **em-dash** (—) is a mark longer than a hyphen used as a punctuation mark in sentences and to set apart a relevant thought. Even after plucking out the line separated by the dash marks, the sentence will be intact and make sense.

Looking out the airplane window at the landmarks—Lake Clarke, Thompson Community College, and the bridge—she couldn't help but feel excited to be home.

The dashes use is similar to that of parentheses or a pair of commas. So, what's the difference? Many believe that using dashes makes the clause within them stand out while using parentheses is subtler. It's advised to not use dashes when commas could be used instead.

Quotation Marks

Quotation marks ("") are used in a number of ways. Here are some instances where quotation marks should be used:

- Dialogue for characters in narratives. When characters speak, the first word should always be capitalized and the punctuation goes inside the quotes. For example:

  Janie said, "The tree fell on my car during the hurricane."

- Around titles of songs, short stories, essays, and chapters in books
- To emphasize a certain word
- To refer to a word as the word itself

Capitalization

Here's a non-exhaustive list of things that should be capitalized:

- The first word of every sentence
- The first word of every line of poetry
- The first letter of proper nouns (World War II)
- Holidays (Valentine's Day)
- The days of the week and months of the year (Tuesday, March)
- The first word, last word, and all major words in the titles of books, movies, songs, and other creative works (In the novel, *To Kill a Mockingbird*, note that *a* is lowercase since it's not a major word, but *to* is capitalized since it's the first word of the title.)
- Titles when preceding a proper noun (President Roberto Gonzales, Aunt Judy)

When simply using a word such as president or secretary, though, the word is not capitalized.

> Officers of the new business must include a *president* and *treasurer*.

Seasons—spring, fall, etc.—are not capitalized.

North, *south*, *east*, and *west* are capitalized when referring to regions but are not when being used for directions. In general, if it's preceded by *the* it should be capitalized.

> I'm from the South.
> I drove south.

Writing Tips

Conciseness

Unfortunately, writers often include extra words and phrases that seem necessary at the time but add nothing to the main idea. This confuses the reader and creates unnecessary repetition. Writing that lacks conciseness is usually guilty of excessive wordiness and redundant phrases.

Here's an example containing both of these issues:

> When legislators decided to begin creating legislation making it mandatory for automobile drivers and passengers to make use of seat belts while in cars, a large number of them made those laws for reasons that were political reasons.

There are several empty or "luff" words here that take up too much space. These can be eliminated while still maintaining the writer's meaning. For example:

- "Decided to begin" could be shortened to "began"
- "Making it mandatory for" could be shortened to "requiring"
- "Make use of" could be shortened to "use"
- "A large number" could be shortened to "many"

In addition, there are several examples of redundancy that can be eliminated:

- "Legislators decided to begin creating legislation" and "made those laws"
- "Automobile drivers and passengers" and "while in cars"
- "Reasons that were political reasons"

These changes are incorporated as follows:

> When legislators began requiring drivers and passengers to use seat belts, many of them did so for political reasons.

Euphemisms

Euphemisms are terms or phrases used to say something indirectly. Often times it's to soften an expression, be polite, or in some cases to be impolite. Eliminating euphemisms can be helpful in writing more concisely.

> Normal expression: He is very short.
>
> Euphemism: He is vertically challenged.

Clichés

A **cliché** is an old, often-used phrase that has lost all originality, humor, or depth due to its overuse. These idioms are all *clichés*:

- A penny for your thoughts
- Head over heels in love
- Give your two cents

It's best to avoid clichés since they are overused and because their elimination can help you be more concise.

Distinguishing Between Formal and Informal Language

It can be helpful to distinguish whether a writer or speaker is using formal or informal language because it can give the reader or listener clues to whether the text is informative, nonfiction, argumentative, or the intended tone or audience. Formal and informal language in written or verbal communication serve different purposes and are often intended for different audiences. Consequently, their tone, word choices, and grammatical structures vary. These differences can be used to identify which form of language is used in a given piece and to determine which type of language should be used for a certain context. Understanding the differences between formal and informal language will also allow a writer or speaker to implement the most appropriate and effective style for a given situation.

Formal language is less personal and more informative and pragmatic than informal language. It is more "buttoned-up" and business-like, adhering to proper grammatical rules. It is used in professional or academic contexts, to convey respect or authority. For example, one would use formal language to write an informative or argumentative essay for school and to address a superior or esteemed professional like a potential employer, a professor, or a manager. Formal language avoids contractions, slang, colloquialisms, and first-person pronouns.

Informal language is often used when communicating with family members, friends, peers, and those known more personally. It is more casual, spontaneous, and forgiving in its conformity to grammatical rules and conventions. Informal language is used for personal emails, some light fiction stories, and some correspondence between coworkers or other familial relationships.

Slang refers to non-standard expressions that are not used in elevated speech and writing. Slang creates linguistic in-groups and out-groups of people, those who can understand the slang terms and those who can't. Slang is often tied to a specific time period. For example, "groovy" and "far out" are connected to the 1970s, and "as if!" and "4-1-1-" are connected to the 1990s. **Colloquial language** is language that is used conversationally or familiarly—e.g., "What's up?"—in contrast to formal, professional, or academic language—"How are you this evening?" Formal language uses sentences that are usually more complex and often in passive voice. Punctuation can differ as well. For example, exclamation points are used to show strong emotion or can be used as an interjection but should be used sparingly in formal writing situations.

Textspeak is a term used to refer to the informal language used in text messages and similar messaging mediums. While often appropriate for use in those contexts, it should be avoided in more formal settings.

Outside of casual conversations, it's important to use formal language both in speaking and writing.

Sensitivity

In speech and writing, it's important to be cognizant as to how your words are perceived by others. Racist, sexist, and other derogatory language should be avoided because it is rude, demeaning, and can severely hurt career opportunities. It may be helpful to adopt a position of being "above reproach", meaning that your words and actions are so pure they cannot be criticized for being insensitive.

Various Homonyms

That/Which

The pronouns *that* and *which* are both used to refer to nouns—but they are not interchangeable. The rule is to use the word *that* in essential clauses and phrases that help convey the meaning of the sentence. Use the word *which* in nonessential (less important) clauses. Typically, *which* clauses are enclosed in commas.

> The morning <u>that I fell asleep in class</u> caused me a lot of trouble.
>
> This morning's coffee, <u>which had too much creamer</u>, woke me up.

Who/Whom

We use the pronouns *who* and *whom* to refer to people. We always use *who* when it is the subject of the sentence or clause. We never use *whom* as the subject; it is always the object of a verb or preposition.

> <u>Who</u> hit the baseball for the home run? (subject)
>
> The baseball fell into the glove of <u>whom</u>? (object of the preposition of)
>
> The umpire called <u>whom</u> "out"? (object of the verb called)

To/Too/Two

> to: a preposition or infinitive (*to walk, to run, walk to the store, run to the tree*)
> too: means also, as well, or very (*She likes cookies, too.; I ate too much.*)
> two: a number (*I have two cookies. She walked to the store two times.*)

There/Their/They're

> there: an adjective, adverb, or pronoun used to start a sentence or indicate place (*There are four vintage cars over there.*)

their: a possessive pronoun used to indicate belonging (*Their car is the blue and white one*.)
they're: a contraction of the words "they are" (*They're going to enter the vintage car show*.)

Its/It's

its: a possessive pronoun (*The elephant had its trunk in the water.*)
it's: a contraction of the words "it is" (*It's an impressive animal.*)

Affect/Effect

affect: as a verb means "to influence" (*How will the earthquake affect your home?*); as a noun means "emotion or mood" (*Her affect was somber.*)
effect: as a verb means "to bring about" (*She will effect a change through philanthropy.*); as a noun means "a result of" (*The effect of the earthquake was devastating.*)

Other pairs of words cause mix-ups but are not necessarily homonyms. Here are a few of those:

Bring/Take

bring: when the action is coming toward (*Bring me the money.*)
take: when the action is going away from (*Take her the money.*)

Can/May

can: means "able to" (*The child can ride a bike.*)
may: asks permission (*The child asked if he may ride his bike.*)

Than/Then

than: a conjunction used for comparison (*I like tacos better than pizza.*)
then: an adverb telling when something happened (*I ate and then slept.*)

Disinterested/Uninterested

disinterested: used to mean "neutral" (*The jury remains disinterested during the trial.*)
uninterested: used to mean "bored" (*I was uninterested during the lecture.*)

Percent/Percentage

percent: used when there is a number involved (*Five percent of us like tacos.*)
percentage: used when there is no number (*That is a low percentage.*)

Fewer/Less

fewer: used for things you can count (*He has fewer playing cards.*)
less: used for things you cannot count, as well as time (*He has less talent. You have less than a minute.*)

Farther/Further

farther: used when discussing distance (*His paper airplane flew farther than mine.*)
further: used to mean "more" (*He needed further information.*)

Lend/Loan

lend: a verb used for borrowing (*Lend me your lawn mower. He will lend it to me.*)
loan: a noun used for something borrowed (*She applied for a student loan.*)

Among/Between

among: used when referring to more than two things (*Surfing is among my favorite hobbies.*)

between: usually used when referring to just two things, or when naming specific distinct items, even if more than two (*She sat between Bill and Ronald.*)

Good/Well

good: an adjective, which modifies a noun or pronoun (*She is a good pianist.*)
well: an adverb that answers the question "how?" (*She plays piano well.*)

Bad/Badly

bad: an adjective, which modifies a noun or pronoun (*That was a bad storm.*)
badly: an adverb that answers the question "how?" (*Donna was hurt badly in the car accident.*)

Hear/Here

hear: a verb that means to perceive sound by using one's ears (*I can hear the birds chirping.*)
here: an adverb meaning at, on, or in this place (*The book was found here.)*

i.e./e.g.

i.e.: short for the Latin phrase *id est,* which means "in other words." (*Our new house is a money pit – i.e., things are constantly breaking and we have spent tens of thousands of dollars on repairs.*)
e.g.: short for the Latin phrase *exempli gratia*, which means "for example." (*The textbook also comes with online features (e.g., interactive quizzes, instructional videos)*).

Lie/Lay

lie: a verb meaning to recline in a flat position, and using it does not require a direct object (*I'm going to lie down after I call Terry.*)
lay: a verb that means to place something in its resting position, and using it requires a direct object (*I usually lay my sweater on the back of the chair.*)

Who's/Whose

who's: a contraction of "who is" (*Who's coming to dinner?*)
whose: indicates possession (*Whose sweater is this?*)

Look at the following sentence:

Who's job is it to protect America's drivers?

The easiest way to check for correct usage is to replace the word *who's* with "who is" and see if the sentence makes sense:

Who is job is it to protect America's drivers?

By changing the contraction to "Who is" the sentence no longer makes sense. Therefore, the correct word must be *whose*.

Your/You're

your: indicates possession (*Your desk is very organized.*)
you're: a contraction for "you are" (*You are our pick for next VP.*)

Look at the following example:

Your going to have to write your congressman if you want to see action.

Again, the easiest way to check correct usage is to replace the word *Your* with "You are" and see if the sentence still makes sense.

You are going to have to write your congressman if you want to see action.

By replacing Your with "You are," the sentence still makes sense. Thus, in this case, the writer should have used "You're."

Note

Some people have problems with these:

- regardless/irregardless
- a lot/alot

Irregardless and *alot* are always incorrect. Don't use them.

Please keep in mind that grammar questions on the actual exam may be hospital related.

Practice Quiz

1. Which sentence contains an error in punctuation or capitalization?
    a. "The show is on," Jackson said.
    b. The Grand Canyon is a national park.
    c. Lets celebrate tomorrow.
    d. Oliver, a social worker, got a new job this month.

2. Which of the following sentences contains an error in usage?
    a. Their words was followed by a signing document.
    b. No one came to the theater that evening.
    c. Several cats were living in the abandoned house down the road.
    d. It rained that morning; they had to cancel the kayaking trip.

3. What type of grammatical error does the following sentence contain?

    It was true, Lyla ate the last cupcake.

a. Subject-verb agreement error
    b. Punctuation error
    c. Shift in verb tense
    d. Split infinitive

4. Which sentence below contains an error in punctuation or capitalization?
    a. Afterwards, we got ice cream down the road.
    b. The word "slacken" means to decrease.
    c. They started building the Hoover dam in 1931.
    d. Matthew got married to his best friend, Maria.

5. Choose the sentence that contains an error in usage. If there are no errors, select Choice *D.*
    a. After her swim, Jeanine saw a blue kid's shovel.
    b. Pistachios are my favorite kind of nut, although they're expensive.
    c. One apple is better than two lemons.
    d. We found three five-dollar bills on the way home.

See answers on the next page.

Answer Explanations

1. C: The correct answer choice is "Lets celebrate tomorrow." *Lets* is supposed to be short for "let us," and therefore needs an apostrophe between the *t* and the *s*: *Let's*.

2. A: This error is marked by a subject/verb agreement. *Words* is plural, so the verb must be plural as well. The correct usage would be: "Their words were followed by a signing document."

3. B: There is a punctuation error. The comma creates a comma splice where a period or a semicolon should be since we have two independent clauses on either side of the comma.

4. C: Choice *C* is the problematic answer; the whole phrase "Hoover Dam" should be capitalized, not just "Hoover."

5. A: Choice *A* has the error in usage because we have a dangling modifier with the phrase "blue kid's shovel." The sentence indicates the kid is blue. We want the sentence to say that the shovel is blue. Therefore, it should be: "After her swim, Jeanine saw a kid's blue shovel."

Biology

Biology is the study of living organisms and the processes that are vital for life.

Biology Basics

Taxonomy is the science behind the biological names of organisms. Biologists often refer to organisms by their Latin scientific names to avoid confusion with common names, such as with fish. Jellyfish, crayfish, and silverfish all have the word "fish" in their name, but belong to three different species. In the eighteenth century, Carl Linnaeus invented a naming system for species that included using the Latin scientific name of a species, called the *binomial*, which has two parts: the *genus*, which comes first, and the *specific epithet*, which comes second. Similar species are grouped into the same genus. The Linnaean system is the commonly used taxonomic system today and, moving from comprehensive similarities to more general similarities, classifies organisms into their species, genus, family, order, class, phylum, and kingdom. *Homo sapiens* is the Latin scientific name for humans.

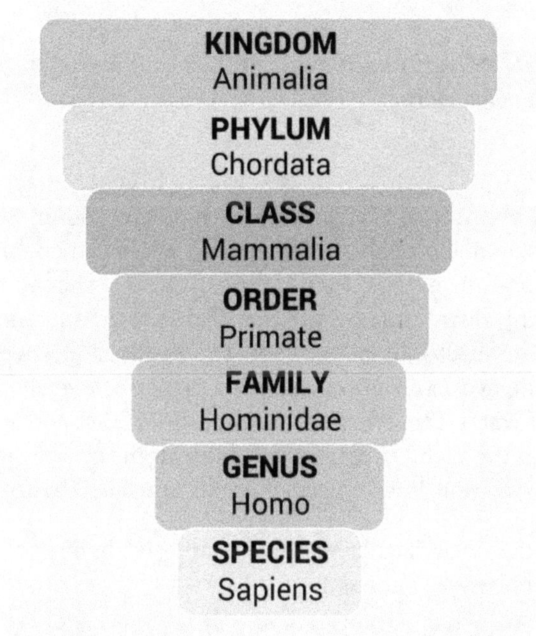

Scientific Method

Human beings are, by nature, very curious. Since long before the scientific method was established, people have been making observations and predicting outcomes, manipulating the physical world to create extraordinary things—from the first man-made fire in 6000 B.C.E. to the satellite that orbited Pluto in 2016. Although the history of the scientific method is sporadic and attributed to many different people, it remains the most reliable way to obtain and utilize knowledge about the observable universe. The scientific method consists of the following steps:

- **Make an observation:** An **observation** is the analysis of information using basic human senses: sight, sound, touch, taste, and smell. Observations can be two different types—qualitative or quantitative. A *qualitative observation* describes what is being observed, such as the color of a house or the smell of a flower. *Quantitative observations* measure what is being observed, such as the number of windows on a house or the intensity of a flower's smell on a scale of 1-5.

- **Create a question:** Observations lead to the identification of a problem, also called an **inference**. Inferences are logical predictions based on experience or education that lead to the formation of a hypothesis.

- **Form a hypothesis:** A **hypothesis** is a testable explanation of an observed scenario and is presented in the form of a statement. It's an attempt to answer a question based on an observation, and it allows a scientist to predict an outcome. A hypothesis makes assumptions on the relationship between two different variables, and answers the question: "If I do this, what happens to that?"

- **Conduct an experiment:** Once a hypothesis has been formed, it must be tested to determine whether it's true or false. To test a hypothesis, one must conduct a carefully designed experiment.

- **Collect and analyze data:** Once the experiment begins, a disciplined scientist must always record the observations in meticulous detail, usually in a journal. Upon reading this journal, a different scientist should be able to clearly understand the experiment and recreate it exactly. The journal includes all **collected data**, or any observed changes.

- **Form a conclusion:** The final step of the scientific method is to make inferences from observed data, which is also known as forming a **conclusion**.

Water

Most cells are primarily composed of water and live in water-rich environments. Since water is such a familiar substance, it is easy to overlook its unique properties. Chemically, water is made up of two hydrogen atoms bonded to one oxygen atom by covalent bonds. The three atoms join to make a V-shaped molecule. Water is a polar molecule, meaning it has an unevenly distributed overall charge due to an unequal sharing of electrons. Due to oxygen's electronegativity and its more substantial positively charged nucleus, hydrogen's electrons are pulled closer to the oxygen. This causes the hydrogen atoms to have a slight positive charge and the oxygen atom to have a slight negative charge. In a glass of water, the molecules constantly interact and link for a fraction of a second due to intermolecular bonding between the slightly positive hydrogen atoms of one molecule and the slightly negative oxygen of a different molecule. These weak intermolecular bonds are called **hydrogen bonds**.

Water has several important qualities, including: cohesive and adhesive behaviors, temperature moderation ability, expansion upon freezing, and diverse use as a solvent.

Cohesion is the interaction of many of the same molecules. In water, cohesion occurs when there is hydrogen bonding between water molecules. Water molecules use this bonding ability to attach to each other and can work against gravity to transport dissolved nutrients to the top of a plant. A network of water-conducting cells can push water from the roots of a plant up to the leaves. Adhesion is the linking of two different substances. Water molecules can form a weak hydrogen bond with, or adhere to, plant cell walls to help fight gravity. The cohesive behavior of water also causes surface tension. If a glass of water is slightly overfull, water can still stand above the rim. This is because of the unique bonding of water molecules at the surface—they bond to each other and to the molecules below them, making it seem like it is covered with an impenetrable film. A raft spider could actually walk across a small body of water due to this surface tension.

Another important property of water is its ability to moderate temperature. Water can moderate the temperature of air by absorbing or releasing stored heat into the air. Water has the distinctive capability of being able to absorb or release large quantities of stored heat while undergoing only a small change in temperature. This is because of the relatively high **specific heat** of water, where specific heat is the amount of heat it takes for one gram of a material to change its temperature by 1 degree Celsius. The specific heat of water is one calorie per gram per degree Celsius, meaning that for each gram of water, it takes one calorie of heat to raise or lower the temperature of water by 1 degree Celsius.

When the temperature of water is reduced to freezing levels, water displays another interesting property: It expands instead of contracts. Most liquids become denser as they freeze because the molecules move around slower and stay closer together. Water molecules, however, form hydrogen bonds with each other as they move together. As the temperature lowers and they begin to move slower, these bonds become harder to break apart. When water freezes into ice, molecules are frozen with hydrogen bonds between them and they take up about 10 percent more volume than in their liquid state. The fact that ice is less dense than water is what makes ice float to the top of a glass of water.

Lastly, the **polarity** of water molecules makes it a versatile solvent. **Ionic compounds**, such as salt, are made up of positively- and negatively-charged atoms, called **cations** and **anions**, respectively. Cations and anions are easily dissolved in water because of their individual attractions to the slight positive charge of the hydrogen atoms or the slight negative charge of the oxygen atoms in water molecules. Water molecules separate the individually charged atoms and shield them from each other so they don't bond to each other again, creating a homogenous solution of the cations and anions. Nonionic compounds, such as sugar, have polar regions, so are easily dissolved in water. For these compounds, the water molecules form hydrogen bonds with the polar regions (hydroxyl groups) to create a homogenous solution. Any substance that is attracted to water is termed **hydrophilic**. Substances that repel water are termed **hydrophobic**.

Biological Molecules

Basic units of organic compounds are often called **monomers**. Repeating units of linked monomers are called **polymers**. The most important large molecules, or polymers, found in all living things can be divided into four categories: carbohydrates, lipids, proteins, and nucleic acids. This may be surprising since there is so much diversity in the outward appearance and physical abilities of living things present on Earth. Carbon (C), hydrogen (H), oxygen (O), nitrogen (N), sulfur (S), and phosphorus (P) are the major elements of most biological molecules. Carbon is a common backbone of large molecules because of its ability to form four covalent bonds.

Carbohydrates

Carbohydrates consist of sugars and polymers of sugars. The simplest sugars are **monosaccharides**, which have the empirical formula of CH_2O. The formula for the monosaccharide glucose, for example, is $C_6H_{12}O_6$. Glucose is an important molecule for cellular respiration, the process of cells extracting energy by breaking bonds through a series of reactions. The individual atoms are then used to rebuild new small molecules. **Polysaccharides** are made up of a few hundred to a few thousand monosaccharides linked together. These larger molecules have two major functions. The first is that they can be stored as starches, such as **glycogen**, and then broken down later for energy. Secondly, they may be used to form strong materials, such as **cellulose**, which is the firm wall that encloses plant cells, and **chitin**, the carbohydrate insects use to build exoskeletons.

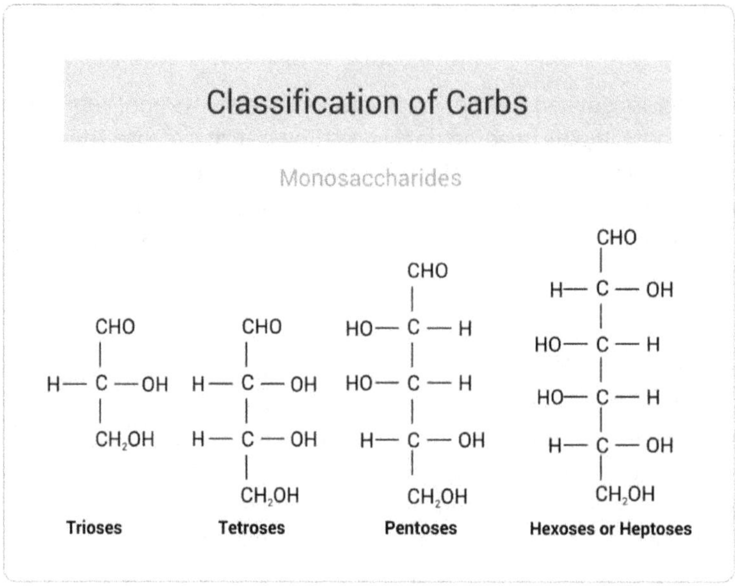

Lipids

Lipids are a class of biological molecules that are **hydrophobic**, meaning they don't mix well with water. They are mostly made up of large chains of carbon and hydrogen atoms, termed **hydrocarbon chains**. When lipids mix with water, the water molecules bond to each other and exclude the lipids because they are unable to form bonds with the long hydrocarbon chains. Because the structure of different lipids is so diverse, they have a wide range of functions, which include energy storage, signaling, structure, protection, and making up the cell membrane. The three most important types of lipids are fats, phospholipids, and steroids.

Fats are made up of two types of smaller molecules: glycerol and fatty acids. **Glycerol** is a chain of three carbon atoms, with a **hydroxyl group** attached to each carbon atom. A hydroxyl group is made up of an oxygen and hydrogen atom bonded together. **Fatty acids** are long hydrocarbon chains that have a backbone of sixteen or eighteen carbon atoms. The carbon atom on one end of the fatty acid is part of a **carboxyl group.** A carboxyl group is a carbon atom that uses two of its four bonds to bond to one oxygen atom (double bond) and uses another one of its bonds to link to a hydroxyl group.

Fats are made by joining three fatty acid molecules and one glycerol molecule.

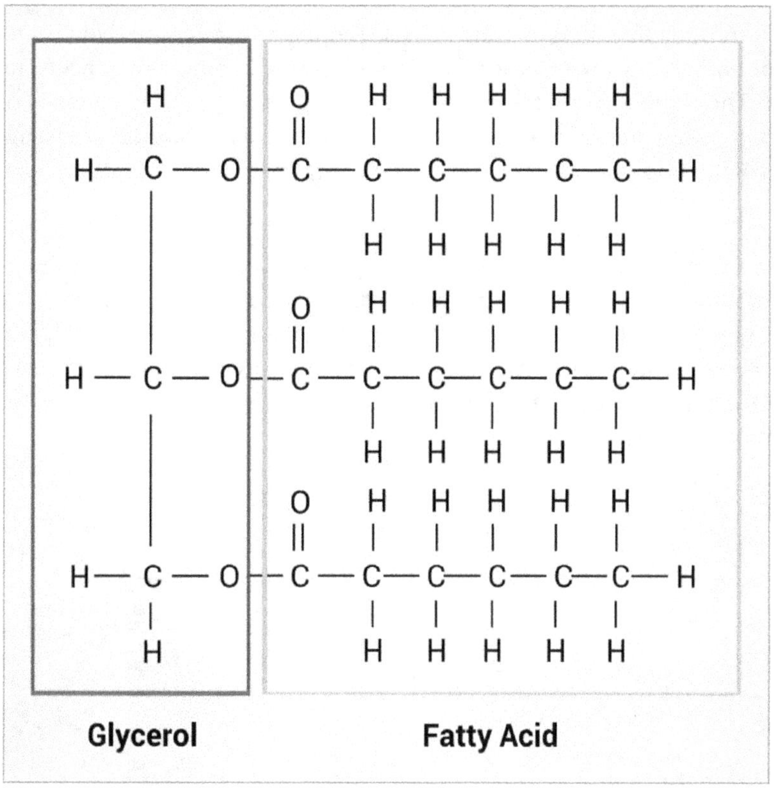

These energy-storage molecules can exist as any of the following types.

- **Saturated fats** have no double bonds within their fatty acid tails. These are solid at room temperature and are mostly animal fats like bacon fat.
- **Unsaturated fats** have double bonds within any of their fatty acid tails. Due to the kinks caused by the double bonds, these fats are liquid at room temperature and are mostly plant fats like olive oil.

Phospholipids are made of two fatty acid molecules linked to one glycerol molecule. A **phosphate group** is attached to a third hydroxyl group of the glycerol molecule. A phosphate group consists of a phosphate atom connected to four oxygen atoms and has an overall negative charge.

Phospholipids have an interesting structure because their fatty acid tails are hydrophobic, but their phosphate group heads are hydrophilic. When phospholipids mix with water, they create double-layered structures, called **bilayers,** that shield their hydrophobic regions from water molecules. Cell membranes are made of phospholipid bilayers, which allow the cells to mix with aqueous solutions outside and inside, while forming a protective barrier and a semi-permeable membrane around the cell.

Steroids are lipids that consist of four fused carbon rings. The different chemical groups that attach to these rings are what make up the many types of steroids. **Cholesterol** is a common type of steroid found in animal cell membranes. Steroids are mixed in between the phospholipid bilayer and help maintain the structure of the membrane and aids in cell signaling.

Proteins

Proteins are essential for most all functions in living beings. The term *protein* is derived from the Greek word *proteios*, meaning *first* or *primary*. All proteins are made from a set of twenty **amino acids**, molecules that are linked in unbranched polymers. The combinations are numerous, which accounts for the diversity of proteins. Amino acids are linked by peptide bonds, while polymers of amino acids are called **polypeptides.** These polypeptides, either individually or in linked combination with each other, fold up to form coils of biologically-functional molecules, called proteins.

There are four levels of protein structure: primary, secondary, tertiary, and quaternary. The **primary structure** is the sequence of amino acids, similar to the letters in a long word. The **secondary structure** is beta sheets, or alpha helices, formed by hydrogen bonding between the polar regions of the polypeptide backbone. **Tertiary structure** is the overall shape of the molecule that results from the interactions between the side chains linked to the polypeptide backbone. **Quaternary structure** is the overall protein structure that occurs when a protein is made up of two or more polypeptide chains.

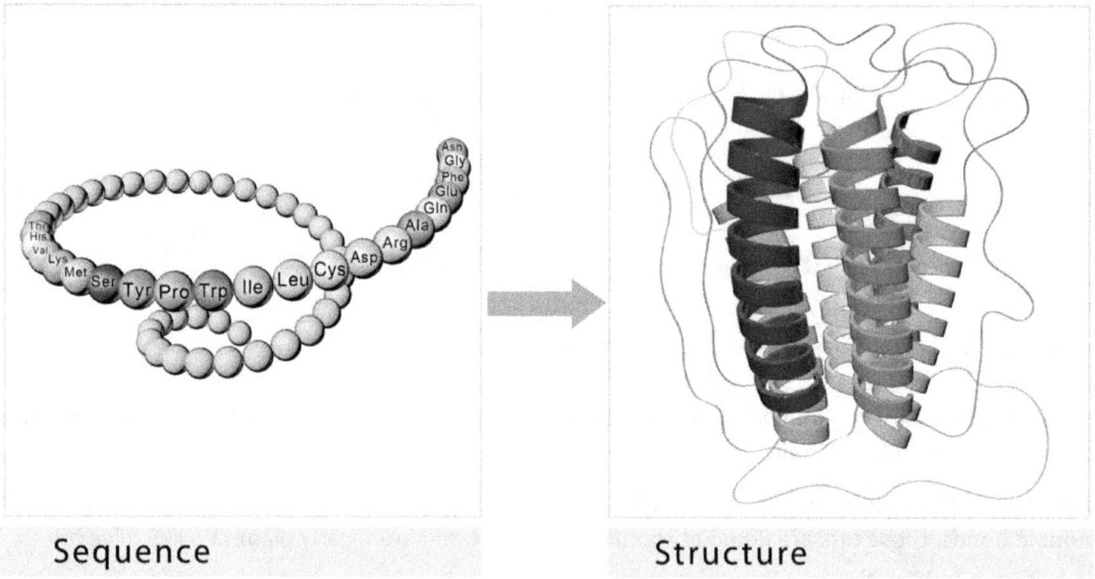

Nucleic Acids

Nucleic acids can also be called **polynucleotides** because they are made up of chains of monomers called **nucleotides.** Nucleotides consist of a five-carbon sugar, a nitrogen-containing base, and a phosphate group. There are two types of nucleic acids: **deoxyribonucleic acid (DNA)** and **ribonucleic acid (RNA)**. Both DNA and RNA enable living organisms to pass on their genetic information and complex components to subsequent generations. While

DNA is made up of two strands of nucleotides coiled together in a double-helix structure, RNA is made up of a single strand of nucleotides that folds onto itself.

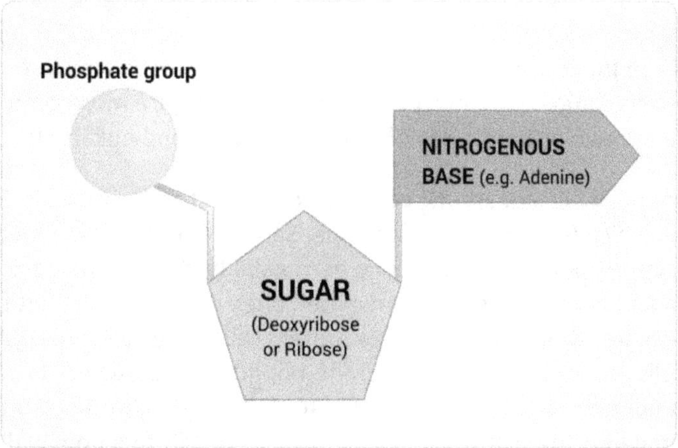

Metabolism

Metabolism is the set of chemical processes that occur within a cell for the maintenance of life. It includes both the synthesizing and breaking down of substances. A **metabolic pathway** begins with a molecule and ends with a specific product after going through a series of reactions, often involving an enzyme at each step. An **enzyme** is a protein that aids in the reaction. **Catabolic pathways** are metabolic pathways in which energy is released by complex molecules being broken down into simpler molecules. Contrast to catabolic pathways are **anabolic pathways**, which use energy to build complex molecules out of simple molecules. With cell metabolism, remember the **first law of thermodynamics**: Energy can be transformed, but it cannot be created or destroyed. Therefore, the energy released in a cell by a catabolic pathway is used up in anabolic pathways.

The reactions that occur within metabolic pathways are classified as either exergonic reactions or endergonic reactions. **Exergonic reactions** end in a release of free energy, while **endergonic reactions** absorb free energy from its surroundings. **Free energy** is the portion of energy in a system, such as a living cell, that can be used to perform work, such as a chemical reaction. It is denoted as the capital letter G and the change in free energy from a reaction or set of reactions is denoted as delta G (ΔG). When reactions do not require an input of energy, they are said to occur spontaneously. Exergonic reactions are considered spontaneous because they result in a negative delta G ($-\Delta G$), where the products of the reaction have less free energy within them than the reactants. Endergonic reactions require an input of energy and result in a positive delta G ($+\Delta G$), with the products of the reaction containing more free energy than the individual reactants. When a system no longer has free energy to do work, it has reached **equilibrium**. Since cells always work, they are no longer alive if they reach equilibrium.

Cells balance their energy resources by using the energy from exergonic reactions to drive endergonic reactions forward, a process called **energy coupling**. **Adenosine triphosphate**, or ATP, is a molecule that is an immediate source of energy for cellular work. When it is broken down, it releases energy used in endergonic reactions and anabolic pathways. ATP breaks down into adenosine diphosphate, or ADP, and a separate phosphate group, releasing energy in an exergonic reaction. As ATP is used up by reactions, it is also regenerated by having a new phosphate group added onto the ADP products within the cell in an endergonic reaction.

Enzymes are special proteins that help speed up metabolic reactions and pathways. They do not change the overall free energy release or consumption of reactions; they just make the reactions occur more quickly as it lowers the activation energy required. Enzymes are designed to act only on specific substrates. Their physical shape fits snugly onto their matched substrates, so enzymes only speed up reactions that contain the substrates to which they are matched.

The Cell

Cells are the basic structural and functional unit of all organisms. They are the smallest unit of matter that is living. While there are many single-celled organisms, most biological organisms are more complex and made up of many different types of cells. There are two distinct types of cells: prokaryotic and eukaryotic.

Prokaryotic cells include bacteria, while **eukaryotic cells** include animal and plant cells. Both types of cells are enclosed by a cell membrane, which is selectively permeable. Selective permeability means essentially that it is a **cell membrane**, which is selectively permeable. Selective permeability means that it acts as a gatekeeper, allowing certain molecules and ions in and out while keeping unwanted ones at bay, at least until they are ready for use. Both contain ribosomes, which are complexes that make protein inside the cell, and DNA. One major difference is that the DNA in eukaryotic cells are enclosed in a membrane-bound **nucleus**, where in prokaryotic cells, DNA is in the **nucleoid**, a region that is not enclosed by a membrane. Another major difference is that eukaryotic cells contain **organelles,** which are membrane-enclosed structures, each with a specific function, while prokaryotic cells do not have organelles.

Organelles Found in Eukaryotic Cells

The following cell organelles are found in both animal and plant cells unless otherwise noted:

Nucleus: The nucleus consists of three parts: nuclear envelope, nucleolus, and chromatin. The **nuclear envelope** is the double membrane that surrounds the nucleus and separates its contents from the rest of the cell. It is porous so substances can pass back and forth between the nucleus and the other parts of the cell. It is also continuous, with the endoplasmic reticulum that is present within the cytosol of the cell. The **nucleolus** is in charge of producing ribosomes. **Chromosomes** are comprised of tightly coiled proteins, RNA, and DNA and are collectively called **chromatin**.

Endoplasmic Reticulum (ER): The ER is a network of membranous sacs and tubes responsible for membrane synthesis and other metabolic and synthetic activities of the cell. There are two types of ER, rough and smooth. **Rough ER** is lined with ribosomes and is the location of protein synthesis. This provides a separate compartment for site-specific protein synthesis and is important for the intracellular transport of proteins. **Smooth ER** does not contain ribosomes and is the location of lipid synthesis.

Flagellum: The flagellum is found in protists and animal cells. It is a cluster of microtubules projected out of the plasma membrane and aids in cell motility.

Centrosome: The centrosome is the area of the cell where microtubules are created and organized for mitosis. Each centrosome contains two **centrioles.**

Cytoskeleton: The cytoskeleton in animal cells is made up of microfilaments, intermediate filaments, and microtubules. In plant cells, the cytoskeleton is made up of only microfilaments and microtubules. These structures reinforce the cell's shape and aid in cell movements.

Microvilli: Microvilli are found only in animal cells. They are protrusions in the cell membrane that increase the cell's surface area. They have a variety of functions, including absorption, secretion, and cellular adhesion.

Peroxisome: A peroxisome contains enzymes that are involved in many of the cell's metabolic functions, one of the most important being the breakdown of fatty acid chains. It produces hydrogen peroxide as a by-product of these processes and then converts the hydrogen peroxide to water.

Mitochondrion: The mitochondrion, considered the cell's powerhouse, is one of the most important structures for maintaining regular cell function. It is where cellular respiration occurs and where most of the cell's ATP is generated.

Lysosome: Lysosomes are found exclusively in animal cells. They are responsible for digestion and can hydrolyze macromolecules.

Golgi Apparatus: The Golgi apparatus is responsible for synthesizing, modifying, sorting, transporting, and secreting cell products. Because of its large size, it was one of the first organelles studied in detail.

Ribosomes: Ribosomes are found either free in the cytosol, bound to the rough ER, or bound to the nuclear envelope. They are also found in prokaryotes. Ribosomes make up a complex that forms proteins within the cell.

Plasmodesmata: Found only in plant cells, plasmodesmata are cytoplasmic channels, or tunnels, that go through the cell wall and connect the cytoplasm of adjacent cells.

Chloroplast: Chloroplasts are plastids found in protists, such as algae and plant cells. It is responsible for photosynthesis, which is the process of converting sunlight to chemical energy that is stored and used later to drive cellular activities.

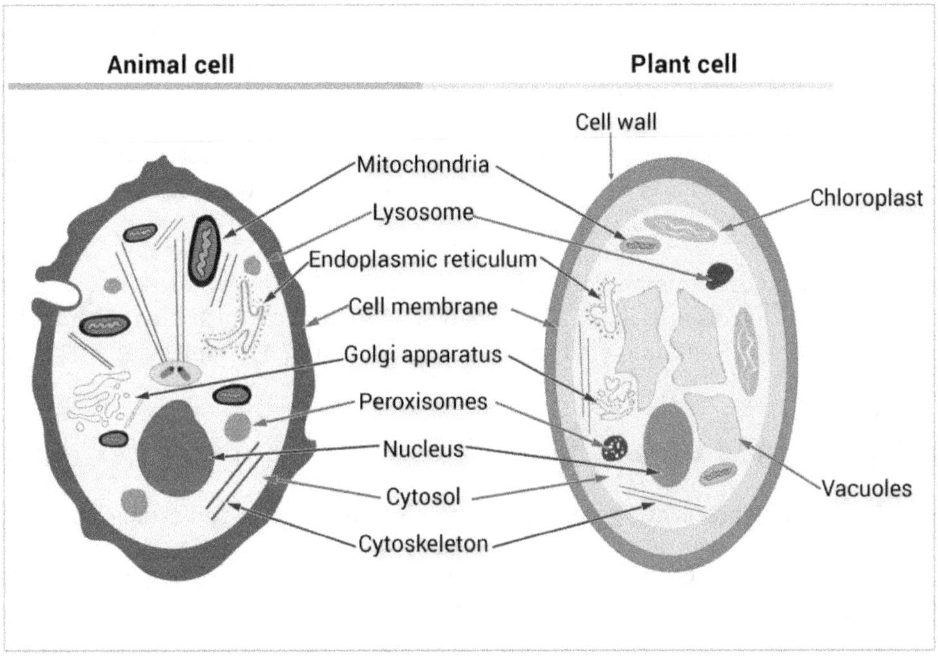

Vacuoles: Vacuoles are membrane-bound organelles found primarily in plant and fungi cells, but also in some animal cells. Vacuoles are filled with water and some enzymes and are important for intracellular digestion and waste removal. The membrane-bound nature of the vacuole allows for the storage of harmful material and poisonous substances. The pressure from the water inside the vacuole also contributes to the structure of plant cells. Animals have food vacuoles that contain the contents of phagocytosis. **Phagocytosis**, or "cellular eating," occurs when a cell engulfs large particles and internalizes them by using vacuoles.

Central Vacuole: A central vacuole is found only in plant cells, and is responsible for storage, breakdown of waste products, and hydrolysis of macromolecules.

Plasma Membrane: The plasma membrane is a phospholipid bilayer that encloses the cell. It is also found in prokaryotes.

Cell Wall: Cell walls are present in fungi, plant cells, and some protists. The cell wall is made up of strong fibrous substances, including cellulose (plants), chitin (fungi) and other polysaccharides, and protein. It is a layer outside of the plasma membrane that protects the cell from mechanical damage and helps maintain the cell's shape.

Cellular Respiration

Cellular respiration is a set of metabolic processes that converts energy from nutrients into ATP. Respiration can either occur aerobically, using oxygen, or anaerobically, without oxygen. While prokaryotic cells carry out respiration in the cytosol, most of the respiration in eukaryotic cells occurs in the mitochondria.

Aerobic Respiration

There are three main steps in aerobic cellular respiration: glycolysis, the citric acid cycle (also known as the Krebs cycle), and oxidative phosphorylation. **Glycolysis** is an essential metabolic pathway that converts glucose to pyruvate and allows for cellular respiration to occur. It does not require oxygen to be present. Glucose is a common molecule used for energy production in cells. During glycolysis, two three-carbon sugars are generated from the splitting of a glucose molecule. These smaller sugars are then converted into pyruvate molecules via oxidation and atom rearrangement. Glycolysis requires two ATP molecules to drive the process forward, but the end product of the process has four ATP molecules, for a net production of two ATP molecules. Also, two reduced nicotinamide adenine dinucleotide (NADH) molecules are created from when the electron carrier oxidized nicotinamide adenine dinucleotide (NAD+) peels off two electrons and a hydrogen atom.

In aerobically-respiring eukaryotic cells, the pyruvate molecules then enter the mitochondrion. Pyruvate is oxidized and converted into a compound called acetyl-CoA. This molecule enters the **citric acid cycle** to begin the process of aerobic respiration.

The citric acid cycle has eight steps. Remember that glycolysis produces two pyruvate molecules from each glucose molecule. Each pyruvate molecule oxidizes into a single acetyl-CoA molecule, which then enters the citric acid cycle. Therefore, two citric acid cycles can be completed and twice the number of ATP molecules are generated per glucose molecule.

Eight Steps of the Citric Acid Cycle

Step 1: Acetyl-CoA adds a two-carbon acetyl group to an oxaloacetate molecule and produces one citrate molecule.

Step 2: Citrate is converted to its isomer isocitrate by removing one water molecule and adding a new water molecule in a different configuration.

Step 3: Isocitrate is oxidized and converted to α-ketoglutarate. A carbon dioxide (CO_2) molecule is released and one NAD+ molecule is converted to NADH.

Step 4: α-Ketoglutarate is converted to succinyl-CoA. Another carbon dioxide molecule is released and another NAD+ molecule is converted to NADH.

Step 5: Succinyl-CoA becomes succinate by the addition of a phosphate group to the cycle. The oxygen molecule of the phosphate group attaches to the succinyl-CoA molecule and the CoA group is released. The rest of the phosphate group transfers to a guanosine diphosphate (GDP) molecule, converting it to guanosine triphosphate (GTP). GTP acts similarly to ATP and can actually be used to generate an ATP molecule at this step.

Step 6: Succinate is converted to fumarate by losing two hydrogen atoms. The hydrogen atoms join a flavin adenine dinucleotide (FAD) molecule, converting it to $FADH_2$, which is a hydroquinone form.

Step 7: A water molecule is added to the cycle and converts fumarate to malate.

Step 8: Malate is oxidized and converted to oxaloacetate. One lost hydrogen atom is added to an NAD molecule to create NADH. The oxaloacetate generated here then enters back into step one of the cycle.

At the end of glycolysis and the citric acid cycles, four ATP molecules have been generated. The NADH and $FADH_2$ molecules are used as energy to drive the next step of oxidative phosphorylation.

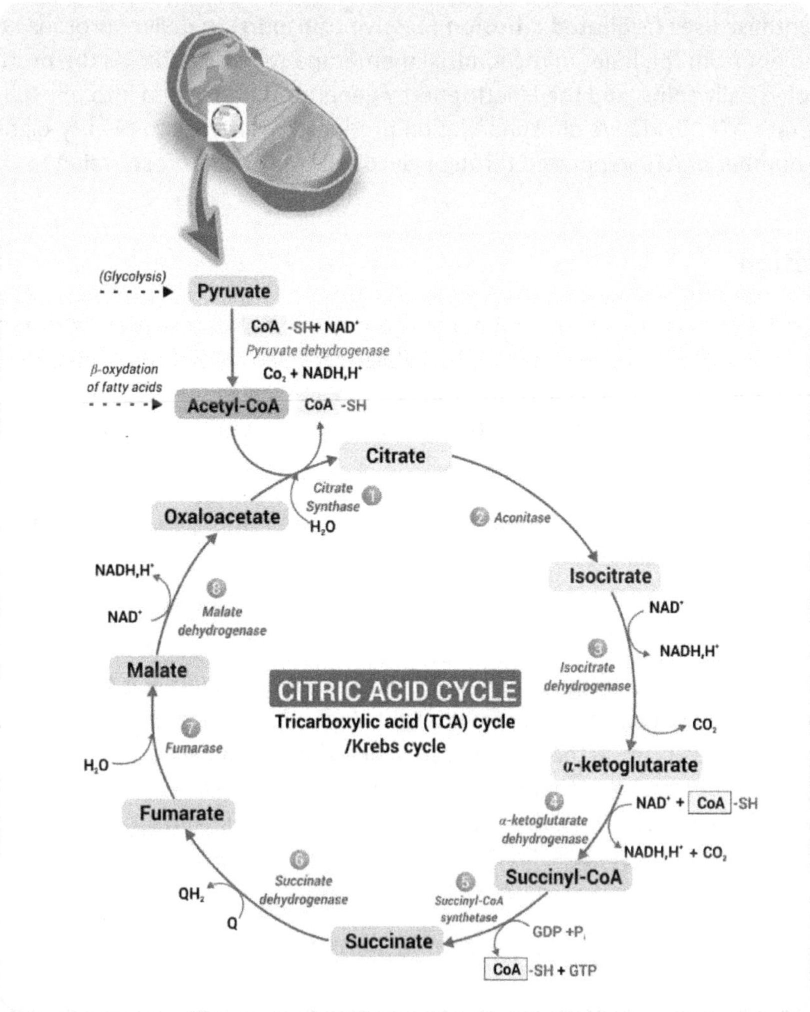

Oxidative Phosphorylation

Oxidative phosphorylation includes two steps: the electron transport chain and chemiosmosis. The inner mitochondrial membrane has four protein complexes, sequenced I to IV, used to transport protons and electrons through the inner mitochondrial matrix. Two electrons and a proton (H+) are passed from each NADH and $FADH_2$ to these channel proteins, pumping the hydrogen ions to the inner-membrane space using energy from the high-energy electrons to create a concentration gradient. NADH and $FADH_2$ also drop their high-energy electrons to the electron transport chain. NAD+ and FAD molecules in the mitochondrial matrix return to the Krebs cycle to pick up materials for the next delivery. From here, two processes happen simultaneously:

1. **Electron Transport Chain:** In addition to complexes I to IV, there are two mobile electron carriers present in the inner mitochondrial membrane, called **ubiquinone** and **cytochrome C.** At the end of this transport chain, electrons are accepted by an O_2 molecule in the matrix, and water is formed with the addition of two hydrogen atoms from chemiosmosis.

2. **Chemiosmosis:** This occurs in an ATP synthase complex that sits next to the four electron transporting complexes. ATP synthase uses **facilitated diffusion** (passive transport) to deliver protons across the concentration gradient from the inner mitochondrial membrane to the matrix. As the protons travel, the ATP synthase protein physically spins, and the kinetic energy generated is invested into phosphorylation of ADP molecules to generate ATP. Oxidative phosphorylation produces twenty-six to twenty-eight ATP molecules, bringing the total number of ATP generated through glycolysis and cellular respiration to thirty to thirty-two molecules.

Anaerobic Respiration

Some organisms do not live in oxygen-rich environments and must find alternate methods of respiration. Anaerobic respiration occurs in certain prokaryotic organisms. They utilize an electron transport chain similar to the aerobic respiration pathway; however, the terminal acceptor molecule is an electronegative substance that is not O_2. Some bacteria, for example, use the sulfate ion (SO_4^{2-}) as the final electron accepting molecule and the resulting byproduct is hydrogen sulfide (H_2S) instead of water.

Muscle cells that reach anaerobic threshold go through lactic acid respiration, while yeasts go through alcohol fermentation. Both processes only make two ATP.

Photosynthesis

Photosynthesis is the process of converting light energy into chemical energy that is then stored in sugar and other organic molecules. It can be divided into two stages: the light-dependent reactions and the Calvin cycle. In plants, the photosynthetic process takes place in the chloroplast. Inside the chloroplast are membranous sacs, called **thylakoids**. Chlorophyll is a green pigment that lives in the thylakoid membranes and absorbs the light energy, starting the process of photosynthesis. The **Calvin cycle** takes place in the **stroma,** or inner space, of the chloroplasts. The complex series of reactions that take place in photosynthesis can be simplified into the following equation:

$$6CO_2 + 12H_2O + \text{Light Energy} \rightarrow C_6H_{12}O_6 + 6O_2 + 6H_2O$$

Basically, carbon dioxide and water mix with light energy inside the chloroplast to produce organic molecules, oxygen, and water. Note that water is on both sides of the equation. Twelve water molecules are consumed during this process and six water molecules are newly formed as byproducts.

The Light Reactions

During the **light reactions**, chlorophyll molecules absorb light energy, or solar energy. In the thylakoid membrane, chlorophyll molecules, together with other small molecules and proteins, form photosystems, which are made up of a reaction-center complex surrounded by a light-harvesting complex. In the first step of photosynthesis, the light-harvesting complex from photosystem II (PSII) absorbs a photon from light, passes the photon from one pigment molecule to another within itself, and then transfers it to the reaction-center complex. Inside the reaction-center complex, the energy from the photon enables a special pair of chlorophyll *a* molecules to release two electrons. These two electrons are then accepted by a primary electron acceptor molecule. Simultaneously, a water molecule is split into two hydrogen atoms, two electrons and one oxygen atom. The two electrons are transferred one by one to the chlorophyll *a* molecules, replacing their released electrons.

The released electrons are then transported down an electron transport chain by attaching to the electron carrier plastoquinone (Pq), a cytochrome complex, and then a protein called plastocyanin (Pc) before they reach photosystem I (PS I). As the electrons pass through the cytochrome complex, protons are pumped into the thylakoid space, providing the concentration gradient that will eventually travel through ATP synthase to make ATP (like in aerobic respiration). PS I absorbs photons from light, similar to PS II. However, the electrons that are released from the chlorophyll *a* molecules in PS I are replaced by the electrons coming down the electron transport chain (from PS II). A primary electron acceptor molecule accepts the released electrons in PS I and passes the electrons onto another electron transport chain involving the protein ferredoxin (Fd).

In the final steps of the light reactions, electrons are transferred from Fd to Nicotinamide adenine dinucleotide phosphate (NADP+) with the help of the enzyme NADP+ reductase and NADPH is produced. The ATP and nicotinamide adenine dinucleotide phosphate-oxidase (NADPH) produced from the light reactions are used as energy to form organic molecules in the Calvin cycle.

The Calvin Cycle

There are three phases in the Calvin cycle: carbon fixation, reduction, and regeneration of the CO_2 acceptor. **Carbon fixation** is when the first carbon molecule is introduced into the cycle, when CO_2 from the air is absorbed by the chloroplast. Each CO_2 molecule enters the cycle and attaches to ribulose bisphosphate (RuBP), a five-carbon sugar. The enzyme RuBP carboxylase-oxygenase, also known as rubisco, catalyzes this reaction. Next, two three-carbon 3-phosphoglycerate sugar molecules are formed immediately from the splitting of the six-carbon sugar.

Next, during the **reduction** phase, an ATP molecule is reduced to ADP and the phosphate group attaches to 3-phosphoglycerate, forming 1,3-bisphosphoglycerate. An NADPH molecule then donates two high-energy electrons to the newly formed 1,3-bisphosphate, causing it to lose the phosphate group and become glyceraldehyde 3-phosphate (G3P), which is a high-energy sugar molecule. At this point in the cycle, one G3P molecule exits the cycle and is used by the plant. However, to regenerate RuBP molecules, which are the CO_2 acceptors in the cycle, five G3P molecules continue in the cycle. It takes three turns of the cycle and three CO_2 molecules entering the cycle to form one G3P molecule.

In the final phase of the Calvin cycle, three RuBP molecules are formed from the rearrangement of the carbon skeletons of five G3P molecules. It is a complex process that involves the reduction of three ATP molecules. At the end of the process, RuBP molecules are again ready to enter the first phase and accept CO_2 molecules.

Although the Calvin cycle is not dependent on light energy, both steps of photosynthesis usually occur during daylight, as the Calvin cycle is dependent upon the ATP and NADPH produced by the light reactions, because that energy can be invested into bonds to create high-energy sugars. The Calvin cycle invests nine ATP molecules and six

NADPH molecules into every one molecule of G3P that it produces. The G3P that is produced can be used as the starting material to build larger organic compounds, such as glucose.

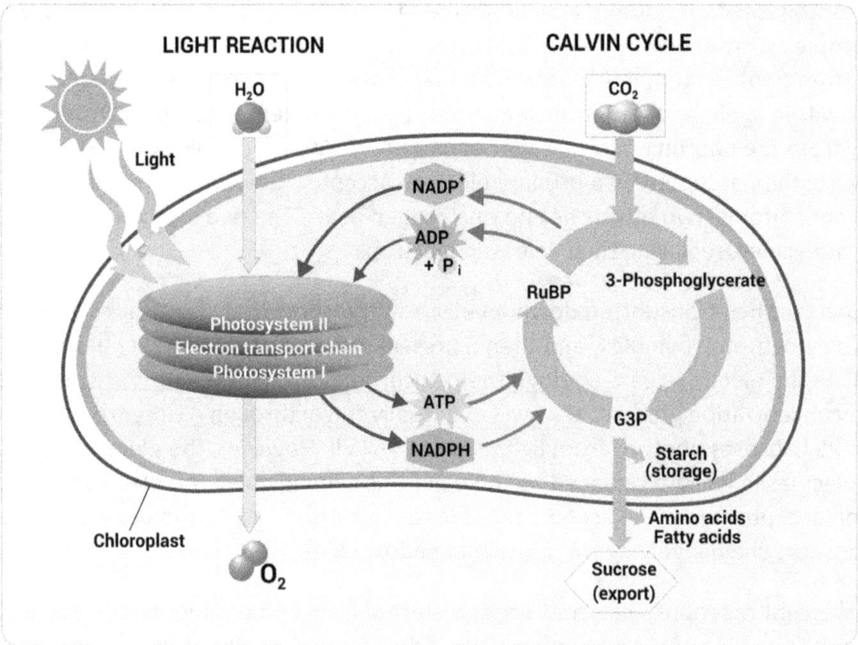

Cellular Reproduction

Cellular reproduction is the process that cells use to divide into two new cells. The ability of a multicellular organism to generate new cells to replace dying and damaged cells is vital for sustaining its life. Bacteria reproduce via **binary fission**, which is a simpler process than eukaryotic division because it doesn't involve splitting a nucleus and doesn't have a web of proteins to pull chromosomes apart. Bacteria copy their DNA in a process called DNA replication, grow, and then the replicated DNA moves to either side, and two new cells are made.

There are two processes by which a eukaryotic cell can divide: mitosis and meiosis. In **mitosis,** the daughter cells produced from parental cell division are identical to each other and the parent. **Meiosis** produces genetically unique haploid cells due to two stages of cell division. Meiosis produces **haploid** cells, or **gametes** (sperm and egg cells), which only have one set of chromosomes. Humans are **diploid** because we have two sets of chromosomes – one from each parent. **Somatic** (body) cells are all diploid and are produced via mitosis.

Mitosis

Mitosis is the division of the genetic material in the nucleus of a cell, and is immediately followed by **cytokinesis**, which is the division of the cytoplasm of the cell. The two processes make up the mitotic phase of the cell cycle. Mitosis can be broken down into five stages: prophase, prometaphase, metaphase, anaphase, and telophase. Mitosis is preceded by **interphase**, where the cell spends the majority of its life while growing and replicating its DNA.

Prophase: During this phase, the mitotic spindles begin to form. They are made up of centrosomes and microtubules. As the microtubules lengthen, the centrosomes move farther away from each other. The nucleolus disappears and the chromatin fibers begin to coil up and form chromosomes. Two sister **chromatids**, which are two identical copies of one chromosome, are joined together at the centromere.

Prometaphase: The nuclear envelope begins to break down and the microtubules enter the nuclear area. Each pair of chromatin fibers develops a **kinetochore**, which is a specialized protein structure in the middle of the adjoined fibers. The chromosomes are further condensed.

Metaphase: The microtubules are stretched across the cell and the centrosomes are at opposite ends of the cell. The chromosomes align at the **metaphase plate**, which is a plane that is exactly between the two centrosomes. The centromere of each chromosome is attached to the kinetochore microtubules that are stretching from each centrosome to the metaphase plate.

Anaphase: The sister chromatids break apart, forming individual chromosomes. The two daughter chromosomes move to opposite ends of the cell. The microtubules shorten toward opposite ends of the cell as well. The cell elongates and, by the end of this phase, there is a complete set of chromosomes at each end of the cell.

Telophase: Two nuclei form at each end of the cell and nuclear envelopes begin to form around each nucleus. The nucleoli reappear and the chromosomes become less condensed. The microtubules are broken down by the cell and mitosis is complete.

Cytokinesis divides the cytoplasm by pinching off the cytoplasm, forming a cleavage furrow, and the two daughter cells then enter interphase, completing the cycle.

Plant cell mitosis is similar except that it lacks centromeres, and instead has a microtubule organizing center. Cytokinesis occurs with the formation of a cell plate.

Meiosis

Meiosis is a type of cell division in which the parent cell has twice as many sets of chromosomes as the daughter cells into which it divides. Although the first stage of meiosis involves the duplication of chromosomes, similar to that of mitosis, the parent cell in meiosis divides into four cells, as opposed to the two produced in mitosis.

Meiosis has the same phases as mitosis, except that they occur twice: once in meiosis I and again in meiosis II. The diploid parent has two sets of homologous chromosomes, one set from each parent. During meiosis I, each chromosome set goes through a process called **crossing over**, which jumbles up the genes on each chromatid. In anaphase one, the separated chromosomes are no longer identical and, once the chromosomes pull apart, each daughter cell is haploid (one set of chromosomes with two non-identical sister chromatids). Next, during meiosis II, the two intermediate daughter cells divide again, separating the chromatids, producing a total of four total haploid cells that each contains one set of chromosomes.

Genetics

Genetics is the study of heredity, which is the transmission of traits from one generation to the next, and hereditary variation. The chromosomes passed from parent to child contain hereditary information in the form of genes. Each gene has specific sequences of DNA that encode proteins, start pathways, and result in inherited traits. In the human life cycle, one haploid sperm cell joins one haploid egg cell to form a diploid cell. The diploid cell is the zygote, the first cell of the new organism, and from then on mitosis takes over and nine months later, there is a fully developed human that has billions of identical cells.

The monk Gregor Mendel is referred to as the father of genetics. In the 1860s, Mendel came up with one of the first models of inheritance, using peapods with different traits in the garden at his abbey to test his theory and develop his model. His model included three laws to determine which traits are inherited; his theories still apply today, after genetics has been studied more in depth.

1. The **Law of Dominance:** Each characteristic has two versions that can be inherited. The gene that encodes for the characteristic has two variations, or alleles, and one is dominant over the other.

2. The **Law of Segregation:** When two parent cells form daughter cells, the alleles segregate and each daughter cell only inherits one of the alleles from each parent.

3. The **Law of Independent Assortment:** Different traits are inherited independent of one another because in metaphase, the set of chromosomes line up in random fashion – mom's set of chromosomes do not line up all on the left or right, there is a random mix.

Organisms contain a **genotype** and a **phenotype**. The genotype is the DNA present in the cells that code for the genes, and the phenotype is the set of observable traits that are expressed. For example, a brown-eyed girl may have genes for both blue and brown eyes, but the actual physical trait expressed is brown eyes. So, the genotype is blue and brown eyes, but the phenotype is brown eyes.

Dominant and Recessive Traits

Each gene has two **alleles**, one inherited from each parent. **Dominant alleles** are noted in capital letters (A) and **recessive alleles** are noted in lower case letters (a). There are three possible combinations of alleles among dominant and recessive alleles: AA, Aa, and aa. If both alleles are identical, the individual is considered **homozygous**; if the two alleles have different sequences, the individual is considered **heterozygous**. In most genes, one allele is considered more dominant than the other and will mask the appearance of the less dominant, or recessive, allele when there is a heterozygous situation. Dominant alleles, when mixed with recessive alleles, will mask the recessive trait. The recessive trait would only appear as the phenotype when the allele combination is aa because a dominant allele is not present to mask it.

Although most genes follow the standard dominant/recessive rules, there are some genes that defy them. Examples include cases of co-dominance, multiple alleles, incomplete dominance, sex-linked traits, and polygenic inheritance.

In cases of **co-dominance**, both alleles are expressed equally. For example, blood type has three alleles: I^A, I^B, and i. I^A and I^B are both dominant to i, but co-dominant with each other. An I^AI^B has AB blood. With incomplete dominance, the allele combination Aa actually makes a third phenotype. An example: certain flowers can be red (AA), white (aa), or pink (Aa).

Punnett Square

For simple genetic combinations, a **Punnett square** can be used to assess the phenotypes of subsequent generations. In a 2 x 2 cell square, one parent's alleles are set up in columns and the other parent's alleles are in rows. The resulting allele combinations are shown in the four internal cells.

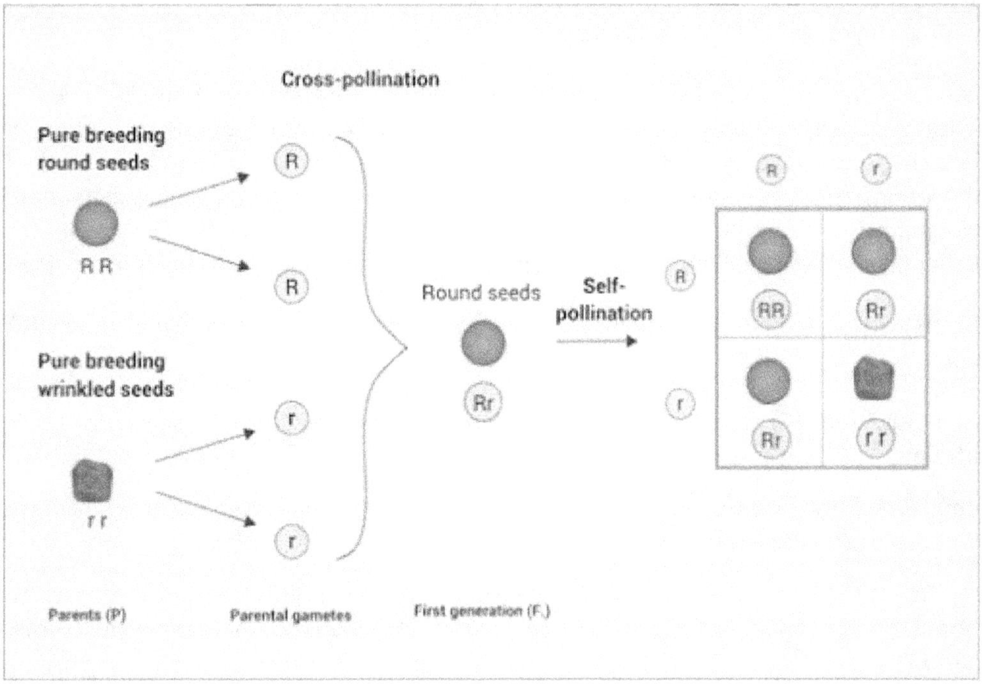

In the example above, two parents with alleles RR and rr, have a 50% chance (2 in 4) of having an offspring with alleles Rr.

Mutations

Genetic **mutations** occur when there is a permanent alteration in the DNA sequence that codes for a specific gene. They can be small, affecting only one base pair, or large, affecting many genes on a chromosome. Mutations are classified as either hereditary, which means they were also present in the parent gene, or acquired, meaning they occurred after the genes were passed down from the parents. Although mutations are not common, they are an important aspect of genetics and variation in the general population.

DNA

DNA is made of nucleotide, and contains the genetic information of a living organism. It consists of two polynucleotide strands that are twisted and linked together in a double-helix structure. The polynucleotide strands are made up of four nitrogenous bases: adenine (A), thymine (T), guanine (G), and cytosine (C). Adenine and guanine are purines while thymine and cytosine are pyrimidines. These bases have specific pairings of A with T, and G with C. The bases are ordered so that these specific pairings will occur when the two polynucleotide strands coil together to form a DNA molecule. The two strands of DNA are described as antiparallel because one strand runs 5′ → 3′ while the other strand of the helix runs 3′ → 5′.

Before chromosome replication and cell division can occur, DNA replication must happen in interphase. There are specific base pair sequences on DNA, called origins of replication, where DNA replication begins. The proteins that begin the replication process attach to this site and begin separating the two strands and creating a replication bubble. Each end of the bubble has a replication fork, which is a Y-shaped area of the DNA that is being unwound. Several types of proteins are important to the beginning of DNA replication. **Helicases** are enzymes responsible for untwisting the two strands at the replication fork. Single-strand binding proteins bind to the separated strands so that they do not join back together during the replication process. While part of the DNA is unwound, the remainder of the molecule becomes even more twisted in response. Topoisomerase enzymes help relieve this strain by breaking, untwisting, and rejoining the DNA strands.

Once the DNA strand is unwound, an initial primer chain of RNA from the enzyme primase is made to start replication. Replication of DNA can only occur in the 5′ → 3′ direction. Therefore, during replication, one strand of the DNA template creates the leading strand in the 5′ → 3′ direction and the other strand creates the lagging strand. While the leading strand is created efficiently and in one piece, the lagging strand is generated in fragments, called **Okazaki fragments**, then are pieced together to form a complete strand by DNA ligase. Following the primer chain of RNA, DNA polymerases are the enzymes responsible for extending the DNA chains by adding on base pairs.

DNA forms the genetic code in the nucleus of eukaryotes, and RNA is the interpreter of that code. RNA exists in the following subtypes:

- **Messenger RNA (mRNA)** copies the DNA into a complementary transcript. This process is called **transcription**.
- **Ribosomal RNA (rRNA)** makes up the protein-making structure called the ribosome, which reads the transcript in a process called **translation.**
- **Transfer RNA (tRNA)** carries amino acids and delivers them to the ribosome. Each three letters of the mRNA transcript, or **codon**, recruits the anti-codon of a tRNA molecule that carries the corresponding amino acid.

Only when a **stop codon** is reached will the ribosome disassemble, thus releasing the assembled protein.

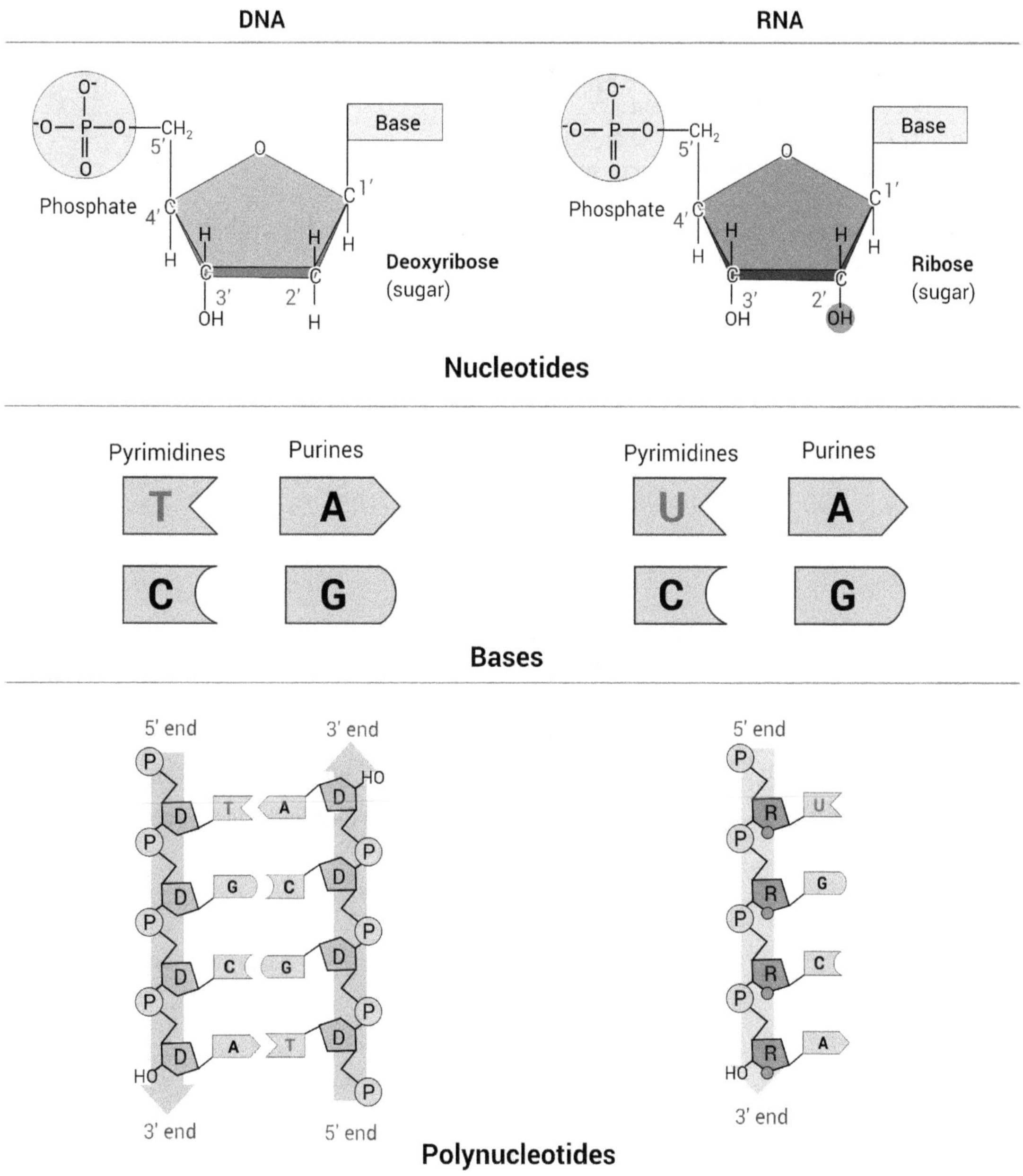

Practice Quiz

1. What is an adaptation?
   a. The original traits found in a common ancestor
   b. Changes that occur in the environment
   c. When one species begins behaving like another species
   d. An inherited characteristic that enhances survival and reproduction

2. If a person with AB blood and a person with O blood have children, what is the probability that their children will have the same phenotype as either parent?
   a. 0%
   b. 25%
   c. 50%
   d. 75%

3. What organelle is the site of protein synthesis?
   a. Nucleus
   b. Smooth ER
   c. Ribosome
   d. Lysosome

4. Which of the following structures is unique to eukaryotic cells?
   a. Cell walls
   b. Nuclei
   c. Cell membranes
   d. Ribosomes

5. Which level of protein structure is defined by the folds and coils of the protein's polypeptide backbone?
   a. Primary
   b. Secondary
   c. Tertiary
   d. Quaternary

See answers on the next page.

Answer Explanations

1. D: Charles Darwin based the idea of adaptation around his original concept of natural selection. He believed that evolution occurred based on three observations: the unity of life, the diversity of life, and the suitability of organisms to their environments. There was unity in life based on the idea that all organisms descended from a common ancestor. Then, as the descendants of common ancestors faced changes in their environments or moved to new environments, they began adapting new features to help them. This concept explained the diversity of life and how organisms were matched to their environments. Natural selection helps to improve the fit between organisms and their environments by increasing the frequency of features that enhance survival and reproduction.

2. A: There is no chance that an offspring will have O blood or AB blood (see Punnett square).

	I^A	I^B
i	$I^A i$	$I^B i$
i	$I^A i$	$I^B i$

3. C: Proteins are synthesized on ribosomes. The ribosome uses messenger RNA as a template, and the transfer RNA brings amino acids to the ribosome where they are synthesized into peptide strands using the genetic code provided by the messenger RNA.

4. B: The structure exclusively found in eukaryotic cells is the nucleus. Animal, plant, fungi, and protist cells are all eukaryotic. DNA is contained within the nucleus of eukaryotic cells, and they also have membrane-bound organelles that perform complex intracellular metabolic activities. Prokaryotic cells (archaea and bacteria) do not have a nucleus or other membrane-bound organelles and are less complex than eukaryotic cells.

5. B: The secondary structure of a protein refers to the folds and coils that are formed by hydrogen bonding between the slightly charged atoms of the polypeptide backbone. The primary structure is the sequence of amino acids, similar to the letters in a long word. The tertiary structure is the overall shape of the molecule that results from the interactions between the side chains that are linked to the polypeptide backbone. The quaternary structure is the complete protein structure that occurs when a protein is made up of two or more polypeptide chains.

Chemistry

Scientific Notation, the Metric System, and Temperature Scales

Scientific Notation

Scientific notation is the conversion of extremely small or large numbers into a format that is easier to comprehend and manipulate. It changes the number into three separate parts: a mathematical sign (+/−), a digit term (known as a **significand**), and an exponential term.

$$Scientific\ notation = (+\ or\ -)\ significand \times exponential\ term$$

To put a number into scientific notation, one should use the following steps:

- Move the decimal point to after the first non-zero number to find the digit number.
- Count how many places the decimal point was moved in step 1.
- Determine if the exponent is positive or negative.
- Create an exponential term using the information from steps 2 and 3.
- Combine the digit term and exponential term to get scientific notation.

For example, to put 0.0000098 into scientific notation, the decimal should be moved so that it lies between the last two numbers: 00000<u>9.8</u>. This creates the digit number:

$$9.8$$

Next, the number of places that the decimal point moved is determined; to get between the 9 and the 8, the decimal was moved six places to the right. It may be helpful to remember that a decimal moved to the right creates a negative exponent, and a decimal moved to the left creates a positive exponent. Because the decimal was moved six places to the right, the exponent is negative.

Now, the exponential term can be created by using the base 10 (this is *always* the base in scientific notation) and the number of places moved as the exponent, in this case:

$$10^{-6}$$

Finally, the digit term and the exponential term can be combined as a product. Therefore, the scientific notation for the number 0.0000098 is:

$$9.8 \times 10^{-6}$$

Standard vs. Metric Systems

The measuring system used today in the United States developed from the British units of measurement during colonial times. The most typically used units in this customary system are those used to measure weight, liquid volume, and length, whose common units are found below. In the customary system, the basic unit for measuring weight is the ounce (oz); there are 16 ounces (oz) in 1 pound (lb) and 2000 pounds in 1 ton. The basic unit for measuring liquid volume is the ounce (oz); 1 ounce is equal to 2 tablespoons (tbsp) or 6 teaspoons (tsp), and there are 8 ounces in 1 cup, 2 cups in 1 pint (pt), 2 pints in 1 quart (qt), and 4 quarts in 1 gallon (gal). For measurements of length, the inch (in) is the base unit; 12 inches make up 1 foot (ft), 3 feet make up 1 yard (yd), and 5280 feet make up 1 mile (mi). However, as there are only a set number of units in the customary system, with extremely large or extremely small amounts of material, the numbers can become awkward and difficult to compare.

Common Customary Measurements		
Length	**Weight**	**Capacity**
1 foot = 12 inches	1 pound = 16 ounces	1 cup = 8 fluid ounces
1 yard = 3 feet	1 ton = 2,000 pounds	1 pint = 2 cups
1 yard = 36 inches		1 quart = 2 pints
1 mile = 1,760 yards		1 quart = 4 cups
1 mile = 5,280 feet		1 gallon = 4 quarts
		1 gallon = 16 cups

Aside from the United States, most countries in the world have adopted the **metric system** embodied in the International System of Units (SI). The three main SI base units used in the metric system are the meter (m), the gram (g), and the liter (L); meters measure length, grams measure mass, and liters measure volume. These are known as the **basic units of measure.**

These three units can use different **prefixes**, which indicate larger or smaller versions of the unit by powers of ten. This can be thought of as making a new unit, which is sized by multiplying the original unit in size by a factor.

These prefixes and associated factors are:

Metric Prefixes			
Prefix	**Symbol**	**Multiplier**	**Exponential**
kilo	k	1,000	10^3
hecto	h	100	10^2
deca	da	10	10^1
no prefix		1	10^0
deci	d	0.1	10^{-1}
centi	c	0.01	10^{-2}
milli	m	0.001	10^{-3}

The correct prefix is then attached to the base. Some examples:

1 milliliter equals .001 liters.

1 kilogram equals 1,000 grams.

Some units of measure are represented as square or cubic units depending on the solution. For example, perimeter is measured in linear units, area is measured in square units, and volume is measured in cubic units.

Also be sure to use the most appropriate unit for the thing being measured. A building's height might be measured in feet or meters while the length of a nail might be measured in inches or centimeters. Additionally, for SI units, the prefix should be chosen to provide the most succinct available value. For example, the mass of a bag of fruit would likely be measured in kilograms rather than grams or milligrams, and the length of a bacteria cell would likely be measured in micrometers rather than centimeters or kilometers.

Temperature Scales

There are three main temperature scales used in science. The scale most often used in the United States is the **Fahrenheit** scale. This scale is based on the measurement of water freezing at 32°F and water boiling at 212°F. The **Celsius** scale uses 0°C as the temperature for water freezing and 100°C for water boiling. The Celsius scale is the most widely used in the scientific community. The accepted measurement by the International System of Units (from the French Système international d'unités), or SI, for temperature is the Kelvin scale. This is the scale employed in thermodynamics, since its zero is the basis for absolute zero, or the unattainable temperature, when matter no longer exhibits degradation.

The conversions between the temperature scales are as follows:

°Fahrenheit to °Celsius: $°C = \frac{5}{9}(°F - 32)$

°Celsius to °Fahrenheit: $°F = \frac{9}{5}(°C) + 32$

°Celsius to Kelvin: $K = °C + 273.15$

Accuracy and Precision

For a hypothesis to be proven true or false, all experiments are subject to multiple trials in order to verify accuracy and precision. A measurement is **accurate** if the observed value is close to the "true value." For example, if someone measured the pH of water at 6.9, this measurement would be considered accurate (the pH of water is 7). On the other hand, a measurement is **precise** if the measurements are consistent—that is, if they are reproducible. If someone had a series of values for a pH of water that were 6.9, 7.0, 7.2, and 7.3, their measurements would not be precise. However, if all measured values were 6.9, or the average of these values was 6.9 with a small range, then their measurements would be precise. Measurements can fall into the following categories:

- Both accurate and precise
- Accurate but not precise
- Precise but not accurate
- Neither accurate nor precise

Atomic Structure and the Periodic Table

Atomic Structure

The structure of an atom has two major components: the atomic nucleus and the atomic shells (also known as **orbitals**). The **nucleus** is found in the center of an atom. The three major subatomic particles are protons, neutrons, and electrons and are found in the atomic nucleus and shells.

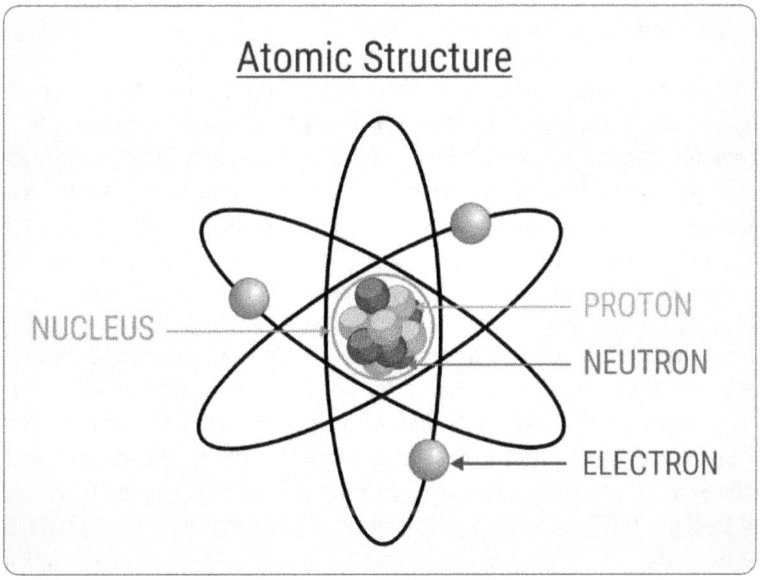

Protons are found in the atomic nucleus and are positively charged particles. The addition or removal of protons from an atom's nucleus creates an entirely different element. **Neutrons** are also found in the atomic nucleus and are neutral particles, meaning they have no net electrical charge. The addition or removal of neutrons from an atom's nucleus does not create a different element but instead creates a lighter or heavier form of that element called an isotope. **Electrons** are found orbiting in the atomic shells around the nucleus and are negatively charged particles. A proton or a neutron has nearly 2,000 times the mass of an electron.

Electrons orbit the nucleus in **atomic shells,** or **electron clouds**, each of which can accommodate a certain number of electrons. For example, the first atomic shell can accommodate two electrons, the second atomic shell can hold a maximum of eight electrons, and the third atomic shell can house a maximum of eight electrons. The negatively charged electrons orbiting the nucleus are attracted to the positively charged protons in the nucleus via electromagnetic force. The attraction of opposite electrical charges gives rise to chemical bonds, which refers to the ways atoms are attached to each other.

The **atomic number** of an atom is determined by the number of protons within the nucleus. When a substance is composed of atoms that all have the same atomic number, it is called an **element**. Elements are arranged by atomic number and grouped by properties in the **Periodic table.**

An atom's **mass number** is determined by the sum of the total number of protons and neutrons in the atom. Most nuclei have a net neutral charge, and all atoms of one type have the same atomic number. However, there are some atoms of the same type that have a different mass number, due to an imbalance of neutrons. These are called **isotopes**. In isotopes, the atomic number, which is determined by the number of protons, is the same, but the mass number, which is determined by adding the protons and neutrons, is different due to the irregular number of neutrons.

An atom can gain a charge by having greater or fewer electrons than protons, and any atom with a charge is referred to as an **ion**. If an ion has more electrons than protons, it has a negative charge and is an **anion**. If an atom has fewer electrons than protons, it has a positive charge and is a **cation**.

Chemical Bonding

Chemical bonding typically results in the formation of a new substance, called a **compound**. Only the electrons in the outermost atomic shell are able to form chemical bonds. These electrons are known as **valence electrons**, and they are what determines the chemical properties of an atom.

Chemical bonding occurs between two or more atoms that are joined together. There are three types of chemical bonds: ionic, covalent, and metallic. The characteristics of the different bonds are determined by how electrons behave in a compound. **Lewis structures** were developed to help visualize the electrons in molecules; they are a method of writing a compound structure formula and including its electron composition. A Lewis symbol for an element consists of the element symbol and a dot for each valence electron. The dots are located on all four sides of the symbol, with a maximum of two dots per side, and eight dots, or electrons, total. The octet rule states that atoms tend to gain, lose, or share electrons until they have a total of eight valence electrons.

Ionic bonds are formed from the electrostatic attractions between oppositely charged atoms. They result from the transfer of electrons from a metal on the left side of the periodic table to a nonmetal on the right side. The metallic substance often has low ionization energy and will transfer an electron easily to the nonmetal, which has a high electron affinity. An example of this is the compound NaCl, which is sodium chloride or table salt, where the Na atom transfers an electron to the Cl atom. Due to strong bonding, ionic compounds have several distinct characteristics. They have high melting and boiling points and are brittle and crystalline. They are arranged in rigid, well-defined structures, which allow them to break apart along smooth, flat surfaces. The formation of ionic bonds is a reaction that is exothermic. In the opposite scenario, the energy it takes to break up a one mole quantity of an ionic compound is referred to as lattice energy, which is generally endothermic. The Lewis structure for NaCl is written as follows:

$$Na + \cdot\ddot{\underset{\cdot\cdot}{Cl}}\colon \rightarrow Na^{+} + \colon\ddot{\underset{\cdot\cdot}{Cl}}\colon^{-}$$

Covalent bonds are formed when two atoms share electrons, instead of transferring them as in ionic compounds. The atoms in covalent compounds have a balance of attraction and repulsion between their protons and electrons, which keeps them bonded together. Two atoms can be joined by single, double, or even triple covalent bonds. As the number of electrons that are shared increases, the length of the bond decreases. Covalent substances have low melting and boiling points and are poor conductors of heat and electricity.

The Lewis structure for Cl_2 is written as follows:

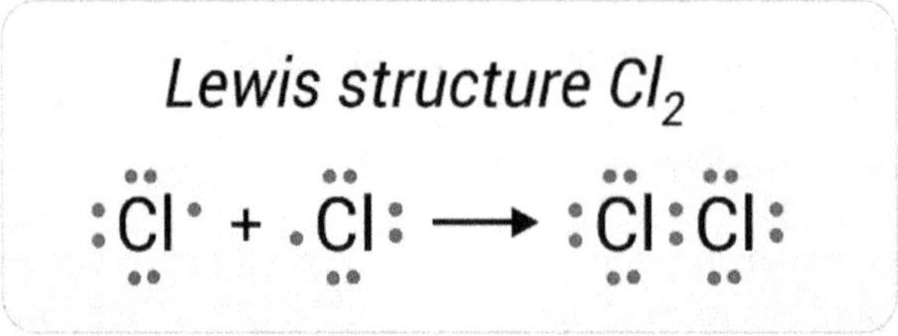

Metallic bonds are formed by electrons that move freely through metal. They are the product of the force of attraction between electrons and metal ions. The electrons are shared by many metal cations and act like glue that holds the metallic substance together, similar to the attraction between oppositely-charged atoms in ionic substances, except the electrons are more fluid and float around the bonded metals and form a sea of electrons.

Metallic compounds have characteristic properties that include strength, conduction of heat and electricity, and malleability. They can conduct electricity by passing energy through the freely moving electrons, creating a **current**. These compounds also have high melting and boiling points. Lewis structures are not common for metallic structures because of the free-roaming ability of the electrons.

Periodic Table

The periodic table catalogues all of the elements known to man, currently 118. It is one of the most important references in the science of chemistry. Information that can be gathered from the periodic table includes the element's atomic number, atomic mass, and chemical symbol. The first periodic table was rendered by Mendeleev in the mid-1800s and was ordered according to increasing atomic mass. The modern periodic table is arranged in order of increasing atomic number. It is also arranged in horizontal rows known as **periods,** and vertical columns known as **families,** or **groups**. The periodic table contains seven periods and eighteen families. Elements in the periodic table can also be classified into three major groups: metals, metalloids, and nonmetals. **Metals** are concentrated on the left side of the periodic table, while **nonmetals** are found on the right side. **Metalloids** occupy the area between the metals and nonmetals.

Due to the fact the periodic table is ordered by increasing atomic number, the electron configurations of the elements show periodicity. As the atomic number increases, electrons gradually fill the shells of an atom. In general, the start of a new period corresponds to the first time an electron inhabits a new shell.

Periodic Table of the Elements

1A	2A	3B	4B	5B	6B	7B	8B	8B	8B	11B	12B	3A	4A	5A	6A	7A	8A
1 H hydrogen 1.008																	2 He helium 4.003
3 Li lithium 6.94	4 Be beryllium 9.012											5 B boron 10.81	6 C carbon 12.01	7 N nitrogen 14.01	8 O oxygen 16.00	9 F fluorine 19.00	10 Ne neon 20.18
11 Na sodium 22.99	12 Mg magnesium 24.31											13 Al aluminum 26.98	14 Si silicon 28.09	15 P phosphorus 30.97	16 S sulfur 32.06	17 Cl chlorine 35.45	18 Ar argon 39.95
19 K potassium 39.10	20 Ca calcium 40.08	21 Sc scandium 44.96	22 Ti titanium 47.88	23 V vanadium 50.94	24 Cr chromium 52.00	25 Mn manganese 54.94	26 Fe iron 55.85	27 Co cobalt 58.93	28 Ni nickel 58.69	29 Cu copper 63.55	30 Zn zinc 65.39	31 Ga gallium 69.72	32 Ge germanium 72.64	33 As arsenic 74.92	34 Se selenium 78.96	35 Br bromine 79.90	36 Kr krypton 83.79
37 Rb rubidium 85.47	38 Sr strontium 87.62	39 Y yttrium 88.91	40 Zr zirconium 91.22	41 Nb niobium 92.91	42 Mo molybdenum 95.96	43 Tc technetium (98)	44 Ru ruthenium 101.1	45 Rh rhodium 102.9	46 Pd palladium 106.4	47 Ag silver 107.9	48 Cd cadmium 112.4	49 In indium 114.8	50 Sn tin 118.7	51 Sb antimony 121.8	52 Te tellurium 127.6	53 I iodine 126.9	54 Xe xenon 131.3
55 Cs cesium 132.9	56 Ba barium 137.3	57-71	72 Hf hafnium 178.5	73 Ta tantalum 180.9	74 W tungsten 183.9	75 Re rhenium 186.2	76 Os osmium 190.2	77 Ir iridium 192.2	78 Pt platinum 195.1	79 Au gold 197.0	80 Hg mercury 200.5	81 Tl thallium 204.4	82 Pb lead 207.2	83 Bi bismuth 209.0	84 Po polonium (209)	85 At astatine (210)	86 Rn radon (222)
87 Fr francium (223)	88 Ra radium (226)	89-103	104 Rf rutherfordium (265)	105 Db dubnium (268)	106 Sg seaborgium (271)	107 Bh bohrium (270)	108 Hs hassium (277)	109 Mt meitnerium (276)	110 Ds darmstadtium (281)	111 Rg roentgenium (280)	112 Cn copernicium (285)	113 Uut ununtrium (284)	114 Fl flerovium (289)	115 Uup ununpentium (288)	116 Lv livermorium (293)	117 Uus ununseptium (294)	118 Uuo ununoctium (294)

Lanthanide Series	57 La lanthanum 138.9	58 Ce cerium 140.1	59 Pr praseodymium 140.9	60 Nd neodymium 144.2	61 Pm promethium (145)	62 Sm samarium 150.4	63 Eu europium 152.0	64 Gd gadolinium 157.2	65 Tb terbium 158.9	66 Dy dysprosium 162.5	67 Ho holmium 164.9	68 Er erbium 167.3	69 Tm thulium 168.9	70 Yb ytterbium 173.0	71 Lu lutetium 175.0
Actinide Series	89 Ac actinium (227)	90 Th thorium 232	91 Pa protactinium 231	92 U uranium 238	93 Np neptunium (237)	94 Pu plutonium (244)	95 Am americium (243)	96 Cm curium (247)	97 Bk berkelium (247)	98 Cf californium (251)	99 Es einsteinium (252)	100 Fm fermium (257)	101 Md mendelevium (258)	102 No nobelium (259)	103 Lr lawrencium (262)

Alkaline Metal	Alkaline Earth	Transition Metal	Basic Metal	Semimetal	Nonmetal	Halogen	Noble Gas	Lanthanide	Actinide

Other trends in the properties of elements in the periodic table are:

Atomic radius: One-half the distance between the nuclei of atoms of the same element

Electronegativity: A measurement of the tendency of an atom to form a chemical bond

Ionization energy: The amount of energy needed to remove an electron from a gas or ion

Electron affinity: The ability or tendency of an atom to accept an electron into its valence shell

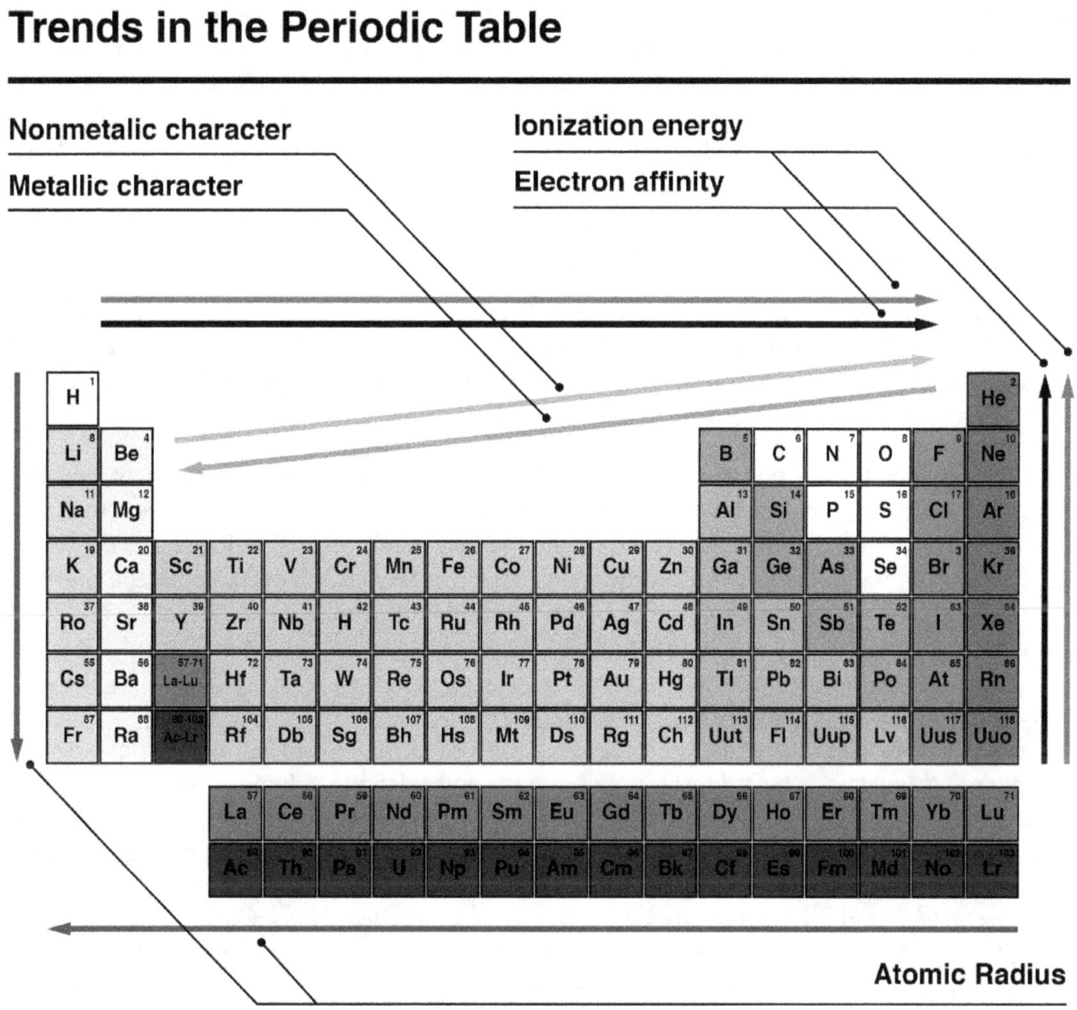

Chemical Equations

Chemical reactions are represented by **chemical equations**. The equations help to explain how the molecules change during the reaction. For example, when hydrogen gas (H_2) combines with oxygen gas (O_2), two molecules of water are formed. The equation is written as follows, where the "+" sign means *reacts with* and the "⟶" means *produces*:

$$2H_2 + O_2 \rightarrow 2H_2O$$

Two hydrogen molecules react with an oxygen molecule to produce two water molecules. In all chemical equations, the quantity of each element on the reactant side of the equation should equal the quantity of the same element on the product side of the equation due to the law of conservation of matter. If this is true, the equation is described as balanced. To figure out how many of each element there is on each side of the equation, the coefficient of the element should be multiplied by the subscript next to the element. Coefficients and subscripts are noted for quantities larger than one. The **coefficient** is the number located directly to the left of the element. The **subscript** is the small-sized number directly to the right of the element.

In the previous equation, on the left side, the coefficient of the hydrogen is two and the subscript is also two, which makes a total of four hydrogen atoms. Using the same method, there are two oxygen atoms. On the right side, the coefficient two is multiplied by the subscript in each element of the water molecule, making four hydrogen atoms and two oxygen atoms. This equation is balanced because there are four hydrogen atoms and two oxygen atoms on each side. The states of the reactants and products can also be written in the equation: gas (g), liquid (l), solid (s), and dissolved in water (aq). If they are included, they are noted in parentheses on the right side of each molecule in the equation.

Reaction Rates, Equilibrium, and Reversibility

Chemical reactions are conveyed using chemical equations. Chemical equations must be balanced with equivalent numbers of atoms for each type of element on each side of the equation. Antoine Lavoisier, a French chemist, was the first to propose the **Law of Conservation of Mass** for the purpose of balancing a chemical equation. The law states, "Matter is neither created nor destroyed during a chemical reaction."

The **reactants** are located on the left side of the arrow, while the **products** are located on the right side of the arrow. Coefficients are the numbers in front of the chemical formulas. Subscripts are the numbers to the lower right of chemical symbols in a formula. To tally atoms, one should multiply the formula's coefficient by the subscript of each chemical symbol. For example, the chemical equation $2\ H_{2+}O_2 \rightarrow 2H_2O$ is balanced. For H, the coefficient of 2 multiplied by the subscript 2=4 hydrogen atoms. For O, the coefficient of 1 multiplied by the subscript 2=2 oxygen atoms. Coefficients and subscripts of 1 are understood and never written.

States of Matter and Factors that Affect Phase Changes

Matter is most commonly found in three distinct states or phases: solid, liquid, and gas. A solid has a distinct shape and a defined volume. A liquid has a more loosely defined shape and a definite volume, while a gas has no definite shape or volume. The *Kinetic Theory of Matter* states that matter is composed of a large number of small particles (specifically, atoms and molecules) that are in constant motion. The distance between the separations in these particles determines the state of the matter: solid, liquid, or gas. In gases, the particles have a large separation and no attractive forces. In liquids, there is moderate separation between particles and some attractive forces to form a loose shape. Solids have almost no separation between their particles, causing a defined and set shape. The constant movement of particles causes them to bump into each other, thus allowing the particles to transfer energy between each other. This bumping and transferring of energy helps explain the transfer of heat and the relationship between pressure, volume, and temperature.

The *Ideal Gas Law* states that pressure, volume, and temperature are all related through the equation: $PV=nRT$, where P is pressure, V is volume, n is the amount of the substance in moles, R is the gas constant, and T is temperature.

Through this relationship, volume and pressure are both proportional to temperature, but pressure is inversely proportional to volume. Therefore, if the equation is balanced, and the volume decreases in the system, pressure needs to proportionately increase to keep both sides of the equation balanced. In contrast, if the equation is unbalanced and the pressure increases, then the temperature would also increase, since pressure and temperature are directly proportional.

When pressure, temperature, or volume change in matter, a change in state can occur. Changes in state include solid to liquid (melting), liquid to gas (evaporation), solid to gas (sublimation), gas to solid (deposition), gas to liquid (condensation), and liquid to solid (freezing). There is one other state of matter called *plasma*, which is seen in lightning, television screens, and neon lights. Plasma is most commonly converted from the gas state at extremely high temperatures.

The amount of energy needed to change matter from one state to another is labeled by the terms for phase changes. For example, the temperature needed to supply enough energy for matter to change from a liquid to a gas is called the *heat of vaporization*. When heat is added to matter in order to cause a change in state, there will be an increase in temperature until the matter is about to change its state. During its transition, all of the added heat is used by the matter to change its state, so there is no increase in temperature. Once the transition is complete, then the added heat will again yield an increase in temperature.

Reaction Rates

The rate of a reaction is the measure of the change in concentration of the reactants or products over a certain period of time. Many factors affect how fast or slow a reaction occurs, such as concentration, pressure, or temperature. As the concentration of a reactant increases, the rate of the reaction also increases, because the frequency of collisions between elements increases. High-pressure situations for reactants that are gases cause the gas to compress and increase the frequency of gas molecule collisions, similar to solutions with higher concentrations. Reactions rates are then increased with the higher frequency of gas molecule collisions. Higher temperatures usually increase the rate of the reaction, adding more energy to the system with heat and increasing the frequency of molecular collisions.

Equilibrium

Equilibrium is described as the state of a system when no net changes occur. Chemical equilibrium occurs when opposing reactions occur at equal rates. In other words, the rate of reactants forming products is equal to the rate of the products breaking down into the reactants — the concentration of reactants and products in the system doesn't change. This happens in **reversible chemical reactions** as opposed to irreversible chemical reactions. In **irreversible chemical reactions**, the products cannot be changed back to reactants. Although the concentrations are not changing in equilibrium, the forward and reverse reactions are likely still occurring. This type of equilibrium is called a **dynamic equilibrium**. In situations where all reactions have ceased, a **static equilibrium** is reached. Chemical equilibriums are also described as homogeneous or heterogeneous. **Homogeneous equilibrium** involves substances that are all in the same phase, while **heterogeneous equilibrium** means the substances are in different phases when equilibrium is reached.

When a reaction reaches equilibrium, the conditions of the equilibrium are described by the following equation, based on the chemical equation $\mathrm{aA} + \mathrm{bB} \leftrightarrow \mathrm{cC} + \mathrm{dD}$:

Catalysts are substances that accelerate the speed of a chemical reaction. A catalyst remains unchanged throughout the course of a chemical reaction. In most cases, only small amounts of a catalyst are needed. Catalysts increase the rate of a chemical reaction by providing an alternate path requiring less activation energy. Activation energy refers to the amount of energy required for the initiation of a chemical reaction.

Catalysts can be homogeneous or heterogeneous. Catalysts in the same phase of matter as its reactants are homogeneous, while catalysts in a different phase than reactants are heterogeneous. It is important to remember catalysts are selective. They don't accelerate the speed of all chemical reactions, but catalysts do accelerate specific chemical reactions.

Solutions and Solution Concentrations

A homogeneous mixture, also called a **solution,** has uniform properties throughout a given sample. An example of a homogeneous solution is salt (the **solute,** or what is being dissolved) fully dissolved in warm water (the **solvent,** the material dissolving the solute). In this example, salt is the **solute,** or the material being dissolved, and water is the **solvent,** or the material dissolving the solute. In this case, any number of samples taken from the parent solution would be identical.

One **mole** is the amount of matter contained in 6.02×10^{23} of any object, such as atoms, ions, or molecules. It is a useful unit of measure for items in large quantities. This number is also known as **Avogadro's number**. One mole of ^{12}C atoms is equivalent to 6.02×10^{23} ^{12}C atoms. Avogadro's number is often written as an inverse mole, or as $6.02 \times 10^{23}/\text{mol}$.

Molarity is the concentration of a solution. It is based on the number of moles of solute in one liter of solution and is written as the capital letter M. A 1.0 molar solution, or 1.0 M solution, has one mole of solute per liter of solution. The molarity of a solution can be determined by calculating the number of moles of the solute and dividing it by the volume of the solution in liters. The resulting number is the mol/L or M for molarity of the solution. Alternatively, **percent concentration** can be written as parts of solute per 100 parts of solvent.

Chemical Reactions

Chemical reactions are characterized by a chemical change in which the starting substances, or reactants, differ from the substances formed, or products. Chemical reactions may involve a change in color, the production of gas, the formation of a precipitate, or changes in heat content. The following are the basic types of chemical reactions:

- **Decomposition Reactions:** A compound is broken down into smaller elements. For example, $2H_2O \rightarrow 2H_2 + O_2$. This is read as, "2 molecules of water decompose into 2 molecules of hydrogen and 1 molecule of oxygen."
- **Synthesis Reactions:** Two or more elements or compounds are joined together. For example, $2H_2 + O_2 \rightarrow 2H_2O$. This is read as, "2 molecules of hydrogen react with 1 molecule of oxygen to produce 2 molecules of water."
- **Single Displacement Reactions:** A single element or ion takes the place of another element in a compound. It is also known as a substitution reaction. For example, $Zn + 2HCl \rightarrow ZnCl_2 + H_2$. This is read as, "zinc reacts with 2 molecules of hydrochloric acid to produce one molecule of zinc chloride and one molecule of hydrogen." In other words, zinc replaces the hydrogen in hydrochloric acid.
- **Double Displacement Reactions:** Two elements or ions exchange a single element to form two different compounds, resulting in different combinations of cations and anions in the final compounds. It is also known as a metathesis reaction. For example, $H_2SO_4 + 2NaOH \rightarrow Na_2SO_4 + 2H_2O$
    - Special types of double displacement reactions include:
        - **Oxidation-Reduction (or Redox) Reactions:** Elements undergo a change in oxidation number. For example, $2S_2O_3{}^{2-}\ (aq) + I_2\ (aq) \rightarrow S_4O_6{}^{2-}\ (aq) + 2I^-\ (aq)$.
        - **Acid-Base Reactions:** Involves a reaction between an acid and a base, which produces a salt and water. For example, $HBr + NaOH \rightarrow NaBr + H_2O$.
        - **Combustion Reactions:** A hydrocarbon (a compound composed of only hydrogen and carbon) reacts with oxygen (O_2) to form carbon dioxide (CO_2) and water (H_2O). For example, $CH_4 + 2O_2 \rightarrow CO_2 + 2H_2O$.

Stoichiometry

Stoichiometry investigates the quantities of chemicals that are consumed and produced in chemical reactions. Chemical equations are made up of reactants and products; stoichiometry helps elucidate how the changes from reactants to products occur, as well as how to ensure the equation is balanced.

Chemical reactions are limited by the amount of starting material, or reactants, available to drive the process forward. The reactant that has the smallest amount of substance is called the limiting reactant. The **limiting reactant** is completely consumed by the end of the reaction. The other reactants are called **excess reactants**. For example, gasoline is used in a combustion reaction to make a car move and is the limiting reactant of the reaction. If the gasoline runs out, the combustion reaction can no longer take place, and the car stops.

The quantity of product that should be produced after using up all of the limiting reactant can be calculated and is called the **theoretical yield of the reaction**. Since the reactants do not always act as they should, the actual amount of resulting product is called the **actual yield**. The actual yield is divided by the theoretical yield and then multiplied by 100 to find the **percent yield** for the reaction.

Solution stoichiometry deals with quantities of solutes in chemical reactions that occur in solutions. The quantity of a solute in a solution can be calculated by multiplying the molarity of the solution by the volume. Similar to chemical equations involving simple elements, the number of moles of the elements that make up the solute should be equivalent on both sides of the equation.

When the concentration of a particular solute in a solution is unknown, a **titration** is used to determine that concentration. In a titration, the solution with the unknown solute is combined with a standard solution, which is a solution with a known solute concentration. The point at which the unknown solute has completely reacted with the known solute is called the **equivalence point**. Using the known information about the standard solution, including the concentration and volume, and the volume of the unknown solution, the concentration of the unknown solute is determined in a balanced equation. For example, in the case of combining acids and bases, the equivalence point is reached when the resulting solution is neutral. HCl, an acid, combines with NaOH, a base, to form water, which is neutral, and a solution of Cl^- ions and Na^+ ions. Before the equivalence point, there are an unequal number of cations and anions and the solution is not neutral.

Oxidation and Reduction

Oxidation and reduction reactions, also known as **redox reactions**, are those in which electrons are transferred from one element to another. Batteries and fuel cells are two energy-related technologies that utilize these reactions. When an atom, ion, or molecule loses its electrons and becomes more positively charged, it is described as being oxidized. When a substance gains electrons and becomes more negatively charged, it is reduced. In chemical reactions, if one element or molecule is oxidized, another must be reduced for the equation to be balanced. Although the transfer of electrons is obvious in some reactions where ions are formed, redox reactions also include those in which electrons are transferred but the products remain neutral.

Keep track of oxidation states or oxidation numbers to ensure the chemical equation is balanced. **Oxidation numbers** are assigned to each atom in a neutral substance or ion. For ions made up of a single atom, the oxidation number is equal to the charge of the ion. For atoms in their original elemental form, the oxidation number is always zero. Each hydrogen atom in an H_2 molecule, for example, has an oxidation number of zero. The sum of the oxidation numbers in a molecule should be equal to the overall charge of the molecule. If the molecule is a positively charged ion, the sum of the oxidation number should be equal to overall positive charge of the molecule. In ionic compounds that have a cation and anion joined, the sum of the oxidation numbers should equal zero.

All chemical equations must have the same number of elements on each side of the equation to be balanced. Redox reactions have an extra step of counting the electrons on both sides of the equation to be balanced. Separating redox reactions into oxidation reactions and reduction reactions is a simple way to account for all of the electrons involved. The individual equations are known as **half-reactions**. The number of electrons lost in the oxidation reaction must be equal to the number of electrons gained in the reduction reaction for the redox reaction to be balanced.

The oxidation of tin (Sn) by iron (Fe) can be balanced by the following half-reactions:

Oxidation: $Sn^{2+} \rightarrow Sn^{4+} + 2e^-$

Reduction: $2Fe^{3+} + 2e^- \rightarrow 2Fe^{2+}$

Complete redox reaction: $Sn^{2+} + 2Fe^{3+} \rightarrow Sn^{4+} + 2Fe^{2+}$

Acids and Bases

Acids and bases are defined in many different ways. An **acid** can be described as a substance that increases the concentration of H^+ ions when it is dissolved in water, as a proton donor in a chemical equation, or as an electron-pair acceptor. A **base** can be a substance that increases the concentration of OH^- ions when it is dissolved in water, accepts a proton in a chemical reaction, or is an electron-pair donor.

pH refers to the power or potential of hydrogen atoms and is used as a scale for a substance's acidity. In chemistry, pH represents the hydrogen ion concentration (written as $[H^+]$) in an aqueous, or watery, solution. The hydrogen ion concentration, $[H^+]$, is measured in moles of H^+ per liter of solution.

The pH scale is a logarithmic scale used to quantify how acidic or basic a substance is. pH is the negative logarithm of the hydrogen ion concentration: pH=-log [H^+]. A one-unit change in pH correlates with a ten-fold change in hydrogen ion concentration. The pH scale typically ranges from zero to 14, although it is possible to have pHs outside of this range. Pure water has a pH of 7, which is considered **neutral**. pH values less than 7 are considered **acidic**, while pH values greater than 7 are considered **basic**, or **alkaline**.

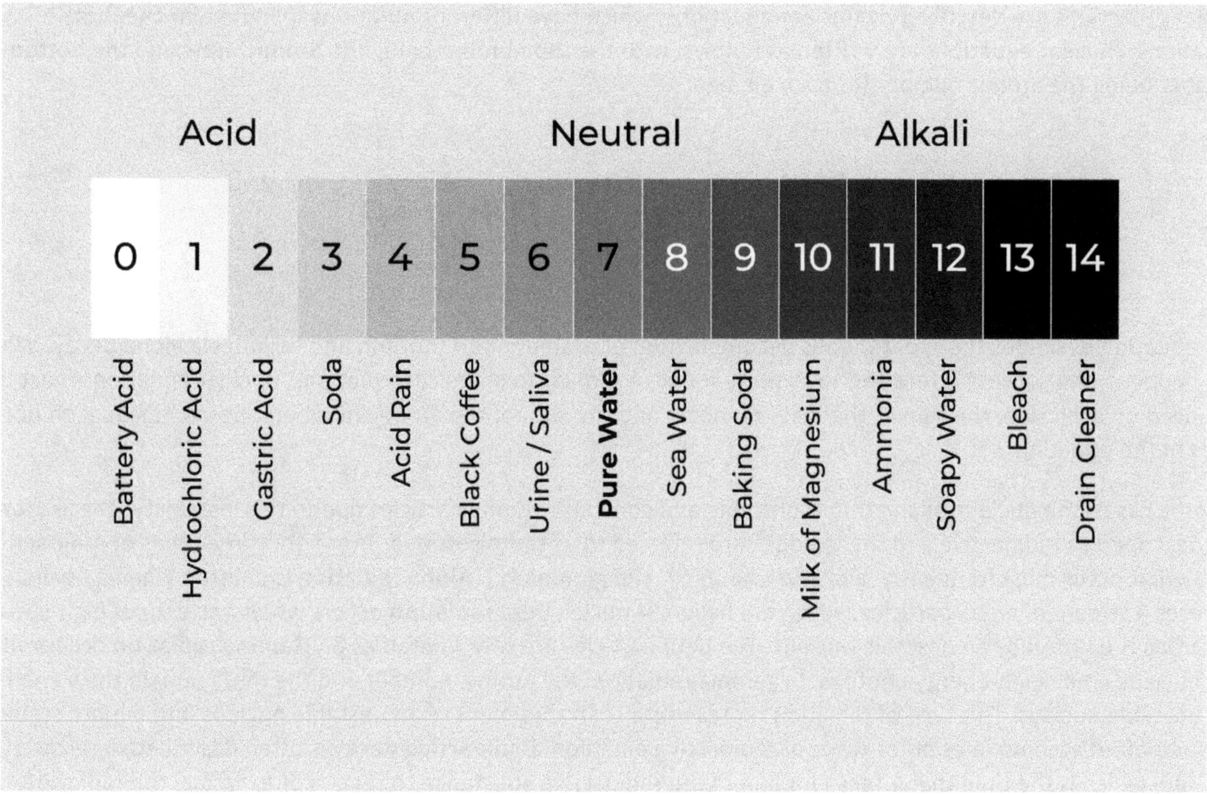

Generally speaking, an acid is a substance capable of donating hydrogen ions, while a base is a substance capable of accepting hydrogen ions. A **buffer** is a molecule that can act as either a hydrogen ion donor or acceptor. Buffers are crucial in the blood and body fluids, and prevent the body's pH from fluctuating into dangerous territory. pH can be measured using a pH meter, test paper, or indicator sticks.

Water can act as either an acid or a base. When mixed with an acid, water can accept a proton and become an H_3O^+ ion. When mixed with a base, water can donate a proton and become an OH^- ion. Sometimes water molecules donate and accept protons from each other; this process is called **autoionization**. The chemical equation is written as follows: $H_2O + H_2O \rightarrow OH^- + H_3O^+$.

Acids and bases are characterized as strong, weak, or somewhere in between. Strong acids and bases completely or almost completely ionize in aqueous solution. The chemical reaction is driven completely forward, to the right side of the equation, where the acidic or basic ions are formed. Weak acids and bases do not completely dissociate in aqueous solution. They only partially ionize and the solution becomes a mixture of the acid or base, water, and the acidic or basic ions. Strong acids are complemented by weak bases, and vice versa. A **conjugate acid** is an ion that forms when its base pair gains a proton. For example, the conjugate acid ${NH_4}^+$ is formed from the base NH_3. The **conjugate base** that pairs with an acid is the ion that is formed when an acid loses a proton. ${NO_2}^-$ is the conjugate base of the acid HNO_2.

Nuclear Chemistry

Nuclear chemistry is the study of reactions in which the nuclei of atoms are transformed and their identities are changed. These reactions can involve large changes in energy—much larger than the energy changes that occur when chemical bonds between atoms are made or broken. Nuclear chemistry is also used to create electricity.

Nuclear reactions are described by nuclear equations, which have different notations than regular chemical equations. Nuclear equations are written as follows, with the top number being the **atomic mass** and the bottom number being the atomic number for each element:

$$^{238}_{92}U \rightarrow \, ^{234}_{90}Th + \, ^{4}_{2}He$$

The equation describes the spontaneous decomposition of uranium into thorium and helium via alpha decay. When this happens, the process is referred to as nuclear decay. Similar to chemical equations, nuclear equations must be balanced on each side; the sum of the mass numbers and the sum of the atomic numbers should be equal on both sides of the equation.

In some cases, the nucleus of an atom is unstable and constantly emits particles due to this instability. These atoms are described as radioactive and the isotopes are referred to as **radioisotopes.** There are three types of radioactive decay that occur most frequently: alpha (α), beta (β), and gamma (γ). **Alpha radiation** is emitted when a nucleus releases a stream of alpha particles, which are helium-4 nuclei. **Beta radiation** occurs when a stream of high-speed electrons is emitted by an unstable nucleus. The beta particles are often noted as β^-. **Gamma radiation** occurs when the nucleus emits high-energy photons. In gamma radiation, the atomic number and the mass remain the same for the unstable nucleus. This type of radiation represents a rearrangement of an unstable nucleus into a more stable one and often accompanies other types of radioactive emission. **Radioactive decay** is often described in terms of its half-life, which is the time that it takes for half of the radioactive substance to react. For example, the radioisotope strontium-90 has a half-life of 28.8 years. If there are 10 grams of strontium-90 to start with, after 28.8 years, there would be 5 grams left.

There are two distinct types of nuclear reactions: fission and fusion reactions. Both involve a large energy release. In **fission** reactions, a large atom is split into two or more smaller atoms. The nucleus absorbs slow-moving neutrons, resulting in a larger nucleus that is unstable. The unstable nucleus then undergoes fission. Nuclear power plants depend on nuclear fission reactions for energy. **Fusion** reactions involve the combination of two or more lighter atoms into a larger atom. Fusion reactions do not occur in Earth's nature due to the extreme temperature and pressure conditions required to make them happen. Fusion products are generally not radioactive. Fusion reactions are responsible for the energy that is created by the Sun.

Biochemistry

Biochemistry deals with the chemistry of organisms. There are four classes of macromolecules that allow organisms to exist: carbohydrates, lipids, proteins, and nucleic acids. Carbon is the backbone of these organic molecules because of its ability to form up to four covalent bonds.

Carbon (C), hydrogen (H), oxygen (O), nitrogen (N), sulfur (S), and phosphorus (P) are the most prevalent elements in these biological molecules. The following chart gives an overview of each organic molecule.

Organic Molecule	Example	Monomer (smallest repeating unit)	Structure	Function
Carbohydrate	• Sugar • Cellulose	Monosaccharide	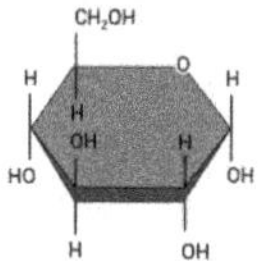 Glucose 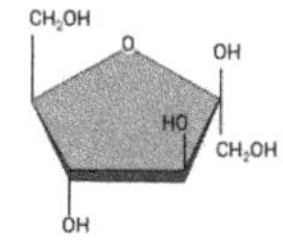 Fructose 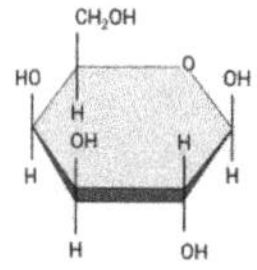 Galactose	• Energy • Structure
Protein	• Actin • Insulin	Amino Acid	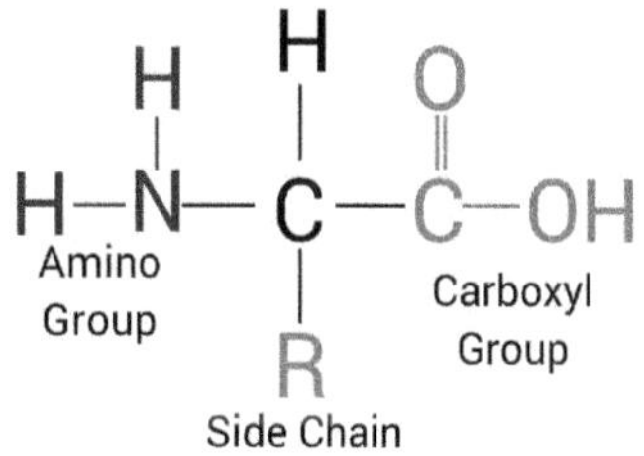 	• Structure • Support • Some hormones
Lipid	• Fat • Oil	Technically none because the glycerol and fatty acids are not repeating.	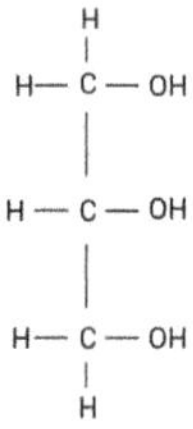 Glycerol 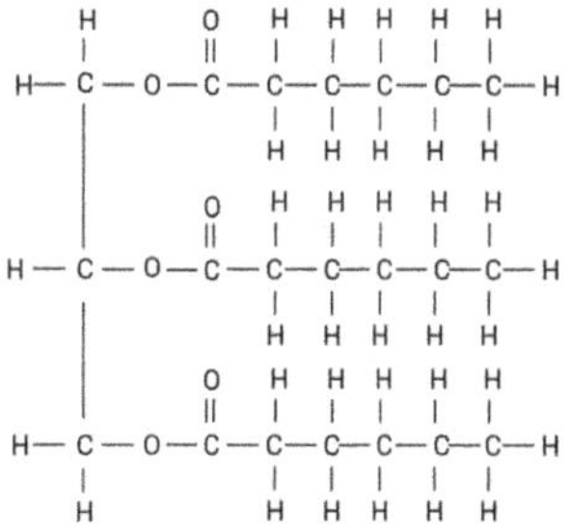 Triglyceride-Saturated	• Long-term energy • Steroid Hormones • Cell membranes

Organic Molecule	Example	Monomer (smallest repeating unit)	Structure	Function
Nucleic Acid	• DNA • RNA	Nucleotide	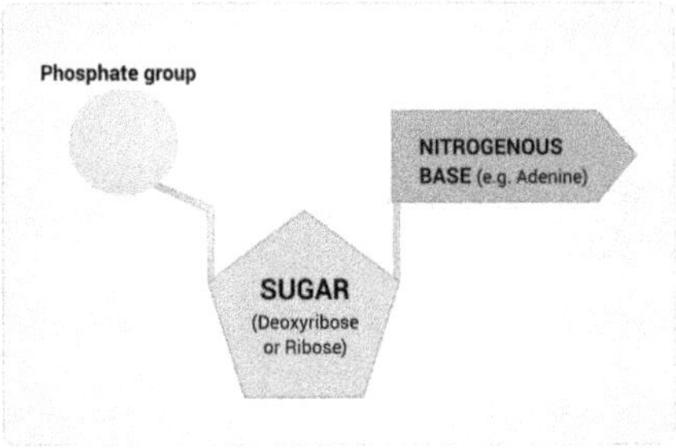	• Genetic code • Makes Protein

Carbohydrates

Carbohydrates are usually sweet, ring-like sugar molecules that are built from carbon (carbo-), oxygen, and hydrogen (-hydrates, meaning water). They can exist as one-ring **monosaccharides,** like glucose, fructose, and galactose, or as two-ring **disaccharides**, like lactose, maltose, and sucrose. These simple sugars can be easily broken down and used via glycolysis to provide a source of quick energy. **Polysaccharides** are repeating chains of monosaccharide rings. They are more complex carbohydrates, and there are several types. For example:

- Plants store energy in the form of **starch**.
- Animals store energy in the form of **glycogen**. Vertebrates store glycogen in the liver and muscles.
- **Cellulose** is the chief structural component of plant cell walls.
- **Chitin** is the chief structural component of fungi cell walls and the exoskeletons of arthropods.

•

• **Glycolysis** is an essential metabolic pathway that converts glucose to pyruvate and allows for cellular respiration to occur. It does not require oxygen to be present. Glucose is a common molecule used for energy production in cells. During glycolysis, two three-carbon sugars are generated from the splitting of a glucose molecule. These smaller sugars are then converted into pyruvate molecules via oxidation and atom rearrangement. Glycolysis requires two ATP molecules to drive the process forward, but the end product of the process has four ATP molecules, for a net production of two ATP molecules. Also, two reduced nicotinamide adenine dinucleotide (NADH) molecules are created from when the electron carrier oxidized nicotinamide adenine dinucleotide ($\mathrm{NAD}+$) peels off two electrons and a hydrogen atom.

Proteins

Proteins are composed of chains of amino acids. There are several different kinds.

Enzymes catalyze chemical reactions in the body.

Storage proteins like albumin in eggs are important for development.

Hormonal proteins are responsible for initiating signal transduction cascades that regulate gene expression.

Motor proteins like actin and myosin are responsible for movement.

Immune proteins like antibodies and antigens are important for fighting disease.

Transport proteins like channel proteins and protein pumps move molecules.

Receptor proteins receive chemical messages like neurotransmitters.

Marker proteins serve as a cell's identification or fingerprint that distinguishes between cells of different types and sources.

Structural proteins like keratin are important for things like spider webs, hair, and feathers.

All proteins are made from a combination of some of all of the same 20 amino acids. The varying amino acids are linked by **peptide bonds** and form the primary structure of the polypeptide, or chain of amino acids. The primary structure is just the string of amino acids. It is the secondary, tertiary, and quaternary structure that determines protein shape and function. The secondary structure can be beta sheets or alpha helices formed by hydrogen bonding between the polar regions of the polypeptide backbone. Tertiary structure results from the interactions between the side chains. Quaternary structure is the overall protein structure that occurs when subunits merge, take the correct shape, and become functional.

The process of breaking down proteins to produce glucose is **gluconeogenesis.**

Lipids

Lipids are mostly nonpolar, hydrophobic molecules that are not soluble in water. **Triglycerides** are a type of lipid with a glycerol backbone attached to three long fatty acid chains.

Phospholipids are also composed of glycerol except they have two fatty acid tails. The third tail is replaced with a hydrophilic phosphate group. The amphipathic nature of this molecule results in a lipid bilayer where the "water-loving" hydrophilic heads face the extracellular matrix and cytoplasm and the "water-hating" hydrophobic tails face each other on the inside.

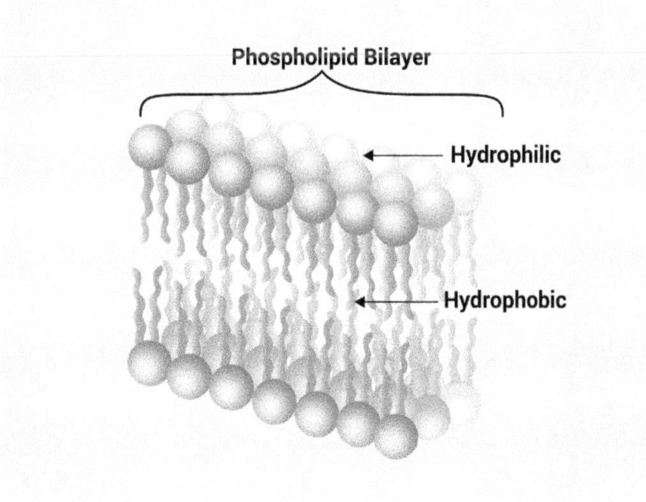

Steroids are another type of lipid. Cholesterol is a steroid that is embedded in animal cell membranes and acts as a fluidity buffer. Steroid hormones such as testosterone and estrogen are responsible for transcriptional regulation in certain cells.

Nucleic acids

Nucleic acids are made of **nucleotides**. Nucleotides consist of a five-carbon sugar, a nitrogen-containing base, and a phosphate group. Deoxyribonucleic acid (DNA) exists as two nucleotide chains arranged in a double helix. Each **deoxyribose** sugar is connected to a nitrogenous base and an electrically-negative phosphate group. The nitrogenous bases are adenine and guanine, the two-ringed purines, and cytosine and thymine, the one-ringed pyrimidines. The double helix is held together by weak hydrogen bonds that connect adenine to thymine and cytosine to guanine. Ribonucleic acid (RNA) has a slightly different structure. It is usually single-stranded, has a **ribose** sugar as opposed to deoxyribose, and contains uracil instead of thymine.

Practice Quiz

1. Which of the following shows the correct order of strength of intermolecular bonds?
   a. London dispersion > hydrogen > dipole-dipole
   b. Hydrogen > London dispersion > dipole-dipole
   c. London dispersion > dipole-dipole > hydrogen
   d. Hydrogen > dipole-dipole > London dispersion

2. Which property of liquids describes how water defies gravity to move upward from the root of a plant through the stem and into the leaves?
   a. Capillary action
   b. Surface tension
   c. High vapor pressure
   d. Solubility

3. Which element's atoms have the greatest number of electrons?
   a. Hydrogen
   b. Iron
   c. Copper
   d. Iodine

4. Which coefficient would fill in the blank in the following equation to correctly balance the chemical reaction between iron oxide and carbon monoxide: $FeO_3 + 3CO \rightarrow Fe + \_\_CO_2$?
   a. 1
   b. 3
   c. 2
   d. 6

5. Which characteristic is NOT a property of water?
   a. If it acts as a base, it donates a proton.
   b. It is amphoteric and can act as an acid or a base.
   c. If it donates a proton, it becomes a conjugate base in the form of hydroxide ions.
   d. If it accepts a proton, it becomes a conjugate acid in the form of hydronium ions.

See answers on the next page.

Answer Explanations

1. D: London dispersion forces are the weakest type of intermolecular attraction. They form between induced dipoles that are temporary and break apart easily. Hydrogen bonds are the strongest type of weak intermolecular attraction. When hydrogen bonds to a highly electronegative atom, the interaction becomes exaggerated and creates a stronger bond than expected. Dipole-dipole interactions are stronger than London dispersion forces because the dipoles are permanently present in the molecular configuration, but they are weaker than hydrogen bonds.

2. A: Capillary action is a combination of adhesion and cohesion and allows water to move up the stem of a plant, so Choice *A* is correct. Adhesion is the attraction of liquid to the container that it is in and cohesion is the attraction of liquid molecules to each other. These intermolecular forces combine to move water upward throughout the plant from the roots. Surface tension, Choice *B,* occurs when the molecules at the surface of a liquid are pulled down into the body of the liquid and a strong interface is created at the surface. Vapor pressure, Choice *C,* involves the ability of a liquid to become a gas. Water does not dissolve the plant stem, so solubility is not involved in the travel of water up the stem, making Choice *D* incorrect.

3. D: Iodine has the greatest number of electrons at 53 electrons. The number of electrons increases in elements going from left to right across the periodic table. Hydrogen, Choice *A,* is at the top left corner of the periodic table, so it has the fewest electrons (one electron). Iron has 26 electrons, copper has 29 electrons, Choices *B* and *C,* respectively.

4. B: For a chemical equation to be balanced, the same quantity of each element must be present on each side of the equation. The left side of the equation contains one iron (Fe) atom, six oxygen atoms, and three carbon atoms. On the right side of the equation, there is also one iron atom; the rest of the oxygen and carbon atoms must be accounted for by the carbon dioxide molecules. Having three carbon dioxide molecules would give three carbon atoms and six oxygen atoms, which is equivalent to the reactants' side of the equation.

5. A: Choice *A* is the correct answer because it is the only one that contains an incorrect statement about the properties of water. Water is amphoteric and can act as an acid or a base, as stated in Choice *B.* When it acts as an acid, it donates a proton to the molecule it is reacting with, and then becomes hydroxide ions and acts as a conjugate base, Choice *C.* When it acts like a base, it accepts a proton, Choice *D,* and becomes hydronium ions, which act as a conjugate acid. When water acts as a base, it does not donate a proton, making Choice *A* the correct answer.

Anatomy and Physiology

General Terminology

Anatomy may be defined as the structural makeup of an organism. The study of anatomy may be divided into microscopic/fine anatomy and macroscopic/gross anatomy. **Fine anatomy** concerns itself with viewing the features of the body with the aid of a microscope, while **gross anatomy** concerns itself with viewing the features of the body with the naked eye. **Physiology** refers to the functions of an organism, and it examines the chemical or physical functions that help the body function appropriately.

Levels of Organization of the Human Body

All the parts of the human body are built of individual units called **cells.** Groups of similar cells are arranged into **tissues**, different tissues are arranged into **organs,** and organs working together form entire **organ systems**. The human body has twelve organ systems that govern circulation, digestion, immunity, hormones, movement, support, coordination, urination & excretion, reproduction (male and female), respiration, and general protection.

Body Cavities

The body is partitioned into different hollow spaces that house organs. The human body contains the following cavities:

- **Cranial cavity:** The cranial cavity is surrounded by the skull and contains organs such as the brain and pituitary gland.
- **Thoracic cavity:** The thoracic cavity is encircled by the sternum (breastbone) and ribs. It contains organs such as the lungs, heart, trachea (windpipe), esophagus, and bronchial tubes.
- **Abdominal cavity:** The abdominal cavity is separated from the thoracic cavity by the diaphragm. It contains organs such as the stomach, gallbladder, liver, small intestines, and large intestines. The abdominal organs are held in place by a membrane called the peritoneum.
- **Pelvic cavity:** The pelvic cavity is enclosed by the pelvis, or bones of the hip. It contains organs such as the urinary bladder, urethra, ureters, anus, and rectum. It contains the reproductive organs as well. In females, the pelvic cavity also contains the uterus.
- **Spinal cavity:** The spinal cavity is surrounded by the vertebral column. The vertebral column has five regions: cervical, thoracic, lumbar, sacral, and coccygeal. The spinal cord runs through the middle of the spinal cavity.

Three Primary Body Planes

A **plane** is an imaginary flat surface. The three primary planes of the human body are frontal, sagittal, and transverse. The **frontal**, or **coronal,** plane is a vertical plane that divides the body or organ into front (anterior) and back (posterior) portions. The **sagittal,** or **lateral,** plane is a vertical plane divides the body or organ into right and left sides. The **transverse** plane is a horizontal plane that divides the body or organ into upper and lower portions. In medical imaging, computed tomography (CT) scans are oriented only in the transverse plane; while magnetic resonance imaging (MRI) scans may be oriented in any of the three planes.

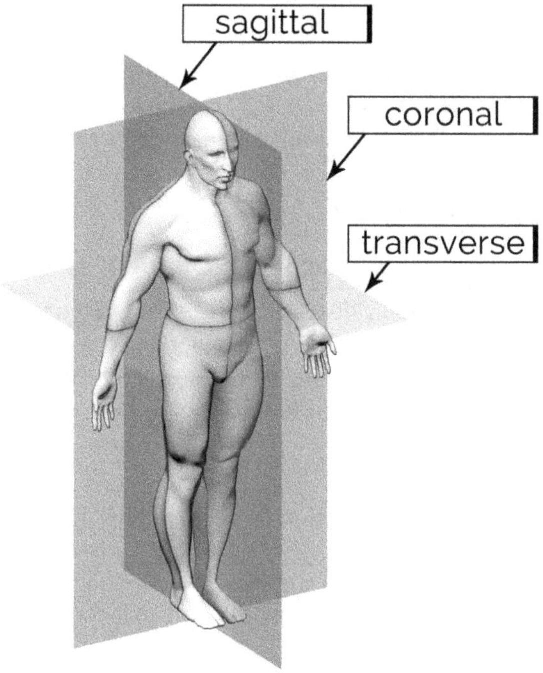

Note the body above is in the **anatomic position**. In anatomic position, the body and head are straight up and down, the feet are close but not touching, and the hands are pointed forward.

Terms of Direction

Medial refers to a structure being closer to the midline of the body. For example, the nose is medial to the eyes.

Lateral refers to a structure being farther from the midline of the body, and it is the opposite of medial. For example, the eyes are lateral to the nose.

Proximal refers to a structure or body part located near an attachment point. For example, the elbow is proximal to the wrist.

Distal refers to a structure or body part located far from an attachment point, and it is the opposite of proximal. For example, the wrist is distal to the elbow.

Anterior means toward the front in humans. For example, the lips are anterior to the teeth. The term **ventral** can be used in place of anterior and refers to the abdominal region, or underside, of an organism.

Posterior means toward the back in humans, and it is the opposite of anterior. For example, the teeth are posterior to the lips. The term **dorsal** can be used in place of posterior and refers to the back or upper side of an organism.

Superior means above and refers to a structure closer to the head. For example, the head is superior to the neck. The terms **cephalic** or **cranial** may be used in place of superior.

Inferior means below and refers to a structure farther from the head, and it is the opposite of superior. For example, the neck is inferior to the head. The term **caudal** may be used in place of inferior and refers to a structure near the tail or posterior of the body.

Superficial refers to a structure closer to the surface. For example, the muscles are superficial because they are just beneath the surface of the skin.

Deep refers to a structure farther from the surface, and it is the opposite of superficial. For example, the femur is a deep structure lying beneath the muscles.

Body Regions

Terms for general locations on the body include:

- Cervical: relating to the neck (can also refer to the cervix, as in cervical cancer)
- Clavicular: relating to the clavicle, or collarbone
- Ocular: relating to the eyes
- Acromial: relating to the shoulder
- Cubital: relating to the elbow
- Brachial: relating to the arm
- Carpal: relating to the wrist
- Thoracic: relating to the chest
- Abdominal: relating to the abdomen
- Pubic: relating to the groin
- Pelvic: relating to the pelvis, or bones of the hip
- Femoral: relating to the femur, or thigh bone
- Geniculate: relating to the knee
- Pedal: relating to the foot
- Palmar: relating to the palm of the hand
- Plantar: relating to the sole of the foot

Abdominopelvic Regions and Quadrants

The **abdominopelvic region** may be defined as the combination of the abdominal and the pelvic cavities. The region's upper border is the breasts and its lower border is the groin region. The region is divided into the following nine sections:

- Right hypochondriac: region below the cartilage of the ribs
- Epigastric: region above the stomach between the hypochondriac regions
- Left hypochondriac: region below the cartilage of the ribs
- Right lumbar: region of the waist
- Umbilical: region between the lumbar regions where the umbilicus, or belly button (navel), is located
- Left lumbar: region of the waist
- Right inguinal: region of the groin
- Hypogastric: region below the stomach between the inguinal regions
- Left inguinal: region of the groin

A simpler way to describe the abdominopelvic area is to divide it into the following quadrants:

- Right upper quadrant (RUQ): Encompasses the right hypochondriac, right lumbar, epigastric, and umbilical regions.
- Right lower quadrant (RLQ): Encompasses the right lumbar, right inguinal, hypogastric, and umbilical regions.
- Left upper quadrant (LUQ): Encompasses the left hypochondriac, left lumbar, epigastric, and umbilical regions.
- Left lower quadrant (LLQ): Encompasses the left lumbar, left inguinal, hypogastric, and umbilical regions.

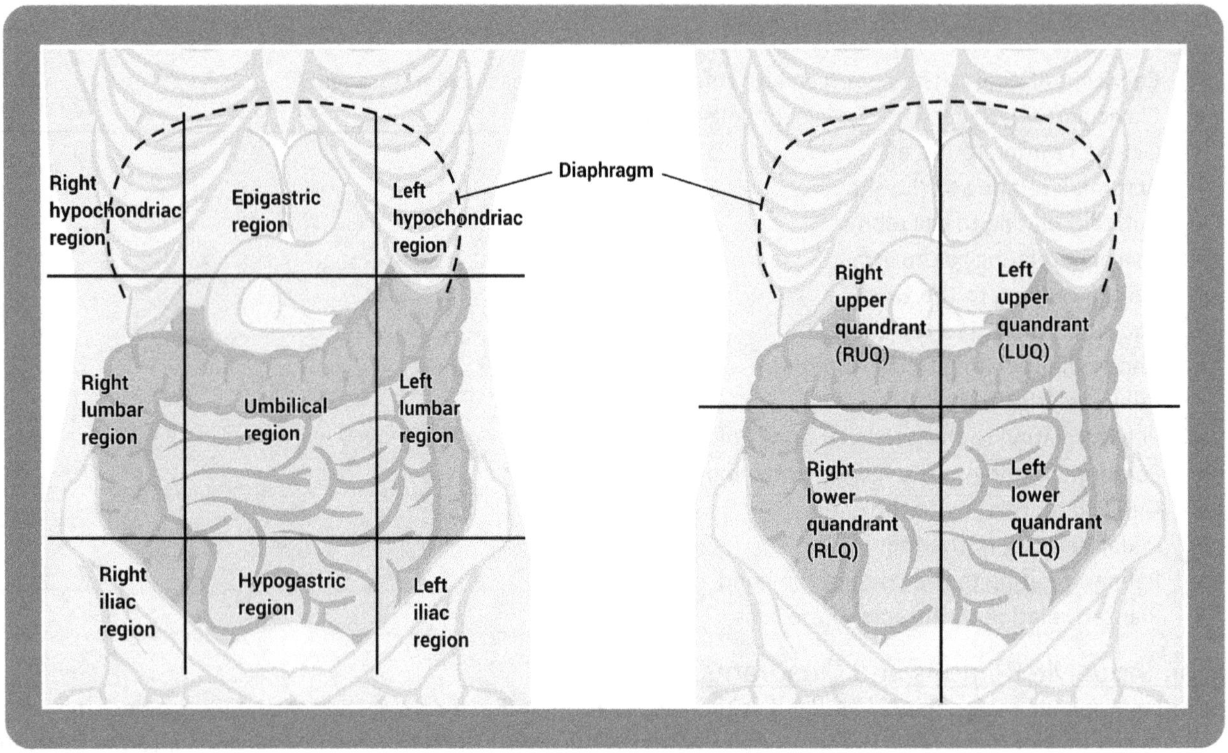

Cytology

Every living organism consists of cells, and cells are the basic unit of life. **Cytology** is the study of cells (usually eukaryotic cells), and is somewhat similar to **histology** (the study of cells and tissues in living organisms). Cells must contain a cell membrane, cytoplasm, and genetic information (usually in a nucleus). The cell membrane forms a barrier between the inside and outside of the cell, envelops the cellular contents, and interfaces with the extracellular fluid through proteins and other structures found in and on the cell membrane.

Eukaryotic cells—those found in plants, animals, and fungi—possess functional units called **organelles**. Each organelle performs one or more specific tasks in the cell. The nucleus contains the cell's genetic material, deoxyribonucleic acid, or DNA, which contains the necessary information for assembling all of the cell's proteins. The rough ER has embedded ribosomes, and it assembles enzymes and proteins. The smooth ER lacks ribosomes, and creates and stores lipids. The Golgi apparatus contains many enzymes; these enzymes allow it to process incoming proteins and package them into small membranous sacs called **vesicles** for transport into and out of the cell. Mitochondria are involved in aerobic cellular respiration, which generates ATP.

There are several other important cellular components that aren't usually classified as organelles, because they lack membranes. Ribosomes serve a vital role by assembling proteins based on the sequence in RNA in a process known as **translation**. The cytoskeleton is a collection of protein filaments; it provides a lattice for intracellular transport and helps maintain the cell's shape. The cytosol is the fluid inside the cell and membrane-bound organelles. Vesicles transport material in or out of the cell. Vacuoles are large, amorphous cell compartments, mostly found in plants and fungi, that store fluid, proteins, and other materials, and maintain the cell's rigidity. Cilia and flagella move fluids past the cell's surface or help with mobility.

Mitosis and Meiosis

The **cell cycle** is the process by which a cell divides and duplicates itself. There are two processes by which a cell can divide itself: mitosis and meiosis. In **mitosis,** the daughter cells that are produced from parental cell division are identical to each other and the parent. **Meiosis** is a unique process that involves two stages of cell division and produces haploid cells, which are cells containing only one set of chromosomes, from diploid parent cells, which are cells containing two sets of chromosomes.

Histology

Histology is the examination of specialized cells and cell groups that perform a specific function by working together. Although there are trillions of cells in the human body, there are only 200 different types of cells. Groups of cells form biological tissues, and tissues combine to form organs, such as the heart and kidney. Organs are structures that have many different functions that are vital to living creatures. There are four primary types of tissue: epithelial, connective, muscle, and neural. Each tissue type has specific characteristics that enable organs and organ systems to function properly.

Muscle: Muscle tissue supports the body and allows it to move, and muscles are special because their cells have the ability to contract. There are three distinct types of muscle tissue: skeletal, smooth, and cardiac. **Skeletal muscle** is voluntary, or under conscious control, and is usually attached to bones. Most body movement is directly caused by the contraction of skeletal muscle. **Smooth muscle** is typically involuntary, or not under conscious control, and may be found in blood vessels, the walls of hollow organs, and the urinary bladder. **Cardiac muscle** is involuntary and found in the heart, which helps propel blood throughout the body.

Nervous: Nervous tissue is unique in that it is able to coordinate information from sensory organs as well as communicate the proper behavioral responses. **Neurons,** or nerve cells, are the workhorses of the nervous system. They communicate via **action potentials** (electrical signals) and **neurotransmitters** (chemical signals).

Epithelial: Epithelial tissue covers the external surfaces of organs and lines many of the body's cavities. Epithelial tissue helps to protect the body from invasion by microbes (bacteria, viruses, parasites), fluid loss, and injury.

Epithelial cell shapes can be:

- Squamous: cells with a flat shape
- Cuboidal: cells with a cubed shape
- Columnar: cells shaped like a column

Epithelial cells can be arranged in four patterns:

- Simple: a type of epithelium composed solely from a single layer of cells
- Stratified: a type of epithelium composed of multiple layers of cells
- Pseudostratified: a type of epithelium that appears to be stratified but actually consists of only one layer of cells

- Transitional: a type of epithelium noted for its ability to expand and contract

Connective: Connective tissue supports and connects the tissues and organs of the body. Connective tissue is composed of cells dispersed throughout a matrix which can be gel, liquid, protein fibers, or salts. The primary protein fibers in the matrix are collagen (for strength), elastin (for flexibility), and reticulum (for support). Connective tissue can be categorized as either **loose** or **dense.** Examples of connective tissue include bones, cartilage, ligaments, tendons, blood, and adipose (fat) tissue.

Integumentary System

The **integumentary system** includes skin, hair, nails, oil glands, and sweat glands. The largest organ of the integumentary system (and of the body), the skin, acts as a barrier and protects the body from mechanical impact, variations in temperature, microorganisms, chemicals, and UV radiation from the sun. It regulates body temperature, peripheral circulation, and excretes waste through sweat. It also contains a large network of nerve cells that relay changes in the external environment to the brain.

Layers of Skin

Skin consists of three layers: the surface **epidermis**, the inner **dermis**, and the subcutaneous **hypodermis** that is below the dermis and contains a layer of fat and connective tissue, which are both important for insulation.

The whole epidermis is composed of epithelial cells that lack blood vessels. The outer epidermis is composed of dead cells, which surround the living cells underneath. The most inner epidermal tissue is a single layer of cells called the **stratum basale,** which is composed of rapidly dividing cells that push old cells to the skin's surface. When being pushed out, the cells' organelles disappear, and they start producing a protein called **keratin**, which eventually forms a tough waterproof layer. This outer layer sloughs off every four to five weeks. The **melanocytes** in the stratum basale produce the pigment melanin, which absorbs UV rays and protects the skin. Skin also produces vitamin D if exposed to sunlight.

The dermis underneath the epidermis contains supporting collagen fibers peppered with nerves, blood vessels, hair follicles, sweat glands, oil glands, and smooth muscles.

Skin's Involvement in Temperature Homeostasis

The skin has a thermoregulatory role in the human body that is controlled by a negative feedback loop. The control center of temperature regulation is the hypothalamus in the brain. When the hypothalamus is alerted by receptors from the dermis, it secretes hormones that activate effectors to keep internal temperature at a set point of 98.6°F (37°C). If the environment is too cold, the hypothalamus will initiate a pathway that induces muscle shivering to release heat energy as well as constrict blood vessels to limit heat loss. In hot conditions, the hypothalamus will initiate a pathway that vasodilates blood vessels to increase heat loss and stimulate sweating for evaporative cooling. Evaporative cooling occurs when the hottest water particles evaporate and leave behind the coolest ones. This cools down the body.

Sebaceous Glands vs. Sweat Glands

The skin also contains oil glands, or **sebaceous glands**, and sweat glands that are **exocrine** because their substances are secreted through ducts. **Endocrine** glands secrete substances into the blood stream instead. Oil glands are attached to hair follicles. They secrete **sebum**, an oily substance that moisturizes the skin, protecting it from water loss. Sebum also keeps the skin elastic. Also, sebum's slight acidity provides a chemical defense against bacterial and fungal infections.

Sweat glands not attached to hair follicles are called **eccrine** glands. They are all over the body, and are the sweat glands responsible for thermoregulation. They also remove bodily waste by secreting water and electrolytes. Sweat glands attached to hair follicles are apocrine glands, and there are far fewer apocrine sweat glands than eccrine sweat glands in the body. **Apocrine** glands are only active post-puberty. They secrete a thicker, viscous substance that is attractive to bacteria, leading to the unpleasant smell in armpits, feet, and the groin. They are stimulated during stress and arousal.

Skeletal System

Axial Skeleton and Appendicular Skeleton

The skeletal system is composed of 206 bones interconnected by tough connective tissue called ligaments. The **axial skeleton** can be considered the north-south axis of the skeleton. It includes the spinal column, sternum, ribs, and skull. There are 80 bones in the axial skeleton, and 33 of them are vertebrae. The ribs make up 12 of the bones in the axial skeleton.

The remaining 126 bones are in the **appendicular skeleton**, which contains bones of the appendages like the collarbone (clavicle), shoulders (scapula), arms, hands, hips, legs, and feet. The arm bones consist of the upper humerus with the radius and ulna that attach to the hands. The wrists, hands, and fingers are composed of the carpals, metacarpals, and phalanges, respectively. The femur attaches to the hips. The patella or kneecap connects the femur to the fibula and tibia. The ankles, feet, and toes are composed of the tarsals, metatarsals, and phalanges, respectively.

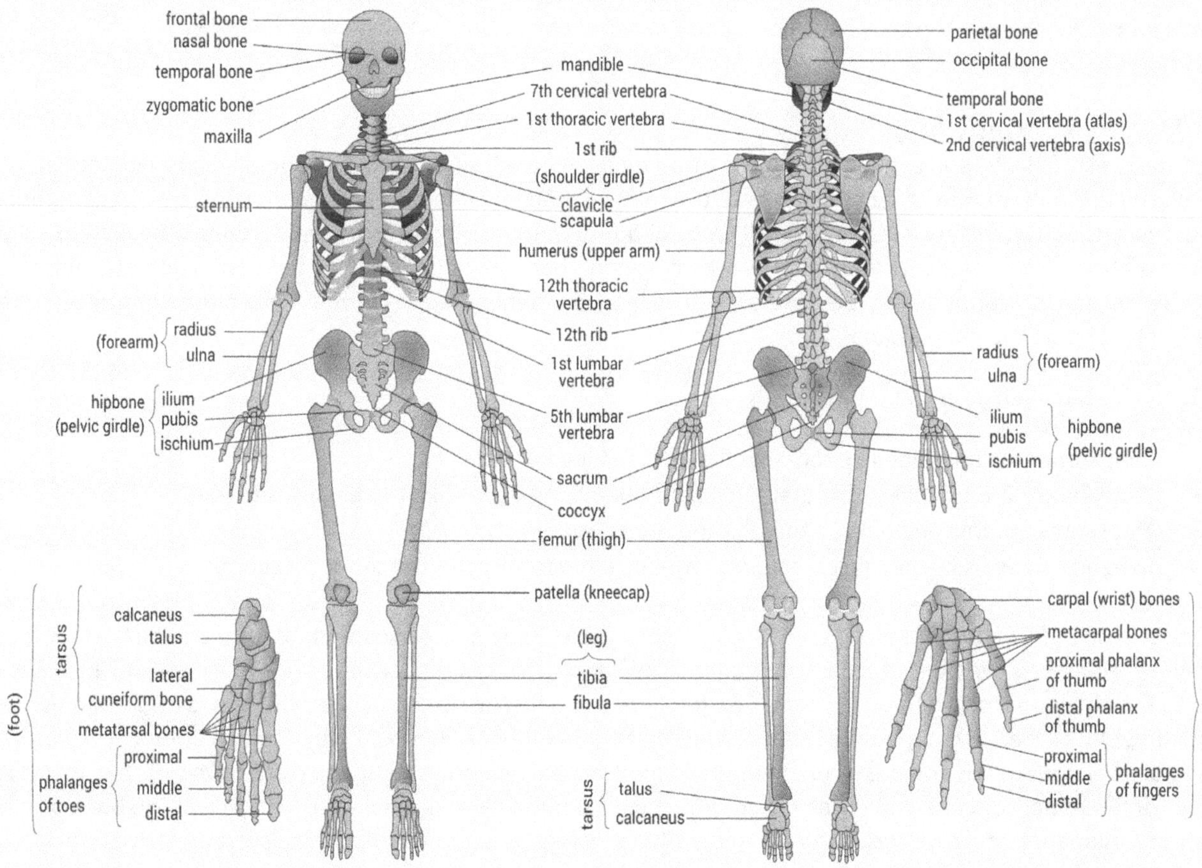

Functions of the Skeletal System

One of the skeletal system's most important functions is to protect vital internal organs. The skull protects the brain, the ribs protect the lungs and heart, the vertebrae protect the spinal column, and the pelvis protects the uterus and other reproductive organs. Yellow bone marrow stores lipids, or fats. Red bone marrow produces red and white blood cells as well as platelets in a process known as **hemopoiesis**. The bones themselves store the essential minerals calcium and phosphorus. The organization of the skeleton allows us to stand upright and acts as a foundation for organs and tissues to attach and maintain their location. This is similar to how the wooden frame of a house has room partitions to designate the type of room and floors that furniture can attach to.

The skeletal system and the muscular system are literally interconnected and allow for voluntary movement. Strong connective tissues called **tendons** attach bones to muscles. Most muscles work in opposing pairs and act as levers. For example, flexing the biceps brings the upper arm and lower arm closer together and flexing the triceps moves them apart. **Synovial joints** are movable joints, and they are rich with cartilage, connective tissue, and synovial fluid, which acts as a lubricant. The majority of joints are synovial joints, and they include hinge joints, like the one at the elbow, which permits flexion and extension.

The vertebrae are **cartilaginous joints**, which have spaces between them filled with cushion-like intervertebral discs that act as shock absorbers. The tight fit between the vertebrae and the intervertebral discs helps to protect the spinal cord inside by limiting the movement between two adjacent vertebrae. However, because there are so many vertebrae, the backbone as a whole is somewhat flexible.

Fibrous joints like those in the skull have fibrous tissue between the bones and no cavity between them. These are fixed joints that are immobile.

Compact and Spongy Bone

Osteoclasts, osteoblasts, and osteocytes are the three types of bone cells. **Osteoclasts** break down old bone, **osteoblasts** make new bone, and **osteocytes** are the mature functional bone cells. Bone is constantly regenerating due to the osteoblasts/osteoclasts that line all types of bones and the blood vessels inside them. The cells exist within a matrix of collagen fibers and minerals. The collagen fibers provide resistance to tension and the minerals provide resistance to compression. Because of the collagen and mineral matrix, bones have ample reinforcement to collectively support the entire human body.

Bones can be classified as any of the following:

- **Long bones** include tube-like rods like the arm and leg bones.
- **Short bones** are tube-like rods that are smaller than long bones like the fingers and toes.
- **Flat bones** are thin and flat like the ribs and breastbone.
- **Irregular bones**, like the vertebrae, are compact and don't fit into the other categories.
-

The outer tissue of the bone is surrounded by connective tissue known as **periosteum**. It appears shiny, smooth, and white. It protects the bone, anchors the bone to the connective tissue that surrounds muscles, and links the bone to the circulatory and nervous system. **Compact bone** is underneath the periosteum and is made of a dense blend of tightly packed osteocytes. It serves as a mineral reservoir of calcium and phosphorus. Compact bones have a **Haversian system** that is composed of embedded blood vessels, lymph vessels, and nerve bundles that span the interior of the bone from one end to the other. Branching from the central canal to the surface of the bone are the **canals of Volkmann,** which deliver materials to peripheral osteocytes. Concentric circles surround the central Haversian canal, and these **lamallae** have gaps between them called **lacunae** where osteocytes are embedded.

In contrast, **spongy bone** is very porous and more flexible than compact bone. It is at the ends of long bones and the central part of flat bones. It looks like a honeycomb, and the open spaces are connected by **trabeculae** which are beams of tissue that add support. They add strength without adding mass.

Cartilage is a very flexible connective tissue made of collagen and flexible elastin. It has no blood vessels and obtains materials via diffusion. It is replaced by bone starting in infancy in a process called **ossification**.

Muscular System

The muscular system is responsible for involuntary and voluntary movement of the body. There are three types of muscle: skeletal, cardiac, and smooth.

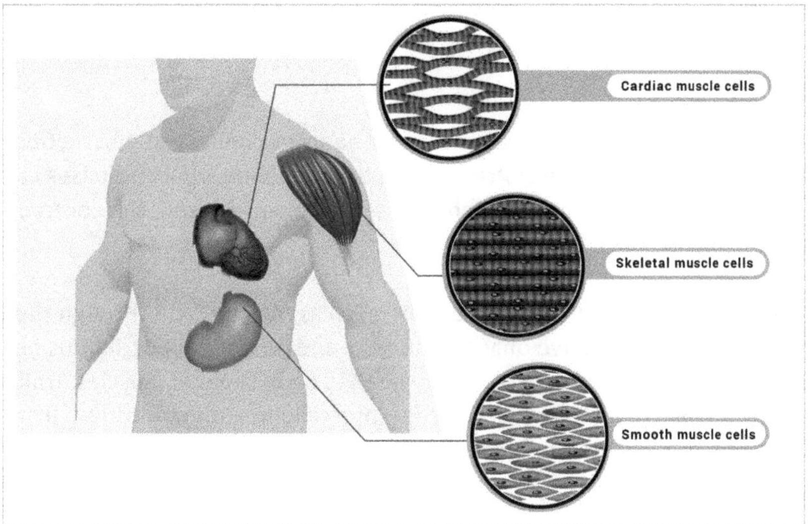

Skeletal Muscles

Skeletal muscles, or **voluntary muscles**, are attached to bones by tendons and are responsible for voluntary movement. The connecting tendons are made up of dense bands of connective tissue and have collagen fibers that firmly attach the muscle to the bone. Their fibers are actually woven into the coverings of the bone and muscle so that they can withstand pressure and tension. They usually work in opposing pairs like the biceps and triceps, for example. Muscles that work together are called **synergists.**

Skeletal muscles are made of bundles of long **fibers** that are composed of cells with many nuclei due to their length. These fibers contain **myofibrils,** and myofibrils are made of alternating **filaments**. The thicker myosin filaments are in between the smaller actin filaments in a unit called a **sarcomere**, and the overlapping regions of these filaments give the muscle its characteristic striated, or striped, appearance. Actin filaments are attached to exterior Z lines, myosin filaments are attached to a central M line, and when a muscle is at rest, there is a gap between the Z line and the myosin filaments. Only when the muscle contracts and the actin filaments slide over the myosin filaments does the myosin reach the Z line, as illustrated in the picture below. This **sliding-filament model of muscle**

contraction is dependent on myosin molecules forming and breaking cross-bridges with actin in order to pull the actin filaments closer to the M line.

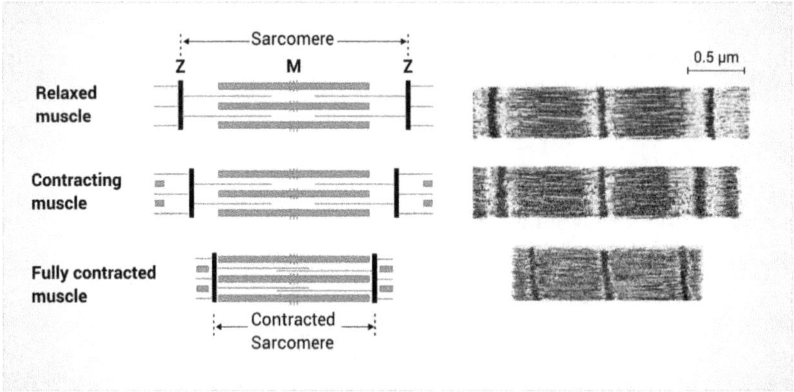

Skeletal muscles are controlled by the nervous system. Motor neurons connect to muscle fibers via neuromuscular junctions. Motor neurons must release the neurotransmitter **acetylcholine**, which releases calcium ions to stimulate myosin cross-bridging and contraction. As the acetylcholine stops being released, the contraction ends.

Smooth Muscles

Smooth muscles are responsible for involuntary movement, such as moving food through the digestive tract and moving blood through vessels. Their cells have only one nucleus and do not have striations because actin and myosin filaments do not have an organized arrangement like they do in skeletal muscles. Unlike skeletal muscle, smooth muscle doesn't rely on neuromuscular junctions for intercellular communication. Instead, they operate via gap junctions, which send impulses directly from cell to cell.

Cardiac Muscles

Cardiac muscle cells are found only in the heart where they control the heart's rhythm and blood pressure. Like skeletal muscle, cardiac muscle has striations, but cardiac muscle cells are smaller than skeletal muscle cells, so they typically have only one nucleus. Like smooth muscle, cardiac muscles do not require neurotransmitter release by motor neurons to function, and they instead operate via gap junctions.

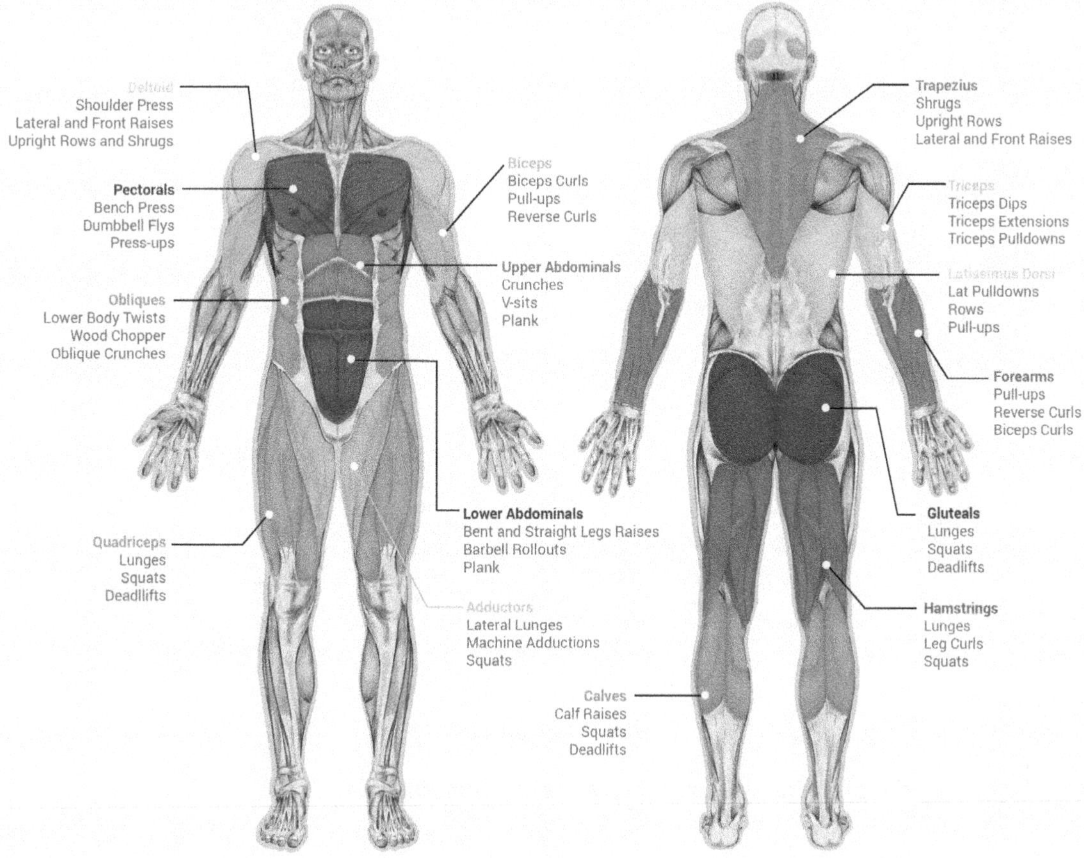

Nervous System

The human nervous system coordinates the body's response to stimuli from inside and outside the body. There are two major types of nervous system cells: neurons and neuroglia. **Neurons** are the workhorses of the nervous system and form a complex communication network that transmits electrical impulses termed **action potentials**, while **neuroglia** connect and support the neurons. Motor neurons use sodium and potassium pumps and channels in order to make action potentials occur.

Although some neurons monitor the senses, some control muscles, and some connect the brain to other neurons, all neurons have four common characteristics:

- **Dendrites:** These receive electrical signals from other neurons across small gaps called *synapses*.
- **Nerve cell body:** This is the hub of processing and protein manufacture for the neuron.
- **Axon:** This transmits the signal from the cell body to other neurons.
- **Terminals:** These bridge the neuron to dendrites of other neurons and deliver the signal via chemical messengers called **neurotransmitters.**

Here is an illustration of this:

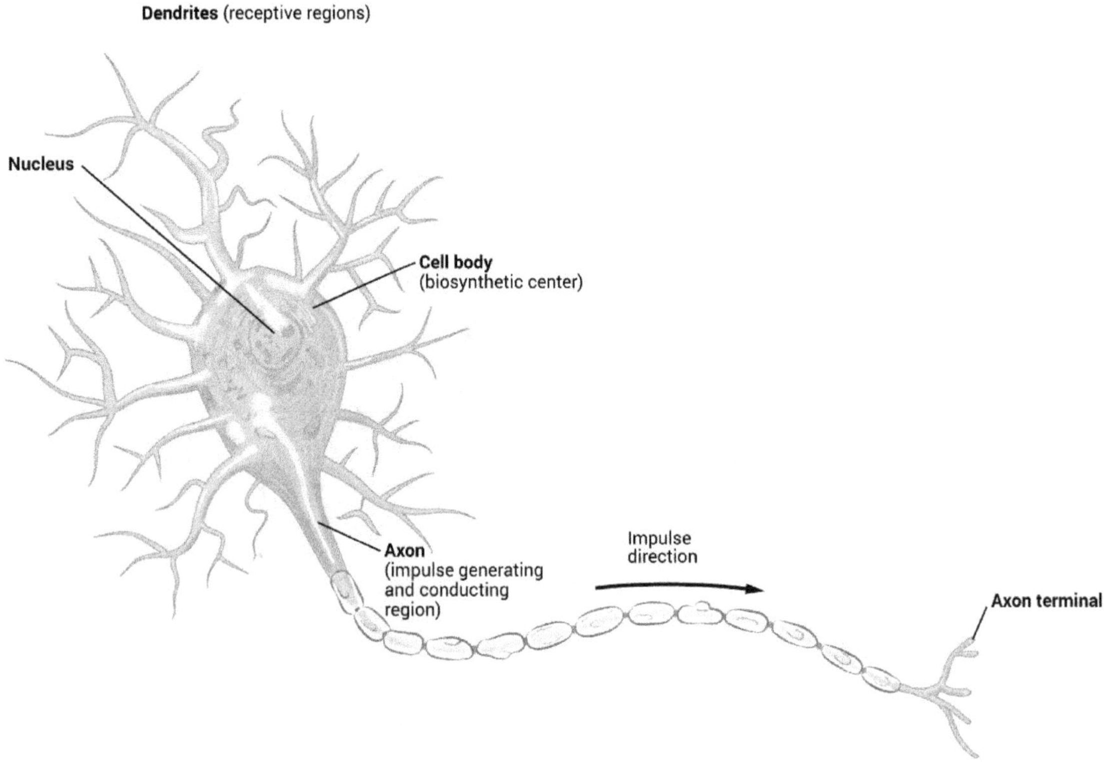

There are two major divisions of the nervous system, central and peripheral:

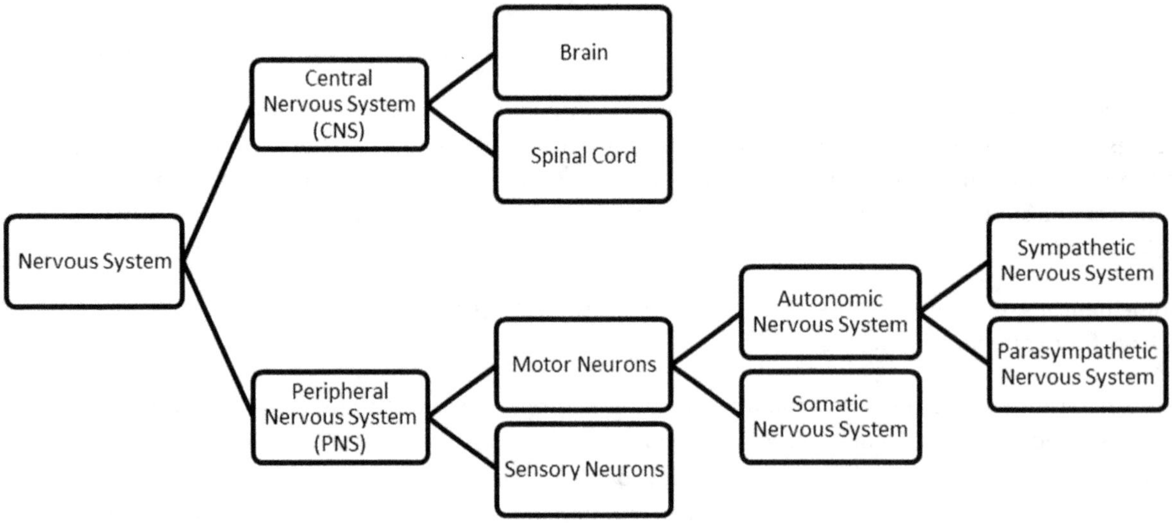

Central Nervous System

The **central nervous system (CNS)** consists of the brain and spinal cord. Three layers of membranes called the meninges cover and separate the CNS from the rest of the body.

The major divisions of the brain are the forebrain, the midbrain, and the hindbrain.

The **forebrain** consists of the cerebrum, the thalamus and hypothalamus, and the rest of the limbic system. The **cerebrum** is the largest part of the brain, and its most well-documented part is the outer cerebral cortex. The cerebrum is divided into right and left hemispheres, and each cerebral cortex hemisphere has four discrete areas, or lobes: frontal, temporal, parietal, and occipital.

The **frontal lobe** governs duties such as voluntary movement, judgment, problem solving, and planning, while the other lobes are more sensory. The **temporal lobe** integrates hearing and language comprehension, the **parietal lobe** processes sensory input from the skin, and the **occipital lobe** processes visual input from the eyes. For completeness, the other two senses, smell and taste, are processed via the olfactory bulbs. The thalamus helps organize and coordinate all of this sensory input in a meaningful way for the brain to interpret.

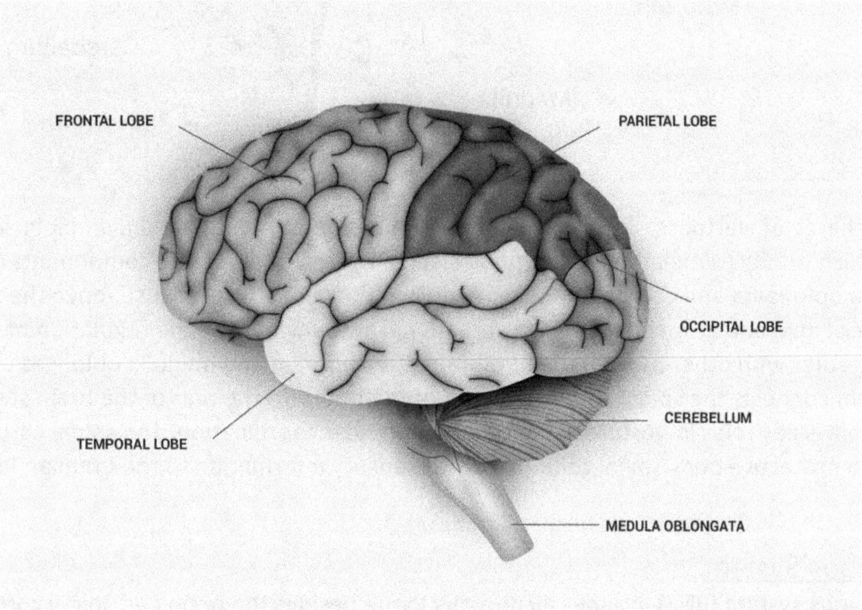

The **hypothalamus** controls the endocrine system and all of the hormones that govern long-term effects on the body. Each hemisphere of the limbic system includes a **hippocampus** (which plays a vital role in memory), an

amygdala (which is involved with emotional responses like fear and anger), and other small bodies and nuclei associated with memory and pleasure.

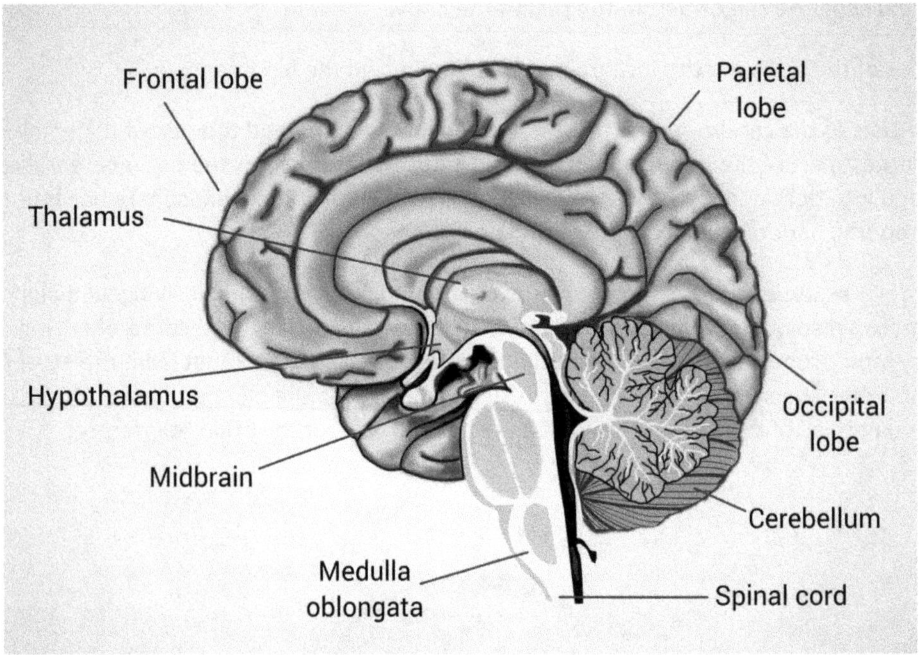

The **midbrain** is in charge of alertness, sleep/wake cycles, and temperature regulation, and it includes the **substantia nigra** which produces melatonin to regulate sleep patterns. The notable components of the **hindbrain** include the **medulla oblongata** and **cerebellum.** The medulla oblongata is located just above the spinal cord and is responsible for crucial involuntary functions such as breathing, swallowing, and the regulation of the heart rate and blood pressure. Together with other parts of the hindbrain, the midbrain and medulla oblongata form the **brain stem**. The brain stem connects the spinal cord to the rest of the brain. To the rear of the brain stem sits the cerebellum, which plays key roles in posture, balance, and muscular coordination. The spinal cord itself, which is encapsulated by the protective bony spinal column, carries sensory information to the brain and motor information to the body.

Peripheral Nervous System

The **peripheral nervous system (PNS)** includes all nervous tissue besides the brain and spinal cord. The PNS consists of the sets of cranial and spinal nerves and relays information between the CNS and the rest of the body. The PNS has two divisions: the autonomic nervous system and the somatic nervous system.

Autonomic Nervous System

The **autonomic nervous system (ANS)** governs involuntary, or reflexive, body functions. Ultimately, the autonomic nervous system controls functions such as breathing, heart rate, digestion, body temperature, and blood pressure.

The ANS is split between parasympathetic nerves and sympathetic nerves. These two nerve types are antagonistic and have opposite effects on the body. **Parasympathetic** nerves predominate resting conditions, and decrease heart rate, decrease breathing rate, prepare digestion, and allow urination and excretion. **Sympathetic** nerves, on the other hand, become active when a person is under stress or excited, and they increase heart rate, increase breathing rates, and inhibit digestion, urination, and excretion.

Somatic Nervous System and the Reflex Arc

The **somatic nervous system (SNS)** governs the conscious, or voluntary, control of skeletal muscles and their corresponding body movements. The SNS contains afferent and efferent neurons. **Afferent** neurons carry sensory messages from the skeletal muscles, skin, or sensory organs to the CNS. **Efferent neurons relay motor messages from the CNS to skeletal muscles, skin, or sensory organs.**

The SNS also has a role in involuntary movements called **reflexes**. A reflex is defined as an involuntary response to a stimulus. They are transmitted via what is termed a **reflex arc**, where a stimulus is sensed by an affector and its afferent neuron, interpreted and rerouted by an interneuron, and delivered to effector muscles by an efferent neuron where they respond to the initial stimulus. A reflex is able to bypass the brain by being rerouted through the spinal cord; the interneuron decides the proper course of action rather than the brain. The reflex arc results in an instantaneous, involuntary response. For example, a physician tapping on the knee produces an involuntary knee jerk referred to as the patellar tendon reflex.

Endocrine System

The **endocrine system** is made up of the ductless tissues and glands that secrete hormones directly into the bloodstream. It is similar to the nervous system in that it controls various functions of the body, but it does so via secretion of hormones in the bloodstream as opposed to nerve impulses. The endocrine system is also different because its effects last longer than that of the nervous system. Nerve impulses are immediate while hormone responses can last for minutes or even days.

The endocrine system works closely with the nervous system to regulate the physiological activities of the other systems of the body in order to maintain homeostasis. Hormone secretions are controlled by tight feedback loops that are generally regulated by the hypothalamus, the bridge between the nervous and endocrine systems. The hypothalamus receives sensory input via the nervous system and responds by stimulating or inhibiting the pituitary gland, which, in turn, stimulates or inhibits several other glands. The tight control is due to hormone secretions.

Hormones are chemicals that bind to specific target cells. Each hormone will only bind to a target cell that has a specific receptor that has the correct shape. For example, testosterone will not attach to skin cells because skin cells have no receptor that recognizes testosterone.

There are two types of hormones: steroid and protein. Steroid hormones are lipid, nonpolar substances, and most are able to diffuse across cell membranes. Once they do, they bind to a receptor that initiates a signal transduction cascade that affects gene expression. Non-steroid hormones bind to receptors on cell membranes that also initiate a signal transduction cascade that affects enzyme activity and chemical reactions.

Major Endocrine Glands

Hypothalamus: This gland is a part of the brain. It connects the nervous system to the endocrine system because it receives sensory information through nerves, and it sends instructions via hormones delivered to the pituitary.

Pituitary Gland: This gland is pea-sized and is found at the bottom of the hypothalamus. It has two lobes called the anterior and posterior lobes. It plays an important role in regulating other endocrine glands. For example, it secretes growth hormone, which regulates growth. Other hormones that are released by this gland control the reproductive system, childbirth, nursing, blood osmolarity, and metabolism.

The hormones and glands respond to each other via feedback loops, and a typical feedback loop is illustrated in the picture below. The hypothalamus and pituitary gland are master controllers of most of the other glands.

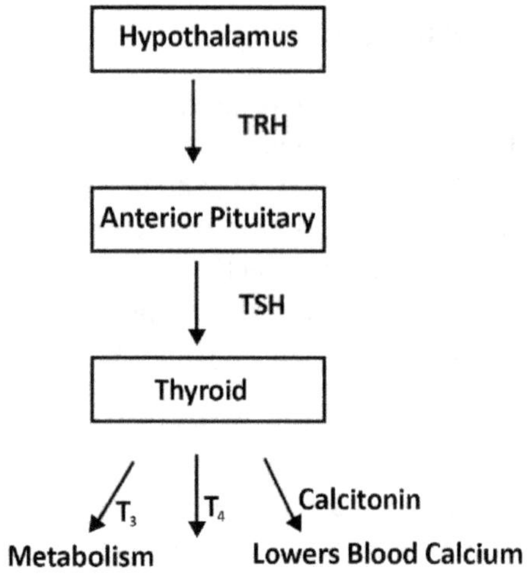

Thymus Gland: This gland is located in the chest cavity, embedded in connective tissue. It produces several hormones that are important for development and maintenance of T lymphocytes, which are important cells for immunity.

Adrenal Gland: One adrenal gland is attached to the top of each kidney. It produces epinephrine and norepinephrine which cause the "fight or flight" response in the face of danger or stress. These hormones raise heart rate, blood pressure, dilate bronchioles, and deliver blood to the muscles. All of these actions increase circulation and release glucose so that the body has an energy burst.

Pineal Gland: The pineal gland secretes melatonin, which is a hormone that regulates the body's circadian rhythm, which governs the natural wake-sleep cycle.

Testes and Ovaries: They secrete testosterone and both estrogen and progesterone, respectively. They are responsible for secondary sex characteristics, gamete development, and female hormones are important for embryonic development.

Thyroid Gland: This gland releases hormones like thyroxine and calcitonin. Thyroxine stimulates metabolism, and calcitonin monitors the amount of circulating calcium. Calcitonin signals the body to regulating calcium from bone reserves as well as kidney reabsorption of calcium.

Parathyroid Glands: These are four pea-sized glands located on the posterior surface of the thyroid. The main hormone that is secreted is called parathyroid hormone (PTH), which influences calcium levels like calcitonin, except it is antagonistic. PTH increases extracellular levels of calcium while calcitonin decreases it.

Pancreas: The pancreas is an organ that has both endocrine and exocrine functions. It functions outside of a typical feedback loop in that blood sugar seems to signal the pancreas itself. The endocrine functions are controlled by the pancreatic **islets of Langerhans**, which are groups of beta cells scattered throughout the gland that secrete insulin to lower blood sugar levels in the body. Neighboring alpha cells secrete glucagon to raise blood sugar. These complementary hormones keep blood sugar in check.

Cardiovascular System

The **cardiovascular system** (also called the **circulatory system**) is a network of organs and tubes that transport blood, hormones, nutrients, oxygen, and other gases to cells and tissues throughout the body. It is also known as the cardiovascular system. The major components of the circulatory system are the blood vessels, blood, and heart.

Blood Vessels

In the circulatory system, **blood vessels** are responsible for transporting blood throughout the body. The three major types of blood vessels in the circulatory system are arteries, veins, and capillaries. **Arteries** carry blood from the heart to the rest of the body. Veins carry blood from the body back to the heart. **Capillaries** connect arteries to veins and form networks that exchange materials between the blood and the cells.

In general, arteries are stronger and thicker than veins, as they withstand high pressures exerted by the blood as the heart pumps it through the body. Arteries control blood flow through either **vasoconstriction** (narrowing of the blood vessel's diameter) or **vasodilation** (widening of the blood vessel's diameter). The smallest arteries, which are farthest from the heart, are called **arterioles.** The blood in veins is under much lower pressures, so veins have valves to prevent the backflow of blood.

Most of the exchange between the blood and tissues takes place through the capillaries. There are three types of capillaries: continuous, fenestrated, and sinusoidal.

Continuous capillaries are made up of epithelial cells tightly connected together. As a result, they limit the types of materials that pass into and out of the blood. Continuous capillaries are the most common type of capillary. **Fenestrated capillaries** have openings that allow materials to be freely exchanged between the blood and tissues. They are commonly found in the digestive, endocrine, and urinary systems. **Sinusoidal capillaries** have larger openings and allow proteins and blood cells through. They are found primarily in the liver, bone marrow, and spleen.

Blood

Blood is vital to the human body. It is a liquid connective tissue that serves as a transport system for supplying cells with nutrients and carrying away their wastes. The average adult human has five to six quarts of blood circulating through their body. Approximately 55% of blood is plasma (the fluid portion), and the remaining 45% is composed of solid cells and cell parts. There are three major types of blood cells:

- Red blood cells, or **erythrocytes**, transport oxygen throughout the body. They contain a protein called **hemoglobin** that allows them to carry oxygen. The iron in the hemoglobin gives the cells and the blood their red colors.
- White blood cells, or **leukocytes**, are responsible for fighting infectious diseases and maintaining the immune system. Monocytes, lymphocytes (including B-cells and T-cells), neutrophils, basophils, and eosinophils compose the white blood cells. All are developed in bone marrow.
    - **Monocytes** eat and destroy invaders like bacteria and viruses.
    - **Lymphocytes** are responsible for antibody creation in the defense against invasive organisms and infections.
    - **Neutrophils**, the most abundant white blood cell, take out bacterial and fungal organisms. They are the first line of defense against infections.
    - **Basophils** and mast cells secrete histamine, the substance responsible for itching associated with allergic diseases.

- **Eosinophils** target parasites and cancer cells and are part of the body's allergic response. They have low phagocytic activity and primarily secrete destructive enzymes.

- **Platelets** are cell fragments that play a central role in the blood clotting process.

All blood cells in adults are produced in the bone marrow—red blood cells and most white blood cells are produced in the red marrow, and some white blood cells are produced in the yellow bone marrow.

Heart

The **heart** is a two-part, muscular pump that forcefully pushes blood throughout the human body. The human heart has four chambers—two upper atria and two lower ventricles separated by a partition called the septum. There is a pair on the left and a pair on the right. Anatomically, *left* and *right* correspond to the sides of the body that the patient themselves would refer to as left and right. Four valves help to section off the chambers from one another. Between the right atrium and ventricle, the three flaps of the **tricuspid valve** keep blood from backflowing from the ventricle to the atrium, similar to how the two flaps of the **mitral valve** work between the left atrium and ventricle. As these two valves lie between an atrium and a ventricle, they are referred to as **atrioventricular (AV) valves**. The other two valves are **semilunar (SL)** and control blood flow into the two great arteries leaving the ventricles. The **pulmonary valve** connects the right ventricle to the pulmonary artery, while the **aortic valve** connects the left ventricle to the aorta.

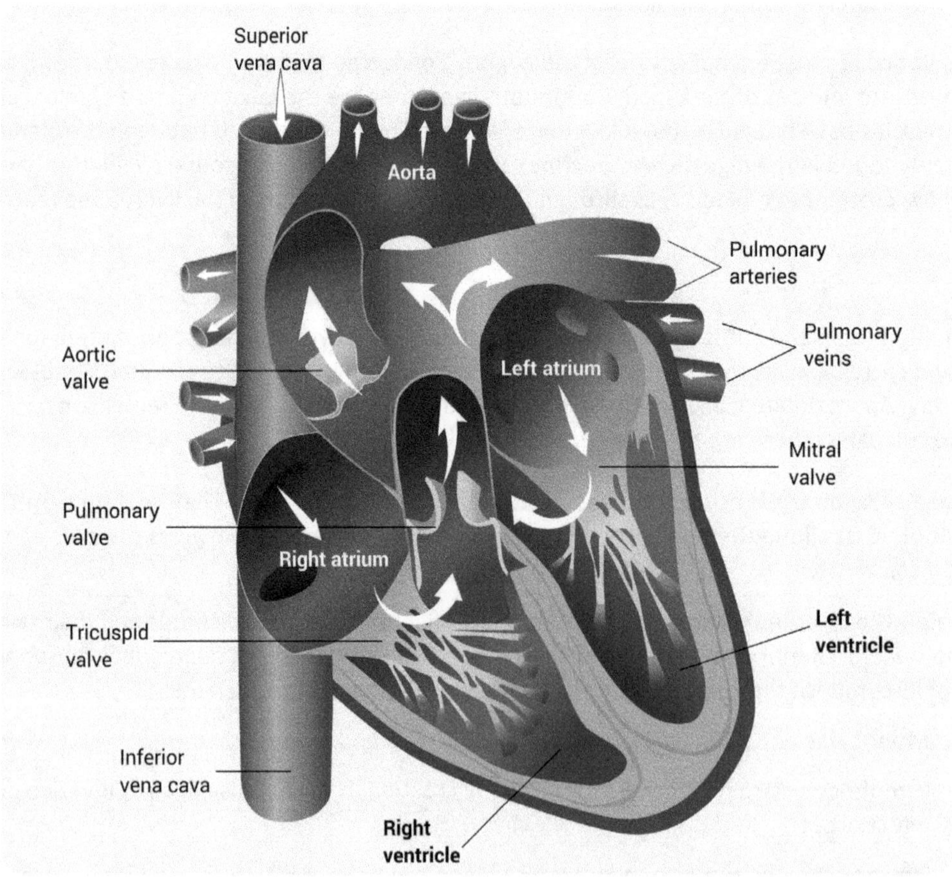

Cardiac Cycle

A **cardiac cycle** is one complete sequence of cardiac activity. The cardiac cycle represents the relaxation and contraction of the heart and can be divided into two phases: diastole and systole. **Diastole** is the phase during which the heart relaxes and fills with blood. It gives rise to the diastolic blood pressure (DBP), which is the bottom number of a blood pressure reading. **Systole** is the phase during which the heart contracts and discharges blood. It gives rise to the systolic blood pressure (SBP), which is the top number of a blood pressure reading. The heart's electrical conduction system coordinates the cardiac cycle.

Types of Circulation

Five major blood vessels manage blood flow to and from the heart: the superior vena cava and inferior vena cava, the aorta, the pulmonary artery, and the pulmonary vein. The superior vena cava is a large vein that drains blood from the head and the upper body. The **inferior vena cava** is a large vein that drains blood from the lower body. The **aorta** is the largest artery in the human body and carries blood from the heart to body tissues. The **pulmonary arteries** carry blood from the heart to the lungs. The **pulmonary veins** transport blood from the lungs to the heart.

In the human body, there are two types of circulation: pulmonary circulation and systemic circulation. **Pulmonary circulation** supplies blood to the lungs. Deoxygenated blood enters the right atrium of the heart and is routed through the tricuspid valve into the right ventricle. Deoxygenated blood then travels from the right ventricle of the heart through the pulmonary valve and into the pulmonary arteries. The pulmonary arteries carry the deoxygenated blood to the lungs. In the lungs, oxygen is absorbed, and carbon dioxide is released. The pulmonary veins carry oxygenated blood to the left atrium of the heart.

Systemic circulation supplies blood to all other parts of the body, except the lungs. Oxygenated blood flows from the left atrium of the heart through the mitral, or bicuspid, valve into the left ventricle of the heart. Oxygenated blood is then routed from the left ventricle of the heart through the aortic valve and into the aorta. The aorta delivers blood to the systemic arteries, which supply the body tissues. In the tissues, oxygen and nutrients are exchanged for carbon dioxide and other wastes. The deoxygenated blood along with carbon dioxide and wastes enter the systemic veins, where they are returned to the right atrium of the heart via the superior and inferior vena cava.

Respiratory System

The **respiratory system** enables breathing and supports the energy-making process in cells. The respiratory system transports an essential reactant, oxygen, to cells so that they can produce energy in their mitochondria via cellular respiration. The respiratory system also removes carbon dioxide, a waste product of cellular respiration. This system is divided into the upper respiratory system and the lower respiratory system. The **upper system** comprises the nose, the nasal cavity and sinuses, and the pharynx. The **lower respiratory system** comprises the larynx (voice box), the trachea (windpipe), the small passageways leading to the lungs, and the lungs.

The pathway of oxygen to the bloodstream begins with the nose and the mouth. Upon inhalation, air enters the nose and mouth and passes into the sinuses where it gets warmed, filtered, and humidified. The throat, or the pharynx, allows the entry of both food and air; however, only air moves into the trachea, or windpipe, since the epiglottis covers the trachea during swallowing and prevents food from entering. The trachea contains mucus and cilia. The mucus traps many airborne pathogens while the cilia act as bristles that sweep the pathogens away toward the top of the trachea where they are either swallowed or coughed out.

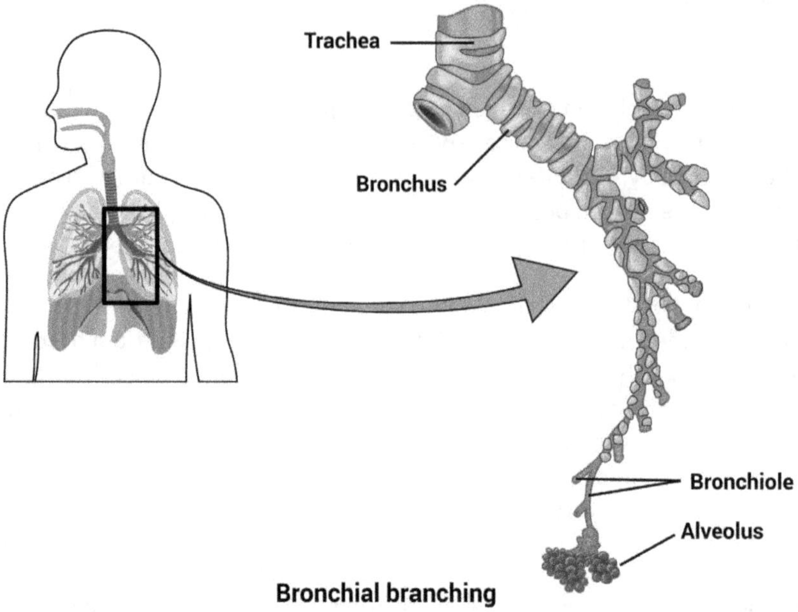

Bronchial branching

The **trachea** itself has two vocal cords at the top that make up the **larynx**. At its bottom, the trachea forks into two major **bronchi**—one for each lung. These bronchi continue to branch into smaller and smaller **bronchioles** before terminating in grape-like air sacs called **alveoli;** these alveoli are surrounded by capillaries and provide the body with an enormous amount of surface area to exchange oxygen and carbon dioxide gases, in a process called **external respiration**.

In total, the lungs contain about 1500 miles of airway passages. The right lung is divided into three lobes (superior, middle, and inferior), and the left lung is divided into two lobes (superior and inferior).

The left lung is smaller than the right lung, likely because it shares its space in the chest cavity with the heart.

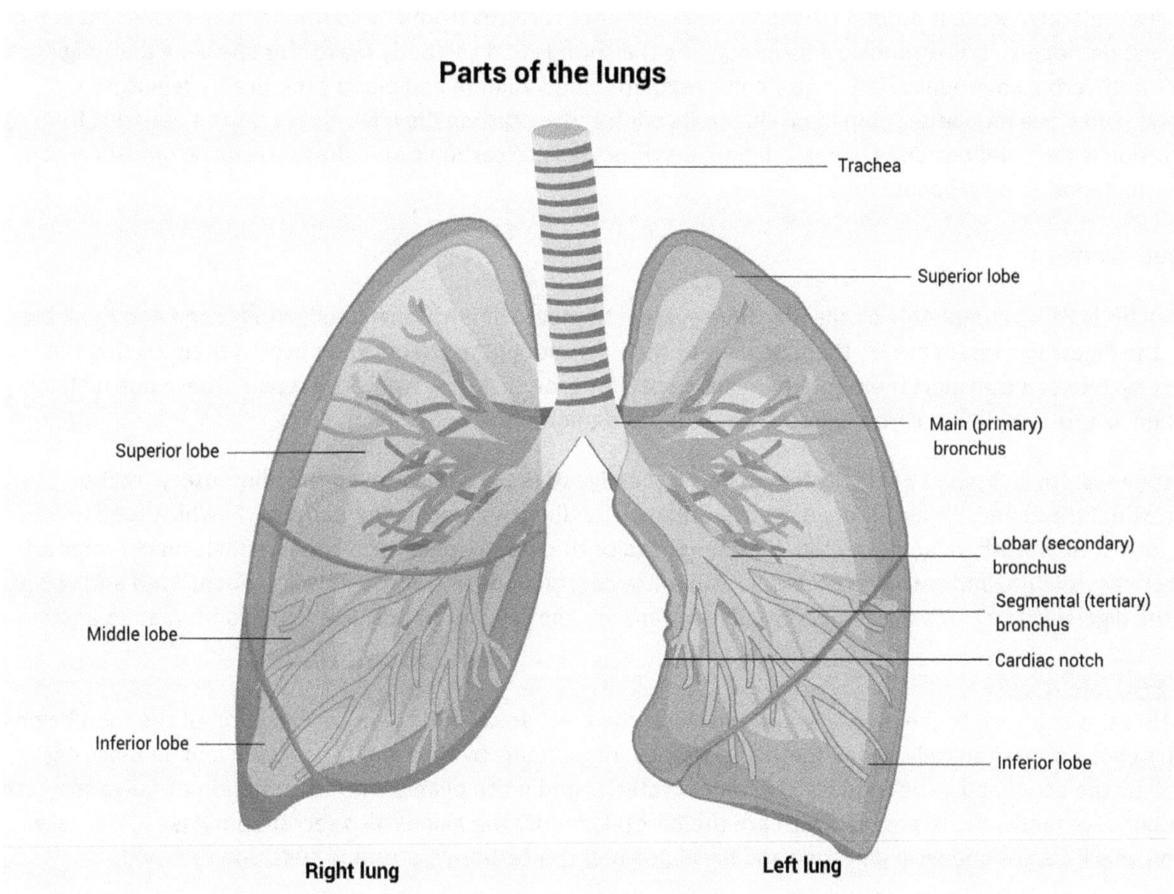

A flat muscle underneath the lungs called the **diaphragm** controls breathing. When the diaphragm contracts, the volume of the chest cavity increases and indirectly decreases its air pressure. This decrease in air pressure creates a vacuum, and the lungs pull in air to fill the space. This process is called negative pressure breathing.

Upon **inhalation** or **inspiration,** oxygen in the alveoli diffuses into the capillaries to be carried by blood to cells throughout the body, in a process called **internal respiration**. A protein called hemoglobin in red blood cells easily bonds with oxygen, removing it from the blood and allowing more oxygen to diffuse in. This protein allows the blood to take in 60 times more oxygen than the body could without it, and this explains how oxygen can become so concentrated in blood even though it is only 21% of the atmosphere. While oxygen diffuses from the alveoli into the capillaries, carbon dioxide diffuses from the capillaries into the alveoli. When the diaphragm relaxes, the elastic lungs snap back to their original shape; this decreases the volume of the chest cavity and increases the air pressure until it is back to normal. This increased air pressure pushes the carbon dioxide waste from the alveoli through **exhalation** or **expiration.**

The autonomic nervous system controls breathing. The medulla oblongata gets feedback regarding the carbon dioxide levels in the blood and will send a message to the diaphragm that it is time for a contraction. While breathing can be voluntary, it is mostly under autonomic control.

Functions of the Respiratory System

The respiratory system has many functions. Most importantly, it provides a large area for gas exchange between the air and the circulating blood. It protects the delicate respiratory surfaces from environmental variations and defends them against pathogens. It is responsible for producing the sounds that the body makes for speaking and singing, as well as for non-verbal communication. It also helps regulate blood volume and blood pressure by releasing vasopressin, and it is a regulator of blood pH due to its control over carbon dioxide release, as the aqueous form of carbon dioxide is the chief buffering agent in blood. Erythrocytes use carbonic anhydrase to convert most carbon dioxide in the blood to bicarbonate ions.

Digestive System

The human body relies completely on the **digestive system** to meet its nutritional needs. After food and drink are ingested, the digestive system breaks them down into their component nutrients and absorbs them so that the circulatory system can transport them to other cells to use for growth, energy, and cell repair. These nutrients may be classified as proteins, lipids, carbohydrates, vitamins, and minerals.

The digestive system is thought of chiefly in two parts: the **digestive tract** (also called the **alimentary tract** or **gastrointestinal tract**) and the accessory digestive organs. The digestive tract is the pathway in which food is ingested, digested, absorbed, and excreted. It is composed of the mouth, pharynx, esophagus, stomach, small and large intestines, rectum, and anus. **Peristalsis**, or wave-like contractions of smooth muscle, moves food and wastes through the digestive tract. The accessory digestive organs are the salivary glands, liver, gallbladder, and pancreas.

Mouth and Stomach

The mouth is the entrance to the digestive system. Here, the mechanical and chemical digestion of the food begins. The food is chewed mechanically by the teeth and shaped into a **bolus** by the tongue so that it can be more easily swallowed by the esophagus. The food also becomes waterier and more pliable with the addition of saliva secreted from the salivary glands, the largest of which are the parotid glands. The glands also secrete **amylase** in the saliva, an enzyme which begins chemical digestion and breakdown of the carbohydrates and sugars in the food.

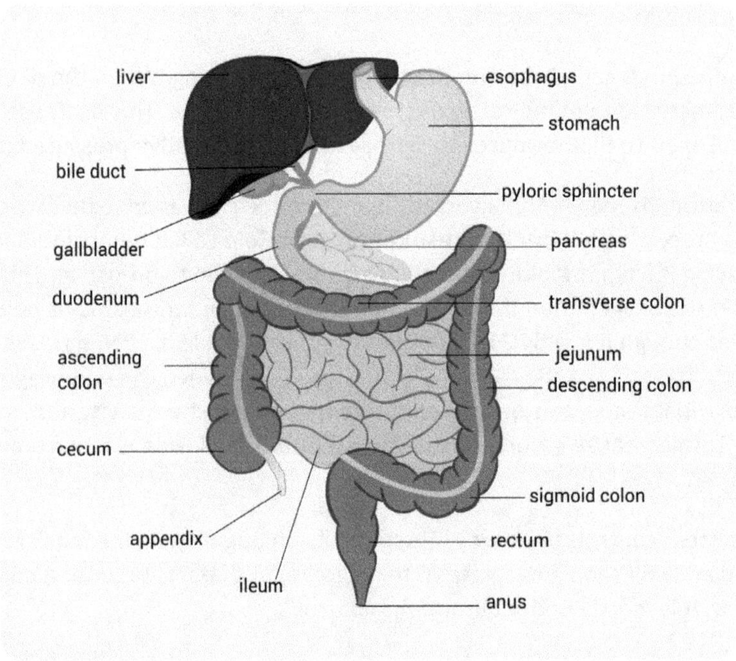

The food then moves through the pharynx and down the muscular esophagus to the stomach.

The stomach is a large, muscular sac-like organ at the distal end of the esophagus. Here, the bolus is subjected to more mechanical and chemical digestion. As it passes through the stomach, it is physically squeezed and crushed while additional secretions turn it into a watery nutrient-filled liquid that exits into the small intestine as **chyme.**

The stomach secretes a great many substances into the **lumen** of the digestive tract. Some cells produce gastrin, a hormone that prompts other cells in the stomach to secrete a gastric acid composed mostly of hydrochloric acid (HCl). The HCl is at such a high concentration and low pH that it denatures most proteins and degrades a lot of organic matter. The stomach also secretes mucous to form a protective film that keeps the corrosive acid from dissolving its own cells. Gaps in this mucous layer can lead to peptic ulcers. Finally, the stomach also uses digestive enzymes like proteases and lipases to break down proteins and fats; although there are some gastric lipases here, the stomach is most known for breaking down proteins.

Small Intestine

The chyme from the stomach enters the first part of the small intestine, the **duodenum,** through the **pyloric sphincter,** and its extreme acidity is partly neutralized by sodium bicarbonate secreted along with mucous. The presence of chyme in the duodenum triggers the secretion of the hormones secretin and cholecystokinin (CCK). Secretin acts on the pancreas to dump more sodium bicarbonate into the small intestine so that the pH is kept at a reasonable level, while CCK acts on the gallbladder to release the **bile** that it has been storing. Bile, a substance produced by the liver and stored in the gallbladder, helps to **emulsify** or dissolve fats and lipids.

Because of the bile (which aids in lipid absorption) and the secreted lipases (which break down fats), the duodenum is the chief site of fat digestion in the body. The duodenum also represents the last major site of chemical digestion in the digestive tract, as the other two sections of the small intestine (the **jejunum** and **ileum**) are instead heavily involved in absorption of nutrients.

The small intestine reaches 40 feet in length, and its cells are arranged in small finger-like projections called **villi.** This is due to its key role in the absorption of nearly all nutrients from the ingested and digested food, effectively transferring them from the lumen of the GI tract to the bloodstream, where they travel to the cells that need them. These nutrients include simple sugars like glucose from carbohydrates, amino acids from proteins, emulsified fats, electrolytes like sodium and potassium, minerals like iron and zinc, and vitamins like D and B12. Vitamin B12's absorption, though it takes place in the intestines, is actually aided by **intrinsic factor** that was released into the chyme back in the stomach.

Large Intestine

The leftover parts of food which remain unabsorbed or undigested in the lumen of the small intestine next travel through the **large intestine**, that may also be referred to as the **large bowel** or **colon.** The large intestine is mainly responsible for water absorption. As the chyme at this stage no longer has anything useful that can be absorbed by the body, it is now referred to as **waste,** and it is stored in the large intestine until it can be excreted from the body. Removing the liquid from the waste transforms it from liquid to solid stool, or **feces.**

This waste first passes from the small intestine to the **cecum**, a pouch that forms the first part of the large intestine. In herbivores, it provides a place for bacteria to digest cellulose, but in humans most of it is vestigial and is known as the appendix. From the cecum, waste next travels up the ascending colon, across the transverse colon, down the descending colon, and through the sigmoid colon to the rectum. The rectum is responsible for the final storage of waste before being expelled through the **anus**. The anal canal is a small portion of the rectum leading through to the anus and the outside of the body.

Pancreas

The **pancreas** has endocrine and exocrine functions. The endocrine function involves releasing the hormone insulin, which decreases blood sugar (glucose) levels, and glucagon, which increases blood sugar (glucose) levels, directly into the bloodstream. Both hormones are produced in the **islets of Langerhans,** insulin in the beta cells and glucagon in the alpha cells.

The exocrine function of the pancreas involves the secretion of inactive digestive enzymes (**zymogens**) from acinar cells into the main pancreatic duct. The main pancreatic duct joins the common bile duct, which empties into the small intestine (specifically the duodenum). The digestive enzymes are then activated and take part in the digestion of carbohydrates, proteins, and fats within chyme (the mixture of partially digested food and digestive juices).

Urinary System

The **urinary system** is made up of the kidneys, ureters, urinary bladder, and the urethra. It is the system responsible for removing waste products and balancing water and electrolyte concentrations in the blood. The urinary system has many important functions related to waste excretion. It regulates the concentrations of sodium, potassium, chloride, calcium, and other ions in the filtrate by controlling the amount of each that is reabsorbed during filtration. The reabsorption or secretion of hydrogen ions and bicarbonate contributes to the maintenance of blood pH. Certain kidney cells can detect any reductions in blood volume and pressure. If that happens, they secrete renin, which activates a hormone that causes increased reabsorption of sodium ions and water, raising volume and pressure. Under hypoxic conditions, kidney cells will secrete erythropoietin in order to stimulate red blood cell production. Kidney cells also synthesize **calcitriol**, which is a hormone derivative of vitamin D3 that aids in calcium ion absorption by the intestinal epithelium.

Under normal circumstances, humans have two functioning **kidneys** in the lower back and on either side of the spinal cord. They are the main organs that are responsible for filtering waste products out of the blood and regulating blood water and electrolyte levels. Blood enters the kidney through the renal artery, and urea and wastes are removed, while water and the acidity/alkalinity of the blood is adjusted. Toxic substances and drugs are also filtered. Blood exits through the renal vein, and the urine waste travels through the ureter to the bladder, where it is stored until it is eliminated through the urethra.

The kidneys have an outer **renal cortex** and an inner **renal medulla** that contain millions of tiny filtering units called **nephrons.** Nephrons have two parts: a glomerulus, which is the filter, and a tubule. The **glomerulus** is a network of capillaries covered by the **Bowman's capsule**, which is the entrance to the tubule. As blood enters the kidneys via the renal artery, the glomerulus allows for fluid and waste products to pass through it and enter the tubule. Blood cells and large molecules, such as proteins, do not pass through and remain in the blood.

The **filtrate** passes through the tubule, which has several parts. The proximal tubule comes first, and then the descending and ascending limbs of the loop of Henle dip into the medulla, followed by the distal tubule and collecting duct. The journey through the tubule involves a balancing act that regulates blood osmolarity, pH, and electrolytes exchange of materials between the tubule and the bloodstream. The final product at the collecting tubule is called urine, and it is delivered to the bladder by the ureter. The most central part of the kidney is the **renal pelvis**, and it acts as a funnel by delivering the urine from the millions of collecting tubules to the **ureters**. The filtered blood exits through the renal vein and is returned to circulation.

Here's a look at the genitourinary system:

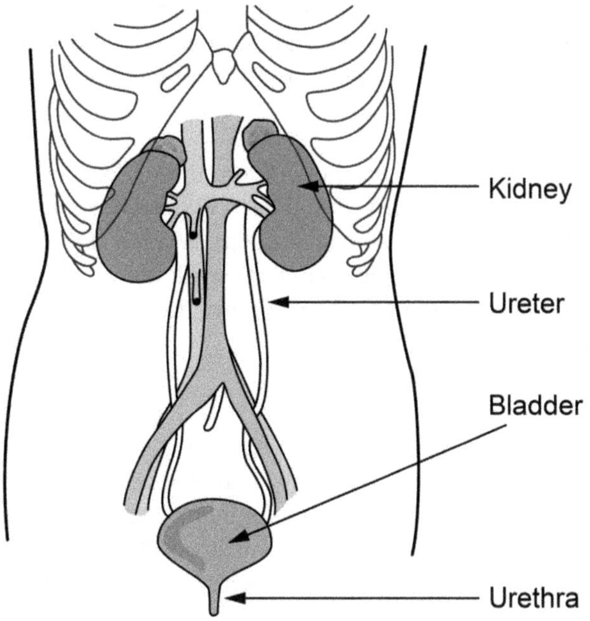

Here's a close up look at the kidney:

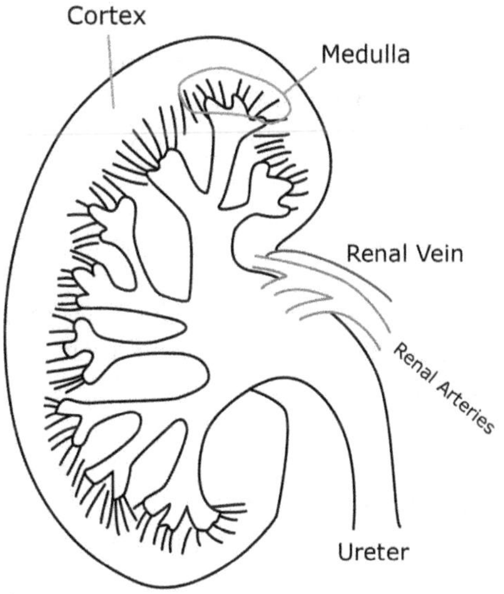

Waste Excretion

Once urine accumulates, it leaves the kidneys. The urine travels through the ureters into the **urinary bladder,** a muscular organ that is hollow and elastic. As more urine enters the urinary bladder, its walls stretch and become thinner so there is no significant difference in internal pressure. The urinary bladder stores the urine until the body is ready for urination, at which time the muscles contract and force the urine through the **urethra** and out of the body.

Reproductive System

The **reproductive system** is responsible for producing, storing, nourishing, and transporting functional reproductive cells, or gametes, in the human body. It includes the reproductive organs, also known as **gonads**, the reproductive tract, the accessory glands and organs that secrete fluids into the reproductive tract, and the **perineal structures**, which are the external genitalia.

Reproduction involves the passing of genes from one generation to the next, and that is accomplished through haploid gametes. Gametes have gone through meiosis and have 23 chromosomes, half the normal number. The male gamete is **sperm**, and the female gamete is an **egg** or **ovum.** When a sperm fertilizes an egg, they create a **zygote,** which is the first cell of a new organism. The zygote has a full set of 46 chromosomes because it received 23 from each parent. Because of gene shuffling during sperm and egg development, sperm and egg chromosome sets are all different, which results in the variety seen in humans.

Male Reproductive System

The entire male reproductive system is designed to generate sperm and produce semen that facilitate fertilization of eggs, the female gametes. The testes are the endocrine glands that secrete **testosterone**, a hormone that is important for secondary sex characteristics and sperm development, or **spermatogenesis**. Testosterone is in the androgen steroid-hormone family. The testes also produce and store 500 million spermatocytes, which are the male gametes, each day. Testes are housed in the **scrotum,** which is a sac that hangs outside the body so that spermatogenesis occurs at cooler and optimal conditions.

The **seminiferous tubules** within the testes produce spermatocytes, which after production travel to **epididymis** where they are stored as they mature. Then, the sperm move to the ejaculatory duct via the vas deferens. The ejaculatory duct contains more than just sperm. The **seminal vesicles** secrete an alkaline substance that will help sperm survive in the acidic vagina. The prostate gland secretes enzymes bathed in a milky white fluid that is important for thinning semen after ejaculation to increase its likelihood of reaching the egg. The **bulbourethral gland**, or **Cowper's gland,** secretes an alkaline fluid that lubricates the urethra prior to ejaculation to neutralize any acidic urine residue.

The sperm, along with all the exocrine secretions, are collectively called **semen.** Their destination is the vagina, and they can only get there if the penis is erect due to arousal and increased circulation. During sexual intercourse, ejaculation will forcefully expel the contents of the semen and effectively deliver the sperm to the egg. The muscular prostate gland is important for ejaculation. Each ejaculation releases 2 to 6 million sperm. Sperm has a whip-like flagellum tail that facilitates movement.

Female Reproductive System

The **vagina** is the passageway that sperm must travel through to reach an egg, the female gamete. Surrounding the vagina are the labia minor and labia major, both of which are folds that protect the urethra, which is used for urination and is part of the urinary system, and the vaginal opening. The **clitoris** is rich in nerve-endings, making it sensitive and highly stimulated during sexual intercourse. It is above the vagina and urethra. An exocrine gland called the **Bartholin's glands** secretes a fluid during arousal that is important for lubrication.

The female gonads are the **ovaries.** Ovaries generally alternate producing one gamete, an egg or oocyte, per month. They are also responsible for secreting the hormones **estrogen** and **progesterone**. Fertilization cannot happen unless the ejaculated sperm finds the egg, which is only available at certain times of the month. Eggs, or ova, develop in the ovaries in clusters surrounded by follicles, and after puberty, they are delivered to the uterus once a month via the **Fallopian tubes**.

The 28-day average journey of the egg to the uterus is called the menstrual cycle, and it is highly regulated by the endocrine system. The regulatory hormones Gonadotropin releasing hormone (GnRH), luteinizing hormone (LH), and follicle-stimulating hormone (FSH) orchestrate the menstrual cycle. Ovarian hormones estrogen and progesterone are also important in timing as well as for vascularization of the uterus in preparation for pregnancy. **Fertilization** usually happens around ovulation, which is when the egg is inside the fallopian tube. The resulting zygote travels down the tube and implants into the uterine wall. The uterus protects and nourishes the developing embryo for nine months until it is ready for the outside environment.

If the egg released is unfertilized, the uterine lining will slough off during **menstruation.** Should a fertilized egg, called a **zygote**, reach the uterus, it will embed itself into the uterine wall due to uterine vascularization that will deliver blood, nutrients, and antibodies to the developing embryo. The uterus is where the embryo will develop for the next nine months. **Mammary glands** are important female reproductive structures because they produce the milk provided for babies during **lactation**. Milk contains nutrients and antibodies that benefit the baby.

Practice Quiz

1. What is the body plane that runs vertically through the body at right angles to the midline?
    a. Coronal
    b. Transverse
    c. Sagittal
    d. Superior

2. Which statement is true?
    a. Ligaments attach skeletal muscles to bone.
    b. Tendons connect bones at joints.
    c. Cartilage adds mechanical support to joints.
    d. Most veins deliver oxygenated blood to cells.

3. Which layer of skin contains sensory receptors and blood vessels?
    a. Epidermis
    b. Dermis
    c. Hypodermis
    d. Subcutaneous

4. What are concentric circles of bone tissue called?
    a. Lacunae
    b. Lamellae
    c. Trabeculae
    d. Diaphysis

5. When deoxygenated blood first enters the heart, which of the following choices is in the correct order for its journey to the aorta?

    I. Tricuspid valve → Lungs → Mitral valve
    II. Mitral valve → Lungs → Tricuspid valve
    III. Right ventricle → Lungs → Left atrium
    IV. Left ventricle → Lungs → Right atrium

    a. I and III only
    b. I and IV only
    c. II and III only
    d. II and IV only

See answers on the next page.

Answer Explanations

1. A: The coronal, or frontal, plane is a vertical plane positioned so that it divides the body into front (ventral) and back (dorsal) regions. The plane is positioned so that the face, kneecap, and toes are on the ventral side, and the vertebrae and heel are on the dorsal side. The coronal plane is one of three body planes. The other two are the transverse and sagittal planes. The transverse plane divides the anatomy into upper (cranial or head) and lower (caudal or tail) regions. The sagittal plane runs front/back perpendicular to the frontal plane and divides the anatomy into right and left regions.

2. C: Cartilage adds mechanical support to joints. It provides a flexible cushion that aids in mobility while offering support. The first two choices are switched—it is ligaments that connect bones at joints and tendons that attach skeletal muscles to bones. Choice *D* is incorrect because arteries, not veins, deliver oxygenated blood.

3. B: The dermis is the skin layer that contains nerves, blood vessels, hair follicles, and glands. These structures are called skin appendages. These appendages are scattered throughout the connective tissue (elastin and collagen), and the connective tissue provides support to the outer layer, the epidermis. The epidermal surface is a thin layer (except feet and palms, where it is thick) of continually regenerating cells that don't have a blood supply of their own, which explains why superficial cuts don't bleed. The hypodermis is the subcutaneous layer underneath the dermis, and it is composed primarily of fat in order to provide insulation.

4. B: In the Haversian system found in compact bone, concentric layers of bone cells are called lamellae. Between the lamellae are lacunae, which are gaps filled with osteocytes. The Haversian canals on the outer regions of the bone contain capillaries and nerve fibers. Spongy (cancellous) bone is on the extremities of long bones, which makes sense because the ends are softer due to the motion at joints (providing flexibility and cushion). The middle of the bone between the two spongy regions is called the diaphysis region. Spongy bone is highly vascular and is the site of red bone marrow (the marrow that makes red blood cells). Long bones, on the other hand, are long, weight-bearing bones like the tibia or femur that contain yellow marrow in adulthood. Trabeculae are dense, collagenous, rod-shaped tissues that add mechanical support to the spongy regions of bone. Muscular trabeculae can be found in the heart and are similar in that they offer physical reinforcement.

5. A: Carbon dioxide-rich blood is delivered from systemic circulation to the right atrium. It is pumped into the right ventricle. The tricuspid valve prevents backflow between the two chambers. From there, the pulmonary artery takes blood to the lungs where diffusion causes gas exchange. Then, oxygenated blood returns to the left atrium before getting pumped into the left ventricle. The mitral valve prevents the backflow of blood from the left ventricle to the atrium. Finally, blood is ejected from the left ventricle through the aorta to enter systemic circulation.

Physics

Nature of Motion

The measurement of an object's movement or change in position (x), over a change in time (t) is an object's **speed.** The **average speed** of an object is defined as the distance that the object travels divided by how long it takes the object to travel that distance.

$$Speed = \frac{distance}{time}$$

Distance is measured in meters, and time is measured in seconds. The standard scientific units for speed and velocity are meters/second (m/s):

$$\frac{\text{meters}}{\text{second}} = \frac{\text{m}}{\text{s}}$$

Units of miles/hour (mph) are also commonly used in America.

Velocity & Acceleration

Velocity

When the direction is included with the speed, it is referred to as the **velocity.** This is because velocity is the measure of the change in distance over the change in time.

For example, a car traveling east and another traveling west can have the same speed of 30 miles per hour (mph), but their velocities are different. If movement eastward is considered positive, then movement westward is negative. Thus, the eastbound car has a velocity of 30 mph while the westbound car has a velocity of -30 mph.

Another example where velocity and speed are different is with a car traveling around a bend in the road. The speed is constant along the road, but the direction (and therefore the velocity) changes continuously.

The fact that velocity has a *magnitude* (speed) and a direction makes it a **vector quantity**. A *vector* is an arrow pointing in the direction of motion, with its length proportional to its magnitude. A measurement such as speed is called a **scalar quantity** because it only has a numeric value without a particular direction.

A "change in position" refers to the difference in location of an object's starting point and an object's ending point. In science, this change is represented by the Greek letter Delta, Δ.

$$velocity\ (v) = \frac{\Delta x}{\Delta t}$$

Average velocity is calculated by averaging the beginning or initial velocity and the ending or final velocity of an object.

Acceleration

While an object's speed measures how fast the object's position will change in a certain amount of time, an object's **acceleration** measures how fast the object's speed will change in a certain amount of time. Acceleration can be thought of as the change in velocity or speed (Δv) divided by the change in the time (Δt).

$$acceleration\ (a) = \frac{\Delta v}{\Delta t}$$

Velocity is measured in meters/second and time is measured in seconds, so the standard unit for acceleration is meters/second^2 (m/s^2).

$$\frac{\text{meters}/\text{second}}{\text{second}} = \frac{\text{meters}}{\text{second}^2} = \frac{\text{m}}{\text{s}^2}$$

Acceleration is expressed by using both magnitude and direction, so it is a vector quantity like velocity. Acceleration is present when an object is slowing down, speeding up, or changing direction, since these represent instances where velocity is changing. This means that forces like friction and gravity accelerate objects and increase or decrease their velocities over time.

Projectile Motion

Projectile motion describes the way in which a projectile will move when the only force acting upon it is gravity. Since the force of Earth's gravity is nearly constant at sea level, its magnitude is approximated as a rate of 9.8 m/s^2. For projectile motion problems, the projectile is assumed to travel a curved path to the ground and ignore air resistance, wind speed, and other such complications.

Projectile motion has two components: horizontal and vertical. Without air resistance, there is no horizontal acceleration, so the horizontal velocity won't change. However, the vertical velocity will change because of gravity's acceleration on the projectile. A sample parabolic curve of projectile motion is shown below.

Projectile Path for a Bullet Fired Horizontally from a Hill (Ignoring Air Resistance)

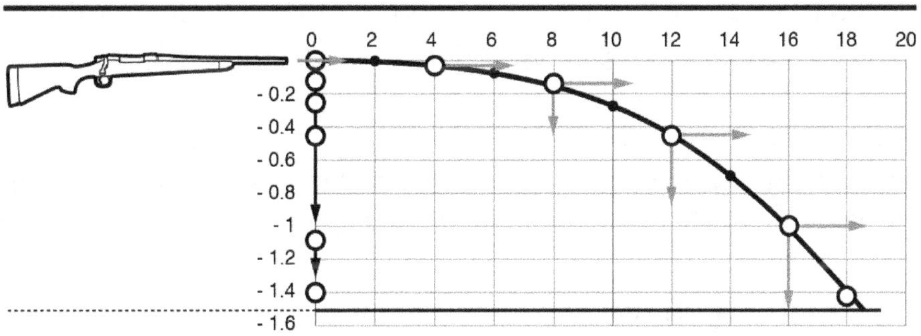

Horizontal distance (d_x) is defined as the relationship between velocity (v_x) and time (t), where x is the movement along the horizontal plane (x-axis).

$$d_x = v_x t$$

Because of the force of gravity, the vertical velocity and position is continuously changing and thus more complicated to calculate. The following equations are different expressions of vertical motion:

$$v_f^2 = v_i^2 + 2ad$$

$$d = \frac{1}{2}at^2 + v_i t$$

$$v_f = v_i + at$$

These equations use v_f as the final velocity, v_i as the initial velocity, a as the acceleration, d as the horizontal distance traveled, and t as the time to describe functions of motion.

Newton's Laws of Motion

Sir Isaac Newton spent a great deal of time studying objects, forces, and how an object's motion responds to forces. Newton made great advancements by using mathematics to describe the motion of objects and to predict future motions of objects by applying his mathematical models to situations. Through his extensive research, Newton is credited for summarizing the basic laws of motion for objects here on Earth. These laws are as follows:

1. The law of inertia: An object in motion will remain in motion, unless acted upon by an outside force. An object at rest remains at rest, unless acted upon by an outside force. Simply put, **inertia** is the natural tendency of an object to continue along with what it is already doing; an outside force would have to act upon the object to make it change its course. This includes an object that is sitting still.

2. $F = ma$: The **force (F)** on an object is equal to the mass (m) multiplied by the acceleration (a) on that object. **Mass (m)** refers to the amount of a substance while acceleration (a) refers to a change in velocity over time.

    - In the case of a projectile falling to Earth's surface, the acceleration is due to gravity.
    - Multiplying an object's mass by its gravitational acceleration gives the special force that is called the object's **weight (W).** Note that weight is a force and is a vector quantity while mass is in kilograms and is a scalar quantity, as it has no acceleration.
    - Forces are typically measured in **Newtons** (N), which are a derived SI unit equal to 1 $\frac{\text{kg}\cdot\text{m}}{\text{s}^2}$. You can find an object's weight in Newtons by multiplying its mass (in kilograms) by the acceleration of gravity ($9.8\ \text{m/s}^2$ for Earth).

3. For every action, there is an equal and opposite reaction. This means that, if a book drops onto a desk, the book will exert a force on the desk due to hitting it, but the desk will also exert an equal force on the book in the opposite direction. This is what sometimes causes fallen objects to bounce once or twice after hitting the ground.

A clear understanding of force is crucial to using Newton's laws of motion. **Forces** are anything acting upon an object either in motion or at rest; this includes friction and gravity. These forces can push or pull on a mass, and they have a magnitude and a direction. Forces are represented by a **vector,** which is the arrow lined up along the direction of the force with its tip at the point of application. The magnitude of the force is represented by the length of the vector. Large forces have long vector lengths.

Friction

Friction is a resistance to movement that always imparts a negative acceleration to an object. Because it accelerates an object in the opposite direction than it wants to go, friction will cause moving objects to slow down and eventually stop. Frictional force depends on several factors including the texture of the two surfaces and the amount of contact force pushing the surfaces together. There are four types of friction: static, sliding, rolling, and fluid friction. **Static friction** occurs between stationary objects, while **sliding friction** occurs when solid objects slide over each other. **Rolling friction** happens when a solid object rolls over another solid object, and **fluid friction** is a friction caused by an object moving through a fluid or through fluid layers. These 'fluids' can be either a gas or a liquid, so this also includes air resistance.

Rotation

Rotating and spinning objects have a special type of movement. A spinning top can move across a table, demonstrating linear motion, but it can also spin in place, demonstrating angular motion. Just as a car moves from place to place by changing its location, its velocity, and its acceleration, so too can a rotating object change its orientation, its angular velocity, and its angular acceleration.

For linear movement, the first thing that is described is the object's displacement. The **displacement** of the object is how far it moves from its starting location; this linear change in location is usually represented by the symbol Δx. However, for the angular movement of a simple solid like a sphere, the distance that its surface travels is not a good measure of its angular movement, since a large sphere would have to rotate a much smaller degree to move the same distance as a small sphere would. This angular distance is referred to as S, or the arc length.

A better measure of angular movement is the **angular displacement *θ*,** which is defined as the angle through which the object will rotate. Because there are a standard 360° in all circles, angular displacement can be used to compare angular movement between objects of different sizes, making it a much more versatile tool than the arc length. However, although a circle can be split up into 360 degrees, it can also be visualized as being split up into 2π **radians,** where radians is a unit similar to degrees that describes angles. The 2π is usually used in physics because a circle's circumference has a value of 2πtimes its radius, and radians is an easier unit to use than is degrees.

The angular displacement can be found by dividing the arc length that an object rotates through by the radius of the object's rotation. For example, if an object completes 1 full rotation, it has rotated through 360°. It has also traveled an arc length equal to its circumference, or $2\pi r$. Plugging this arc length S into the equation below, it can be seen that the angular displacement is 2π, which is correct since it is equal to the 360° as discussed previously.

$$angular\ displacement\ (\theta) = \frac{S}{r}$$

The angular speed or **angular velocity, w,** is the measure of how quickly the object is rotating, and w is defined as the angular displacement that is accomplished in a certain amount of time, as shown below.

$$angular\ speed\ (\omega) = \frac{\Delta\theta}{\Delta t}$$

Similar to linear velocity, angular velocity may accelerate due to external forces, and this angular acceleration is given by the variable α. Its equation, the change in angular velocity over a change in time, is given below.

$$angular\ acceleration\ (\alpha) = \frac{\Delta\omega}{\Delta t}$$

When objects are exhibiting circular motion, they also demonstrate the **conservation of angular momentum,** meaning that the angular momentum of a system is always constant, regardless of the placement of the mass. **Rotational inertia** can be affected by how far the mass of the object is placed with respect to the center of rotation (**axis of rotation**). The larger the distance between the mass and the center of rotation, the slower the rotational velocity. Conversely, if the mass is closer to the center of rotation, the rotational velocity increases. A change in one affects the other, thus conserving the angular momentum. This holds true if no external forces act upon the system.

Uniform Circular Motion

Circular motion is similar in many ways to linear (straight line) motion; however, there are a few additional points to note. In uniform circular motion, a spinning object is always linearly accelerating because it is always changing direction. The force causing this constant acceleration on or around an axis is called the **centripetal force,** and it is often associated with centripetal acceleration. Centripetal force always pulls toward the axis of rotation; this means that the force will always pull towards the center of the rotation circle. The relationship between the velocity (v) of an object and the radius (r) of the circle is **centripetal acceleration**, and the equation is as follows:

$$centripetal\ acceleration\ (a_c) = \frac{v^2}{r}$$

According to Newton's law, force is the combination of two factors, mass and acceleration. This is demonstrated by centripetal force. Centripetal force is shown mathematically by using the mass of an object (m), the velocity (v), and the radius (r).

$$centripetal\ force\ (F_c) = \frac{mv^2}{r}$$

Kinetic Energy and Potential Energy

The two primary forms of energy are kinetic energy and potential energy. **Kinetic energy**, or KE, involves the energy of motion, and is easily found for Newtonian physics by an object's mass in kilograms and velocity in meters per second. Kinetic energy can be calculated using the following equation:

$$KE = \frac{1}{2}mv^2$$

Potential energy represents the energy possessed by an object by virtue of its position. In the classical example, an object's gravitational potential energy can be found as a simple function of its height or by what distance it drops. Potential energy, or PE, may be calculated using the following equation:

$$PE = mgh$$

Both kinetic energy and potential energy are scalar quantities measured in **Joules**. One Joule is the amount of energy that can push an object with 1 Newton of force for 1 meter, so it is also referred to as a Newton-meter. As mentioned previously, the **Law of Conservation of Energy** states that energy can neither be created nor destroyed. Therefore, potential and kinetic energy can be transformed into one another, depending on an object's speed and position.

Linear Momentum and Impulse

Motion creates something called **momentum.** This is a calculation of an object's mass multiplied by its velocity. Momentum can be described as the amount an object wants to continue moving along its current course.

Momentum in a straight line is called linear momentum. Just as energy can be transferred and conserved, so too can momentum.

Changing the expression of Newton's second law of motion yields a new expression.

$$Force(F) = ma = m \times \frac{\Delta v}{\Delta t}$$

If both sides of the expression are multiplied by the change in time, the law produces the impulse equation.

$$F\Delta t = m\Delta v$$

This equation shows that the amount of force during a length of time creates an **impulse.** This means that if a force acts on an object during a given amount of time, it will have a determined impulse. However, if the same change in velocity happens over a longer amount of time, the required force is much smaller, due to the conservation of momentum.

$$p = mv$$

Linear momentum, p, is found by multiplying the mass of an object by its velocity. Since momentum, like mass and energy, is conserved, Newton's 2nd law can be restated for multiple objects. In this form, it can be used to understand the energy of objects that have interacted, since the conservation of momentum implies that the momentum before and after an interaction must be the same. This is best demonstrated in the case of elastic collision, where an object of mass m_1 with velocity v_1 collides with an object of mass m_2 with velocity v_2 and both object end with velocities v_1' and v_2', respectively.

$$m_1v_1' + m_2v_2' = m_1v_1 + m_2v_2$$

Universal Gravitation

Newton's **law of universal gravitation** addresses the universality of gravity. Gravity acts as a force at a distance and causes all bodies in the universe to attract each other.

The **force of gravity (F_g)** is proportional to the masses of two objects (m_1 and m_2) and inversely proportional to the square of the distance (r^2) between them. (G is the proportionality constant). This is shown in the following equation:

$$F_g = G\frac{m_1m_2}{r^2}$$

All objects falling within the Earth's atmosphere are all affected by the force of gravity, so their rates of acceleration will be equal to 9.8 $\mathrm{m/s^2}$, or gravity. Therefore, if two objects are dropped from the same height at the same time, they should hit the ground at the same time. This is irrespective of mass, since the previous kinetics equations don't include mass, so a bowling ball and a feather would theoretically fall at identical rates. Unfortunately, in the Earth's atmosphere, air resistance would slow the feather much more than the bowling ball, so the bowling ball would fall faster, but this effect can be minimized in a vacuum. In other words, without air resistance or other external forces acting on the objects, gravity will affect every object on the Earth with the same rate of acceleration.

Waves and Sound

Waves are periodic disturbances in a gas, liquid, or solid that are created as energy is transmitted. Each part of a wave has a different name and is used in different calculations. The four parts of a wave are the crest, the trough, the amplitude, and the wavelength. The **crest** is the highest point, while the **trough** is the lowest. The **amplitude** is the distance between a peak and the average of the wave; it is also the distance between a trough and the average of the wave, but an amplitude is always positive, since it is an absolute value. Finally, the distance between one wave and the exact same place on the next wave is the **wavelength.**

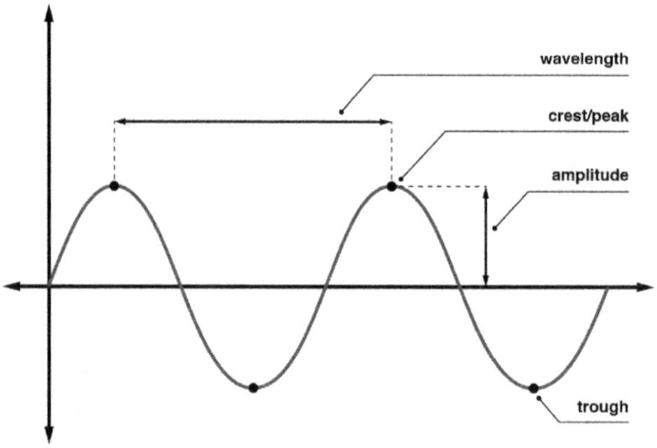

With amplitude and wavelength, it is possible to describe any wave, but an important question still remains unanswered: How fast is the wave traveling? A wave's speed can be shown as either its period or its frequency. A wave's period, T, is how long it takes for the wave to travel one wavelength, while a wave's frequency, f, is how many wavelengths are traveled in one second. These are inversely related, so they are reciprocals of each other, as shown below.

$$f = \frac{1}{T} \text{ and } T = \frac{1}{f}$$

The largest categories of waves are electromagnetic waves and mechanical waves. **Electromagnetic waves** can transmit energy through a vacuum and do not need a medium to travel through, examples of which are light, radio, microwaves, gamma rays, and other forms of electromagnetism. **Mechanical waves** can only transmit energy through another form of matter called a medium. The particles of the medium are shifted as the wave moves through the medium, and can be anything from solids to liquids to gasses. Examples of mechanical waves include auditory sounds heard by human ears in the air as well as percussive shocks like earthquakes.

There are two different forms of waves: transverse and longitudinal waves. **Transverse** waves are waves in which particles of the medium move in a direction perpendicular to the direction waves move, as in most electromagnetic waves. **Compression**, or longitudinal, waves are waves in which the particles of the medium move in a direction parallel to the direction the waves move, as in most mechanical waves. A good example of a longitudinal wave is sound. Waves travel within a medium at a speed that is determined by the wavelength (λ) and frequency (f) of the wave.

$$v = f\lambda$$

There is a proportional relationship between the amplitude of a wave and the potential energy in the wave. This means the taller the wave, the more stored energy it is transmitting.

Light

Light is an electromagnetic wave that is created by electric and magnetic interactions. Like other electromagnetic waves, light does not need a medium to travel. Light energy can be absorbed and changed into heat, reflected, or even transmitted.

A wave is reflected when it collides with a surface and bounces off, unharmed. The **law of reflection** shows that an **incident ray** (the wave that hits the surface) will bounce off the surface and become a reflected ray (the wave that leaves the surface). Because the wave doesn't lose any energy, the angle at which it hits the surface will be identical to the angle at which it leaves the surface, so the interaction produces identical waves. This is the definition of **reflection**.

On the other hand, a wave is refracted when a wave collides with a surface and bends, such as when the medium it is traveling through changes. Examples of **refraction** include the bending of light as it passes through a prism and sunlight passing through raindrops to create a rainbow.

To understand refraction, a 'normal' line is drawn perpendicular to the surface that the wave will hit. The angle created between the normal line and the incident ray is the angle of incidence, while the angle of reflection is the opposite and equal angle formed between the normal line and the reflected ray. The refraction of light depends on the varying speeds and densities of different media. As light passes through different media, the wave will bend toward or away from the normal line, depending on the material it is transitioning to. **Snell's law** describes this behavior mathematically in the equation that follows:

$$n_1 \sin \theta_1 = n_2 \sin \theta_2$$

In this equation, n is the index of refraction and θ is the angle of refraction. The **index of refraction** determines the amount of light that bends or refracts when it encounters a medium. Materials that interact with and change the wave more will have higher indices of refraction, and any material's index of refraction can be found by the following equation.

$$n = \frac{c}{v_s}$$

Because the speed of light in a vacuum, c, is constant, it can be used to show how much a material will interact with a wave. The **refractive index, n,** shows how much the speed of light is changed when it travels through the material at a new velocity of v_s.

Optics

Spherical mirrors change the way light reflects. Lenses and curved mirrors are made to focus light in certain ways. There are several terms used to describe and define mirrors and lenses. The **principal axis** is a reference line that usually passes through the center of the curve of the mirror or lens. The **vertex, V,** is the point where the mirror is crossed by the principal axis. The sphere which contains the curve of the mirror has a center called the **center of curvature (C)**. The **focal point (F)** is halfway between the center of curvature and the vertex.

The **focal length (f)** is measured by how far the focal point is from the mirror. The following graphic shows a visual representation of these terms in a concave mirror.

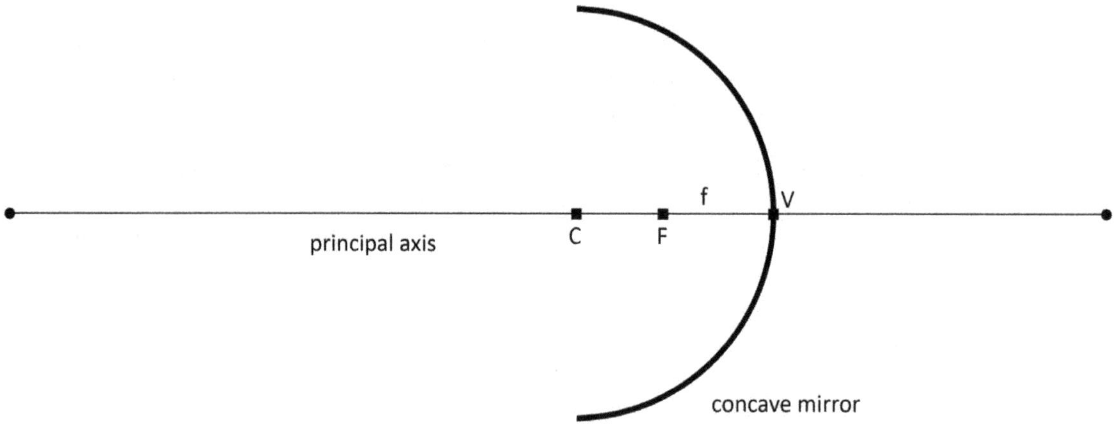

The focal lengths of concave mirrors are positive. Concave mirrors can produce images of various shapes and sizes as well as of different orientations based on the focal length of the mirror and the placement of the object. Convex mirrors differ from concave mirrors in that they have negative focal lengths. The other main difference is that convex mirrors always form images that are reduced in size and upright.

Lenses are pieces of transparent material molded to refract light rays to create an image. There are two types of lenses. Convex lenses, also called **converging lenses**, have positive focal lengths. Concave lenses, or **diverging lenses**, conversely have negative focal lengths. Images in convex lenses can look different depending on the focal length of the lens and where the object is located. Convex lenses only create images that are upright and smaller in size than the object.

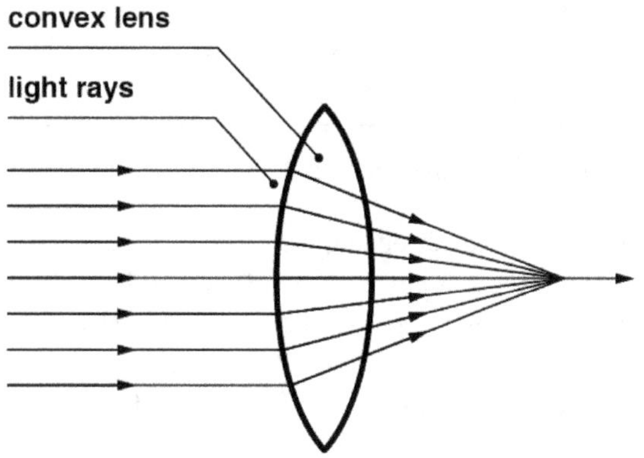

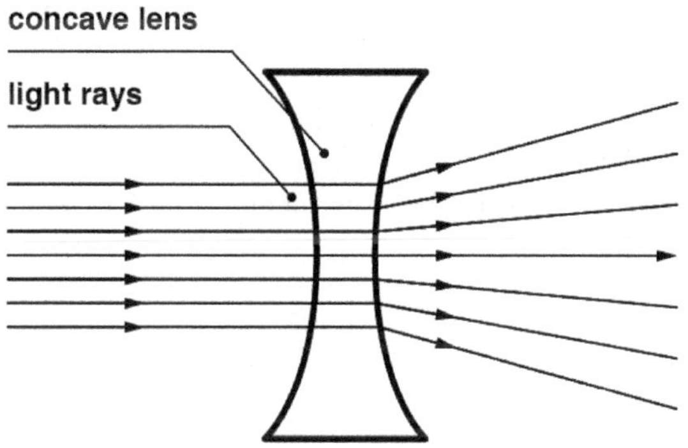

Atomic Structure

All known matter is made of atoms. Atoms have a nucleus composed of **protons** (with a positive charge) and **neutrons** (with no net charge), which is surrounded by a cloud of **electrons** (with negative charges). Since protons have a positive charge and neutrons have a neutral charge, an atom's nucleus typically has an overall positive electrical charge, but because electrons orbiting the nucleus have an overall negative charge, an atom with equal numbers of protons and electrons is considered stable.

The properties of an atom vary with the number of electrons and their arrangement in shells around the nucleus. Electrons are organized into distributions of subshells called **electron configurations**. Subshells fill from the inside (closest to the nucleus) to the outside and are lettered starting with "k." The strength of the bond between the nucleus and the electron is called the **binding energy**. The binding energy is stronger for those shells located closer to the nucleus.

The number of electrons in each shell can be determined using the following equation using n for the shell number:

$$2n^2$$

The Nature of Electricity

The nature of electricity is based on the atoms of a given material, as objects develop electric charges when their atoms gain or lose electrons. The electrons that are in the furthest shell from an atom's nucleus are the most likely to interact, so they are specially termed **valence electrons**. If the electrons are tightly bound to their atoms, the material is an **insulator** because, like rubber, wood, and glass, the material prevents electrons from flowing freely. However, if the electrons are loosely bound to the atoms, the material is a **conductor** because, like iron and other metals, the electrons can flow freely throughout the material.

It is important to note that opposite charges attract each other, while like charges repel each other. Interestingly, the repulsive force between two electrons is equivalent to the attractive force between an electron and a proton (only in different directions). Coulomb described these repellant and attractive forces between two objects in his namesake law. This electrical **Coulomb force, *F*,** is determined by multiplying the charges of the two objects, q_1 and q_2, by a constant, k, and dividing by the distance they are from one another squared, r^2.

$$F = \frac{kq_1q_2}{r^2}$$

If the force is negative, then the objects attract each other because $q_1$and $q_2$are of opposite charges. If the force is positive, then the objects repel each other because q_1 and q_2 are of the same charge.

An electric charge naturally produces an electric field around itself. Electric fields can vary in strength and magnitude depending on the type of charge (positive or negative) that generates the field. The nature of electric fields can be tested using a test charge. Mathematically, the magnitude of an electric field (E) can be found using the following equation:

$$E = \frac{F}{q_o}$$

Where F is the force a test charge would undergo, and q_o is the magnitude of the test charge. Electric fields are vector quantities; this means they have both a magnitude and a direction. In the case of electric fields, it is the convention to define the direction of the field vector as the way a positive test charge would move when positioned in the electric field: towards a negative charge and away from other positive charges.

An **electric circuit** is usually comprised of circuit elements joined by a wire or other object that allows an electric charge to move along the path without interruption — this moving electric charge is called an electric **current.** However, constant electric currents may only exist in a complete circuit if there is a voltage difference in the circuit. **Voltage** is literally the distance that a circuit's electrical force could move one electron, but voltage can be visualized as how much energy a certain part of the circuit has available to push around electrons. Electrons will flow from regions of higher voltage to regions of lower voltage, so it is the difference in voltages between two parts of a circuit that makes a current actually flow.

In other words, voltage difference is the difference in potential energy between two places measured in **volts (*V*),** while a circuit is a closed path through which electrons can flow. Because every atom has positive charges that pull on electrons and resist their flow, most real circuits have a **resistance** level, measured in **ohms**, which is described as the opposition to the flow of electric charge. The amount of current that can flow through a circuit depends on the voltage difference and how well the wire resists the flow of electricity. **Ohm's law** gives us the relationship between voltage (V), current in amperes (I), and resistance in ohms (R).

$$V = I \times R$$

Series Circuits (A) and Parallel Circuits (B)

Practical circuits have numerous loads which can be hooked up "in series" (A) or "in parallel" (B), as shown below.

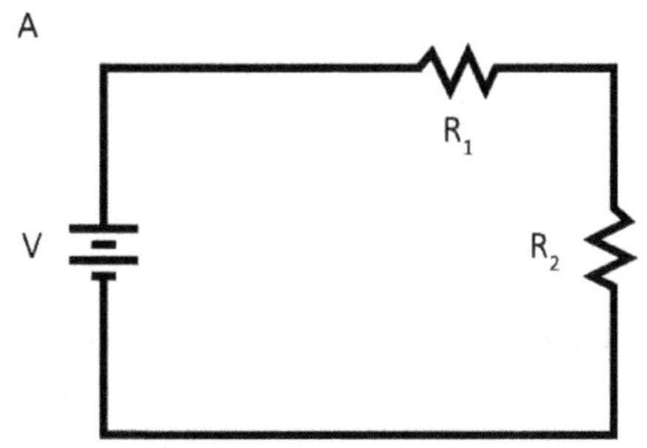

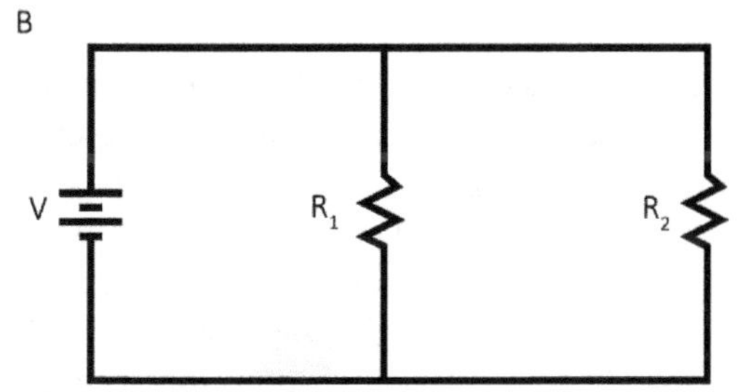

To determine the total voltage requirement for circuits with multiple component loads (in series or in parallel), it is necessary to find the equivalent resistance of the circuits.

Series circuits put resistors in a row or series so that current must flow from one to the other, while **parallel circuits** run resistors in parallel sections so that current can flow through one or the other. In a series circuit like the one in A, the voltage drops across each resistor, but the current is the same in all of them. The current must be the same across each resistor, as according to Ampere's law, the electrons in the current must continue flowing throughout the wire and not build up or disappear. In other words, the electrons going into the resistor must all go out so that the "flow in equals flow out."

The current through each resistor is the same, and the total voltage (V) equals the drop across R_1 plus the drop across R_2. The equivalent resistance is determined by solving Ohm's law for voltage:

$$V = V_1 + V_2 = IR_1 + IR_2 = I(R_1 + R_2) = IR_{eq}$$

Thus, in a series circuit, the equivalent resistance is equal to the sum of the component resistances, and this relation holds for any number of resistors in a series.

In a parallel circuit like the one in (B), the voltage is the same across each resistor because each is attached directly to the power source and the ground. The electric current is divided between the loads depending on their resistances, since it can flow through either of them, but not both. If the resistance is the same in both loads, then the same amount of current passes through each one. If the resistance is different in each load, then more current passes through the load with the lower resistance, since energy takes the path of least resistance.

The **equivalent resistance (R_{eq})** of the parallel circuit is determined by solving Ohm's law for the current through each resistor, setting it equal to the total current (R_t), and remembering that the voltages are all the same:

$$I_t = \frac{V}{R_{eq}} = \frac{V}{R_1} + \frac{V}{R_2} \quad \textbf{or} \quad \frac{1}{R_{eq}} = \frac{1}{R_1} + \frac{1}{R_2} \quad \textbf{so} \quad R_{eq} = \frac{1}{\frac{1}{R_1} + \frac{1}{R_2}}$$

In a parallel circuit, the equivalent resistance is equal to one over the sum of the reciprocals of the component resistances.

Magnetism and Electricity

Magnetism can occur naturally in certain types of materials like iron, nickel, and cobalt. If two straight rods are made from iron, they will usually have a naturally negative end (pole) and a positive end (pole). These charged poles react just like any charged item: opposite charges attract and like charges repel. They will attract each other when set up positive to negative, but if one rod is turned around, the two rods will repel each other due to the alignment of negative to negative and positive to positive.

Magnetic fields can also be created and amplified by using an electric current. The force of attraction between two magnetic fields is measured in **Teslas**. The relationship between magnetic forces and electrical forces can be explored by sending an electric current through a stretch of wire, which creates an electromagnetic force around the wire from the charge of the current, as long as the flow of electricity is sustained. This magnetic force can also attract and repel other items with magnetic properties. Depending upon the strength of the current in the wire, a smaller or larger magnetic force can be generated around this wire. As soon as the current is cut off, the magnetic force also stops. When a magnetic field produces an electric current, this is called an **electromagnetic induction**.

Practice Quiz

1. Velocity is a measure of which of the following?
    a. Speed with direction
    b. The change in speed over the change in time
    c. Acceleration with direction
    d. All of the above

2. Which of the following correctly lists the subatomic particles in an atom?
    a. Protons carry no charge in the nucleus, neutrons carry a negative charge in the nucleus, and electrons surround the nucleus in a cloud and carry a positive charge.
    b. Protons carry a positive charge in the nucleus, neutrons have no charge in the nucleus, and electrons have a negative charge and are found in a cloud surrounding the nucleus.
    c. Protons carry a positive charge in the nucleus, electrons have a negative charge in the nucleus, and neutrons have a negative charge and surround the nucleus in a cloud.
    d. Protons carry a positive charge, and they surround the nucleus in a cloud. The nucleus contains negatively charged electrons and neutrons, which carry no charge.

3. Which of the following equations is not an accurate representation of Ohm's Law?
    a. $V = I \times R$
    b. $R = \frac{V}{I}$
    c. $I = \frac{V}{R}$
    d. $V = \frac{R}{I}$

4. A football is kicked so that it leaves the punter's toe at a horizontal angle of 45 degrees. Ignoring any spin or tumbling, at what point is the vertical velocity of the football at a minimum?

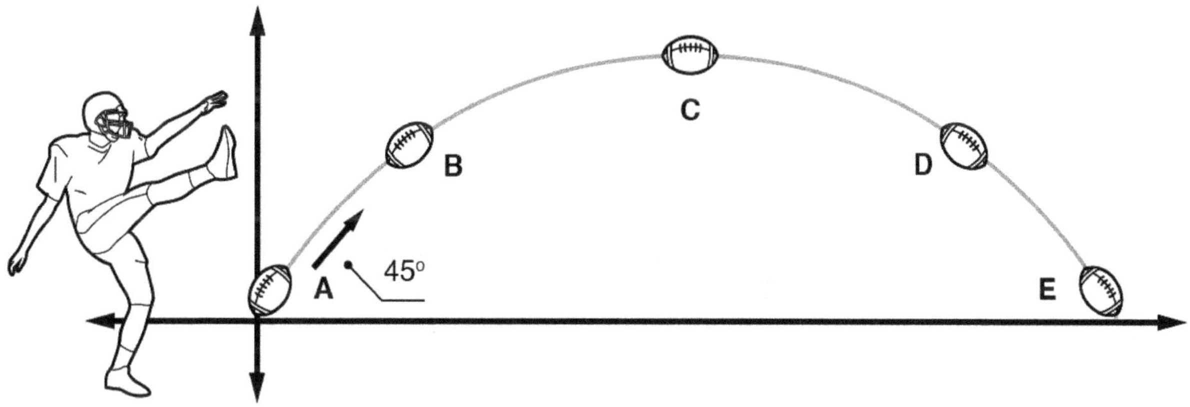

    a. At Point A
    b. At Point C
    c. At Points B and D
    d. At Points A and E

5. A cannonball is dropped from a height of 10 meters off of the ground. What is its approximate velocity just before it hits the ground?
   a. $9.81\ m/s$
   b. $14\ m/s$
   c. $32\ m/s$
   d. $1\ m/s$

6. The energy from electricity results from which of the following?
   a. The atomic structure of matter
   b. The ability to do work
   c. The neutrons in an atom
   d. Conductive materials like metals

7. Electric power can be measured in which of the following units?
   a. Volts
   b. Amperes
   c. Ohms
   d. Watts

8. Which of the following is true regarding series circuits?
   a. The voltage drops across each resistor, but the current is the same in all of them.
   b. The voltage is the same across each resistor, but the current drops after each of them.
   c. The voltage drops across each resistor, and the current drops in each of them.
   d. The voltage and current are the same across each of them in the series.

See answers on the next page.

Answer Explanations

1. A: Velocity is a measure of speed with direction. To calculate velocity, find the distance covered and the time it took to cover that distance; change in position over the change in time. A standard measurement for velocity is in meters per second ($\mathrm{m/s}$). The change in velocity over change in time is acceleration, while acceleration with direction has no specific name.

2. B: The structure of atoms is as follows: The central nucleus contains protons and neutrons. Protons have a positive charge (+1), and neutrons are neutral, so they do not carry a charge. Around the nucleus is a cloud, which contains electrons in rings called orbitals. Electrons are negatively charged (–1), and those in the outermost ring — farthest from the nucleus — tend to be easier to remove from the atom.

3. D: Ohm's Law describes the relation between voltage and amperage, where voltage is a measure of electromotive potential much like potential energy of motion in kinetics. Amperage measures the electric current or the flow rate of 1 coulomb of electrons in a second. The basic law is $V = I \times R$, but this can be manipulated in the following ways:

$$I = \frac{V}{R} \quad \text{or} \quad V = I \times R \quad \text{or} \quad R = \frac{V}{I}$$

4. B: The vertical velocity is at a minimum at the top of its arc. The acceleration due to gravity reduces the upwards velocity every moment after the kick until an instant where the ball has zero vertical velocity. Afterwards the vertical velocity increases downwards until it collides with the ground.

5. B: Remember that the cannonball at rest, y meters off the ground, has a potential energy of $PE = mgy$. As it falls, the potential energy is converted to kinetic energy until (at ground level) the kinetic energy is equal to the total original potential energy:

$$\frac{1}{2}mv^2 = mgy$$

Rearranged to solve for velocity, the equation is:

$$v = \sqrt{2gy}$$

This makes sense because all objects fall at the same rate, so the velocity must be independent of the mass; thus, Choice *D* is incorrect. Plugging the values into the equation, the result is 14 m/s. Remember, *g* is approximately $9.8\ m/s^2$.

6. A: The physical structure of the atoms that compose matter lends itself to the production of electricity. The arrangement of the subatomic particles and the associated charges—mainly the negatively charged electrons in the cloud—are associated with the ability to create an electric current, which can be harnessed to do work.

7. D: The difference in potential between two separate points is a measure of volts. Amperes indicate the number of electrons that pass a specific point per second. Ohms measure the resistance to flow (essentially electrical friction). Watts are a measure of power or the rate at which electrical energy is used or converted into another type of energy. Watts are often converted to kilowatts or, when expressing power rates, kilowatt-hours.

8. B: When devices are connected in a series circuit, the voltage is the same across each device (or resistor) in the loop, but the current drops after each device. Recall that for lightbulbs connected in series, this is observed by a decrease in the brightness of each successive bulb. This is one of the disadvantages of a series circuit. In contrast, the current increases with the addition of each resistor in parallel circuits.

HESI A2 Practice Test #1

Mathematics

1. Which of the following is equivalent to the value of the digit 3 in the number 792.134?
    a. 3×10
    b. 3×100
    c. $\frac{3}{10}$
    d. $\frac{3}{100}$

2. Add $101{,}694 + 623$.
    a. 103,317
    b. 102,317
    c. 102,417
    d. 102,427

3. How would the number 847.89632 be written if rounded to the nearest hundredth?
    a. 847.90
    b. 900
    c. 847.89
    d. 847.896

4. What is the sum of $\frac{1}{3}$ and $\frac{2}{5}$?
    a. $\frac{3}{8}$
    b. $\frac{11}{15}$
    c. $\frac{11}{30}$
    d. $\frac{4}{5}$

5. Add and express in reduced form: $\frac{7}{12} + \frac{5}{9}$
    a. $1\frac{5}{36}$
    b. $\frac{13}{9}$
    c. $\frac{41}{36}$
    d. $1\frac{4}{9}$

6. How would $\frac{4}{5}$ be written as a percent?
    a. 40%
    b. 125%
    c. 90%
    d. 80%

7. Subtract $7{,}236 - 978$.
   a. 6,268
   b. 5,258
   c. 6,358
   d. 6,258

8. What are all the factors of 12?
   a. 12, 24, 36
   b. 1, 2, 4, 6, 12
   c. 12, 24, 36, 48
   d. 1, 2, 3, 4, 6, 12

9. Which fractions are equivalent, or would fill the same portion on a number line?
   a. $\frac{2}{4}$ and $\frac{3}{8}$
   b. $\frac{1}{2}$ and $\frac{4}{8}$
   c. $\frac{3}{6}$ and $\frac{3}{5}$
   d. $\frac{2}{4}$ and $\frac{5}{8}$

10. Subtract $653.4 - 59.38$.
   a. 595.92
   b. 594.11
   c. 594.02
   d. 593.92

11. Subtract and express in reduced form: $\frac{19}{24} - \frac{1}{6}$
   a. $\frac{5}{8}$
   b. $\frac{18}{6}$
   c. $\frac{15}{24}$
   d. $\frac{1}{3}$

12. If $-3(x + 4) = x + 8$, what is the value of x?
   a. $x = 4$
   b. $x = 2$
   c. $x = 5$
   d. $x = -5$

13. Multiply 346×13.
   a. 4,598
   b. 4,468
   c. 4,498
   d. 4,568

14. If $4x - 3 = 5$, what is the value of x?
   a. 1
   b. 2
   c. 3
   d. 4

15. A grocery store is selling individual bottles of water, and each bottle contains 750 milliliters of water. If a customer purchases 12 bottles, what conversion will correctly determine how many liters the customer will take home?
   a. 100 milliliters equals 1 liter
   b. 1,000 milliliters equals 1 liter
   c. 1,000 liters equals 1 milliliter
   d. 10 liters equals 1 milliliter

16. At the beginning of the day, Xavier has 20 apples. At lunch, he meets his sister Emma and gives her half of his apples. After lunch, he stops by his neighbor Jim's house and gives him 6 of his apples. He then uses $\frac{3}{4}$ of his remaining apples to make an apple pie for dessert at dinner. At the end of the day, how many apples does Xavier have left?
   a. 1
   b. 2
   c. 4
   d. 6

17. 12 is 40% of what number?
   a. 24
   b. 28
   c. 34
   d. 30

18. $3\frac{2}{3} - 1\frac{4}{5} =$
   a. $1\frac{13}{15}$
   b. $\frac{14}{15}$
   c. $2\frac{2}{3}$
   d. $\frac{4}{5}$

19. What is $\frac{660}{100}$ rounded to the nearest integer?
   a. 67
   b. 66
   c. 7
   d. 6

20. Which of the following is largest?
   a. -0.45
   b. -0.096
   c. -0.3
   d. -0.313

21. What is the value of b in this equation?

$$5b - 4 = 2b + 17$$

a. 13
b. 24
c. 7
d. 21

22. Katie works at a clothing company and sold 192 shirts over the weekend. One-third of the shirts that were sold were patterned and the rest were solid. Which mathematical expression would calculate the number of solid shirts Katie sold over the weekend?

a. $192 \times \frac{1}{3}$
b. $192 \div \frac{1}{3}$
c. $192 \times (1 - \frac{1}{3})$
d. $192 \div 3$

23. Arrange the following numbers from least to greatest value:

$$0.85, \frac{4}{5}, \frac{2}{3}, \frac{91}{100}$$

a. $0.85, \frac{4}{5}, \frac{2}{3}, \frac{91}{100}$
b. $\frac{4}{5}, 0.85, \frac{91}{100}, \frac{2}{3}$
c. $\frac{2}{3}, \frac{4}{5}, 0.85, \frac{91}{100}$
d. $0.85, \frac{91}{100}, \frac{4}{5}, \frac{2}{3}$

24. Divide and reduce $\frac{5}{13} \div \frac{25}{169}$.

a. $\frac{13}{5}$
b. $\frac{65}{25}$
c. $\frac{25}{65}$
d. $\frac{5}{13}$

25. Express $\frac{54}{15}$ as a mixed number, reduced to lowest terms.

a. $3\frac{3}{5}$
b. $3\frac{1}{15}$
c. $3\frac{3}{54}$
d. $3\frac{1}{54}$

26. In the problem $5 \times 6 + 4 \div 2 - 1$, which operation should be completed first?
    a. Multiplication
    b. Addition
    c. Division
    d. Subtraction

27. Express $8\frac{3}{7}$ as an improper fraction.
    a. $\frac{11}{7}$
    b. $\frac{21}{8}$
    c. $\frac{5}{3}$
    d. $\frac{59}{7}$

28. Express $11\frac{5}{8}$ as an improper fraction.
    a. $\frac{55}{8}$
    b. $\frac{93}{8}$
    c. $\frac{16}{11}$
    d. $\frac{19}{5}$

29. Round to the nearest tenth: 8.067.
    a. 8.07
    b. 8.1
    c. 8.00
    d. 8.11

30. When rounding 245.2678 to the nearest thousandth, which place value would be used to decide whether to round up or round down?
    a. Ten-thousandths
    b. Thousandths
    c. Hundredths
    d. Thousands

31. Carey bought 184 pounds of fertilizer to use on her lawn. Each segment of her lawn required $11\frac{1}{2}$ pounds of fertilizer to do a sufficient job. If a student was asked to determine how many segments could be fertilized with the amount purchased, what operation would be necessary to solve this problem?
    a. Multiplication
    b. Division
    c. Addition
    d. Subtraction

32. Which of the following is an equivalent measurement for 1.3 cm?
    a. 0.13 m
    b. 0.013 m
    c. 0.13 mm
    d. 0.013 mm

33. Alan currently weighs 200 pounds, but he wants to lose weight to get down to 175 pounds. What is this difference in kilograms? (1 pound is approximately equal to 0.45 kilograms.)
    a. 9 kg
    b. 11.25 kg
    c. 78.75 kg
    d. 90 kg

34. $\frac{14}{15}+\frac{3}{5}-\frac{1}{30}=$
    a. $\frac{19}{15}$
    b. $\frac{43}{30}$
    c. $\frac{4}{3}$
    d. $\frac{3}{2}$

35. Which value is NOT equivalent to the others?
    a. $18:12$
    b. $\frac{6}{4}$
    c. $4:3$
    d. $\frac{36}{24}$

36. Express 517 in Roman numerals.
    a. CXVII
    b. DCIIV
    c. DXVII
    d. VDVII

37. Convert 1500 hours into a 12-hour clock time.
    a. 3:00 p.m.
    b. 9:00 a.m.
    c. 3:00 a.m.
    d. 9:00 p.m.

38. $\frac{5}{3} \times \frac{7}{6} =$

a. $\frac{3}{5}$

b. $\frac{18}{3}$

c. $\frac{45}{31}$

d. $\frac{35}{18}$

39. Which common denominator would be used to evaluate $\frac{2}{3} + \frac{4}{5}$?

a. 15
b. 3
c. 5
d. 10

40. What time is 10:00 a.m. in military (24-hour clock) time?

a. 0100 hours
b. 1000 hours
c. 1200 hours
d. 0200 hours

41. 1 kilometer is how many centimeters?

a. 100 cm
b. 1,000 cm
c. 10,000 cm
d. 100,000 cm

42. What is $(2 \times 20) \div (7 + 1) + (6 \times 0.01) + (4 \times 0.001)$?

a. 5.064
b. 5.64
c. 5.0064
d. 48.064

43. The value of 6×12 is the same as:

a. $2 \times 4 \times 4 \times 2$
b. $7 \times 4 \times 3$
c. $6 \times 6 \times 3$
d. $3 \times 3 \times 4 \times 2$

44. A piggy bank contains 12 dollars' worth of nickels. A nickel weighs 5 grams, and the empty piggy bank weighs 1,050 grams. What is the total weight of the full piggy bank?

a. 1,110 grams
b. 1,200 grams
c. 2,250 grams
d. 2,200 grams

45. Last year, the New York City area received approximately $27\frac{3}{4}$ inches of snow. The Denver area received approximately 3 times as much snow as New York City. How much snow fell in Denver?

a. 60 inches
b. $27\frac{1}{4}$ inches
c. $9\frac{1}{4}$ inches
d. $83\frac{1}{4}$ inches

46. How many pints are in 15 gallons?

a. 45 pts.
b. 100 pts.
c. 120 pts.
d. 15 pts.

47. A patient has a temperature of 37.4 °C. What is this on the Fahrenheit scale?

a. 99.23 °F
b. 99.32 °F
c. 98.32 °F
d. 98.23 °F

48. What is the solution to the following problem in decimal form?

$$\frac{3}{5} \times \frac{7}{10} \div \frac{1}{2}$$

a. 0.042
b. 84%
c. 0.84
d. 0.42

49. 20 is 40% of what number?

a. 60
b. 8
c. 200
d. 50

50. Give a numerical expression for the following: "Six less than three times the sum of twice a number and one."

a. $2x + 1 - 6$
b. $3x + 1 - 6$
c. $3(x + 1) - 6$
d. $3(2x + 1) - 6$

51. In an office, there are 50 workers. A total of 60% of the workers are women. The chances of a woman wearing a skirt is 50%. If no men wear skirts, how many workers are wearing skirts?

a. 12
b. 15
c. 16
d. 20

52. What is the solution to $7\frac{5}{8} - 3\frac{1}{5}$?

a. $4\frac{17}{40}$
b. $10\frac{33}{40}$
c. $4\frac{11}{20}$
d. $6\frac{29}{40}$

53. $52.3 \times 10^{-3} =$

a. 0.00523
b. 0.0523
c. 0.523
d. 523

54. Jessica buys 10 cans of paint. Red paint costs $1 per can, and blue paint costs $2 per can. In total, she spends $16. How many red cans did she buy?

a. 2
b. 3
c. 4
d. 5

55. A farmer owns two (non-adjacent) square plots of land, which he wishes to fence. The area of one is 1,000 square feet, while the area of the other is 10 square feet. How much fencing does he need, in feet?

a. 44
b. $40\sqrt{10}$
c. $440\sqrt{10}$
d. $44\sqrt{10}$

Reading Comprehension

The next five questions are based on the following passage:

> My gentleness and good behaviour had gained so far on the emperor and his court, and indeed upon the army and people in general, that I began to conceive hopes of getting my liberty in a short time. I took all possible methods to cultivate this favourable disposition. The natives came, by degrees, to be less apprehensive of any danger from me. I would sometimes lie down, and let five or six of them dance on my hand; and at last the boys and girls would venture to come and play at hide-and-seek in my hair. I had now made a good progress in understanding and speaking the language. The emperor had a mind one day to entertain me with several of the country shows, wherein they exceed all nations I have known, both for dexterity and magnificence. I was diverted with none so much as that of the rope-dancers, performed upon a slender white thread, extended about two feet, and twelve inches from the ground. Upon which I shall desire liberty, with the reader's patience, to enlarge a little.
>
> This diversion is only practised by those persons who are candidates for great employments, and high favour at court. They are trained in this art from their youth, and are not always of noble birth, or liberal education. When a great office is vacant, either by death or disgrace (which often happens), five or six of those candidates petition the emperor to entertain his majesty and the court with a dance on the rope; and whoever jumps the highest, without falling, succeeds in the

office. Very often the chief ministers themselves are commanded to show their skill, and to convince the emperor that they have not lost their faculty. Flimnap, the treasurer, is allowed to cut a caper on the straight rope, at least an inch higher than any other lord in the whole empire. I have seen him do the summerset several times together, upon a trencher fixed on a rope which is no thicker than a common packthread in England. My friend Reldresal, principal secretary for private affairs, is, in my opinion, if I am not partial, the second after the treasurer; the rest of the great officers are much upon a par.

Excerpt adapted from *Gulliver's Travels into Several Remote Nations of the World* by Jonathan Swift

1. Which of the following statements best summarizes the central purpose of this text?
   a. Gulliver details his fondness for the archaic, yet interesting, practices of his captors.
   b. Gulliver conjectures about the intentions of the aristocratic sector of society.
   c. Gulliver becomes acquainted with the people and practices of his new surroundings.
   d. Gulliver's differences cause him to become penitent around new acquaintances.

2. What is the word *principal* referring to in the following text?

   My friend Reldresal, principal secretary for private affairs, is, in my opinion, if I am not partial, the second after the treasurer; the rest of the great officers are much upon a par.

   a. Primary or chief
   b. An acolyte
   c. An individual who provides nurturing
   d. One in a subordinate position

3. What can the reader infer from this passage?

   I would sometimes lie down, and let five or six of them dance on my hand; and at last the boys and girls would venture to come and play at hide-and-seek in my hair.

   a. The children tortured Gulliver.
   b. Gulliver traveled because he wanted to meet new people.
   c. Gulliver is considerably larger than the children who are playing around him.
   d. Gulliver has a genuine love and enthusiasm for people of all sizes.

4. What is the significance of the word *mind* in the following passage?

   The emperor had a mind one day to entertain me with several of the country shows, wherein they exceed all nations I have known, both for dexterity and magnificence.

   a. The ability to think
   b. A collective vote
   c. A definitive decision
   d. A mythological question

5. Which of the following assertions does NOT support the fact that games are a commonplace event in this culture?
   a. My gentleness and good behavior ... short time.
   b. They are trained in this art from their youth ... liberal education.
   c. Very often the chief ministers themselves are commanded to show their skill ... not lost their faculty.
   d. Flimnap, the treasurer, is allowed to cut a caper on the straight rope ... higher than any other lord in the whole empire.

6. As summer approaches, drowning incidents will increase. Drowning happens very quickly and silently. Most people assume that drowning is easy to spot, but a person who is drowning doesn't make noise or wave his arms. Instead, he will have his head back and his mouth open, with just his face out of the water. A person who is truly in danger of drowning is not able to wave his arms in the air or move much at all. Recognizing these signs of drowning can prevent tragedy.

The main purpose of this passage is to:

a. Explain the dangers of swimming
b. Show how to identify the signs of drowning
c. Explain how to be a lifeguard
d. Compare the signs of drowning

The next three questions are based on the following passage:

This excerpt is an adaptation from "The 'Hatchery' of the Sun-Fish" — Scientific American, #711

I have thought that an example of the intelligence (instinct?) of a class of fish which has come under my observation during my excursions into the Adirondack region of New York State might possibly be of interest to your readers, especially as I am not aware that anyone except myself has noticed it, or, at least, has given it publicity.

The female sun-fish (called, I believe, in England, the roach or bream) makes a "hatchery" for her eggs in this wise. Selecting a spot near the banks of the numerous lakes in which this region abounds, and where the water is about 4 inches deep, and still, she builds, with her tail and snout, a circular embankment 3 inches in height and 2 thick. The circle, which is as perfect a one as could be formed with mathematical instruments, is usually a foot and a half in diameter; and at one side of this circular wall an opening is left by the fish of just sufficient width to admit her body.

The mother sun-fish, having now built or provided her "hatchery," deposits her spawn within the circular enclosure, and mounts guard at the entrance until the fry are hatched out and are sufficiently large to take charge of themselves. As the embankment, moreover, is built up to the surface of the water, no enemy can very easily obtain an entrance within the enclosure from the top; while there being only one entrance, the fish is able, with comparative ease, to keep out all intruders.

I have, as I say, noticed this beautiful instinct of the sun-fish for the perpetuity of her species more particularly in the lakes of this region; but doubtless the same habit is common to these fish in other waters.

7. What is the purpose of this passage?

a. To show the effects of fish hatcheries on the Adirondack region
b. To persuade the audience to study ichthyology (fish science)
c. To depict the sequence of mating among sun-fish
d. To enlighten the audience on the habits of sun-fish and their hatcheries

8. How is the circle that keeps the larvae of the sun-fish safe made?

a. It is formed with mathematical instruments.
b. The sun-fish builds it with her tail and snout.
c. It is provided to her as a "hatchery" by Mother Nature.
d. The sun-fish builds it with her larvae.

9. The author included the third paragraph in the passage to achieve which of the following effects?
   a. To complicate the subject matter
   b. To express a bias
   c. To insert a counterargument
   d. To conclude a sequence and add a final detail

Questions 10–19 are based on the following passage:

In the quest to understand existence, modern philosophers must question if humans can fully comprehend the world. Classical western approaches to philosophy tend to hold that one can understand something, be it an event or object, by standing outside of the phenomenon and observing it. It is then by unbiased observation that one can grasp the details of the world. This seems to hold true for many things. Scientists conduct experiments and record their findings, and thus many natural phenomena become comprehensible. However, several of these observations were possible because humans used tools in order to make these discoveries.

This may seem like an extraneous matter. After all, people invented things like microscopes and telescopes in order to enhance their capacity to view cells or the movement of stars. While humans are still capable of seeing things, the question remains if human beings have the capacity to fully observe and see the world in order to understand it. It would not be an impossible stretch to argue that what humans see through a microscope is not the exact thing itself but rather a human interpretation of it.

This would seem to be the case in the "Business of the Holes" experiment conducted by Richard Feynman. To study the way electrons behave, Feynman set up a barrier with two holes and a plate. The plate was there to indicate how many times the electrons would pass through the hole(s). Rather than casually observing the electrons acting under normal circumstances, Feynman discovered that electrons behave in two totally different ways depending on whether or not they are observed. The electrons that were observed had passed through either one of the holes or were caught on the plate as particles. However, electrons that weren't observed acted as waves instead of particles and passed through both holes. This indicated that electrons have a dual nature. Electrons seen by the human eye act like particles, while unseen electrons act like waves of energy.

This dual nature of the electrons presents a conundrum. While humans now have a better understanding of electrons, the fact remains that people cannot entirely perceive how electrons behave without the use of instruments. We can only observe one of the mentioned behaviors, which only provides a partial understanding of the entire function of electrons. Therefore, we're forced to ask ourselves whether the world we observe is objective or if it is subjectively perceived by humans. Or, an alternative question: can humans understand the world only through machines that will allow them to observe natural phenomena?

Both questions humble humanity's capacity to grasp the world. However, those ideas don't take into account that many phenomena have been proven by human beings without the use of machines, such as the discovery of gravity. Like all philosophical questions, whether humanity's reason and observation alone can understand the universe can be approached from many angles.

10. The word *extraneous* in paragraph two can be best interpreted as meaning which one of the following?
    a. Indispensable
    b. Bewildering
    c. Superfluous
    d. Exuberant

11. What is the author's motivation for writing the passage?
    a. Bring to light an alternative view on human perception by examining the role of technology in human understanding.
    b. Educate the reader on the latest astroparticle physics discovery and offer terms that may be unfamiliar to the reader.
    c. Argue that humans are totally blind to the realities of the world by presenting an experiment that proves that electrons are not what they seem on the surface.
    d. Reflect on opposing views of human understanding.

12. Which of the following best describes how paragraph four is structured?
    a. It offers one solution, questions the solution, and then ends with an alternative solution.
    b. It presents an inquiry, explains the detail of that inquiry, and then offers a solution.
    c. It presents a problem, explains the details of that problem, and then ends with more inquiry.
    d. It gives a definition, offers an explanation, and then ends with an inquiry.

13. For the classical approach to understanding to hold true, which of the following is required?
    a. A telescope is needed.
    b. The person observing must prove their theory beyond a doubt.
    c. Multiple witnesses must be present.
    d. The person observing must be unbiased.

14. Which best describes how the electrons in the experiment behaved like waves?
    a. The electrons moved up and down like ocean waves.
    b. The electrons passed through both holes and then onto the plate.
    c. The electrons converted to photons upon touching the plate.
    d. Electrons were seen passing through one hole or the other.

15. The author mentions gravity in the last paragraph in order to do what?
    a. To show that different natural phenomena test man's ability to grasp the world
    b. To prove that since man has not measured it with the use of tools or machines, humans cannot know the true nature of gravity
    c. To demonstrate an example of natural phenomena humans discovered and understood without the use of tools or machines
    d. To show an alternative solution to the nature of electrons that humans have not thought of yet

16. Which situation best parallels the revelation of the dual nature of electrons discovered in Feynman's experiment?
   a. A man is born color-blind and grows up observing everything in lighter or darker shades. With the invention of special goggles he puts on, he discovers that there are other colors in addition to different shades.
   b. The coelacanth was thought to be extinct, but a live specimen was just recently discovered. There are now two living species of coelacanth known, and both are believed to be endangered.
   c. In the Middle Ages, blacksmiths added carbon to iron, thus inventing steel. This important discovery would have its biggest effects during the industrial revolution.
   d. The x-ray machine was invented to help doctors better examine and treat broken bones. It was put to use in hospitals and medical centers.

17. Which statement about technology would the author likely disagree with?
   a. Technology can help expand the field of human vision.
   b. Technology renders human observation irrelevant.
   c. Developing tools used in observation and research indicates growing understanding of our world itself.
   d. Studying certain phenomena necessitates the use of tools and machines.

18. As it is used in paragraph 4, the word *conundrum* most nearly means:
   a. Platitude
   b. Enigma
   c. Solution
   d. Hypothesis

19. What is the author's purpose in paragraph 3?
   a. To prove to the audience the thesis of the passage by providing evidence suggesting that electrons behave differently when observed by the human eye
   b. To propose that the experiment conducted was not ethically done and to provide evidence that a new experiment should be conducted in order to reach the truth
   c. To introduce the topic to the audience in a manner that puts it into a practical as well as historical understanding
   d. To pose a question relating to the topic about whether humans fully observe phenomena in an objective or subjective sense

Questions 20–24 are based on the following passage:

> The Middle Ages were a time of great superstition and theological debate. Many beliefs were developed and practiced, while some died out or were listed as heresy. Boethianism is a Medieval theological philosophy that attributes sin to gratification and righteousness with virtue and God's providence. Boethianism holds that sin, greed, and corruption are means to attain temporary pleasure, but that they inherently harm the person's soul as well as other human beings.
>
> In *The Canterbury Tales,* we observe more instances of bad actions punished than goodness being rewarded. This would appear to be some reflection of Boethianism. In the "Pardoner's Tale," all three thieves wind up dead, which is a result of their desire for wealth. Each wrongdoer pays with their life, and they are unable to enjoy the wealth they worked to steal. Within his tales, Chaucer gives reprieve to people undergoing struggle, but also interweaves stories of contemptible individuals being cosmically punished for their wickedness. The thieves idolize physical wealth, which leads to their downfall. This same theme and ideological principle of Boethianism is repeated in the "Friar's Tale," whose summoner character attempts to gain further wealth by partnering with a demon. The summoner's refusal to repent for his avarice and corruption leads to the demon

dragging his soul to Hell. Again, we see the theme of the individual who puts faith and morality aside in favor for a physical prize. The result, of course, is that the summoner loses everything.

The examples of the righteous being rewarded tend to appear in a spiritual context within the *Canterbury Tales*. However, there are a few instances where we see goodness resulting in physical reward. In the "Prioress's Tale," we see corporal punishment for barbarism and a reward for goodness. The Jews are punished for their murder of the child, giving a sense of law and order (though racist) to the plot. While the boy does die, he is granted a lasting reward by being able to sing even after his death, a miracle that marks that the murdered youth led a pure life. Here, the miracle represents eternal favor with God.

Again, we see the theological philosophy of Boethianism in Chaucer's *The Canterbury Tales* through acts of sin and righteousness and the consequences that follow. When pleasures of the world are sought instead of God's favor, we see characters being punished in tragic ways. However, the absence of worldly lust has its own set of consequences for the characters seeking to obtain God's favor.

20. What would be a potential reward for living a good life, as described in Boethianism?
  a. A long life sustained by the good deeds one has done over a lifetime
  b. Wealth and fertility for oneself and the extension of one's family line
  c. Vengeance for those who have been persecuted by others who have a capacity for committing wrongdoing
  d. God's divine favor for one's righteousness

21. What might be the main reason why the author chose to discuss Boethianism through examining *The Canterbury Tales*?
  a. *The Canterbury Tales* is a well-known text.
  b. *The Canterbury Tales* is the only known fictional text that contains use of Boethianism.
  c. *The Canterbury Tales* presents a manuscript written in the medieval period that can help illustrate Boethianism through stories and show how people of the time might have responded to the idea.
  d. Within each individual tale in *The Canterbury Tales*, the reader can read about different levels of Boethianism and how each level leads to greater enlightenment.

22. What "ideological principle" is the author referring to in the middle of the second paragraph when talking about the "Friar's Tale"?
  a. The principle that the act of ravaging another's possessions is the same as ravaging one's soul
  b. The principle that thieves who idolize physical wealth will be punished in an earthly sense as well as eternally
  c. The principle that fraternization with a demon will result in one losing everything, including their life
  d. The principle that a desire for material goods leads to moral malfeasance punishable by a higher being

23. Which of the following words, if substituted for the word *avarice* in paragraph two, would least change the meaning of the sentence?
  a. Perniciousness
  b. Pithiness
  c. Covetousness
  d. Precariousness

24. Based on the passage, what view does Boethianism take on desire?
   a. Desire does not exist in the context of Boethianism.
   b. Desire is a virtue and should be welcomed.
   c. Having desire is evidence of demonic possession.
   d. Desire for pleasure can lead toward sin.

25. Technology has been invading cars for the last several years, but there are some new high tech trends that are pretty amazing. It is now standard in many car models to have a rear-view camera, hands-free phone and text, and a touch screen digital display. Music can be streamed from a paired cell phone, and some displays can even be programmed with a personal photo. Sensors beep to indicate there is something in the driver's path when reversing and changing lanes. Rain-sensing windshield wipers and lights are automatic, leaving the driver with little to do but watch the road and enjoy the ride. The next wave of technology will include cars that automatically parallel park, and a self-driving car is on the horizon. These technological advances make it a good time to be a driver.
It can be concluded from this paragraph that:
   a. Technology will continue to influence how cars are made.
   b. Windshield wipers and lights are always automatic.
   c. It is standard to have a rear-view camera in all cars.
   d. Technology has reached its peak in cars.

Questions 26–35 are based upon the following passage:

The following is an excerpt from Common Sense by Thomas Payne.

> MANKIND being originally equals in the order of creation, the equality could only be destroyed by some subsequent circumstance; the distinctions of rich, and poor, may in a great measure be accounted for, and that without having recourse to the harsh, ill-sounding names of oppression and avarice. Oppression is often the CONSEQUENCE, but seldom or never the MEANS of riches; and though avarice will preserve a man from being necessitously poor, it generally makes him too timorous to be wealthy.
>
> But there is another and greater distinction, for which no truly natural or religious reason can be assigned, and that is, the distinction of men into KINGS and SUBJECTS. Male and female are the distinctions of nature, good and bad the distinctions of heaven; but how a race of men came into the world so exalted above the rest, and distinguished like some new species, is worth enquiring into, and whether they are the means of happiness or of misery to mankind.
>
> In the early ages of the world, according to the scripture chronology, there were no kings; the consequence of which was, there were no wars; it is the pride of kings which throw mankind into confusion. Holland without a king hath enjoyed more peace for this last century than any of the monarchical governments in Europe. Antiquity favors the same remark; for the quiet and rural lives of the first patriarchs hath a happy something in them, which vanishes away when we come to the history of Jewish royalty.
>
> Government by kings was first introduced into the world by the Heathens, from whom the children of Israel copied the custom. It was the most prosperous invention the Devil ever set on foot for the promotion of idolatry. The Heathens paid divine honors to their deceased kings, and the Christian world hath improved on the plan, by doing the same to their living ones. How impious is the title of sacred majesty applied to a worm, who in the midst of his splendor is crumbling into dust!
>
> As the exalting one man so greatly above the rest cannot be justified on the equal rights of nature, so neither can it be defended on the authority of scripture; for the will of the Almighty, as declared

by Gideon and the prophet Samuel, expressly disapproves of government by kings. All anti-monarchical parts of scripture have been very smoothly glossed over in monarchical governments, but they undoubtedly merit the attention of countries which have their governments yet to form. "Render unto Caesar the things which are Caesar's" is the scripture doctrine of courts, yet it is no support of monarchical government, for the Jews at that time were without a king, and in a state of vassalage to the Romans.

Now three thousand years passed away from the Mosaic account of the creation, till the Jews under a national delusion requested a king. Till then their form of government (except in extraordinary cases, where the Almighty interposed) was a kind of republic administered by a judge and the elders of the tribes. Kings they had none, and it was held sinful to acknowledge any being under that title but the Lord of Hosts. And when a man seriously reflects on the idolatrous homage which is paid to the persons of kings, he need not wonder that the Almighty, ever jealous of his honor, should disapprove of a form of government which so impiously invades the prerogative of heaven.

26. According to the passage, what role does avarice, or greed, play in wealth and poverty?
   a. Avarice makes a man poor.
   b. Avarice is the consequence of wealth.
   c. Avarice prevents a man from being poor, but makes him too fearful to be wealthy.
   d. Avarice is what drives a person to be wealthy.

27. Of these distinctions, which does the author believe to be beyond natural or religious reason?
   a. Good and bad
   b. Male and female
   c. Human and animal
   d. Kings and subjects

28. According to the passage, what are the Heathens responsible for?
   a. Government by kings
   b. Quiet and rural lives of patriarchs
   c. Paying divine honors to their living kings
   d. Equal rights of nature

29. Which of the following best states Paine's rationale for the denouncement of monarchy?
   a. It is against the laws of nature.
   b. It is against the equal rights of nature and is denounced in scripture.
   c. Despite scripture, a monarchical government is unlawful.
   d. Neither the law nor scripture denounce monarchy.

30. Based on the passage, what is the best definition of the word *idolatrous*?
   a. Worshipping kings
   b. Being deceitful
   c. Sinfulness
   d. Engaging in illegal activities

31. What is the essential meaning of the following passage:

> And when a man seriously reflects on the idolatrous homage which is paid to the persons of kings, he need not wonder that the Almighty, ever jealous of his honor, should disapprove of a form of government which so impiously invades the prerogative of heaven.

a. God disapproves of the irreverence of a monarchical government.
b. With careful reflection, men should realize that heaven is not promised.
c. God will punish those that follow a monarchical government.
d. Belief in a monarchical government cannot coexist with belief in God.

32. Based on the passage, what is the best definition of the word *timorous* in the first paragraph?
a. Being full of fear
b. A characteristic of shyness
c. Being able to see through someone
d. Being full of anger and hatred

33. The author's attitude toward the subject can best be described as:
a. Indifferent and fatigued
b. Impassioned and critical
c. Awed and enchanted
d. Enraged and sulky

34. The main purpose of the fourth paragraph is:
a. To persuade the audience that heathens were more advanced than Christians
b. To explain how monarchs came into existence and how Christians adopted the same system
c. To describe the divinity of English monarchs and how it is their birthright to be revered
d. To counteract the preceding paragraph by giving proof of the damage monarchs can cause

35. According to this passage, what does the author say the basis is for men having equal status at one time but that changing later on?
a. All men are created equal by God and separated by man-made ideas
b. All men are created equal by God and God separates some men for greater things
c. It was the common consensus that men were equal
d. The king is the one who establishes the roles of men and women and makes them not equal

Questions 36–45 are based on the following passages:

Passage I

Lethal force, or deadly force, is defined as the physical means to cause death or serious harm to another individual. The law holds that lethal force is only acceptable when you or another person are in immediate and unavoidable danger of death or severe bodily harm. For example, a person could be beating a weaker person in such a way that they are suffering severe enough trauma that could result in death or serious harm. This would be an instance where lethal force would be acceptable and possibly the only way to save that person from irrevocable damage.

Another example of when to use lethal force would be when someone enters your home with a deadly weapon. The intruder's presence and possession of the weapon indicate malicious intent and the ability to inflict death or severe injury upon you and your loved ones. Again, lethal force can be used in this situation. Lethal force can also be applied to prevent the harm of another individual. If a woman is being brutally assaulted and is unable to fend off an attacker, lethal force can be used to defend her as a last-ditch effort. If she is in immediate jeopardy of rape, harm, and/or death, lethal force could be the only response that could effectively deter the assailant.

The key to understanding the concept of lethal force is the term *last resort*. Deadly force cannot be taken back; it should be used only to prevent severe harm or death. The law does distinguish whether the means of one's self-defense is fully warranted or if the individual goes out of control in the process. If you continually attack the assailant after they are rendered incapacitated, this would be causing unnecessary harm, and the law can bring charges against you. Likewise, if you kill an attacker unnecessarily after defending yourself, you can be charged with murder. This would move lethal force beyond necessary defense, making it no longer a last resort but rather a use of excessive force.

Passage II

Assault is an unlawful and intentional act that causes reasonable apprehension in another individual, either by an imminent threat or by initiating offensive contact. Assaults can vary, encompassing physical strikes, threatening body language, and even provocative language. In the case of the latter, even if a hand has not been laid, it is still considered an assault because of its threatening nature.

Let's look at an example. A homeowner is angered because his neighbor blows fallen leaves onto his freshly mowed lawn. Irate, the homeowner gestures a fist to his fellow neighbor and threatens to bash his head in for littering on his lawn. The homeowner's physical motions and verbal threats herald a physical threat against the other neighbor. These factors classify the homeowner's action as an assault. If the neighbor hits the threatening homeowner in retaliation, that would constitute an assault as well because he physically hit the homeowner.

Assault also centers on the involvement of weapons in a conflict. If someone fires a gun at another person, this could be interpreted as an assault unless the shooter acted in self-defense. If an individual drew a gun or a knife on someone with the intent to harm them, that would be considered assault. However, it's also considered an assault if someone simply aims a weapon, loaded or not, at another person in a threatening manner.

36. What is the purpose of the second passage?
   a. To inform the reader about what assault is and how it is committed
   b. To inform the reader about how assault is a minor example of lethal force
   c. To disprove the previous passage concerning lethal force
   d. To recount an incident in which the author was assaulted

37. According to the passages, using lethal force would be legal in which of the following situations?
   a. A disgruntled cashier yells obscenities at a customer.
   b. A thief is seen running away with stolen cash.
   c. A man is attacked in an alley by another man with a knife.
   d. A woman punches another woman in a bar.

38. Given the information in the passages, which of the following must be true about assault?
   a. Assault charges are more severe than unnecessary use of force charges.
   b. There are various forms of assault.
   c. Smaller, weaker people cannot commit assaults.
   d. Assault is justified only as a last resort.

39. Which of the following, if true, would most seriously undermine the explanation proposed by the author of Passage I in the third paragraph?
    a. An instance of lethal force in self-defense is not absolutely absolved from blame. The law considers the necessary use of force at the time it is committed.
    b. An individual who uses lethal force under necessary defense is in direct compliance of the law under most circumstances.
    c. Lethal force in self-defense should be forgiven in all cases for the peace of mind of the primary victim.
    d. The use of lethal force is not evaluated on the intent of the user but rather the severity of the primary attack that warranted self-defense.

40. Based on the passages, what can be inferred about the relationship between assault and lethal force?
    a. An act of lethal force always leads to a type of assault.
    b. An assault will result in someone using lethal force.
    c. An assault with deadly intent can lead to an individual using lethal force to preserve their well-being.
    d. If someone uses self-defense in a conflict, it is called deadly force; if actions or threats are intended, it is called assault.

41. Which of the following best describes the way the passages are structured?
    a. Both passages open by defining a legal concept and then continue to describe situations that further explain the concept.
    b. Both passages begin with situations, introduce accepted definitions, and then cite legal ramifications.
    c. Passage I presents a long definition while the Passage II begins by showing an example of assault.
    d. Both cite specific legal doctrines, then proceed to explain the rulings.

42. What can be inferred about the role of intent in lethal force and assault?
    a. Intent is irrelevant. The law does not take intent into account.
    b. Intent is vital for determining the lawfulness of using lethal force but not for assault.
    c. Intent is very important for determining both lethal force and assault; intent is examined in both parties and helps determine the severity of the issue.
    d. The intent of the assailant is the main focus for determining legal ramifications; it is used to determine if the defender was justified in using force to respond.

43. The author uses the example in the second paragraph of Passage II in order to do what?
    a. To demonstrate two different types of assault by showing how each specifically relates to the other
    b. To demonstrate a single example of two different types of assault, then adding in the third type of assault in the example's conclusion
    c. To prove that the definition of lethal force is altered when the victim in question is a homeowner and his property is threatened
    d. To suggest that verbal assault can be an exaggerated crime by the law and does not necessarily lead to physical violence

44. As it is used in the second passage, the word *apprehension* most nearly means:
    a. Pain
    b. Exhaustion
    c. Fear
    d. Honor

45. One of the main purposes of the last paragraph in the first passage is to state:
   a. How assault is different when used in the home versus when it is used out in public
   b. A specific example of lethal force so that the audience will know what it looks like
   c. Why police officers defend those who use lethal force but do not defend those who use assault
   d. The concept of lethal force as a last resort and the point at which it can cross a line from defense to manslaughter

46. Jerome K. Jerome's humorous account of a boating holiday, Three Men in a Boat, was published in 1889. Originally intended as a serious travel guide, the work became a prime example of a comic novel. Read the passage below, noting the word in italics. Answer the question that follows.

> I felt rather hurt about this at first; it seemed somehow to be a sort of slight. Why hadn't I got housemaid's knee? Why this invidious reservation? After a while, however, less grasping feelings prevailed. I reflected that I had every other known malady in the pharmacology, and I grew less selfish, and determined to do without housemaid's knee. Gout, in its most malignant stage, it would appear, had seized me without my being aware of it; and *zymosis* I had evidently been suffering with from boyhood. There were no more diseases after *zymosis*, so I concluded there was nothing else the matter with me. —Jerome K. Jerome, *Three Men in a Boat*

Which definition best fits the word *zymosis*?
   a. Discontent
   b. An infectious disease
   c. Poverty
   d. Bad luck

Questions 47–53 are based on the following passage:

> Over a period of nearly fifteen years, genetic scientists worked diligently to map out the human genome. An international effort, the goal of which was not perhaps clear to many laypeople at the start, the Human Genome Project sought to identify, map, and sequence all genes found in human DNA to better understand the function and form of each genetic marker. More specifically, the goal was to garner a stronger understanding of everything from disease and predisposition to specific diseases to physical and personality traits. As a result of this work, we've seen significant impact across medical and health fields, which have been able to apply the knowledge to improving both human health and physiological performance.
>
> Over the course of the project, scientists were able to determine that there are approximately 20,500 human genes. In identifying these, scientists were also able to determine their order and then further establish their locations and create linkage maps that help connect the genes to different characteristics that are observable over several generations of a family.
>
> As a result of the work, there have been major advances in medicine that have facilitated the treatment of disease. Because many diseases are related to changes in our genes, scanning and searching for those mutations can help detect diseases early. Early detection is vital in the treatment of many diseases, such as cancer. In addition, genetic testing can identify a predisposition toward a certain disease or condition and, in turn, individuals can act preemptively to address the issue. For example, many women who test positive for a mutation in a BRCA gene, the breast cancer genes, have opted to get mastectomies prior to developing cancer. In this way, genomics works toward helping to prevent diseases in the first place.

Similarly, genomics can help with the diagnosis of disease, particularly when it's something incredibly rare. The research has enabled scientists to identify approximately 2000 different disease genes. What this means for doctors is that when patients come in with an array of symptoms, yet a diagnosis still seems to elude them, genomic research has enabled patients to be diagnosed more quickly and more accurately—in seconds—facilitating faster treatment.

Those treatments, with the help of genomic research, are growing more effective as well. Prior to this research, we've all likely witnessed medication having different effects on different people, and genomic research explains that. Pharmacogenomics, specifically, researches how genes impact the liver's ability to metabolize different drugs. These variations are normal, but until this research, they were unpredictable, meaning sometimes doctors were unsure if a medication dose would be beneficial, toxic, or have no positive impact at all. Now, doctors are able to respond to these differences and modify dosages. Similarly, pharmaceutical researchers are able to develop more effective medications. In fact, more than 250 medications come with pharmacogenomic information, so doctors can appropriately prescribe medication based on a patient's genetics.

Perhaps one of the most significant medical changes is the potential shift from treating to curing when it comes to disease management. Most medicine—even modern medicine—is designed to treat or mitigate conditions. However, a greater understanding of genomics means doctors can identify the gene mutation or variation responsible for the disease and remove it. Using enzymes—in one case, the Cas9 enzyme—doctors can attack the specific part of the gene that carries the mutation and ultimately remove the disease. This kind of gene editing may be the future of medicine, especially as it becomes more affordable.

All in all, genomic research has single-handedly changed the current landscape for medicine, with even more hope on the horizon.

47. The BRCA gene is an example to demonstrate which benefit of genomics?
    a. Disease treatment
    b. Disease eradication
    c. Tailored medicine
    d. Preventive medicine

48. Tangible evidence of the success for pharmacogenomics in paragraph 5 is best seen in which sentence?
    a. " ... we've all likely witnessed medication having different effects on different people ..."
    b. "... more than 250 medications come with pharmacogenomic information ..."
    c. "... variations are normal, but until this research, they were unpredictable ..."
    d. "... doctors are able to respond to these differences and modify dosages."

49. What strategy does the author use throughout the passage to demonstrate the value of the Human Genome Project?
    a. Including genetic mutations
    b. Listing concrete applications for the research
    c. Citing medical researchers
    d. Presenting and refuting the opposition

50. Cas9 will facilitate which of the following?
    a. Pharmacogenomics
    b. Disease diagnosis
    c. Gene editing
    d. Disease detection

51. Based on the language in the passage, how does the author feel about genomic research?
    a. Hopeful
    b. Resigned
    c. Opposed
    d. Concerned

52. What is the author's primary point in the passage?
    a. To persuade readers to support genomic research
    b. To inform readers about how DNA mapping changed medicine
    c. To describe medical treatments that use genomics
    d. To prove the value of scientific research

53. "The research has enabled scientists to identify approximately 2000 different disease genes" is an example of which of the following?
    a. A main idea
    b. A topic sentence
    c. A supporting detail
    d. A statistic

Use the passage below for questions 54 through 55:

Caribbean Island Destinations

Do you want to vacation at a Caribbean island destination? Who wouldn't want a tropical vacation? Visit one of the many Caribbean islands where visitors can swim in crystal blue waters, swim with dolphins, or enjoy family-friendly or adult-only resorts and activities. Every island offers a unique and picturesque vacation destination. Choose from these islands: Aruba, St. Lucia, Barbados, Anguilla, St. John, and so many more. A Caribbean island destination will be the best and most refreshing vacation ever ... no regrets!

54. What is the topic of the passage?
    a. Caribbean island destinations
    b. Tropical vacation
    c. Resorts
    d. Activities

55. What is/are the supporting detail(s) of this passage?
    a. Cruising to the Caribbean
    b. Local events
    c. Family or adult-only resorts and activities
    d. All of the above

Vocabulary

1. What word meaning "on the opposite side" best fits in the following sentence:

Although the patient's right knee had been hurting for a few months, he started experiencing ________ hip pain two weeks ago.

a. Bilateral
b. Ipsilateral
c. Contralateral
d. Lateral

2. Select the correct meaning of the underlined word in the following sentence:

The patient's stomach appeared distended.

a. Enlarged or expanded
b. Sunken or concave
c. Soft and flaccid
d. Discolored or blotchy

3. What word meaning "rapidly or abruptly" best fits in the following sentence:

When the school group arrived, the noise level in the waiting room rose _______________.

a. Concisely
b. Precipitously
c. Contingently
d. Preemptively

4. What word meaning "open" best fits in the following sentence:

After the obstruction was removed, the patient's bowel was ____________.

a. Patent
b. Potent
c. Evident
d. Exude

5. What is the best definition for *symmetrical*?
a. Having two sides
b. Uniform across an axis
c. Uneven sides
d. Disproportionate

6. Select the correct meaning of the underlined word in the following sentence:

After the trauma, new symptoms of the woman's <u>latent</u> infection emerged.

a. Chronic and debilitating
b. Acute but not necessarily severe
c. Present but not active or visible
d. Uncontrollable or volatile

7. What is the best definition for *labile*?
a. Inflexible
b. Reliable
c. Concerned
d. Subject to change

8. Select the meaning of the underlined word in the following sentence.

The warning label clearly stated "do not <u>ingest</u>" because it could be toxic.

a. Touch
b. Consume
c. Inhale
d. Spill

9. Select the correct meaning of the underlined word in the following sentence:

The nurse explained the symptoms of the patient's <u>acute</u> illness and recommended increasing fluid intake.

a. Serious with a poor prognosis
b. Sudden or rapid onset
c. Debilitating and contagious
d. Chronic and slow to resolve

10. What word meaning "severe and harmful" best fits in the following sentence:

The patient was quarantined because the doctor was concerned he had a ____________ disease.

a. Patent
b. Innocuous
c. Latent
d. Virulent

11. What is the best definition of the word *adverse*?
a. Unpredictable
b. Agitated
c. Undesirable
d. Progressive

12. What word meaning "so gradual that it's hardly apparent" best fits in the following sentence:

The nurse explained that atherosclerosis and coronary artery disease often have a(n) _________ onset.

a. Precipitous
b. Insidious
c. Incipient
d. Paroxysmal

13. The doctor's _______________ concern was the patient's lack of appetite.
a. Compensatory
b. Bilateral
c. Primary
d. Impending

14. What word meaning "closer to the trunk" best fits in the following sentence:

The knee is _________ to the ankle.

a. Dorsal
b. Distal
c. Proximal
d. Ventral

15. What word meaning "impenetrable" best fits in the following sentence:

Due to the contagious nature of the patient's infection, the nursing staff was told to don _____________ masks and gloves.

a. Impotent
b. Hygienic
c. Impervious
d. Impending

16. Select the correct meaning of the underlined word in the following sentence:

The <u>etiology</u> of the disease is currently unknown.

a. Prognosis or outlook
b. Origin or cause
c. Mechanism of transmission
d. Incidence in the population

17. Select the meaning of the underlined word in the following sentence:

Unfortunately, the patient's insurance does not cover <u>preexisting</u> conditions.

a. During
b. Prior
c. Post
d. Distal

18. What word meaning "feverish" best fits in the following sentence:

The ________ baby was difficult to sooth.

a. Febrile
b. Futile
c. Libel
d. Liable

19. What is the best definition for *apply*?
a. Adhere
b. Continue
c. Stop
d. Utilize

20. Select the correct meaning of the underlined word in the following sentence:

The <u>viscosity</u> of the patient's synovial fluid was abnormal.

a. A fluid's cellular and nutrient profile
b. A fluid's thickness or resistance to flow
c. A fluid's color and transparency
d. A fluid's sedimentation rate

21. What word meaning "on one's back" best fits in the following sentence:

The surgeon informed the patient that he would be __________ during the procedure.

a. Prone
b. Supine
c. Dorsal
d. Ventral

22. What is the best definition for *urinate*?
a. Stand
b. Excrete
c. Divulge
d. Pump

23. Select the meaning of the underlined word in the following sentence:

The doctor instructed the nurse to remove the <u>subcutaneous</u> tick head from the patient's leg.

a. Under skin
b. Below knee
c. Above foot
d. Round

24. What word meaning "wound with irregular borders" best fits in the following sentence:

The rock climber got a serious ________ on his arm when the boulder moved.

a. Incision
b. Laceration
c. Contusion
d. Avulsion

25. Select the correct meaning of the underlined word in the following sentence:

The patient's father had a history of chronic <u>renal</u> disease.

a. Relating to the pancreas
b. Relating to the liver
c. Relating to the kidney
d. Relating to hormones

26. Which word meaning "removal of necrotic tissue" best fits in the following sentence:

The biker was hopeful that after his knee ___________, he would be in less pain.

a. Debridement
b. Arthroscopy
c. Distension
d. Laparoscopy

27. Select the correct meaning of the underlined word in the following sentence:

During her internship at the hospital, Cassandra got to <u>triage</u> a lot of patients.

a. Diagnose or identify a problem
b. Develop an effective treatment plan
c. Evaluate and gather relevant medical history
d. Sort based on problem severity

28. What word meaning "susceptible to" best fits in the following sentence:

The malnourished child was _________ to rickets.

a. Impended
b. Invariable
c. Prognosticated
d. Predisposed

29. What is the best definition of the word *instigate*?
a. Initiate
b. Prevent
c. Investigate
d. Assent

30. Select the correct meaning of the underlined word in the following sentence:

    The nurse noted that the baby appeared <u>indolent.</u>

    a. Underweight
    b. Agitated
    c. Lethargic
    d. Alert

31. What word referring to "blood vessels that carry deoxygenated blood back to the heart" best fits in the following sentence:

    The nurse was concerned about possible occlusions in the patient's __________.

    a. Capillaries
    b. Arteries
    c. Ventricles
    d. Veins

32. Select the correct meaning of the underlined word in the following sentence:

    The medication had a <u>buccal</u> route of administration.

    a. Under the tongue
    b. In the rectum
    c. Through the nasal cavity
    d. Inside the cheek

33. Which word meaning "teacher" best fits in the following sentence:

    The class __________ is an expert in her field.

    a. Student
    b. Instructor
    c. Pupil
    d. Detective

34. What is the best definition of the word *expectorate*?
    a. To cough out phlegm
    b. To suppress a phlegm production
    c. To stifle a cough
    d. Yellowish or green sputum

35. Select the correct meaning of the underlined word in the following sentence:

    He likes to bike to work because his <u>residence</u> is only a few blocks away.

    a. Home
    b. Area
    c. Doctor
    d. Hotel

36. What is the best definition of the word *relinquish*?
    a. Stop repeatedly
    b. Give again
    c. Punish again
    d. Give up

37. What is the best definition of the word *germinate*?
    a. Lengthen
    b. Infect
    c. Develop
    d. Ail

38. What is the best definition of the word *indemnity?*
    a. Insurance
    b. Punishment
    c. Affinity
    d. Insolation

39. Select the correct meaning of the underlined word in the following sentence:

    Immediately after the holiday, staff interest grew <u>rampant</u>.

    a. Stagnant
    b. Mildly
    c. Unrestrained
    d. Wearily

40. Select the correct meaning of the underlined word in the following sentence:

    An increased pupil size is considered an <u>ominous</u> sign.

    a. Unequivocal
    b. Promising
    c. Auspicious
    d. Threatening

41. What word meaning "low blood sugar" best fits in the following sentence:

    A patient with diabetes did not receive breakfast so the nurse was concerned he might have ______________.

    a. Hypoglycemia
    b. Ketoacidosis
    c. Diabetic coma
    d. Hyperglycemia

42. What is the best definition of the word *observed*?
    a. Watched
    b. Hunted
    c. Scared
    d. Sold

43. What word meaning “sleepy yet arousable to verbal stimuli” best fits in the following sentence:

The ______________ patient was difficult to move to into the room.

a. Comatose
b. Delirious
c. Somnolent
d. Stuporous

44. What word meaning “coughing up blood” best fits in the following sentence:

A patient with tuberculosis should be monitored for ________________.

a. Hematopoiesis
b. Hemoptysis
c. Hematemesis
d. Hematochezia

45. What is the best definition of the word *engorge*?
a. Nourish
b. Squeeze
c. Consume
d. Swell

46. What word meaning “mourning after loss” best fits in the following sentence:

The nurse referred the mother to __________ counseling.

a. Bereavement
b. Disposition
c. Depression
d. Belligerent

47. What word meaning “excessive thirst” best fits in the following sentence:

A common side effect of antispasmodics is __________________.

a. Anuria
b. Polyploidy
c. Polydipsia
d. Polyurea

48. What is the best definition of the word *sentient*?
a. Kind and genial
b. Aging or dying
c. Able to feel or perceive
d. Nostalgic

49. Select the correct meaning of the underlined word in the following sentence:

The patient had a history of anxiety, emphysema, and a peptic ulcer.

a. Relating to ingestion
b. Relating to defecation
c. Relating to digestion
d. Relating to the pancreas

50. What word meaning "a muscle contraction that does not cause a change in muscle length" best fits in the following sentence:

The strength training protocol called for many ____________ exercises.

a. Isometric
b. Isotonic
c. Isokinetic
d. Plyometric

Grammar

1. Select the best word for the blank in the following sentence:

Tom couldn't decide which shirt to ___.

a. ware
b. where
c. wear
d. were

2. Identify the adjective clause in the following sentence.

A boy who loves to ride bikes gets plenty of exercise.

a. A boy who loves
b. Who loves to ride bikes
c. To ride bikes
d. Gets plenty of exercise

3. Identify the adverbial clause in the following sentence.

I want to work in the garden longer unless you are too tired.

a. I want to work in the garden
b. In the garden
c. Are too tired
d. Unless you are too tired

4. Identify the noun phrase in the following sentence.

The actor and actress rode in the long black limousine.

a. Actor and actress
b. Rode in the
c. The long black limousine
d. Actress rode in

5. If you were to rewrite the sentence below, starting with "Walking through Paris," what would the next words be?

Armani got lost when she walked around Paris.

a. you can get lost.
b. Armani found herself lost.
c. she should have gotten lost.
d. is about getting lost.

6. Which sentence does NOT include a gerund phrase?
a. Swimming several laps is a great way to get exercise.
b. The best way to swim quickly is using the flippers.
c. I can swim farther than the coach can in three minutes.
d. Learning to swim is not as difficult as you imagine it to be.

7. Which of the following sentences includes a nonessential appositive phrase?
a. Carrie Fisher, my second cousin, was an actress in the movie *Star Wars*.
b. The actor Harrison Ford also plays a lead role in *Star Wars*.
c. The movie *Star Wars* is about two hours long.
d. The movie *Star Wars* has become legendary.

8. Which of the following sentences highlights an absolute phrase?
a. One of my favorite activities is going camping in the forest.
b. The fire crackling, it is so exciting to be enveloped in nature.
c. The best drinks, hot cocoa and coffee, are served at campfires.
d. I love camping because it is the best experience for school-age children.

9. If you were to rewrite the sentence below, beginning with Phoenix buried his cat, what would the next words be?

After his cat died, Phoenix buried the cat with her favorite toys in his backyard.:

a. in his backyard before she died.
b. after she died in the backyard.
c. with her favorite toys after she died.
d. after he buried her toys in the backyard.

10. If you were to rewrite the sentence below, beginning with Tears streamed down my eyes, what would the next words be?

While I was in the helicopter, I saw the sunset, and tears streamed down my eyes.:

a. while I watched the helicopter fly into the sunset.
b. because the sunset flew up into the sky.
c. because the helicopter was facing the sunset.
d. when I saw the sunset from the helicopter.

For the next two questions, select the answer choice that best corrects the underlined portion of the sentence:

11. It is necessary for instructors to offer tutoring to any students who need extra help in the class.
a. to any students who need extra help in the class.
b. for any students needs extra help in the class.
c. with any students who need extra help in the class.
d. for any students needed extra help in the class.

12. Because many people feel there are too many distractions to get any work done, I actually enjoy working from home.
a. Because many people
b. While many people
c. Maybe many people
d. With most people

Directions for questions 13-14: Rewrite the sentence in your head following the directions given below.

13. Student loan debt is at an all-time high, which is why many politicians are using this issue to gain the attention and votes of students, or anyone with student loan debt.

Rewrite, beginning with Student loan debt is at an all-time high. The next words will be which of the following:

a. because politicians want students' votes.
b. , so politicians are using the issue to gain votes.
c. , so voters are choosing politicians who care about this issue.
d. , and politicians want to do something about it.

14. Seasoned runners often advise new runners to get fitted for better quality running shoes because new runners often complain about minor injuries like sore knees or shin splints.

Rewrite, beginning with Seasoned runners often advise new runners to get fitted for better quality running shoes. The next words will be which of the following:

a. to help them avoid minor injuries
b. because they know better
c. , so they can run further
d. to complain about running injuries

15. What is the noun phrase in the following sentence?

Charlotte's new German Shepherd puppy is energetic.

a. Puppy
b. Charlotte
c. German Shepherd puppy
d. Charlotte's new German Shepherd puppy

16. Which sentence shows grammatically correct parallelism?
a. He is the clown who inflated balloons and honked his nose.
b. He is the clown who inflated balloons and who honked his nose.
c. He is the clown that inflated balloons and who honked his nose.
d. He is the clown that inflated balloons and that honked his nose.

17. Which sentence shows grammatically correct parallelism?
a. My grandparents have been traveling and sightseeing.
b. My grandparents has been traveling and sightseeing.
c. My grandparents were traveling and have been sightseeing.
d. My grandparents have been traveling and they're sightseeing.

18. Which sentence shows grammatically correct subordination?
a. The building was sturdy and solid; it crumbled during the earthquake.
b. The building was study and solid although it crumbled during the earthquake.
c. The building was sturdy and solid, it crumbled during the earthquake.
d. Despite being sturdy and solid, the building crumbled during the earthquake.

19. Which sentence is grammatically correct?
a. Every morning we would wake up, ate breakfast, and broke camp.
b. Every morning we would wake up, eat breakfast, and broke camp.
c. Every morning we would wake up, eat breakfast, and break camp.
d. Every morning we would wake up, ate breakfast, and break camp.

20. Polls show that more and more people in the US distrust the government and view it as dysfunctional and corrupt. Every election, the same people are voted back into office.

Which word or words would best link these sentences?

a. Not surprisingly,
b. Understandably,
c. And yet,
d. Therefore,

21. A student wants to rewrite the following sentence:

Entrepreneurs use their ideas to make money.

He wants to use the word *money* as a verb, but he isn't sure which word ending to use. What is the appropriate suffix to add to *money* to complete the following sentence?

Entrepreneurs __________ their ideas.

a. –ize
b. –ical
c. –en
d. –ful

22. Glorify, fortify, gentrify, acidify

Based on the preceding words, what is the correct meaning of the suffix *–fy*?

a. Marked by, given to
b. Doer, believer
c. Make, cause, cause to have
d. Process, state, rank

23. After a long day at work, Tracy had dinner with her family, and then took a walk to the park.

What are the transitional words in the preceding sentence?

a. After, then
b. At, with, to
c. Had, took
d. A, the

24. Robert needed to find at least four sources for his final project, so he searched several library databases for reliable academic research.

Which words function as nouns in the preceding sentence?

a. Robert, sources, project, databases, research
b. Robert, sources, final, project, databases, academic, research
c. Robert, sources, project, he, library, databases, research
d. Sources, project, databases, research

25. Which sentence has a misplaced modifier?
a. The children love their cute and cuddly teddy bears.
b. Teddy bears are cute and cuddly; the children love them.
c. Cute and cuddly, the children love their teddy bears.
d. Cute and cuddly, the teddy bears are loved by many children.

26. Which of the following uses correct spelling?
   a. Jed was disatisfied with the acommodations at his hotel, so he requested another room.
   b. Jed was dissatisfied with the accommodations at his hotel, so he requested another room.
   c. Jed was dissatisfied with the accomodations at his hotel, so he requested another room.
   d. Jed was disatisfied with the accommodations at his hotel, so he requested another room.

27. Which example shows correct comma usage for dates?
   a. The due date for the final paper in the course is Monday, May 16, 2016.
   b. The due date for the final paper in the course is Monday, May 16 2016.
   c. The due date for the final project in the course is Monday, May, 16, 2016.
   d. The due date for the final project in the course is Monday May 16, 2016.

28. Which sentence shows grammatically correct parallelism?
   a. The puppies enjoy chewing and to play tug-o-war.
   b. The puppies enjoy to chew and playing tug-o-war.
   c. The puppies enjoy to chew and to play tug-o-war.
   d. The puppies enjoy chewing and playing tug-o-war.

29. At last night's company function, in honor of Mr. Robertson's retirement, several employees spoke kindly about his career achievements.

In the preceding sentence, what part of speech is the word *function*?

   a. Adjective
   b. Adverb
   c. Verb
   d. Noun

30. Which of the examples uses the correct plural form?
   a. Tomatos
   b. Analysis
   c. Cacti
   d. Criterion

31. Which of the following examples uses correct punctuation?
   a. The moderator asked the candidates, "Is each of you prepared to discuss your position on global warming?".
   b. The moderator asked the candidates, "Is each of you prepared to discuss your position on global warming?"
   c. The moderator asked the candidates, 'Is each of you prepared to discuss your position on global warming?'
   d. The moderator asked the candidates, "Is each of you prepared to discuss your position on global warming"?

32. Select the best word for the blank in the following sentence.

Garth _____ many pets that he cares for.

   a. has
   b. had
   c. have
   d. haves

33. In which of the following sentences does the word *part* function as an adjective?
   a. The part Brian was asked to play required many hours of research.
   b. She parts ways with the woodsman at the end of the book.
   c. The entire team played a part in the success of the project.
   d. Ronaldo is part Irish on his mother's side of the family.

34. All of Shannon's family and friends helped her to celebrate her 50th birthday at Café Sorrento.

   Which of the following is the complete subject of the preceding sentence?

   a. Family and friends
   b. All
   c. All of Shannon's family and friends
   d. Shannon's family and friends

35. Which of the following sentences uses second person point of view?
   a. I don't want to make plans for the weekend before I see my work schedule.
   b. She had to miss the last three yoga classes due to illness.
   c. Pluto is no longer considered a planet because it is not gravitationally dominant.
   d. Be sure to turn off all of the lights before locking up for the night.

36. As the tour group approached the bottom of Chichen Itza, the prodigious Mayan pyramid, they became nervous about climbing its distant peak.

   Based on the context of the sentence, which of the following words shows the correct meaning of the word *prodigious*?

   a. Very large
   b. Famous
   c. Very old
   d. Fancy

37. Which of the following sentences correctly uses a hyphen?
   a. Last-year, many of the players felt unsure of the coach's methods.
   b. Some of the furniture she selected seemed a bit over - the - top for the space.
   c. Henry is a beagle-mix and is ready for adoption this weekend.
   d. Geena works to maintain a good relationship with her ex-husband to the benefit of their children.

38. Which of the following examples correctly uses quotation marks?
   a. "A Wrinkle in Time" was one of my favorite novels as a child.
   b. Though he is famous for his roles in films like "The Great Gatsby" and "Titanic," Leonardo DiCaprio finally won his first Oscar in 2016.
   c. Sylvia Plath's poem "Daddy" will be the subject of this week's group discussion.
   d. "The New York Times" reported that many fans are disappointed in some of the trades made by the Yankees this off-season.

39. Which of the following sentences shows correct word usage?
   a. It's often been said that work is better then rest.
   b. Its often been said that work is better then rest.
   c. It's often been said that work is better than rest.
   d. Its often been said that work is better than rest.

Directions for questions 40-41: Rewrite the sentence in your head following the directions given below. Keep in mind that your new sentence should be well written and should have essentially the same meaning as the original sentence.

40. There are many risks in firefighting, including smoke inhalation, exposure to hazardous materials, and oxygen deprivation, so firefighters are outfitted with many items that could save their lives, including a self-contained breathing apparatus.

Rewrite, beginning with So firefighters. The next words will be which of the following?

a. are exposed to lots of dangerous situations.
b. need to be very careful on the job.
c. wear life-saving protective gear.
d. have very risky jobs.

41. Though social media sites like Facebook, Instagram, and Snapchat have become increasingly popular, experts warn that teen users are exposing themselves to many dangers such as cyberbullying and predators.

Rewrite, beginning with Experts warn that. The next words will be which of the following?

a. Facebook is dangerous.
b. they are growing in popularity.
c. teens are using them too much.
d. they can be dangerous for teens.

42. While studying vocabulary, a student notices that the words *circumference*, *circumnavigate*, and *circumstance* all begin with the prefix *circum–*. The student uses her knowledge of affixes to infer that all of these words share what related meaning?

a. Around, surrounding
b. Travel, transport
c. Size, measurement
d. Area, location

Directions for questions 43–50: Select the best version of the underlined part of the sentence. If there is no mistake, choose Correct as is.

43. Those are also memories that my siblings and me have now shared with our own children.

a. Those are also memories that I and my siblings
b. Those are also memories that me and my siblings
c. Those are also memories that my siblings and I
d. *Correct as is*

44. Ginger was born and raised in the Maywood neighborhood of Chicago, Illinois in 1955.

a. in Chicago, Illinois of Maywood in 1955.
b. in the Maywood neighborhood, of Chicago, Illinois in 1955.
c. in Maywood neighborhood of Chicago, Illinois, in 1955.
d. *Correct as is*

45. Virginia was attracted to the Committee's approach toward the new legislature.

a. Committies' approach
b. Committees approach
c. Committees' approach
d. *Correct as is*

46. Franz went to a high school five minutes from his house. He played in the marching band.

a. Franz went to a high school five minutes from his house and played in the marching band.
b. Franz went to a high school five minutes from his house but played in the marching band.
c. Franz went to a high school five minutes from his house, he played in the marching band.
d. *Correct as is*

47. After school, the news team was held by a press conference that shed light on the parking lot issues.

a. holds a press conference
b. held a press conference
c. holding a press conference
d. *Correct as is*

48. In 2015; seven years later, it was finally revealed that their dog, Bear, was part Husky.

a. In 2015. Seven years later,
b. In 2015, seven years later,
c. In 2015 seven years later,
d. *Correct as is*

49. Last week, my teacher shared this information with me "One day these rules won't matter, but what's inside your head and heart will."

a. with me. "One day these rules won't matter, but what's inside your head and heart will."
b. with me: "One day these rules won't matter, but what's inside your head and heart will."
c. with me: "One day these rules won't matter, but what's inside your head and heart will".
d. *Correct as is*

50. Society raising it's children to be decent human beings with something valuable to contribute to the world.

a. raising its children to be
b. raises its children to be
c. raising its' children to be
d. *Correct as is*

Directions for the next five questions: Select the best version of the underlined part of the sentence. The first choice is the same as the original sentence. If you think the original sentence is best, choose the first answer.

51. I won't go to the party unless some of my friends go.

Rewrite, beginning with I will go the party. The next words will be:

a. if I want to.
b. if my friends go.
c. since a couple of my friends are going.
d. unless people I know go.

52. He had a broken leg before the car accident, so it took him a long time to recover.

    Rewrite, beginning with He took a long time to recover from the car accident. The next words will be:

    a. from his two broken legs.
    b. after he broke his leg.
    c. because he already had a broken leg.
    d. since he broke his leg again afterward.

53. We had a party the day after Halloween to celebrate my birthday.

    Rewrite, beginning with It was my birthday. The next words will be:

    a. , so we celebrated with a party the day after Halloween.
    b. the day of Halloween so we celebrated with a party.
    c. , and we celebrated with a Halloween party the day after.
    d. a few days before Halloween, so we threw a party.

54. Over time, certain traits develop in animals that enable them to thrive in these environments.

    Rewrite, beginning with Animals thrive in these environments. The next words will be:

    a. over a certain amount of time with changing traits.
    b. which contain traits that allow animals to thrive.
    c. and animals have changing traits over time.
    d. due to certain traits in them that develop over time.

55. I've sat through many lectures and always come away learning something.

    Rewrite, beginning with I have always learned something. The next words will be:

    a. from the many lectures I've sat through.
    b. when I sit through lectures.
    c. and have sat through many lectures.
    d. from going away to many lectures.

Biology

1. Which is true regarding DNA?
    a. It is the genetic code.
    b. It provides energy.
    c. It is single-stranded.
    d. All of the above

2. Which is the cellular organelle used to tag, package, and ship out proteins destined for other cells or locations?
    a. The Golgi apparatus
    b. The lysosome
    c. The centrioles
    d. The mitochondria

3. How do cellulose and starch differ?
   a. Cellulose and starch are proteins with different R groups.
   b. Cellulose is a polysaccharide made up of glucose molecules, and starch is a polysaccharide made up of galactose molecules.
   c. Cellulose and starch are both polysaccharides made up of glucose molecules, but they are connected with different types of bonds.
   d. Cellulose and starch are the same molecule, but cellulose is made by plants and starch is made by animals.

4. Esther is left-handed. Hand dominance is a genetic factor. If being right-handed is a dominant trait over being left-handed, which of the following must NOT be applied about Esther's parents?
   a. Her parents are both right-handed.
   b. Her parents are both left-handed.
   c. Only one parent is right-handed.
   d. All of the above can be true.

5. What is the probability of *AaBbCcDd* × *AAbbccDD* having a child with genotype *AAbbccDD*?
   a. $\frac{1}{2}$
   b. $\frac{1}{4}$
   c. $\frac{1}{8}$
   d. $\frac{1}{16}$

6. Which statement regarding meiosis is correct?
   a. Meiosis produces four diploid cells.
   b. Meiosis contains two cellular divisions separated by interphase II.
   c. Meiosis produces cells with two sets of chromosomes.
   d. Crossing over occurs in the prophase of meiosis I.

7. What molecule serves as the hereditary material for prokaryotic and eukaryotic cells?
   a. Proteins
   b. Carbohydrates
   c. Lipids
   d. DNA

8. What is a product of photosynthesis?
   a. Water
   b. Sunlight
   c. Oxygen
   d. Carbon dioxide

9. What is cellular respiration?
   a. Making high-energy sugars
   b. Breathing
   c. Breaking down food to release energy
   d. Sweating

10. Which one of the following can perform photosynthesis?
    a. Mold
    b. Ant
    c. Mushroom
    d. Algae

11. Which taxonomic system is commonly used to describe the hierarchy of similar organisms today?
    a. Aristotle system
    b. Linnaean system
    c. Cesalpino system
    d. Darwin system

12. What is the Latin specific name for humans?
    a. *Homo sapiens*
    b. *Homo erectus*
    c. *Canis familiaris*
    d. *Homo habilis*

13. What organelles have two layers of membranes?
    a. Nucleus, chloroplast, mitochondria
    b. Nucleus, Golgi apparatus, mitochondria
    c. ER, chloroplast, lysosome
    d. Chloroplast, lysosome, Golgi apparatus

14. When human cells divide by meiosis, how many chromosomes do the resulting cells contain?
    a. 96
    b. 54
    c. 46
    d. 23

15. Which is an organelle found in a plant cell but not an animal cell?
    a. Mitochondria
    b. Chloroplast
    c. Golgi body
    d. Nucleus

16. Which of the following cannot be found in a human cell's genes?
    a. Sequences of amino acids to be transcribed into mRNA
    b. Lethal recessive traits like sickle cell anemia
    c. Mutated DNA
    d. DNA that codes for proteins the cell doesn't use

17. What are the net products of anaerobic glycolysis?
    a. 2 pyruvate molecules, 2 NADH molecules, and 2 ATP molecules
    b. 2 pyruvate molecules, 2 NADH molecules, and 4 ATP molecules
    c. 2 pyruvate molecules, 2 NAD+ molecules, and 2 ATP molecules
    d. 2 pyruvate molecules, 2 NAD+ molecules, and 4 ATP molecules

18. Which of the following correctly states the relationship between the glucose molecules that initially enter into glycolysis and the number of rounds of the citric acid cycle that can be completed?
   a. One round of the citric acid cycle can be completed for each glucose molecule that enters glycolysis.
   b. One round of the citric acid cycle can be completed for every 2 glucose molecules that enter glycolysis.
   c. Two rounds of the citric acid cycle can be completed for each glucose molecule that enters glycolysis.
   d. One round of the citric acid cycle can be completed for every 4 glucose molecules that enter glycolysis.

19. What are the two steps of oxidative phosphorylation?
   a. Electron transport chain and citric acid cycle
   b. Krebs cycle and electron transport chain
   c. Proton pump and facilitated diffusion
   d. Electron transport chain and chemiosmosis

20. Where is the nucleolus located in both plant and animal cells?
   a. Near the chloroplast
   b. Inside the mitochondria
   c. Inside the nucleus
   d. Attached to the cell membrane

21. In which organelle do eukaryotes carry out aerobic respiration?
   a. Golgi apparatus
   b. Nucleus
   c. Mitochondrion
   d. Cytosol

22. What kind of energy do plants use in photosynthesis to create chemical energy?
   a. Light
   b. Electric
   c. Nuclear
   d. Cellular

23. What type of biological molecule includes monosaccharides?
   a. Proteins
   b. Carbohydrates
   c. Nucleic acids
   d. Lipids

24. What are the molecular "energy" investments necessary for every G3P molecule produced by the Calvin cycle?
   a. 9 ATP molecules and 6 NADPH molecules
   b. 9 ATP molecules and 6 $NADP^+$ molecules
   c. 6 ATP molecules and 9 $NADP^+$ molecules
   d. 6 ATP molecules and 9 NADPH molecules

25. What does the cell membrane do?
   a. Builds proteins
   b. Breaks down large molecules
   c. Contains the cell's DNA
   d. Controls which molecules are allowed in and out of the cell

26. Describe the synthesis of the lagging strand of DNA.
    a. DNA polymerases synthesize DNA continuously after initially attaching to a primase.
    b. DNA polymerases synthesize DNA discontinuously in pieces called Okazaki fragments after initially attaching to primases.
    c. DNA polymerases synthesize DNA discontinuously in pieces called Okazaki fragments after initially attaching to RNA primers.
    d. DNA polymerases synthesize DNA discontinuously in pieces called Okazaki fragments which are joined together in the end by a DNA helicase.

27. Which structure is NOT found in prokaryotic cells?
    a. Cell wall
    b. Nucleus
    c. Cell membrane
    d. Vacuole

Questions 28–30 pertain to the passage:

Greenhouses are glass structures that people grow plants in. They allow plants to survive and grow even in the cold winter months by providing light and trapping warm air inside. Light is allowed in through the clear glass walls and roof. Warm air comes in as sunlight through the glass roof. The sunlight is converted into heat, or infrared energy, by the surfaces inside the greenhouse. This heat energy then takes longer to pass back through the glass surfaces and causes the interior of the greenhouse to feel warmer than the outside climate.

Plants may grow better inside a greenhouse versus outside for several reasons. There is more control of the temperature and humidity of the environment inside the greenhouse. The carbon dioxide produced by plants is trapped inside the greenhouse and can increase the rate of photosynthesis of the plants. There are also fewer pests and diseases inside the greenhouse.

Figure 1 below shows how a greenhouse works.

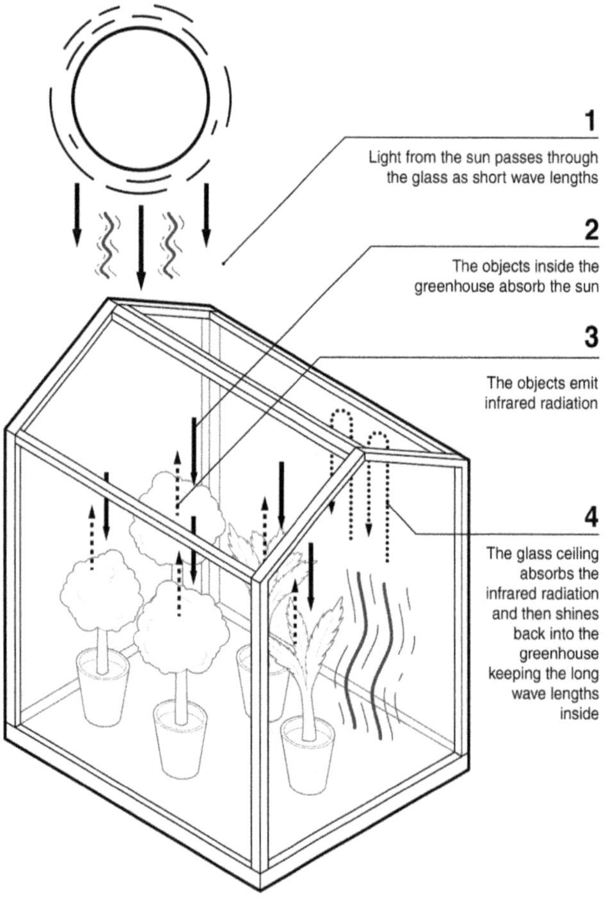

Scientist A wants to compare how a tomato plant grows inside a greenhouse versus outside a greenhouse.

Figure 2 below shows a graph of her results over 3 months.

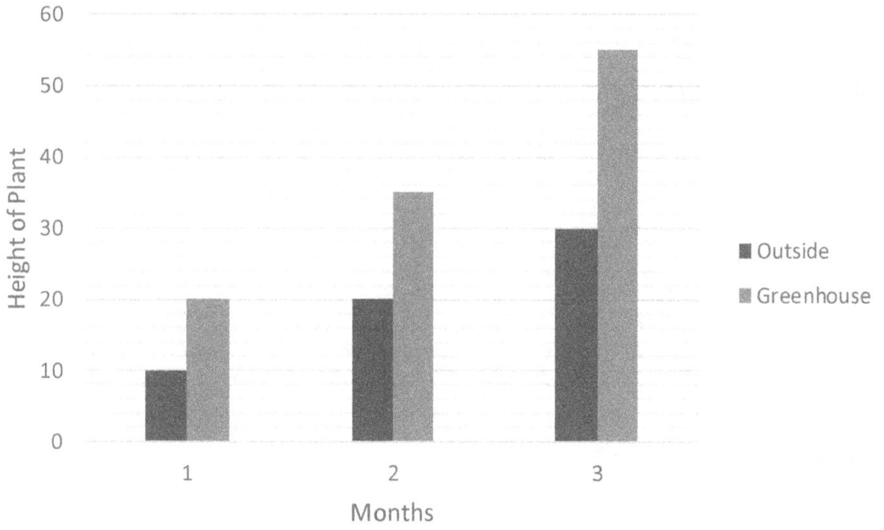

28. Looking at Figure 1, what gets trapped inside the greenhouse that helps plants grow?
    a. Short-wavelength IR
    b. Long-wavelength IR
    c. Cold air
    d. Water

29. Which plant grew taller from Scientist A's experiment?
    a. The plant outside grew taller.
    b. Both plants grew to the same height.
    c. Both plants remained the same height for three months.
    d. The plant inside the greenhouse grew taller.

30. What gets converted to heat inside a greenhouse?
    a. Water
    b. Sunlight
    c. Plants
    d. Oxygen

Chemistry

1. How many centimeters is 0.78 kilometers?
    a. 7.8 cm
    b. 0.078 cm
    c. 78,000 cm
    d. 780 cm

2. Which of the following correctly matches a category of protein with a physiologic example?
    a. Keratin is a structural protein.
    b. Antigens are hormonal proteins.
    c. Channel proteins are marker proteins.
    d. Actin is a transport protein.

3. Most catalysts found in biological systems are which of the following?
   a. Special lipids called cofactors
   b. Special proteins called enzymes
   c. Special lipids called enzymes
   d. Special proteins called cofactors

4. Which statement is true regarding atomic structure?
   a. Protons orbit around a nucleus.
   b. Neutrons have a positive charge.
   c. Electrons are in the nucleus.
   d. Protons have a positive charge.

5. The acceleration of a falling object due to gravity has been proven to be 9.8 m/s^2. A scientist drops a cactus four times and measures the acceleration with an accelerometer and gets the following results: 9.79 m/s^2, 9.81 m/s^2, 9.80 m/s^2, and 9.78 m/s^2. Which of the following accurately describes the measurements?
   a. They're both accurate and precise.
   b. They're accurate but not precise.
   c. They're precise but not accurate.
   d. They're neither accurate nor precise.

6. Which is NOT a disaccharide?
   a. Sucrose
   b. Lactose
   c. Maltose
   d. Mannose

7. How many mL of a 12.0 M stock solution of HCl should be added to water to create 250 mL of a 1.50 M solution of HCl?
   a. 31.2 mL
   b. 30.3 mL
   c. 31.35 mL
   d. 31.3 mL

8. If a reading is above the curve on a solubility curve, the solvent is considered to be which of the following?
   a. Unsaturated
   b. Supersaturated
   c. Stable
   d. Saturated

9. Which of the following correctly lists the maximum number of electrons that the first three orbitals can accommodate?
   a. 2, 4, 8
   b. 1, 4. 8
   c. 2, 2, 8
   d. 2, 8, 8

10. Which of the following is true regarding ionic bonds?
    a. The metallic substance usually transfers an electron to the nonmetal.
    b. The metallic substance often has a high electron affinity.
    c. The ionic substances formed have low melting and boiling points because of the relatively weak bonds.
    d. The formation of ionic bonds is an endothermic reaction.

11. What is the most electronegative element?
    a. Hydrogen
    b. Fluorine
    c. Oxygen
    d. Chlorine

12. In covalent bonding, how does the number of electrons involved in bonding affect bond length?
    a. The more electrons shared, the longer the bond.
    b. The more electrons shared, the shorter the bond.
    c. The more electrons transferred, the longer the bond.
    d. The more electrons transferred, the shorter the bond.

13. Which is the metric prefix for 10^{-3}?
    a. Milli
    b. Centi
    c. Micro
    d. Deci

14. Which of the following statements is true regarding Lewis structures for metallic compounds?
    a. Lewis structures are most accurate for metallic compounds because of the natural way electrons in metallic substances arrange themselves in rather predictable, geometric arrangements.
    b. Lewis structures are not common for metallic compounds because of the free-roaming ability of the electrons.
    c. A Lewis symbol for an element entering a metallic bond can have dots on just the bonded side of the compound, for a maximum of two dots.
    d. Lewis structures help visualize the electrons in metallic compounds more easily than in covalent structures where the electron sharing cannot be depicted well.

15. What is ionization energy?
    a. One-half the distance between the nuclei of atoms of the same element
    b. A measurement of the tendency of an atom to form a chemical bond
    c. The amount of energy needed to remove a valence electron from a gas or ion
    d. The ability or tendency of an atom to accept an electron into its valence shell

16. For gaseous reactants, how does decreasing the pressure in the system affect the reaction rate?
    a. The reaction rate increases because the frequency of collisions increases.
    b. The reaction rate increases because the frequency of collisions decreases.
    c. The reaction rate decreases because the frequency of collisions increases.
    d. The reaction rate decreases because the frequency of collisions decreases.

17. What can be said about the reaction described by the following generic chemical equation?

$$aA(s) + bB(aq) \leftrightarrow cC(s) + dD(aq)$$

a. The reaction is in static equilibrium.
b. The reaction is in dynamic equilibrium.
c. The reaction is in heterogenous equilibrium.
d. The reaction is in homogenous equilibrium.

18. Based on collision theory, what is the effect of temperature on the rate of chemical reaction?
a. Increasing the temperature slows the reaction.
b. Decreasing the temperature speeds up the reaction.
c. Increasing the temperature speeds up the reaction.
d. Collision theory and temperature are unrelated.

19. Burning a piece of paper is what type of change?
a. Chemical change
b. Physical change
c. Sedimentary change
d. Potential change

20. Which of the following is true?
a. A base acts as a proton donor in a chemical equation.
b. A base is an electron-pair acceptor in a chemical equation.
c. An acid increases the concentration of H^+ ions when it is dissolved in water.
d. An acid increases the concentration of OH^- ions when it is dissolved in water.

21. Which of the following is a synthesis reaction?
a. $2NO + O_2 \rightarrow 2NO_2$
b. $H_2CO_3 \rightarrow H_2O + CO_2$
c. $Mg + 2HCl \rightarrow MgCl_2 + H_2$
d. $Zn + 2HCl \rightarrow ZnCl_2 + H_2$

22. What type of reaction is $CH_4 + 2\,O_2 \rightarrow CO_2 + 2\,H_2O$?
a. Substitution Reaction
b. Combustion Reaction
c. Redox Reaction
d. Acid-Base Reaction

23. What is the percent yield for the reaction that produces 45 grams of CaO if 65 grams were expected out of the reaction $CaCO_3 \rightarrow CaO + CO_2$?
a. 6.9%
b. 69%
c. 144%
d. 14.4%

24. Which of the following statements is true?
   a. When an atom, ion, or molecule loses its electrons and becomes more positively charged, it has been reduced.
   b. When an atom, ion, or molecule loses its electrons and becomes more positively charged, it has been oxidized.
   c. When an atom, ion, or molecule loses its electrons and becomes more negatively charged, it has been oxidized.
   d. When an atom, ion, or molecule loses its electrons and becomes more negatively charged, it has been reduced.

25. Which of the following correctly shows a conjugate acid paired with its conjugate base?
   a. H_2SO_4 (acid) and HSO_4^- (conjugate base)
   b. HSO_4^- (acid) and H_2SO_4 (conjugate base)
   c. H_2SO_4 (acid) and HSO_4^+ (conjugate base)
   d. HSO_4^+ (acid) and H_2SO_4 (conjugate base)

26. Ice is a crystalline solid made up of repeating units of water molecules. Which choice does NOT describe a property of an ice cube?
   a. Has an exact melting point
   b. Breaks across a plane
   c. Becomes soft before it melts
   d. Breaks all bonds at the same time when it melts

27. What is the molecular formula for the molecule represented in the following Lewis diagram?

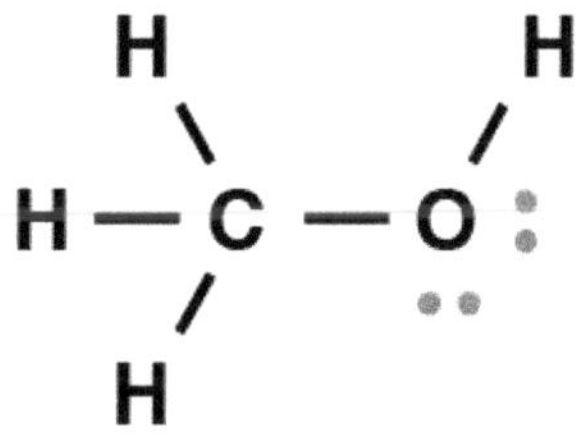

   a. $CH_3 - H_2O$
   b. CH_3
   c. CH_3O
   d. CH_3OH

28. What type of solid is a semiconductor similar to silicon?
   a. Metallic solid
   b. Neutral solid
   c. Ionic solid
   d. Covalent network solid

29. What type of reaction occurs when fossil fuels react with oxygen gas?
   a. Combustion
   b. Combination
   c. Vaporization
   d. Solidification

30. A piece of bone from an animal found at a site in New Mexico was dated using a radioactive carbon-14 method. It was determined that the bone contained 5.0 dpm (disintegrations per minute) per gram of carbon. If the half-life of carbon is 5730 years and the amount of carbon found in living animals is 15.0 dpm per gram of carbon, how old is the animal bone?

a. 6000 years
b. 5000 years
c. 20,000 years
d. 9,000 years

Anatomy and Physiology

1. Eosinophils are best described as which of the following?

a. A type of leukocyte that secretes histamine, which stimulates the inflammatory response.
b. The most abundant type of leukocyte that secretes substances that are toxic to pathogens.
c. A type of leukocyte found under mucous membranes that defends against multicellular parasites.
d. A type of circulating leukocyte that is aggressive and has high phagocytic activity.

2. Which of the following is one of the functions of the stratum basale layer of the epidermis?

a. Repelling water
b. Protecting against UV rays
c. Producing keratin
d. Producing oil to lubricate and protect the skin

3. Tendons connect what?

a. Muscle to muscle
b. Bone to bone
c. Muscle to bone
d. Muscle to ligament

4. How does cartilage obtain nutrients?

a. A network of fine capillaries
b. An extensive network of internal vasculature
c. Carrier proteins
d. Diffusion

5. In terms of levels of organization in the body, what is the next level up from cells? In other words, groups of cells are arranged into which of the following?

a. Organ systems
b. Atoms
c. Organs
d. Tissues

6. Which of the following is NOT one of the functions of sebum?

a. Protecting the skin from water loss
b. Moisturizing the skin
c. Helping with thermoregulation by assisting with evaporative cooling
d. Providing a chemical defense against bacterial and fungal infections

7. Which of the following statements accurately describes the basics of the sliding filament model of muscle contraction?
   a. Myosin filaments form and break cross-bridges with actin in order to pull the actin filaments closer to the M line.
   b. Actin filaments form and break cross-bridges with myosin in order to pull the myosin filaments closer to the M line.
   c. Myosin filaments form and break cross-bridges with actin in order to pull the actin filaments closer to the Z line.
   d. Actin filaments form and break cross-bridges with myosin in order to pull the myosin filaments closer to the Z line.

8. What is one of the characteristics of transitional epithelial tissue that differentiates it from other types of epithelial tissue?
   a. It is composed solely from a single layer of cells.
   b. It appears to be stratified, but it actually consists of only one layer of cells.
   c. It helps protect the body from invasions of microbes like bacteria and parasites.
   d. It can expand and contract.

9. What structures are made by the body's white blood cells to fight bacterial infections?
   a. Antibodies
   b. Antibiotics
   c. Vaccines
   d. Red blood cells

10. Which blood component is chiefly responsible for oxygen transport?
   a. Platelets
   b. Red blood cells
   c. White blood cells
   d. Plasma cells

11. Which of the following is NOT a bone of the axial skeleton?
   a. Sternum
   b. Mandible
   c. Ilium
   d. Atlas

12. Where does sperm maturation take place in the male reproductive system?
   a. Seminal vesicles
   b. Prostate gland
   c. Epididymis
   d. Vas deferens

13. Which hormone in the female reproductive system is responsible for progesterone production?
   a. FSH
   b. LH
   c. hCG
   d. Estrogen

14. Which epithelial tissue makes up the cell layer found in a capillary bed?
    a. Squamous
    b. Cuboidal
    c. Columnar
    d. Stratified

15. When considering anatomical direction, what is the position of the clavicle relative to the humerus?
    a. Lateral
    b. Medial
    c. Distal
    d. Inferior

16. Which structure serves as the electrical stimulator of the cardiac muscle?
    a. The sinoatrial node
    b. The left ventricle
    c. The aorta
    d. The tricuspid valve

17. How many neurons generally make up a sensory pathway?
    a. 1
    b. 2
    c. 3
    d. 4

18. In which part of the eye does visual processing begin?
    a. Cornea
    b. Optic nerve
    c. Retina
    d. Eyelid

19. Receptors in the dermis help the body maintain homeostasis by relaying messages to what area of the brain?
    a. The cerebellum
    b. The brain stem
    c. The pituitary gland
    d. The hypothalamus

20. The radius and ulna are to the humerus what the tibia and fibula are to the _________.
    a. mandible
    b. femur
    c. scapula
    d. carpal

21. The primary function of the endocrine system is to maintain which of the following?
    a. Heartbeat
    b. Respiration
    c. Electrolyte and water balance
    d. Homeostasis

22. Which of the following hormones is primarily responsible for regulating metabolism?
    a. Insulin
    b. Testosterone
    c. Adrenaline
    d. Thyroid hormone

23. Which characteristics are true for skeletal muscle?
    I. Contain sarcomeres
    II. Have multiple nuclei
    III. Are branched

    a. I only
    b. I and II only
    c. I, II, and III
    d. II and III only

24. Which nerve pathway is the simplest, and bypasses the brain?
    a. Autonomic
    b. Reflex arc
    c. Somatic
    d. Sympathetic

25. Using anatomical terms, what is the relationship of the sternum relative to the deltoid?
    a. Medial
    b. Lateral
    c. Superficial
    d. Posterior

26. Which of the following areas of the body has the highest density of sweat glands?
    a. Upper back
    b. Arms
    c. Palms/soles of the feet
    d. Head

27. Which statement is NOT true regarding brain structure?
    a. The corpus callosum connects the hemispheres.
    b. Broca's and Wernicke's areas are associated with speech and language.
    c. The cerebellum is important for long-term memory storage.
    d. The brainstem is responsible for involuntary movement.

28. Which is the first event to happen in a primary immune response?
    a. Macrophages ingest pathogens and present their antigens.
    b. Neutrophils aggregate and act as cytotoxic, nonspecific killers of pathogens.
    c. B lymphocytes make pathogen-specific antibodies.
    d. Helper T cells secrete interleukins to activate pathogen-fighting cells.

29. Which of the following is NOT considered to be a primary function of the proprioceptive system?
   a. Provide awareness of position and kinesthesia within the surroundings.
   b. Produce coordinated reflexes to maintain muscle tone and balance.
   c. Provide peripheral feedback information to the central nervous system to help modify movements and motor response.
   d. Provide cushioning to joints during impact.

30. Which of the following correctly explains the order of how muscle spindles sense the rate and magnitude of increasing muscle tension as the muscle lengthens?
   a. The muscle spindle is stretched, sensory neurons in the spindle are activated, an impulse is sent to the spinal cord, and motor neurons that innervate extrafusal fibers are signaled to relax.
   b. The muscle spindle is stretched, motor neurons in the spindle are activated, an impulse is sent to the spinal cord, and sensory neurons that innervate extrafusal fibers are signaled to relax.
   c. Sensory neurons in the spindle are activated, the muscle spindle is stretched, an impulse is sent to the spinal cord, and motor neurons that innervate extrafusal fibers are signaled to relax.
   d. The muscle spindle is stretched, sensory neurons in the spindle are activated, an impulse is sent to the spinal cord, and sensory neurons that innervate intrafusal fibers are signaled to relax.

Physics

1. Circular motion occurs around what?
   a. The center of mass
   b. The center of matter
   c. An elliptical
   d. An axis

2. Which of the following is true of an object at rest on Earth?
   a. It has no forces acting upon it.
   b. It has no gravity acting upon it.
   c. It is in transition.
   d. It is in equilibrium.

3. Which statement is true regarding electrostatic charges?
   a. Like charges attract.
   b. Like charges repel.
   c. Like charges are neutral.
   d. Like charges neither attract nor repel.

4. Which is NOT a form of energy?
   a. Light
   b. Sound
   c. Heat
   d. Mass

5. Which of the following is a vector quantity?
   a. Mass
   b. Length
   c. Velocity
   d. Speed

6. Why would a pencil appear to bend at the water line in a glass of water?
   a. The wood of the pencil becomes warped from being in the water.
   b. It appears to bend because of the refraction of light traveling from air to water.
   c. The pencil temporarily bends because of its immersion into separate mediums.
   d. The reflection of the light from water to a human's pupil creates the illusion of a warping object.

7. What is the current when a 3.0 V battery is wired across a lightbulb that has a resistance of 6.0 ohms?
   a. 0.5 A
   b. 18.0 A
   c. 0.5 J
   d. 18.0 J

8. The law of the conservation of energy states which of the following?
   a. Energy should be stored in power cells for future use.
   b. Energy will replenish itself once exhausted.
   c. Energy cannot be created or destroyed.
   d. Energy should be saved because it can run out.

9. Running electricity through a wire generates which of the following?
   a. A gravitational field
   b. A frictional field
   c. An acoustic field
   d. A magnetic field

10. Which of the following depicts a form of potential energy?
   a. The light given off by a lamp
   b. The gravitational pull of a black hole
   c. The heat from a microwaved burrito
   d. The motion of a pendulum

11. A car is traveling at a constant velocity of $25\ m/s$. How long does it take the car to travel 45 kilometers in a straight line?
   a. 1 hour
   b. 3,600 seconds
   c. 1,800 seconds
   d. 900 seconds

12. A ship is traveling due east at a speed of $1\ m/s$ against a current flowing due west at a speed of $0.5\ m/s$. How far has the ship travelled from its point of departure after two hours?
   a. 1.8 kilometers west of its point of departure
   b. 3.6 kilometers west of its point of departure
   c. 1.8 kilometers east of its point of departure
   d. 3.6 kilometers east of its point of departure

13. A car is driving along a straight stretch of highway at a constant speed of 60 km/hr when the driver slams the gas pedal to the floor, reaching a speed of 132 km/hr in 10 seconds. What's the average acceleration of the car after the engine is floored?

a. 1 m/s^2
b. 2 m/s^2
c. 3 m/s^2
d. 4 m/s^2

14. A spaceship with a mass of 100,000 kilograms is far away from any planet. To accelerate the craft at the rate of 0.5 m/s^2, what is the rocket thrust?

a. 98.1 N
b. 25,000 N
c. 50,000 N
d. 75,000 N

15. The gravitational acceleration on Earth averages 9.81 m/s^2. An astronaut weighs 1,962 N on Earth. The diameter of Earth is six times the diameter of its moon. What's the mass of the astronaut on Earth's moon?

a. 100 kilograms
b. 200 kilograms
c. 300 kilograms
d. 400 kilograms

16. Jerome ran out of gas and is pushing his car to the gas station down the road. Ignoring friction and air resistance, at what rate is his car accelerating?

a. 2.6 meters per second
b. 1.5 meters per second
c. 1.5 meters per second squared
d. 15 meters per second squared

17. The skater is shown spinning in Figure (a), then bringing in her arms in Figure (b). Which sequence accurately describes what happens to her angular velocity?

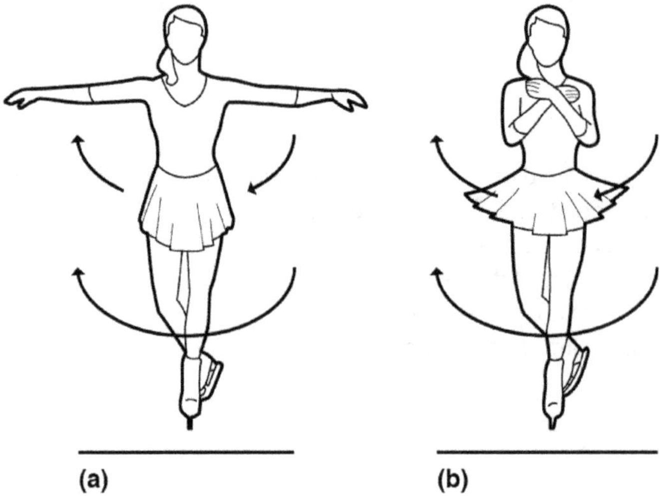

a. Her angular velocity decreases from (a) to (b).
b. Her angular velocity doesn't change from (a) to (b).
c. Her angular velocity increases from (a) to (b).
d. It's not possible to determine what happens to her angular velocity if her weight is unknown.

18. Which of the following is the minimum requirements of what must be present in order for current to flow?
a. A closed path for electrons
b. A battery and an open circuit
c. A closed path for electrons and a voltage
d. A battery or generator

19. The pendulum is held at point A, and then released to swing to the right. At what point does the pendulum have the greatest kinetic energy?

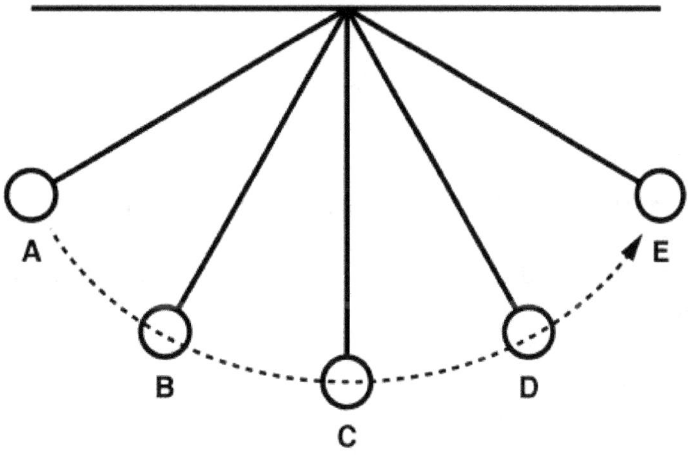

a. At Point B
b. At Point C
c. At Point D
d. At Point E

20. Which statement is true of the total energy of the pendulum?

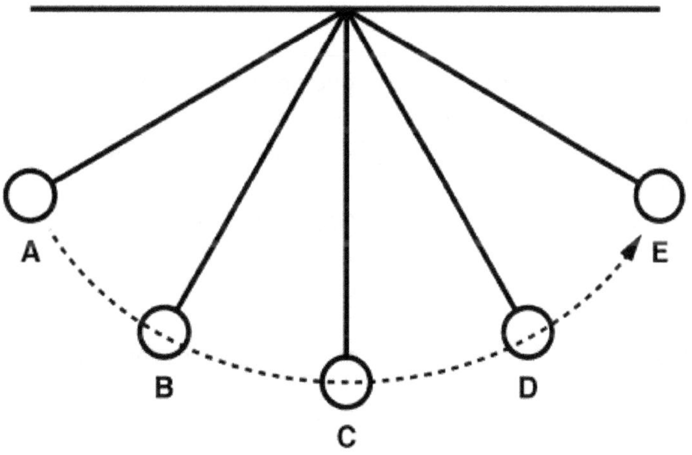

a. Its total energy is at a maximum and equal at Points A and E.
b. Its total energy is at a maximum at Point C.
c. Its total energy is the same at Points A, B, C, D, and E.
d. The total energy can't be determined without knowing the pendulum's mass.

21. Which of the following factors of projectile motion will remain constant across most, if not all, real-world examples of projectile motion?
a. The initial angle at which the projectile is released
b. The initial velocity with which the projectile is released
c. The acceleration the projectile undergoes after it is released
d. The length of time for which the projectile is in air

22. Noble gases like argon and xenon are known to be chemically inert, meaning they do not readily undergo chemical reactions. How many valence electrons do such elements possess?
a. Three
b. Four
c. Six
d. Eight

23. A racecar announcer reports that a racer's average velocity for the first ten laps of a race was 90 mph. Is this an accurate reporting of velocity?
a. Yes, the announcer reported the distance travelled by the racecar for a defined unit of time, which is how velocity is calculated.
b. No, velocity can only be calculated for a specific instance in time, and it therefore makes no sense to report someone's average velocity.
c. No, the announcer did not provide a direction for the racecar's movement; proper velocity measurements consist of both a speed and the direction of that speed.
d. No, velocity cannot be calculated using only a part of an object's motion; the racecar's actual average velocity could only be calculated once the race was over, and the car had come to rest again.

24. Which of the following physical quantities is considered a vector quantity?
a. Pressure
b. Force
c. Temperature
d. Mass

25. A negatively charged body is connected through a conductor to a positively charged body. Which of the following statements accurately describes the flow of electrons in such a system?
a. Electrons would remain stable, as the electrons from either body would repel electrons from the other, oppositely charged body.
b. Electrons would flow from the negative body to the positive body due to the lack of electrons present in the positive body.
c. Electrons would flow from the positive body to the negative body due to the lack of electrons present in the negative body.
d. Electrons from both bodies would flow into the conductor, connecting to each other and neutralizing the charge of either body.

26. For maximum torque to be applied, a man pushing a merry-go-round should hold the arm of the ride at which angle from the direction he applies force?
   a. 0°
   b. 30°
   c. 45°
   d. 90°

27. Which of the following statements accurately reflects the difference between specular and diffuse reflections?
   a. Specular reflections occur when light rays interact with a smooth surface like a mirror, whereas diffuse reflections occur when light rays interact with rougher surfaces.
   b. Specular reflections involve reflections that occur under a single source of light, whereas diffuse reflections occur only when multiple sources of light are present.
   c. Specular reflections occur when there is only a single angle of light present, whereas diffuse reflections occur when there are multiple angles of light present.
   d. Specular reflections occur when light bounces off multiple surfaces, whereas diffuse reflections occur when light bounces off a single surface.

28. Two students argue over the nature of light. One of them claims light acts like a particle, while the other insists light acts like a wave. According to our current understanding of the physics of light, which of these students is correct?
   a. The student who claims light acts like a particle.
   b. The student who insists light acts like a wave.
   c. Both students are correct.
   d. Neither student is correct.

29. A student slides a 2 kg brick across a floor at 10 m/s. If the coefficient of kinetic friction between the brick and the floor is 0.70, what is the magnitude of the kinetic friction acting on the brick, given that $F_f = \mu_k F_N$, $F_N = mg$, and $g = 10$?
   a. 0.14 N
   b. 0.35 N
   c. 14 N
   d. 35 N

30. A curling stone weighing 20 kgs hits a steel hockey puck weighing 1 kg with an acceleration of 2.0 m/s^2. Which of the following forces is greater?
   a. The force the curling stone imparts on the steel hockey puck
   b. The force the hockey puck imparts on the curling stone
   c. The force of friction that is imparted on both the curling stone and the steel hockey puck
   d. The force the curling stone imparts on the steel hockey puck and the force the steel hockey puck imparts on the curling stone are equally great.

Answer Explanations #1

Mathematics

1. D: Digits to the left of the decimal point represent the digit value times increasing multiples of 10 (first 1, then 10, 100, 1,000, and so on). Digits to the right of the decimal point represent the digit value divided by increasing multiples of 10 (first $\frac{1}{10}$, then $\frac{1}{100}$, $\frac{1}{1000}$, and so on). So the second digit to the right of the decimal point equals the digit value divided by 100.

2. B: Set up the problem and add each column, starting on the far right (ones). Add, carrying anything over 9 into the next column to the left. Solve from right to left.

3. A: The hundredths place value is located two digits to the right of the decimal point (the digit 9 in the original number). The digit to the right of the place value is examined to decide whether to round up or keep the digit. In this case, the digit 6 is greater than 5, so the hundredth place is rounded up. When rounding up, if the digit to be increased is a 9, the digit to its left is increased by one and the digit in the desired place value is made a zero. Therefore, the number is rounded to 847.90.

4. B: Fractions must have like denominators to be added. The common denominator is the least common multiple (LCM) of the two original denominators. In this case, the LCM is 15, so both fractions should be changed to equivalent fractions with a denominator of 15. Multiply the bottom of each fraction by whatever number is needed to produce 15, and multiply the top of each fraction by that same number:

$$\frac{1 \times 5}{3 \times 5} = \frac{5}{15} \text{ and } \frac{2 \times 3}{5 \times 3} = \frac{6}{15}$$

Now, add the numerators and keep the denominator the same:

$$\frac{5}{15} + \frac{6}{15} = \frac{11}{15}$$

5. A: Find a common denominator. 36 is a multiple of both 12 and 9, so we can use that. Multiply the top and bottom of each fraction by whatever number it takes to make the bottom 36.

$$\frac{7}{12} \times \frac{3}{3} + \frac{5}{9} \times \frac{4}{4} = \frac{21}{36} + \frac{20}{36}$$

Now add the numerators, keeping the same denominator.

$$\frac{21 + 20}{36} = \frac{41}{36}$$

Convert to a mixed number.

$$\frac{41}{36} = 1\frac{5}{36}$$

The numerator and denominator (5 and 36) do not have any factors in common, so this fraction can't be reduced.

6. D: To convert a fraction to a percent, we can first convert the fraction to a decimal. To do so, divide the numerator by the denominator: $4 \div 5 = 0.8$. To convert a decimal to a percent, multiply by 100:

$$0.8 \times 100 = 80\%$$

7. D: Set up the problem, with the larger number on top. Begin subtracting with the far-right column (ones). Borrow 10 from the column to the left when necessary.

8. D: A given number divides evenly by each of its factors to produce an integer (no decimals). To find the factors of 12, determine what whole numbers when multiplied equal 12. $1x12$, $2x6$, and $3x4$ are all the ways to multiply to 12 using whole numbers, so the factors of 12 are: 1, 2, 3, 4, 6, 12.

9. B: $\frac{1}{2}$ is the same fraction as $\frac{4}{8}$, and both would fill up the same portion of a number line.

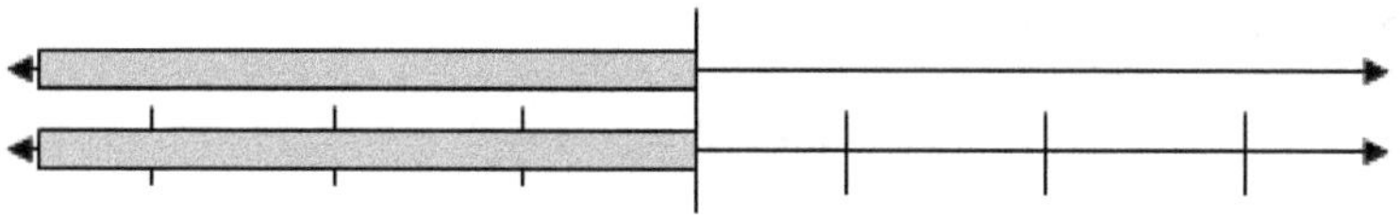

None of the other choices represent a pair of equivalent fractions, as seen below.

Choice *A:*

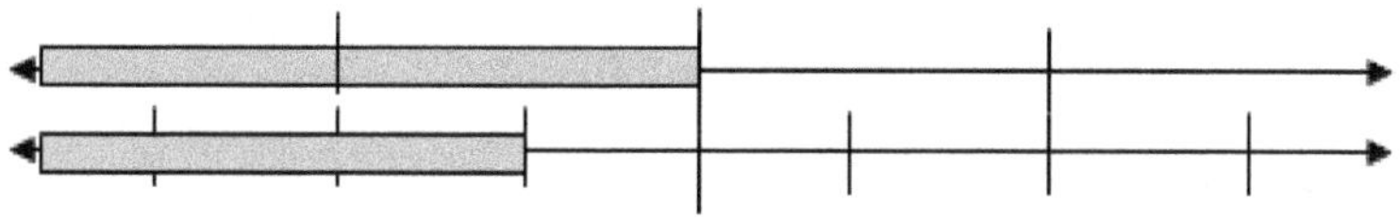

Choice *C:*

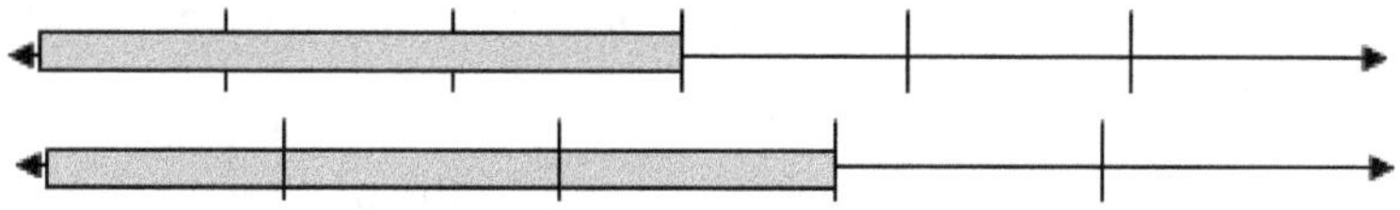

Choice *D:*

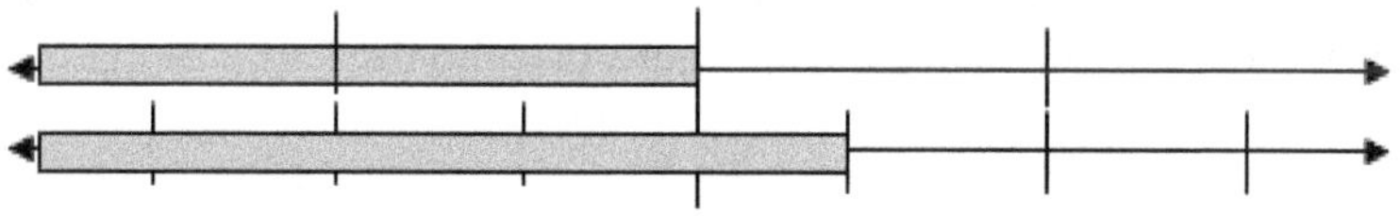

10. C: Set up the problem, with the larger number on top and numbers lined up at the decimal point. Insert 0 in any blank spots to the right of the decimal as placeholders. Begin subtracting with the far-right column. Borrow 10 from the column to the left when necessary.

11. A: Set up the problem and find a common denominator for both fractions.

$$\frac{19}{24} - \frac{1}{6}$$

Multiply the second fraction to convert to a common denominator.

$$\frac{19}{24} - \frac{1}{6} \times \frac{4}{4}$$

Once over the same denominator, subtract across the top.

$$\frac{19 - 4}{24} = \frac{15}{24}$$

Reduce by dividing the numerator and denominator by a common factor (3).

$$\frac{15}{24} = \frac{5}{8}$$

12. D: First, distribute the –3 on the left side:

$$-3x - 12 = x + 8$$

Subtract x from both sides:

$$-4x - 12 = 8$$

Add 12 to both sides to isolate the variable:

$$-4x = 20$$

Finally, divide both sides by –4 to solve:

$$x = -5$$

13. C: Line up the numbers (the number with the most digits on top) to multiply. Begin with the right column on top and the right column on bottom.

Move one column left on top and multiply by the far-right column on the bottom. Remember to carry over after you multiply.

Starting on the far-right column, on top, repeat this pattern for the next digit left on the bottom. Write the answers below the first line of answers. Remember to begin with a zero placeholder.

Continue the pattern.

Add the answer rows together, making sure they are still lined up correctly.

14. B: When solving for x, add 3 to both sides to get $4x = 8$. Then divide both sides by 4 to get $x = 2$.

15. B: $12 \times 750 = 9{,}000$

Therefore, there are 9,000 milliliters of water, which must be converted to liters. 1,000 milliliters equals 1 liter; therefore, 9 liters of water are purchased.

16. A: This problem can be solved using basic arithmetic. Xavier starts with 20 apples, then gives his sister half, which is 20 divided by 2.

$$\frac{20}{2} = 10$$

He then gives his neighbor 6, so 6 is subtracted from 10.

$$10 - 6 = 4$$

Finally, he uses $\frac{3}{4}$ of his remaining apples to make a pie. Since $\frac{3}{4}$ of 4 is 3, he uses 3 apples, so 3 is subtracted from 4.

$$4 - 3 = 1$$

17. D: 40% is $\frac{4}{10}$. The number itself must be $\frac{10}{4}$ of 12, or $\frac{10}{4} \times 12 = 10 \times 3 = 30$.

18. A: Convert these numbers to improper fractions: $\frac{11}{3} - \frac{9}{5}$. Take 15 as a common denominator.

$$\frac{11}{3} - \frac{9}{5} = \frac{55}{15} - \frac{27}{15} = \frac{28}{15} = 1\frac{13}{15}$$

19. C: Dividing by 100 means shifting the decimal point of the numerator to the left by 2. The result is 6.6 and rounds to 7.

20. B: Because these decimals are all negative, the number that is the largest will be the number whose absolute value is the smallest, as that will be the negative number that is "least negative" (closest to zero). To figure out which number has the smallest absolute value, look at the first non-zero digits. The first non-zero digit in Choice *B* is in the hundredths place. The other three all have non-zero digits in the tenths place, so Choice *B* is closest to zero; thus, it is the largest of the four negative numbers.

21. C: To solve for the value of b, isolate the variable b on one side of the equation.

Start by moving the lower value of –4 to the other side by adding 4 to both sides:

$$5b - 4 = 2b + 17$$

$$5b - 4 + 4 = 2b + 17 + 4$$

$$5b = 2b + 21$$

Then subtract $2b$ from both sides:

$$5b - 2b = 2b + 21 - 2b$$

$$3b = 21$$

Then, divide both sides by 3 to get the value of b:

$$\frac{3b}{3} = \frac{21}{3}$$

$$b = 7$$

22. C: $\frac{1}{3}$ of the shirts sold were patterned. Therefore, $1 - \frac{1}{3}$ (that is, $\frac{2}{3}$) of the shirts sold were solid. A fraction of something is calculated with multiplication, so $192 \times (1 - \frac{1}{3})$ solid shirts were sold. (We could calculate that this equals 128, but that's not necessary for this question.)

23. C: For each fraction, we can divide the numerator by the denominator to find a decimal value. $4/5 = 0.8$, $2/3 \approx 0.67$, and $91/100 = 0.91$. Ordering these from least to greatest gives us 0.67, 0.8, 0.85, and 0.91, which matches Choice *C*.

24. A: Set up the division problem.

$$\frac{5}{13} \div \frac{25}{169}$$

Flip the second fraction and multiply.

$$\frac{5}{13} \times \frac{169}{25}$$

Simplify and reduce with cross-multiplication.

$$\frac{1}{1} \times \frac{13}{5}$$

Multiply across the top and across the bottom to solve.

$$\frac{1 \times 13}{1 \times 5} = \frac{13}{5}$$

25. A: Divide 54 by 15:

$$\begin{array}{r} 3 \\ 15\overline{)54} \\ -45 \\ \hline 9 \end{array}$$

The result is 3 with a remainder of 9, which is equivalent to $3\frac{9}{15}$. Reduce the fraction $\frac{9}{15}$ for the final answer, $3\frac{3}{5}$.

26. A: Using the order of operations, multiplication and division are computed first from left to right. Multiplication is on the left; therefore, multiplication should be performed first.

27. D: The original number was $8\frac{3}{7}$. Multiply the denominator by the whole number portion. Add the numerator, and put the total over the original denominator.

$$\frac{(8 \times 7) + 3}{7} = \frac{59}{7}$$

28. B: The original number was $11\frac{5}{8}$. Multiply the denominator by the whole number portion. Add the numerator, and put the total over the original denominator.

$$\frac{(8 \times 11) + 5}{8} = \frac{93}{8}$$

29. B: To round 8.067 to the nearest tenth, use the digit in the hundredths place. The 6 in the hundredths place is greater than 5, so round up in the tenths place.

$$8.067$$

The 0 becomes a 1. Drop the digits after it.

$$8.1$$

30. A: We use the place value to the right of the thousandths place, which would be the ten-thousandths place. The value in the thousandths place is 7. The number in the place value to its right is greater than 4, so the 7 is bumped up to 8. Everything to its right is removed, giving us 245.268.

31. B: This is a division problem because the original amount needs to be split up into equal amounts. Although it's not required to answer the test question, we could solve Carey's problem as follows. The mixed number $11\frac{1}{2}$ should be converted to an improper fraction first:

$$11\frac{1}{2} = \frac{(11 \times 2) + 1}{2} = \frac{23}{2}$$

Carey needs to determine how many times $\frac{23}{2}$ goes into 184. This is a division problem:

$$184 \div \frac{23}{2} = ?$$

The fraction can be flipped, and the problem turns into multiplication:

$$184 \times \frac{2}{23} = \frac{368}{23}$$

This improper fraction can be simplified into 16 because $368 \div 23 = 16$. The answer is 16 lawn segments.

32. B: 100 cm is equal to 1 m. 1.3 divided by 100 is 0.013. Therefore, 1.3 cm is equal to 0.013 m. Because 1 cm is equal to 10 mm, 1.3 cm is equal to 13 mm.

33. B: Using the conversion rate $1\ lb = 0.45\ kg$, 25 is multiplied by 0.45 to convert the projected weight loss from 25 pounds to 11.25 kg.

34. D: Start by taking a common denominator of 30.

$$\frac{14}{15} = \frac{28}{30}$$

$$\frac{3}{5} = \frac{18}{30}$$

$$\frac{1}{30} = \frac{1}{30}$$

Add and subtract the numerators for the next step.

$$\frac{28}{30} + \frac{18}{30} - \frac{1}{30} = \frac{28 + 18 - 1}{30} = \frac{45}{30} = \frac{3}{2}$$

In the last step the 15 is factored out from the numerator and denominator.

35. C: A ratio written as $a:b$ has an equivalent fractional form of $\frac{a}{b}$. Therefore, $18:12$ is equivalent to $\frac{18}{12}=\frac{3}{2}$. $\frac{6}{4}$ reduces to $\frac{3}{2}$. $\frac{36}{24}$ reduces to $\frac{3}{2}$ as well. Choice *C* is $4:3$, which is the same as $\frac{4}{3}$. This option is not equal to the other three values.

36. C: Break down the number into parts:

$$517 = 500 + 10 + 5 + 2$$

500 is represented by D, 10 is represented by X, 5 is represented by V, and 2 is represented by II. Combine these to form DXVII.

37. A: For military (24-hour) times of 1300 and higher, subtract 12 from the hours (the first two digits) and make the time p.m. For 1500, we find $15 - 12 = 3$, so the time is 3:00 p.m.

38. D: To take the product of two fractions, just multiply the numerators and denominators.

$$\frac{5}{3} \times \frac{7}{6} = \frac{5 \times 7}{3 \times 6} = \frac{35}{18}$$

The numerator and denominator have no common factors, so this is simplified completely.

39. A: A common denominator must be found. The least common denominator is 15 because it has both 5 and 3 as factors. The fractions must be rewritten using 15 as the denominator.

40. B: Anything before noon converts over from its a.m. value.

41. D: There are 1,000 meters per kilometer, and 100 centimeters per meter, so we can calculate:

$$1\text{ km} \times \frac{1{,}000\text{ m}}{1\text{ km}} \times \frac{100\text{ cm}}{1\text{ m}} = 100{,}000\text{ cm}$$

42. A: Operations within the parentheses must be completed first. Division is completed next, and finally, addition. When adding decimals, digits within each place value are added together. Therefore, the expression is evaluated as:

$$(2 \times 20) \div (7 + 1) + (6 \times 0.01) + (4 \times 0.001)$$

$$40 \div 8 + 0.06 + 0.004$$

$$5 + 0.06 + 0.004 = 5.064$$

43. D: By rearranging and grouping the factors in Choice *D*, we can notice that $3 \times 3 \times 4 \times 2 = (3 \times 2) \times (4 \times 3) = 6 \times 12$, which is what we were looking for. Alternatively, each of the answer choices could multiplied out and compared to the original value. 6×12 has a value of 72. The answer choices respectively have values of 64, 84, 108, and 72, so answer *D* is the correct choice.

44. C: A dollar contains 20 nickels. Therefore, if there are 12 dollars' worth of nickels, there are $12 \times 20 = 240$ nickels. Each nickel weighs 5 grams. Therefore, the weight of the nickels is $240 \times 5 = 1{,}200$ grams. To find the total weight of the filled piggy bank, add the weight of the nickels and the weight of the empty bank:

$$1{,}200 + 1{,}050 = 2{,}250\text{ grams.}$$

45. D: To find Denver's total snowfall, multiply $27\frac{3}{4}$ by 3. To do this, convert the mixed number into an improper fraction.

$$27\frac{3}{4} = \frac{27 \times 4 + 3}{4} = \frac{111}{4}$$

Therefore, Denver had approximately $\frac{3 \times 111}{4} = \frac{333}{4}$ inches of snow. The improper fraction can be converted back into a mixed number through division.

$$\frac{333}{4} = 83\ \frac{1}{4}\text{ inches}$$

46. C: List out and set up equivalencies.

$$8\text{ pts} = 1\text{ gal}$$

Set up the equivalencies with the initial values.

$$\frac{15\text{ gal}}{1} \times \frac{8\text{ pts}}{1\text{ gal}}$$

Cross-cancel units then multiply across the top and the bottom.

$$\frac{15\ \times 8\text{ pts}}{1} = 120\text{ pts}$$

47. B: Set up the equation for converting Celsius to Fahrenheit.

$$°\text{F} = \frac{9}{5} \times °\text{C} + 32$$

Fill in the givens.

$$°\text{F} = \frac{9}{5} \times 37.4 + 32$$

Solve the equation in in parentheses. Multiply, then add.

$$°\text{F} = 67.32 + 32$$

$$°\text{F} = 99.32\ °\text{F}$$

48. C: The first step in solving this problem is expressing the result in fraction form. Multiplication and division are typically performed in order from left to right, but they can be performed in any order. For this problem, let's start with the division operation between the last two fractions. When dividing one fraction by another, invert or flip the second fraction and then multiply the numerators and denominators.

$$\frac{7}{10} \times \frac{2}{1} = \frac{14}{10}$$

Next, multiply the first fraction by this value:

$$\frac{3}{5} \times \frac{14}{10} = \frac{42}{50}$$

In this instance, to find the decimal form, we can multiply the numerator and denominator by 2 to get 100 in the denominator.

$$\frac{42}{50} \times \frac{2}{2} = \frac{84}{100}$$

In decimal form, this would be expressed as 0.84.

49. D: Setting up a proportion is the easiest way to represent this situation. The proportion is $\frac{20}{x} = \frac{40}{100}$, and cross-multiplication can be used to solve for x. Here, $40x = 2{,}000$, so $x = 50$. The answer can also be found by viewing the two fractions as equivalent, knowing that 20 is half of 40, and 50 is half of 100.

50. D: "Sum" means the result of adding, so "the sum of twice a number and one" can be written as $2x + 1$. Next, "three times the sum of twice a number and one" would be $3(2x + 1)$. Finally, "six less than three times the sum of twice a number and one" would be $3(2x + 1) - 6$.

51. B: If 60% of 50 workers are women, then there are 30 women working in the office. If half of them are wearing skirts, then that means 15 women wear skirts. Since nobody else wears skirts, this means there are 15 people wearing skirts.

52. A: Convert the mixed fractions to improper fractions: $\frac{61}{8} - \frac{16}{5}$. Subtract using 40 as a common denominator, and rewrite to get rid of the improper fraction:

$$\frac{61}{8} - \frac{16}{5} = \frac{305}{40} - \frac{128}{40} = \frac{177}{40} = 4\frac{17}{40}$$

53. B: Multiplying by 10^{-3} means moving the decimal point three places to the left, putting in zeros as necessary.

54. C: We know that red cans are $1 each and blue cans are $2 each. Since the total cost is $16, we can say that $r \times 1 + b \times 2 = 16$, where r is the number of red cans and b is the number of blue cans. We can write this equation more simply as $r + 2b = 16$.

Because Jessica buys 10 cans total, we know that $r + b = 10$, so $b = 10 - r$. Substituting in $10 - r$ for b in the original equation, we get $r + 2(10 - r) = 16$. Simplifying and solving for r, we find:

$$r + 20 - 2r = 16$$

$$20 - r = 16$$

$$r = 4$$

55. D: The first field has an area of 1,000 square feet, so the length of one side is $\sqrt{1{,}000} = \sqrt{100}\sqrt{10} = 10\sqrt{10}$. Since there are four sides to a square, the total perimeter is $40\sqrt{10}$. The second square has an area of 10 square feet, so the length of one side is $\sqrt{10}$, and the perimeter is $4\sqrt{10}$. Adding these together gives:

$$40\sqrt{10} + 4\sqrt{10} = (40 + 4)\sqrt{10} = 44\sqrt{10}$$

Reading Comprehension

1. C: Choice *C* is the correct answer because it most extensively summarizes the entire passage. While Choices *A* and *B* are reasonable possibilities, they reference portions of Gulliver's experiences, not the whole. Choice *D* is incorrect because Gulliver doesn't express repentance or sorrow in this particular passage.

2. A: Principal refers to *chief* or *primary* within the context of this text. Choice *A* is the answer that most closely aligns with this definition. Choices *B* and *D* make reference to a helper or follower, while Choice *C* doesn't meet the description of Reldresal from the passage.

3. C: One can reasonably infer that Gulliver is considerably larger than the children who were playing around him because multiple children could fit into his hand. Choice *A* is incorrect because there is no indication of stress in Gulliver's tone. Choices *B* and *D* aren't the best answer because though Gulliver seems fond of his new acquaintances, he didn't travel there with the intention of meeting new people or to express a definite love for them in this particular portion of the text.

4. C: The emperor made a definitive decision to expose Gulliver to their native customs. In this instance, the word *mind* was not related to a vote, question, or cognitive ability.

5. A: The assertion in Choice *A* does *not* support the fact that games are a commonplace event in this culture because it mentions conduct, not games. Choices *B*, *C*, and *D* are incorrect because these do support the fact that games are a commonplace event.

6. B: The point of this passage is to show what drowning looks like. Choice *A* is incorrect because while drowning is a danger of swimming, the passage doesn't include any other dangers. The passage is not intended for lifeguards specifically, but for a general audience, so Choice *C* is incorrect. There are a few signs of drowning, but the passage does not compare them; thus, Choice *D* is incorrect.

7. D: Choice *A* is incorrect because although the Adirondack region is mentioned in the text, there is no cause or effect relationships between the region and fish hatcheries depicted here. Choice *B* is incorrect because the text does not have an agenda, but rather is meant to inform the audience. Finally, Choice *C* is incorrect because the text says nothing of how sun-fish mate.

8. B: The text explains in the second paragraph that the female sun-fish "builds, with her tail and snout, a circular embankment 3 inches in height and 2 thick." Choice *A* is used in the text as a simile.

9. D: The concluding sequence is expressed in the phrase "[t]he mother sun-fish, having now built or provided her 'hatchery.'" The final detail is the way in which the sun-fish guards the enclosure.

10. C: *Extraneous* most nearly means *superfluous*, or *trivial*. Choice *A*, *indispensable*, is incorrect because it means the opposite of *extraneous*. Choice *B*, *bewildering*, means *confusing* and is not relevant to the context of the sentence. Finally, Choice *D* is incorrect because although the prefix of the word is the same, ex-, the word exuberant means elated or enthusiastic, and is irrelevant to the context of the sentence.

11. A: This is a challenging question because the author's purpose is somewhat open-ended. The author concludes by stating that the questions regarding human perception and observation can be approached from many angles. Thus, they do not seem to be attempting to prove one thing or another. Choice *B* is incorrect because nothing suggests that the electron experiment is related to astroparticle physics, or that the discovery is recent. Choice *C* is a broad generalization that does not reflect accurately on the writer's views. While the author does appear to reflect on opposing views of human understanding, Choice *D*, the best answer is Choice *A*.

12. C: The beginning of this paragraph literally "presents a conundrum," explains the problem of partial understanding, and then ends with more questions, or inquiry. There is no solution offered in this paragraph, making Choices *A* and *B* incorrect. Choice *D* is incorrect because the paragraph does not begin with a definition.

13. D: Looking back in the text, the author describes that classical philosophy holds that understanding can be reached by careful observation. This will not work if they are overly invested or biased in their pursuit. Choices *A* and *C* are in no way related and are completely unnecessary. A specific theory is not necessary to understanding, according to classical philosophy mentioned by the author. Again, the key to understanding is observing the phenomena outside of it, without bias or predisposition. Thus, Choice *B* is wrong.

14. B: Choices *A* and *C* are incorrect because such movement is not mentioned at all in the text. In the passage, the author says that electrons that were physically observed appeared to pass through one hole or another. Remember, the electrons that were observed doing this were described as acting like particles. Therefore, Choice *D* is incorrect. Recall that the plate actually recorded electrons passing through both holes simultaneously and hitting the plate. This behavior, the electron activity that wasn't seen by humans, was characteristic of waves. Thus, Choice *B* is the correct answer.

15. C: The author mentions "gravity" to demonstrate an example of natural phenomena humans discovered and understood without the use of tools or machines. Choice *A* mirrors the language in the beginning of the paragraph but is incorrect in its intent. Choice *B* is incorrect; the paragraph mentions nothing of "not knowing the true nature of gravity." Choice *D* is incorrect as well. There is no mention of an "alternative solution" in this paragraph.

16. A: The important thing to keep in mind is that we must choose a scenario that best parallels, or is most similar to, the discovery of the experiment mentioned in the passage. The important aspects of the experiment can be summed up like so: humans directly observed one behavior of electrons, and then, through analyzing a tool (the plate that recorded electron hits), discovered that there was another electron behavior that could not be physically seen by human eyes. This summary best parallels the scenario in Choice *A*. Like Feynman, the colorblind person can observe one aspect of the world but through the special goggles (a tool), he is able to see a natural phenomenon that he could not physically see on his own. While Choice *D* is compelling, the x-ray helps humans see the broken bone, but it does not necessarily reveal that the bone is broken in the first place. The other choices do not parallel the scenario in question. Therefore, Choice *A* is the best choice.

17. B: The author would not agree that technology renders human observation irrelevant. Choice *A* is incorrect because much of the passage discusses how technology helps humans observe what cannot be seen with the naked eye; therefore, the author would agree with this statement. This line of reasoning is also why the author would agree with Choice *D,* making it incorrect as well. As indicated in the second paragraph, the author seems to think that humans create inventions and tools with the goal of studying phenomena more precisely. This indicates increased understanding as people recognize limitations and develop items to help bypass the limitations and learn. Therefore, Choice *C* is incorrect as well.

18. B: The word *conundrum* most nearly means *enigma*, which is a mystery or riddle. *Platitude* means a banal or overused saying. *Solution* is incorrect here; and *hypothesis* implies a theory or assumption, so this is also incorrect.

19. A: The thesis' best evidence is found in this paragraph because of the experiment depicting how electrons behave in a dual nature. Choice *B* is incorrect; the paragraph mentions nothing about the experiment being unethical. Choice *C* is incorrect; this is characteristic of the first paragraph. Choice *D* is incorrect; this is more characteristic of the second paragraph.

20. D: The author explains that Boethianism is a Medieval theological philosophy that attributes sin to temporary pleasure and righteousness with virtue and God's providence. Other than Choice *D*, the choices listed are all physical things. While these could still be divine rewards, Boethianism holds that the reward for being virtuous is God's favor. It is also stressed in the article that physical pleasures cannot be taken into the afterlife. Therefore, the best choice is *D*, God's favor.

21. C: Choices *A* and *B* are generalized statements, and we have no evidence to support Choice *B*. Choice *D* is very compelling, but it looks at Boethianism in a way that the author does not. The author does not mention "different levels of Boethianism" when discussing the tales, only that the concept appears differently in different tales. Boethianism also doesn't focus on enlightenment.

22. D: Choice *A* is incorrect; while the text does mention thieves ravaging others' possessions, it is only meant as an example and not as the principle itself. Choice *B* is incorrect for the same reason as Choice *A*. Choice *C* is mentioned in the text and is part of the example that proves the principle, but it is not the principle itself.

23. C: The word *avarice* most nearly means *covetousness*, or extremely desirous of money or wealth. Choice *A* means evil or mischief and does not relate to the context of the sentence. Choice *B* is also incorrect, because *pithiness* means shortness or conciseness. Choice *D* is close because *precariousness* means dangerous or instability, which goes well with the context. However, we are told of the summoner's specific characteristic of greed, which makes Choice *C* the best answer.

24. D: Boethianism acknowledges desire as something that leads out of holiness, so Choice *A* is incorrect. Choice *B* is incorrect because in the passage, Boethianism is depicted as being wary of desire and anything that binds people to the physical world. Choice *C* can be eliminated because the author never says that desire indicates demonic possession.

25. A: The passage discusses recent technological advances in cars and suggests that this trend will continue in the future with self-driving cars. Choice *B* and *C* are not true, so these are both incorrect. Choice *D* is also incorrect because the passage suggests continuing growth in technology, not a peak.

26. C: In the final sentence of the first paragraph, it is stated that avarice can prevent a man from being necessitously poor, but too timorous, or fearful, to achieve real wealth. According to the passage, avarice does not tend to make a person very wealthy. The passage states that oppression, not avarice, is the consequence of wealth. The passage does not state that avarice drives a person's desire to be wealthy.

27. D: Paine believes that the distinction that is beyond a natural or religious reason is between king and subjects. Choice *A* is incorrect because he states that the distinction between good and bad is made in heaven. Choice *B* is incorrect because he states that the distinction between male and female is natural. Choice *C* is incorrect because he does not mention anything about the distinction between humans and animals.

28. A: The passage states that the Heathens were the first to introduce government by kings into the world. Choice *B* is incorrect because the quiet lives of patriarchs came before the Heathens introduced this type of government, and Paine puts it in opposition to government by kings. Choice *C* is incorrect because it was Christians, not Heathens, who paid divine honors to living kings. Heathens honored deceased kings. Choice *D* is incorrect because, while equal rights of nature are mentioned in the paragraph, they are not mentioned in relation to the Heathens.

29. B: Paine doesn't say it is against the laws of nature, so Choice *A* is incorrect. He cites parts of scripture that he claims denounce monarchy, so Choices *C* and *D* are incorrect.

30. A: To be *idolatrous* is to worship someone or something other than God, in this case, kings. Choice *B* is incorrect because it is not defined as being deceitful. Choice *C* is incorrect because, while idolatry is considered a sin, it is an example of a sin, not a synonym for it. Choice *D* is incorrect because, while idolatry may have been considered illegal in some cultures, it is not a definition for the term.

31. A: The essential meaning of the passage is that the Almighty, God, disapproves of this type of government. Choice *B* is incorrect because, while heaven is mentioned, it is done so to suggest that the monarchical government is irreverent, not that heaven isn't promised. Choice *C* is incorrect because God's disapproval is mentioned, not his punishment. Choice *D* is incorrect because the passage refers to the Jewish monarchy, which required both belief in God and kings, and the tendency of monarchies to gloss over the anti-monarchical passages of scripture to support their form of government.

32. A: The word *timorous* means being full of fear. The author concludes that extreme greed (avarice) makes people too afraid to be prosperous.

33. B: The author's attitude is closest to Choice *B,* impassioned and critical. Choice *A* is incorrect; the author is not indifferent or fatigued—on the contrary, there is a lot of energy and some underlying passion in the writing. Choice *C* is incorrect; the word *enchanted* means delighted, and the author is more critical and concerned of a monarchial government than enchanted with it. Choice *D* is not the best answer; although the author is passionate and critical of a monarchy, there is more logic than anger coming from the words.

34. B: Choice *A* is incorrect; the author does not agree that heathens were more advanced than Christians in this paragraph; the paragraph only explains the catalyst of the monarchial systems. Choice *C* is incorrect; the author would in fact disagree with the divinity of English monarchs. Choice *D* is incorrect; the paragraph does believe that monarchs cause damage, but the paragraph does not act as a counterargument to the one preceding it.

35. D: The author clearly states that God created men equal and that no one was elevated above anyone else until the nation of Israel, and other heathen nations, chose to put a king over them as their ruler. This is seen as something bad to the author because he says that God would not share his authority with anyone else. God did not create the role of kings, Choice *B*, but according to the author he warned against it. The common consensus was clearly not that all men were equal, Choice *C*, otherwise they would not have created one man to be the king. Since the author says it was a sin to have a king, Choice *D* could not be correct either.

36. A: The purpose is to inform the reader about what assault is and how it is committed. Choice *B* is incorrect because the passage does not state that assault is a lesser form of lethal force, only that an assault can use lethal force, or alternatively, lethal force can be utilized to counter a dangerous assault. Choice *C* is incorrect because the passage is informative and does not have a set agenda. Finally, Choice *D* is incorrect because although the author uses an example in order to explain assault, it is not indicated that this is the author's personal account.

37. C: If the man being attacked in an alley used lethal force in self-defense against the man with a knife, it would not be considered illegal. The presence of a deadly weapon indicates malicious intent, and because the individual is isolated in an alley, lethal force in self-defense may be the only way to preserve his life. Choices *A* and *B* can be ruled out because in these situations no one is in danger of immediate death or bodily harm by someone else. Choice *D* is an assault and does exhibit intent to harm, but this situation isn't severe enough to merit lethal force; there is no intent to kill.

38. B: As discussed in the second passage, there are several forms of assault, like assault with a deadly weapon, verbal assault, or threatening posture or language. Choice *A* is incorrect because the author does not mention what the charges are on assaults; therefore, we cannot assume that they are more or less than unnecessary use of force charges. Choice *C* is incorrect because anyone is capable of assault; the author does not state that one group of people cannot commit assault. Choice *D* is incorrect because assault is never justified. Self-defense resulting in lethal force can be justified.

39. D: The statement in Choice *D* would most undermine the last part of the passage because it directly contradicts how the law evaluates the use of lethal force. Choices *A* and *B* are stated in the paragraph, so they do not undermine the explanation from the author. Choice *C* does not necessarily undermine the passage, but it does not support the passage either. It is more of an opinion that does not offer strength or weakness to the explanation.

40. C: Choice *C* is correct because it clearly establishes what both assault and lethal force are and gives the specific way in which the two concepts meet. Choice *A* is incorrect because lethal force doesn't necessarily result in assault. This is also why Choice *B* is incorrect. Not all assaults would necessarily be life-threatening to the point where lethal force is needed for self-defense. Choice *D* is compelling but ultimately incorrect; the statement touches on aspects of the two ideas but fails to present the concrete way in which the two are connected to each other.

41. A: Choice *D* is incorrect because while the passages utilize examples to help explain the concepts discussed, the author doesn't indicate that they are specific court cases. It's also clear that the passages don't open with examples, but instead, they begin by defining the terms addressed in each passage. This eliminates Choice *B,* and ultimately reveals Choice *A* to be the correct answer. Choice *A* accurately outlines the way both passages are structured. Because the passages follow a nearly identical structure, Choice *C* can easily be ruled out.

42. C: Choices *A* and *B* are incorrect because it is clear in both passages that intent is a prevailing theme in both lethal force and assault. Choice *D* is compelling, but if a person uses lethal force to defend himself or herself, the intent of the defender is also examined in order to help determine if there was excessive force used. Choice *C* is correct because it states that intent is important for determining both lethal force and assault, and that intent is used to gauge the severity of the issues. Remember, just as lethal force can escalate to excessive use of force, there are different kinds of assault. Intent dictates several different forms of assault.

43. B: The example is used to demonstrate a single example of two different types of assault and then adds in a third type of assault in its conclusion. The example mainly provides an instance of "threatening body language" and "provocative language" with the homeowner gesturing threats to his neighbor. It ends the example by adding a third type of assault: physical strikes. This example is used to show the variant nature of assaults. Choice *A* is incorrect because it doesn't mention the "physical strike" assault at the end and is not specific enough. Choice *C* is incorrect because the example does not say anything about the definition of lethal force or how it might be altered. Choice *D* is incorrect because the example mentions nothing about cause and effect.

44. C: The word *apprehension* most nearly means fear. The passage indicates that "assault is an unlawful and intentional act that causes reasonable fear/anxiety in another individual, either by an imminent threat or by initiating offensive contact." The creation of fear in another individual seems to be a property of assault.

45. D: The last paragraph of the first passage states what the term "last resort" means and how it's distinguished in the eyes of the law.

46. B: The correct answer is an infectious disease. By reading and understanding the context of the passage, all other options can be eliminated since the author restates zymosis as disease.

47. D: The ability to identify the BRCA gene enables doctors to prevent cancer by removing the site of the cancer. As such, it functions as preventive medicine. Choice *A* is incorrect. Knowing which gene mutation causes breast cancer does not help with treatment because the cancer can still occur if preventive action isn't taken. Choice *B* is incorrect. Being able to identify the gene and prevent the disease from forming does not eradicate it. Choice *C* is incorrect. Tailored medicine enables doctors to tailor treatments based on a person's genetic makeup. Identifying the BRCA gene does not enable tailored medicine because the treatment is used on any and all individuals with the gene mutation.

48. B: The fact that there are more than 250 medications tailored to match genetic specifications demonstrates how powerful and successful pharmacogenomics has been. Choice *A* is incorrect. Although likely true, it may demonstrate the need for pharmacogenomics but not the successes. Choice *C* and Choice *D* are incorrect. They discuss how pharmacogenomics helps but do not support the success.

49. B: The passage lists the very real and concrete changes to medicine introduced and created based on genomic information. Choice *A* is incorrect. Genetic mutations and their identification are valuable; however, it's the treatment and response to those mutations that demonstrate the true power of genomics. Choice *C* is incorrect. Medical researchers are not cited. Choice *D* is incorrect. The author does not discuss the opinions of those who oppose such research.

50. C: Paragraph 6 states clearly that the potential of Cas9 is to enable gene editing to eradicate diseases before they start. Choice *A* is incorrect. Cas9 is a naturally occurring enzyme and does not need pharmaceuticals. Choice *B* is incorrect. Cas9 facilitates treatment, not diagnosis. Choice *D* is incorrect because, again, it facilitates treatment, not detection.

51. A: The very last line of the passage indicates that the author is hopeful for future advancements. Choice *B* is incorrect. Resigned would suggest defeated, and the author is the opposite of that. Choice *C* and Choice *D* are incorrect. The author is neither opposed nor concerned. Both of these would contradict the hopeful tone and language used within the passage.

52. B: The author presents information that discusses gene research and the application to inform readers. Choice *A* is incorrect. There is no language to persuade readers to support or oppose further gene research. Choice *C* is incorrect. Although medical treatments are described, it's done to support the overall goal of providing information. The procedures are not described in enough detail to make the passage descriptive. Choice *D* is incorrect. That goal is very general, and the passage is quite specific and related to gene research and medicine.

53. C: The fact that researchers have identified 2000 different disease genes supports the larger idea that genomic research has facilitated disease identification and diagnosis. Choice *A* is incorrect. A main idea is a larger idea or statement, such as genomics have facilitated disease diagnosis. Choice *B* is incorrect. A topic sentence establishes the main focus of a paragraph. In this case, the main topic of the paragraph is disease diagnosis. Choice *D* is incorrect. Statistics analyze and interpret the significance of data. The 2000 number is the approximate number of diseases, not a number for that is being analyzed along with other data to determine significance.

54. A: The topic of the passage is Caribbean island destinations. The topic of the passage can be described in a one- or two-word phrase. Remember, when paraphrasing a passage, it is important to include the topic. Paraphrasing is when one puts a passage into their own words.

55. C: Family or adult-only resorts and activities are supporting details in this passage. Supporting details are details that help readers better understand the main idea. They answer questions such as who, what, where, when, why, or how. In this question, cruises and local events are not discussed in the passage, whereas family and adult-only resorts and activities support the main idea.

Vocabulary

1. C: As a prefix, *contra-* means opposite or against. In this case, *contralateral* means on the opposite side of the body.

2. A: *Distended* means enlarged or expanded. A *distended* stomach or other organ is bloated or swollen because of internal pressure.

3. B: *Precipitously* means rapidly, abruptly, or steeply. *Concisely* means in a few words or efficiently worded, *contingently* refers to something that will occur only if something else happens first, and *preemptively* means something taken as a precaution or measure against an anticipated risk or problem, often as a way to try and prevent it.

4. A: In a medical context, a *patent* vessel is unobstructed and open. An atherosclerotic vessel with deposited plaques would probably not be *patent.*

5. B: Symmetrical describes an object that is uniform across an axis. The body is symmetrical because it is the same across a horizontal axis: there are two eyes, arms, legs, etc. Choice *A* is incorrect because something that has two sides is bilateral. Choices *C* and *D* are incorrect because symmetry requires the sides be even and proportional.

6. C: A *latent* disease is present but not detectable in a symptomatic way. It may be dormant, but it has the potential to become symptomatic in the future with discernable manifestations for the patient.

7. D: Labile means something is subject to change. A labile patient describes someone whose emotions change rapidly and easily. Choice *A* is incorrect because inflexible means rigid and unchanging, which is the opposite of labile. Choice *B* is incorrect because reliable means steady, which is the opposite of labile. Choice *C* is incorrect because concerned describes someone who is worried or anxious.

8. B: To ingest means to consume, or swallow. Toxic materials should not be ingested because they can cause significant harm to the body. Choice *A* is incorrect because while toxic materials should not be touched, it is not the same as ingesting. Choice *C* is incorrect because inhale means to breathe in. Choice *D* is incorrect because spill refers to material that has been knocked out of its container.

9. B: Acute illnesses have a sudden or rapid onset. An *acute* illness is the opposite of a *chronic* one, which is a disease that the patient has had for a long time. A sinus infection is an acute illness, while multiple sclerosis is a chronic one.

10. D: *Virulent* means sever and harmful. *Patent* means open, *innocuous* means harmless, and *latent* means dormant.

11. C: An adverse reaction to a medication is an *undesirable* side effect or consequence of taking the drug.

12. B: *Insidious* means so gradual that it's hardly apparent. *Precipitous* means rapid or steep, *incipient* means emergent or at an initial state, and *paroxysmal* means a sudden intensification or recurrence of symptoms, as in a paroxysmal attack of a muscle spasm in the lumbar spine.

13. C: Primary means first or main; the doctor's main concern was about a lack of appetite, which normally indicates an illness. Choice *A* is incorrect because compensatory describes a payment to make up for a loss. Choice *B* is incorrect because bilateral means that an object has two sides. Choice *D* is incorrect because impending means that something is about to happen.

14. C: *Proximal* means closer to the trunk. *Distal* is the opposite of proximal. *Distal* means further from the trunk (usually down an extremity). *Dorsal* means relating to the back, and *ventral* means relating to the front.

15. C: *Impervious* means impenetrable. *Impotent,* in the medical context, means unable to achieve sexual arousal (for a man). In general, the word means powerless. *Hygienic* means sanitary. *Impending* means imminent.

16. B: *Etiology* refers to the cause or origin of a disease or condition. Some diseases have an unknown etiology.

17. *B:* Preexisting means prior; it is a condition that has existed before now. The prefix pre- means before. Choice *A* is incorrect because during refers to something occurring now, or throughout the duration of something else.

Choice *C* is incorrect because post means after, which is the opposite of preexisting. Choice *D* is incorrect because distal refers to a position away from the center of the body.

18. A: *Febrile* means feverish. *Futile* means pointless, *libel* is printed defamation of someone's character, and *liable* means responsible, especially in a legal sense.

19. D: To apply means to utilize; a doctor would apply pressure to a wound to stop bleeding. Choice *A* is incorrect because to adhere means to comply with something, usually a set of rules. Choice *B* is incorrect because to continue means to keep doing something. Choice *C* is incorrect because stop means to come to an end.

20. B: *Viscosity* refers to a fluid's thickness or resistance to flow. A viscous fluid is in contrast to a runny one. For example, honey is more viscous than water.

21. B: *Supine* refers to the position where one is lying on their back, face up. *Prone* is the position on one's stomach.

22. B: Urinate means to excrete; it is the excretion, or discharge, of urine from the body. Choice *A* is incorrect because stand means to be upright on the feet. Choice *C* is incorrect because divulge means to reveal information. Choice *D* is incorrect because pump means to move liquid through force.

23. A: Subcutaneous means under the skin. The prefix sub- means below or under, while cutaneous relates to the skin. Choice *B* is incorrect because the tibia or shin is below the knee, while the tick may be below the knee, the sentence does not provide that information and that's not what subcutaneous means. Choice *C* is incorrect because while the leg is above the foot, that's not what subcutaneous means. Choice *D* is incorrect because round means circular.

24. B: A *laceration* is a wound with irregular edges. An *incision* is a more precise cut, as in one made by a surgeon using a scalpel during surgery. A *contusion* is a bruise and an *avulsion* is a type of fracture where a piece of the bone is ripped off.

25. C: *Renal* means relating to the kidneys. The renal blood vessels serve the kidneys.

26. A: *Debridement* refers to the removal of necrotic tissue. An arthroscopy is a type of surgical procedure on a joint using a camera and small scope, *distension* is swelling or bloating, and a *laparoscopy* is a surgical procedure that involves the insertion of a fiberoptic instrument.

27. D: *Triage* means to sort based on severity. Patients entering the ER need to be triaged so that they are treated in order of urgency.

28. D: *Predisposed* means inclined to a specific condition or action.

29. A: *Instigate* means to initiate or bring about an action. *Prevent* is the opposite of this, making Choice *B* incorrect. While *investigate* sounds similar, it doesn't mean the same thing as instigate, making Choice *C* incorrect. *Assent* means to agree, making Choice *D* incorrect.

30. C: *Indolent* can mean lethargic, lazy, or aversive to activity.

31. D: Arteries bring blood from the heart to the tissues, and veins return the blood to the heart from the tissues.

32. D: *Buccal* means relating to the cheek. An example of a medication with a buccal route of administration is nitroglycerine in the treatment of angina.

33. B: *Instructor* refers to a person who teaches something, a teacher. Choices *A* and *C*, student and pupil, are synonyms referring to those who are taught by instructors. A detective is a person who investigates crime, making Choice *D* incorrect.

34. A: To *expectorate* is to cough out phlegm. Someone with pneumonia may expectorate in the sink.

35. A: A *residence* is where someone lives; it's their home. In the sentence, the man bikes to work because he lives close to the office.

36. D: To *relinquish* something is to give it up or cease to claim it. For example, a spouse trying to be more considerate may relinquish the TV remote so that their partner can choose a show.

37. C: To *germinate* is to develop or come into existence. A novel marketing idea might germinate at a business lunch. In a botany context, it also means to sprout or bud.

38. A: *Indemnity* is an insurance or other security or safeguard against a financial burden or loss.

39. C: *Rampant* means unrestrained. *Stagnant* means still or unchanging, like a body of water with no active flow. *Wildly* means exaggerated and without discipline, and *mildly* means meekly or slightly.

40. D: Something that is ominous is *threatening*. Choices *B* and *C*, *promising* and *auspicious*, are antonyms of ominous. *Unequivocal* refers to something that is *unambiguous* or absolutely certain.

41. A: *Hypo-* means "below" or "beneath," and *glycemia* comes from glucose, so it refers to low blood sugar.

42. A: To *observe* is to watch or examine with one's eyes.

43. C: *Somnolent* means sleepy but arousable to verbal stimuli. Someone *comatose* is unresponsive to stimuli. Someone *delirious* is either ecstatic or mentally disturbed and seeing illusions. *Stuporous* means slowed, dulled, or impaired consciousness.

44. B: *Hemoptysis* refers to coughing up blood. The suffix *-ptysis* means spitting of matter, and the prefix *hemo-* refers to blood.

45. D: A tissue that is *engorged* is swollen with fluid. For example, a new mom will have breasts engorged with milk to nurture her baby.

46. A: *Bereavement* refers to mourning after a loss. *Disposition* is someone's personality or affect, *depression* is a state of a low mood, and *belligerent* means aggressive and hostile.

47. C: *Polydipsia* refers to excessive thirst. *Poly-* means "many" or "multiple" and the suffix *-dipsia* refers to thrist.

48. C: A *sentient* being is living and able to perceive or feel something and respond.

49. C: *Peptic* means relating to digestion. *Peptic* comes from *pepsin,* which is a stomach enzyme that helps degrade proteins.

50. A: Isometric contractions don't cause a change in muscle length. The prefix *iso-* means "same" and *-metric* refers to length.

Grammar

1. C: While all of these words are spelled similarly and sound the same, the correct answer is Choice *C*, *wear*, which means to cover or equip. We wear clothes. Choice *A*, *ware*, refers to an item that is created or manufactured. Choice *B* is incorrect because *where* asks for a specific location. Choice *D*, *were*, is the second person plural version of *to be*, so it is completely irrelevant to the sentence.

2. B: The clause *who loves to ride bikes* is a restrictive adjective clause modifying the noun *boy*. Choice *A* is incorrect because *a boy who loves* is a phrase, not a clause. Choice *C* is incorrect because *to ride bikes* is an infinitive phrase and does not have a subject. Choice *D* is incorrect because *gets plenty of exercise* is not a clause; it has no subject.

3. D: The adverbial clause *unless you are too tired* modifies the verb *want*. Choice *A* is incorrect because *I want to work in the garden* is an independent clause. Choice *B* is incorrect because *in the garden* has no subject and is a prepositional phrase. Choice *C* is incorrect because *are too tired* is not a clause because it has no subject.

4. C: A noun phrase is a noun and all of its modifiers; in this case, *long* and *black* are adjectives modifying the noun *limousine* and *the* is an article modifying *limousine*. Choice *A* is incorrect because it identifies the compound subject of the sentence. Choice *B* is incorrect because it includes the verb *rode*. Choice *D* is incorrect because it includes a subject and a verb, and phrases do not have both.

5. B: Choice *B* is correct because the idea of the original sentences is Armani getting lost while walking through Paris. Choice *A* is incorrect because it replaces third person with second person. Choice *C* is incorrect because the word *should* indicates an obligation to get lost. Choice *D* is incorrect because it is not specific to the original sentence but instead makes a generalization about getting lost.

6. C: Choice *A* is incorrect because *swimming several laps* is a gerund phrase serving as the noun subject of the sentence. Choice *B* is incorrect because *using the flippers* is a gerund phrase serving as the noun object of the sentence. Choice *D* is incorrect because *learning to swim* is a gerund phrase serving as the noun subject of the sentence.

7. A: *My second cousin* is a nonessential appositive phrase renaming *Carrie Fisher*. Because it is nonessential, it is set off by commas in the sentence. Choice *B* is incorrect because *Harrison Ford* is an essential appositive explaining which actor is being discussed. Choice *C* is incorrect because there is no appositive phrase in the sentence. Choice *D* is incorrect because *Star Wars* is an essential appositive explaining which movie is being discussed.

8. B: *The fire crackling* is an absolute phrase that includes a participle following a noun and has nothing to do with the rest of the sentence but cannot stand alone as its own sentence. Choice *A* is incorrect because *going camping in the forest* is a gerund phrase serving as the noun object of the sentence. Choice *C* is incorrect because *hot cocoa and coffee* is a nonessential appositive phrase renaming *the best drinks*. Choice *D* is incorrect because *for school-age children* is a prepositional phrase.

9. C: Choice *C* is correct because it shows that Phoenix buried his cat with her favorite toys after she died, which is true of the original statement. Although Choices *A*, *B*, and *D* mention a backyard, the meanings of these choices are skewed. Choice *A* says that Phoenix buried his cat alive, which is incorrect. Choice *B* says his cat died in the backyard, which we do not know to be true. Choice *D* says Phoenix buried his cat after he buried her toys, which is also incorrect.

10. D: Choice *D* is correct because it expresses the sentiment of a moment of joy bringing tears to one's eyes as one sees a sunset while in a helicopter. Choice *A* is incorrect because it implies that the person was outside of the helicopter watching it from afar. Choice *B* is incorrect because the original sentence does not portray the sunset flying up into the sky. Choice *C* is incorrect because, while the helicopter may have been facing the sunset, this is not the reason that tears were in the speaker's eyes.

11. A: Choice *B* and *D* drop the word *who* and use the wrong tense of the verb *need*. Choice *C* incorrectly uses the preposition *with*.

12. B: Choice *B* uses the best choice of words to create a subordinate and independent clause. In Choice *A*, *because* makes it seem like this is the reason the person enjoys working from home, which is incorrect. In Choice *C*, the word *maybe* creates two independent clauses, which would need to be joined by a semicolon, not a comma. Choice *D* uses *with*, which does not make grammatical sense.

13. B: The original sentence focuses on how politicians are using the student debt issue to their advantage, so Choice *B* is the best answer choice. Choice *A* says politicians want students' votes but suggests that it is the reason for student loan debt, which is incorrect. Choice *C* shifts the focus to voters, when the sentence is really about politicians. Choice *D* is vague and doesn't best restate the original meaning of the sentence.

14. A: This answer best matches the meaning of the original sentence, which states that seasoned runners offer advice to new runners because they have complaints of injuries. Choice *B* may be true, but it doesn't mention the complaints of injuries by new runners. Choice *C* may also be true, but it does not match the original meaning of the sentence. Choice *D* does not make sense in the context of the sentence.

15. D: A noun phrase consists of the noun and all of its modifiers. In this case, the subject of the sentence is the noun *puppy*, but it is preceded by several modifiers—adjectives that give more information about what kind of puppy, which are also part of the noun phrase. Thus, Choice *A* is incorrect. Charlotte refers to the owner and modifies the word puppy, so Choice *B* is false. Choice *C* is incorrect because it contains some, but not all, of the modifiers pertaining to the puppy.

16. A: Choice *B* is not grammatically incorrect, but the repetition of the word *who* is unnecessary and awkward in this sentence. Choice *C* uses *that* before one verb and *who* before the other to refer to the same subject. Like Choice *B*, Choice *D* unnecessarily repeats the pronoun, creating an awkward sentence.

17. A: Choice *B* is incorrect because the singular verb *has* doesn't match the plural noun *grandparents*. Choice *C* is incorrect because *were traveling* does not match with *have been sightseeing*. Choice *D* is incorrect because the tenses of the verbs do not match and because it's missing a comma before *and*.

18. D: Choice *A* is grammatically correct, but it doesn't convey the connection between the two statements. Choice *B* implies that the building was still sturdy and solid after crumbling in the earthquake because the word *although* is misplaced. Choice *C* is incorrect because it uses a comma to join two independent clauses.

19. C: This sentence uses verbs in a parallel series, so each verb must follow the same pattern. In order to fit with the helping verb *would*, each verb must be in the present tense. In Choices *A, B*, and *D*, one or more of the verbs switches to past tense. Only Choice *C* remains in the same tense, maintaining the pattern.

20. C: The second sentence tells of an unexpected outcome of the first sentence. Choice *A,* Choice *B,* and Choice *D* indicate a logical progression, which does not match this surprise. Only Choice *C* indicates this unexpected twist.

21. A: Only two of these suffixes, *–ize* and *–en*, can be used to form verbs, so Choices *B* and *D* are incorrect. Those choices create adjectives. The suffix *–ize* means "to convert or turn into." The suffix *–en* means "to become." Because this sentence is about converting ideas into money, *money* plus *–ize* or *monetize* is the most appropriate word to complete the sentence, so Choice *C* is incorrect.

22. C: The suffix *-fy* means to make, cause, or cause to have. Choices *A, B*, and *D* are incorrect because they show meanings of other suffixes. Choice *A* shows the meaning of the suffix *-ous*. Choice *B* shows the meaning of the suffix *–ist*, and Choice *D* shows the meaning of the suffix *-age*.

23. A: *After* and *then* are transitional words that indicate time or position. Choice *B* is incorrect because the words *at, with,* and *to* are used as prepositions in this sentence, not transitions. Choice *C* is incorrect because the words *had* and *took* are used as verbs in this sentence. In Choice *D, a* and *the* are used as articles in the sentence.

24. A: Choice *A* includes all of the words functioning as nouns in the sentence. Choice *B* is incorrect because it includes the words *final* and *academic,* which are functioning as adjectives in this sentence. The word *he* makes Choice *C* incorrect because it is a pronoun. This example also includes the word *library*, which can function as a noun, but is functioning as an adjective modifying the word *databases* in this sentence. Choice *D* is incorrect because it leaves out the proper noun *Robert*.

25. C: The dependent adjective clause *cute and cuddly* does not modify *the children*, it modifies *teddy bears*. The modifier is misplaced. Choice *A* does not contain a misplaced modifier. It is a grammatically correct independent clause. Choice *B* does not have a misplaced modifier. It is a grammatically correct compound sentence with two independent clauses joined with a semicolon. Choice *D* does not have a misplaced modifier. The modifier *cute and cuddly* correctly modifies *teddy bears*. The sentence is grammatically correct.

26. B: *Dissatisfied* and *accommodations* are both spelled correctly in Choice *B*. These are both considered commonly misspelled words. One or both words are spelled incorrectly in Choices *A, C,* and *D*.

27. A: It is necessary to put a comma between the date and the year. It is also required to put a comma between the day of the week and the month. Choice *B* is incorrect because it is missing the comma between the day and year. Choice *C* is incorrect because it adds an unnecessary comma between the month and date. Choice *D* is missing the necessary comma between day of the week and the month.

28. D: To create parallelism, make both verbal gerunds. Choice *A* is incorrect. *Chewing* is a gerund and *to play* is an infinitive. Choice *B* is incorrect. *To chew* is an infinitive and *playing* is a gerund. Choice *C* is incorrect. *To chew* and *to play* are both infinitives, but they do not match with the verb *enjoy*.

29. D: In Choice *D,* the word *function* is a noun. While the word *function* can also act as a verb, in this particular sentence it is acting as a noun as the object of the preposition *at*. Choices *A* and *B* are incorrect because the word *function* cannot be used as an adjective or adverb.

30. C: *Cacti* is the correct plural form of the word *cactus*. Choice *A* (*tomatos*) includes an incorrect spelling of the plural of *tomato*. Both Choice *B* (*analysis*) and Choice *D* (*criterion*) are incorrect because they are in singular form. The correct plural form for these choices would be *criteria* and *analyses*.

31. B: The example sentences feature a direct quotation that requires the use of double quotation marks Also, the end punctuation, in this case a question mark, should be contained within the quotation marks. Choice *A* is incorrect because there is an unnecessary period after the quotation mark. Choice *C* is incorrect because it uses single quotation marks, which are used for a quote within a quote. Choice *D* is incorrect because it places the punctuation outside of the quotation marks.

32. A: Choice *A* is correct because *has* is the same tense and number as the subject *Garth*, so the verb and subject agree. Choice *B* is incorrect because *had* is past tense while the sentence is clearly present tense, indicated by *that he cares for*. Choice *C* incorrectly uses *have*, which is plural and doesn't agree with the singular subject. Choice *D* is incorrect because *haves* is a plural noun indicating people with possessions, not a verb as is needed here.

33. D: In Choice *D,* the word *part* functions as an adjective that modifies the word *Irish*. Choices *A* and *C* are incorrect because the word *part* functions as a noun in these sentences. Choice *B* is incorrect because the word *part* functions as a verb.

34. C: *All of Shannon's family and friends* is the complete subject because it includes who or what is doing the action in the sentence as well as the modifiers that go with it. Choice *A* is incorrect because it only includes the simple subject of the sentence. Choices *A, B,* and *D* are incorrect because they only include part of the complete subject.

35. D: Choice *D* directly addresses the reader, so it is in second person point of view. This is an imperative sentence since it issues a command; imperative sentences have an understood *you* as the subject. Choice *A* uses first person pronouns *I* and *my*. Choices *B* and *C* are incorrect because they use third person point of view.

36. A: The word *prodigious* is defined as very impressive, amazing, or large. In this sentence, the meaning can be drawn from the words *they became nervous about climbing its distant peak*, as this would be an appropriate reaction upon seeing a very large peak that's far in the distance. Choices *B, C,* and *D* do not accurately define the word *prodigious*, so they are incorrect.

37. D: Choice *D* correctly places a hyphen after the prefix *ex* to join it to the word *husband.* Many words that begin with the prefixes *great, trans, ex, all,* and *self* require a hyphen. Choices *A* and *C* place hyphens in words where they are not needed. *Beagle mix* would only require a hyphen if coming before the word *Henry*, since it would be serving as a compound adjective in that instance. Choice *B* contains hyphens that are in the correct place but are formatted incorrectly since they include spaces between the hyphens and the surrounding words.

38. C: Choice *C* is correct because quotation marks should be used for the title of a short work such as a poem. Choices *A, B,* and *D* are incorrect because the titles of novels, films, and newspapers should be placed in italics, not quotation marks.

39. C: This question focuses on the correct usage of the commonly confused word pairs of *it's/its* and *then/than. It's* is a contraction for *it is* or *it has*. *Its* is a possessive pronoun. The word *than* shows comparison between two things. *Then* is an adverb that conveys time. Choice *C* correctly uses *it's* and *than*. *It's* is a contraction for *it has* in this sentence, and *than* shows comparison between *work* and *rest*. None of the other answers choices use both of the correct words.

40. C: The original sentence states that firefighting is dangerous, making it necessary for firefighters to wear protective gear. The portion of the sentence that needs to be rewritten focuses on the gear, not the dangers, of firefighting. Choices *A, B,* and *D* all discuss the danger, not the gear, so *C* is the correct answer.

41. D: The original sentence states that though the sites are popular, they can be dangerous for teens, so *D* is the best choice. Choice *A* does state that there is danger, but it doesn't identify teens and limits it to just one site. Choice *B* repeats the statement from the beginning of the sentence, and Choice *C* says the sites are used too much, which is not the point made in the original sentence.

42. A: The affix *circum–* originates from Latin and means *around or surrounding*. It is also related to other round words, such as circle and circus. The rest of the choices do not relate to the affix *circum–* and are therefore incorrect.

43. C: The rule for *me* and *I* is that one should use *I* when it is the subject pronoun of a sentence and *me* when it is the object pronoun of the sentence. Break the sentence up to see if *I* or *me* should be used. To say "Those are memories that I have now shared" is correct, rather than "Those are memories that me have now shared." Choice *A* is incorrect because *my siblings* should come before *I*.

44. D: Choice *D* is correct because there should be a comma between the city and state. Choice *A* is incorrect because the order of the sentence designates that Chicago, Illinois is in Maywood, which is incorrect. Choice *B* is incorrect because the comma after neighborhood interrupts the phrase "the Maywood neighborhood of Chicago." Choice *C* is incorrect because a comma after *Illinois* is unnecessary.

45. D: Choice *D* is correct because the *Committee* is one entity, therefore the possession should show the "Committee's approach" with the apostrophe between the *y* and the *s*. Choice *A* is incorrect because the word *Committies* is spelled wrong. Choice *B* is incorrect because the word *Committees* should not be plural and should have an apostrophe to show possession. Choice *C* is incorrect because the apostrophe indicates that the word *Committees* is plural.

46. A: Choice *A* is correct because the conjunction *and* is the best way to combine the two independent clauses. Choice *B* is incorrect because the conjunction *but* indicates a contrast, and there is no contrast between the two clauses. Choice *C* is incorrect because the introduction of the comma after *house* with no conjunction creates a comma splice. Choice *D* is incorrect because the word *he* becomes repetitive since the two clauses can be joined together.

47. B: Choice *B* is correct because it provides the correct verb tense and also makes sense within the context of the passage. Choice *A* is incorrect because the verb tense is inconsistent with the rest of the sentence. Choice *C* is incorrect because, with this use of the sentence, it would create a fragment because the verb *holding* has no helping verb in front of it. Choice *D* is incorrect because it changes the meaning of the sentence.

48. B: Choice *A* is incorrect because *In 2015* is a fragment, not a sentence. Choice *C* is incorrect because there should be a comma after introductory phrases in general, such as "In 2015," and Choice *C* omits a comma. Choice *D* is incorrect because there should be an independent clause on either side of a semicolon, and the phrase "In 2015" is not an independent clause.

49. B: Here, a colon is used to introduce an explanation. Colons either introduce explanations or lists. Additionally, the quote ends with the punctuation inside the quotes, unlike Choice *C*.

50. B: The word *raising* in Choice *A* makes the sentence grammatically incorrect. Choice *C* adds an apostrophe at the end of *its*. While adding an apostrophe to most words would indicate possession, adding *'s* to the word *it* indicates a contraction. The possessive form of the word *it* is *its*. The contraction *it's* denotes *it is*. Thus, Choice *D* is incorrect.

51. B: Choice *B* is correct because like the original sentence, it expresses their plan to go to the party if friends also go. Choice *A* is incorrect because it does not follow the meaning of the original sentence. Choice *C* is incorrect because it states that their friends are going, even though that is not known. Choice *D* is incorrect because it would make the new sentence mean the opposite of the original sentence.

52. C: Choice *C* is correct because the original sentence states that his recovery time was long because his leg was broken before the accident. Choice *A* is incorrect because there is no indication that the man had two broken legs. Choice *B* is incorrect because it indicates that he broke his leg during the car accident, not before. Choice *D* is incorrect because there is no indication that he broke his leg after the car accident.

53. A: Choice *A* is correct because it expresses the fact that the birthday and the party were both after Halloween. Choice *B* is incorrect because it says that the birthday was on Halloween, even though that was not stated in the original sentence. Choice *C* is incorrect because it says the party was specifically a Halloween party and not a birthday party. Choice *D* is incorrect because the party was after Halloween, not before.

54. D: The best answer is Choice *D* because it keeps the original meaning of the sentence with the transitional phrase *due to*. Choice *A* is incorrect; the sentence says that the animals thrive *with* these changing traits over time, but it does not say the animals thrive *because of* these traits. Choice *B* is incorrect because the sentence suggests it is the *environments* and not the *animals* that contain the traits. Choice *C* is incorrect; it says that animals thrive and that they have changing traits that develop, but it fails to show a connection between the two.

55. A: Choice *A* is correct because the meaning is the closest in similarity to the original; there is learning that occurs from the past lectures the speaker has sat through. Choice *B* is incorrect because it changes the tense of the act of sitting through lectures. Choice *C* is incorrect because it uses the conjunction *and* which fails to connect the two clauses. Choice *D* is incorrect because although it uses similar language, it changes the meaning to say that the speaker *goes away* to lectures.

Biology

1. A: Choice *B* is incorrect because DNA does not provide energy—that's the job of carbohydrates and glucose. Choice *C* is incorrect because DNA is double-stranded. Because Choices *B* and *C* are incorrect, Choice *D,* all of the above, is incorrect.

2. A: The Golgi apparatus is designed to tag, package, and ship out proteins destined for other cells or locations. The centrioles typically play a large role only in cell division when they ratchet the chromosomes from the mitotic plate to the poles of the cell. The mitochondria are involved in energy production and are the powerhouses of the cell. The cell structure responsible for cellular storage, digestion, and waste removal is the lysosome. Lysosomes are like recycle bins. They are filled with digestive enzymes that facilitate catabolic reactions to regenerate monomers.

3. C: Cellulose and starch are both polysaccharides, which are long chains of glucose molecules. However, they are connected by different types of bonds, which gives them different structures and different functions.

4. D: Let's label *R* as the right-handed allele and r as the left-handed allele. Esther has to have the combination rr since she's left-handed. She had to get at least one recessive allele from each parent. So, mom could either be Rr or rr (right-handed or left-handed), and dad can also be Rr or rr. As long as each parent carries one recessive allele, it is possible that Esther is left-handed. Therefore, all answer choices are possible.

5. D: The probability of each specified genotype can be determined by individual Punnett squares. Each probability should then be then multiplied (law of multiplication) to find the value, which in this case is $\frac{1}{2} \times \frac{1}{2} \times \frac{1}{2} \times \frac{1}{2} = \frac{1}{16}$.

	A	a
A	AA	Aa
A	AA	Aa

	B	b
b	Bb	bb
b	Bb	bb

	C	c
c	Cc	cc
c	Cc	cc

	D	d
D	DD	Dd
D	DD	Dd

Probabilities: AA=$\frac{1}{2}$ bb=$\frac{1}{2}$ cc=$\frac{1}{2}$ DD=$\frac{1}{2}$

6. D: Choice *A* is incorrect because meiosis produces haploid cells. Choice B is incorrect because there is no interphase II. Otherwise, gametes would be diploid instead of haploid. Choice *C* is incorrect because the resulting cells only have one set of chromosomes. Choice *D* is the only correct answer because each chromosome set goes through a process called crossing over, which jumbles up the genes on each chromatid, during meiosis I.

7. D: DNA serves as the hereditary material for prokaryotic and eukaryotic cells.

8. C: Water, Choice *A*, is a reactant that gets sucked up by the roots. Carbon dioxide, Choice *D*, is a reactant that goes into the stomata. Sunlight, Choice *B*, inputs energy into the reaction in order to create the high-energy sugar.

9. C: Cellular respiration is the process of breaking down food to release energy. Breathing, Choice *B*, is not cellular respiration; breathing is an action that takes place at the organism level with the respiratory system. Making high-energy sugars, Choice *A*, is photosynthesis, not cellular respiration. Sweating, Choice *D*, is perspiration, and has nothing to do with cellular respiration.

10. D: Algae can perform photosynthesis. One indicator that a plant is able to perform photosynthesis is the color green. Plants with the pigment chlorophyll are able to absorb the warmer colors of the light spectrum but are unable to absorb green. That's why they appear green. Choices *A* and *C* are types of fungi and are therefore not able to perform photosynthesis. Fungi obtain energy from food in their environment. An ant, Choice *B*, is also unable to perform photosynthesis since it is an animal.

11. B: The Linnaean system is the most commonly used taxonomic system today. It classifies species based on their similarities and moves from comprehensive to more general similarities. The system is based on the following order: species, genus, family, order, class, phylum, and kingdom.

12. A: *Homo* is the human genus. *Sapiens* are the only remaining species in the Homo genus.

13. A: The nucleus, chloroplast, and mitochondria are all bound by two layers of membrane. The Golgi apparatus, lysosome, and ER only have one membrane layer.

14. D: Human gametes each contain 23 chromosomes. This is referred to as a haploid, which is a cell that has half the number of chromosomes as the original germ cell (46). Germ cells are diploid precursors of the haploid egg and sperm. Meiosis has two major phases, each of which is characterized by sub-phases similar to mitosis. In Meiosis I, the DNA of the parent cell is duplicated in interphase, just like in mitosis. Starting with prophase I, things become a little different. Two homologous chromosomes form a tetrad, cross over, and exchange genetic content. Each shuffled chromosome of the tetrad migrates to the cell's poles, and two haploid daughter cells are formed. In Meiosis II, each daughter undergoes another division more similar to mitosis (with the exception of the fact that there is no interphase), resulting in four genetically-different cells, each with only half of the chromosomal material of the original germ cell.

15. B: Plants use chloroplasts to turn light energy into glucose. Animal cells do not have this ability. Chloroplasts can be found in the plant cell but not the animal cell.

16. A: Human genes are strictly DNA and do not include proteins or amino acids. A human's genome and collection of genes will include even their recessive traits, mutations, and unused DNA.

17. A: The net products of anaerobic glycolysis from one 6-carbon glucose molecule are two 3-carbon pyruvate molecules, two reduced nicotinamide adenine dinucleotide (NADH) molecules, which are created when the electron carrier oxidized nicotinamide adenine dinucleotide (NAD+) peels off two electrons and a hydrogen atom, and two ATP molecules. Glycolysis requires two ATP molecules to drive the process forward, and since the gross end product is four ATP molecules, the net is two ATP molecules.

18. C: Glycolysis produces two pyruvate molecules per glucose molecule that gets broken down because glucose is a 6-carbon sugar and pyruvate is a 3-carbon sugar. Each pyruvate molecule oxidizes into a single acetyl-CoA molecule, which then enters the citric acid cycle. Therefore, two citric acid cycles can be completed per glucose molecule that initially entered glycolysis.

19. D: Oxidative phosphorylation includes two steps: the electron transport chain and chemiosmosis. These two processes help generate ATP molecules by transferring two electrons and a proton (H^+) from each NADH and $FADH_2$ to channel proteins, pumping the hydrogen ions to the inner-membrane space using energy from the high-energy electrons to create a concentration gradient. In chemiosmosis, ATP synthase uses facilitated diffusion to deliver protons across the concentration gradient from the inner mitochondrial membrane to the matrix.

20. C: The nucleolus is always located inside the nucleus. It contains important hereditary information about the cell that is critical for the reproductive process. Chloroplasts, Choice *A,* are only located in plant cells. The nucleolus is not found in the mitochondria, Choice *B,* or attached to the cell membrane, Choice *D.*

21. C: The mitochondrion is often called the powerhouse of the cell and is one of the most important structures for maintaining regular cell function. It is where aerobic cellular respiration occurs and where most of the cell's ATP is generated. The number of mitochondria in a cell varies greatly from organism to organism and from cell to cell. Cells that require more energy, like muscle cells, have more mitochondria.

22. A: Photosynthesis is the process of converting light energy into chemical energy, which is then stored in sugar and other organic molecules. The photosynthetic process takes place in the thylakoids inside chloroplasts in plants. Chlorophyll is a green pigment in the thylakoid membranes that absorbs photons from light.

23. B: Carbohydrates consist of sugars. The simplest sugar molecule is called a monosaccharide and has the molecular formula of CH_2O, or a multiple of that formula. Monosaccharides are important molecules for cellular respiration. Their carbon skeleton can also be used to rebuild new small molecules. Lipids are fats, proteins are formed via amino acids, and nucleic acid is found in DNA and RNA.

24. A: The Calvin cycle is dependent upon the ATP and NADPH produced by the light reactions. Nine ATP molecules and six NADPH molecules are invested into the Calvin cycle for every one molecule of glyceraldehyde 3-phosphate (G3P) produced. In the endergonic reduction reaction, NADPH uses energy from ATP to add a hydrogen to each molecule of 3-phosphoglycerate. This converts the six molecules of 3-PGA into the 3-carbon sugar G3P. ATP supplies energy by donating a phosphate group (Pi) (becoming ADP), and NADPH loses a hydrogen to become $NADP^+$.

25. D: The cell membrane surrounds the cell and regulates which molecules can move in and out of the cell. Ribosomes are cellular machines that build proteins, Choice *A*. Lysosomes break down large molecules, Choice *B*. The nucleus contains the cell's DNA, Choice C.

26. C: The lagging strand of DNA falls behind the leading strand because of its discontinuous synthesis. DNA helicase unzips the DNA helices so that synthesis can take place, and RNA primers are created by the RNA primase for the polymerases to attach to and build from. The lagging strand is synthesizing DNA in a direction that is hard for the polymerase to build, so multiple primers are laid down so that the entire length of DNA can be synthesized simultaneously. These short pieces of DNA being synthesized are known as Okazaki fragments and are joined together by DNA ligase.

27. B: Prokaryotic cells (archaea and bacteria) do not have a nucleus or other membrane-bound organelles and are less complex than eukaryotic cells. The nucleus is exclusively found in eukaryotic cells. Animal, plant, fungi, and protist cells are all eukaryotic. DNA is contained within the nucleus of eukaryotic cells, and they also have membrane-bound organelles that perform complex intracellular metabolic activities.

28. B: Sunlight comes into the greenhouse as short-wavelength IR. As it is absorbed by surfaces in the greenhouse, it is converted to long-wavelength IR. The long-wavelength IR gets trapped inside the greenhouse and bounces off the surfaces and glass and remains inside the greenhouse. Since short-wavelength IR can enter the greenhouse, it also has the ability to leave the greenhouse, making Choice *A* incorrect. The greenhouse feels warmer, not cooler, than outside, so Choice *C* is incorrect. Water is not involved in the reaction noted in Figure 1, so Choice *D* is also incorrect.

29. D: The graph in Figure 2 shows that the greenhouse plant grew taller than the outside plant. The bars representing the greenhouse plant are taller at three time points that Scientist A measured. Greenhouses trap sunlight, warm air, and gases such as CO2 inside the greenhouse, so plants have an increased rate of photosynthesis, allowing them to grow faster. The plants are also protected from pests inside the greenhouse.

30. B: Sunlight enters the greenhouse as short-wavelength IR and gets converted to long-wavelength IR. This process also gives off heat and makes the greenhouse feel warmer than the outside climate. Water and oxygen, Choices *A* and *D,* are not involved in this reaction. The plants remain the same and do not get converted into anything else, Choice *C.*

Chemistry

1. C: Conversion within the metric system is as simple as the movement of decimal points. The prefix *kilo-* means "one thousand," or three zeros, so the procedure to convert kilometers to the primary unit (meters) is to move the decimal point three units to the right. To get to centimeters, the decimal point must be moved an additional two places to the right: $0.78 \rightarrow 78{,}000$. Choice *A* is false because the decimal point has only been moved one place to right. Choice *B* is incorrect because the decimal point is moved one unit in the wrong direction. Choice *D* is false because the decimal has only been moved three units to the right. The problem can also be solved by using the following conversion equation:

$$0.78 \text{ km} \times \frac{1{,}000 \text{ m}}{1 \text{ km}} \times \frac{100 \text{ cm}}{1 \text{ m}} = 78{,}000 \text{ cm}$$

The kilometer (km) units cancel each other out, as do the meter (m) units. The only units left are centimeters (cm).

2. A: Keratin is a structural protein and it is the primary constituent of things like hair and nails. Choice *B* is incorrect because antigens are immune proteins that help fight disease. Hormonal proteins are responsible for initiating the signal transduction cascade to regulate gene expression. Choice *C* is incorrect because channel proteins are transport proteins that help move molecules into and out of a cell. Marker proteins help identify or distinguish a cell. Lastly, Choice *D* is incorrect because actin, like myosin, is a motor protein because it is involved in the process of muscle contraction.

3. B: Biological catalysts are termed *enzymes*, which are proteins with conformations that specifically manipulate reactants into positions which decrease the reaction's activation energy. Lipids do not usually affect reactions, and cofactors, while they can aid or be necessary to the proper functioning of enzymes, do not make up the majority of biological catalysts.

4. D: An atom is structured with a nucleus in the center that contains neutral neutrons and positive protons. Surrounding the nucleus are orbiting electrons that are negatively charged. Choice *D* is the only correct answer.

5. B: The set of results is close to the actual value of the acceleration due to gravity, making the results accurate. However, there is a different value recorded every time, so the results aren't precise, which makes Choice *B* the correct answer.

6. D: Sucrose, lactose, and maltose are disaccharides. Mannose is a monosaccharide.

7. D: Preparing a solution from a stock is simply a process of dilution by adding a certain amount of the stock to water. The amount of stock to use can be calculated using a formula and algebra with the given values for the stock molarity (12.0 M), the diluted volume (250 ml), and diluted molarity (1.50 M):

$$V_S = \frac{M_D V_D}{M_S}$$

$$\mathrm{V_S} = \frac{(1.50\ \mathrm{M})(250\ \mathrm{ml})}{12.0\ \mathrm{M}} = 31.3\ \mathrm{ml}$$

Because the given values are written to three significant figures, the answer should also be written in three significant figures, making Choice *D* the correct answer. The other answer choices are either incorrect values or reported to an incorrect number of significant figures.

8. B: When a solution is on the verge of—or in the process of—crystallization, it is called a *supersaturated* solution. This can also occur in a solution that seems stable, but if it is disturbed, the change can begin the crystallization process. To display the relationship between the mass of a solute that a solvent holds and a given temperature, a *solubility curve* is used. If a reading is on the solubility curve, the solvent is *saturated*; it is full and cannot hold more solute. If a reading is above the curve, the solvent is *supersaturated* and unstable from holding more solute than it should. If a reading is below the curve, the solvent is *unsaturated* and could hold more solute. Choices *A, C*, and *D* are all stable, whereas Choice *B* is unstable.

9. D: Electrons orbit the nucleus of the atom in atomic shells or orbitals. The first atomic shell, closest to the nucleus, can accommodate two electrons. The second atomic shell can hold a maximum of eight electrons, and the third atomic shell can house a maximum of eighteen electrons. The tendency to want to fill the outer orbital completely (called the valence shell), or get rid of a sole electron in the valence shell, influences the degree to which an atom will readily form chemical bonds.

10 A: The metallic substance in an ionic bond often has low ionization energy. Coupled with the fact that the nonmetal has a high electron affinity, the metallic substance readily transfers an electron to the nonmetal. Choice *B* is incorrect because it is the nonmetallic substance, not the metallic one, that has a high electron affinity. Choice *C* is incorrect because ionic bonds are very strong. As such, ionic compounds have high melting and boiling points and are brittle and crystalline. Lastly, Choice *D* is incorrect because the reactions that form ionic bonds are exothermic.

11. B: Electronegativity, or the measure of an atom's tendency to attract a bonding pair of electrons, doesn't quite follow the general trend in the periodic table, so the order should be memorized. Although it generally increases diagonal from the lower left corner to the upper right corner, some of the common elements do not fall along this diagonal. The most electronegative element is fluorine. The following order of decreasing electronegativity should be helpful:

$$\mathrm{F > O > Cl > N > Br > I > S > C > H > metals}$$

12. B: Unlike in ionic bonds where electrons are transferred between the bonding atoms, covalent bonds are formed when two atoms share electrons. The atoms in covalent compounds are bonded together because of the balance of attraction and repulsion between their protons and electrons. Two atoms can be joined by single, double, or triple covalent bonds. As the number of electrons that are shared increases, the length of the bond decreases because the atoms are held together more closely.

13. A: The metric prefix for 10^{-3} is "milli." 10^{-3} is $\frac{1}{10^3}$ or $\frac{1}{1{,}000}$ or 0.001. If this were grams, 10^{-3} would represent 1 milligram or $\frac{1}{1{,}000}$ of a gram. For multiples of 10, the prefixes are as follows: $\mathrm{deca} = 10^1$, $\mathrm{hecta} = 10^2$, $\mathrm{kilo} = 10^3$,

$\text{mega} = 10^6$, $\text{giga} = 10^9$, $\text{tera} = 10^{12}$, $\text{peta} = 10^{15}$, and so on. For sub-units of 10, the prefixes are as follows: $\text{deci} = 10^{-1}$, $\text{centi} = 10^{-2}$, $\text{milli} = 10^{-3}$, $\text{micro} = 1^{-6}$, $\text{nano} = 10^{-9}$, $\text{pico} = 10^{-12}$, $\text{femto} = 10^{-15}$, and so on. Metric units are usually abbreviated by using the first letter of the prefix (except for micro, which is the Greek letter mu, or μ). Abbreviations for multiples greater than 10^3 are capitalized.

14. B: Metallic compounds can conduct electricity by creating a current, which is formed by passing energy through the freely moving electrons. The electrons are shared by many metal cations and are more fluid than those in ionic structures. They float around the bonded metals and form a sea of electrons. Lewis structures are not usually depicted for metallic structures because of this free-roaming ability of the electrons.

15. C: The qualitative definition of ionization energy is the amount of energy needed to remove the most loosely-bound valence electron from a gaseous atom or molecule to form a cation. Choice *A,* refers to atomic radius, Choice *B* refers to electronegativity, and Choice *D* refers to electron affinity. All four of these properties follow trends on the periodic table.

16. D: Recall that the rate of a reaction is the measure of the change in concentration of the reactants or products over a certain period of time. When the reactants are in the gaseous state, increases in pressure increase the frequency of collisions between molecules because they are compressed; therefore, the reaction rate increases because of these increased interactions and collisions. The reverse is true when pressure decreases; thus, the reaction rate decreases because there are fewer collisions between the gas molecules.

17. C: Equilibrium occurs when the rate of reactants forming products is equal to the rate of the products reverting back to the reactants. In equilibrium conditions, the concentration of reactants and products in the system doesn't change. The reaction shown is an example of heterogenous equilibrium because the substances are in different phases when equilibrium is reached. If, for example, the reactants and products were all gases, as in the conversion of sulfur dioxide to sulfur trioxide, and equilibrium is reached, it is considered homogenous equilibrium. There is not enough information provided in the equation to decide whether the system is in static or dynamic equilibrium because there is no indication about the whether the forward and reverse reactions are still occurring (dynamic equilibrium), or if all reactions have ceased (static equilibrium). Therefore, Choices *A* and *B* are incorrect.

18. C: Increasing temperature increases the rate of reactions due to increases in the kinetic energy of atoms and molecules. This increased movement results in increased collisions between reactants (with each other as well as with enzymes), which is the cause of the rate increase.

19. A: A chemical change alters the chemical makeup of the original object. When a piece of paper burns, it cannot be returned to its original chemical makeup because it has formed new materials. Physical change refers to changing a substance's form, but not the composition of that substance. In physical science, sedimentary change and potential change are not terms used to describe any particular process.

20. C: An acid increases the concentration of H^+ ions when it is dissolved in water. It is a proton donor in a chemical equation, or it acts an electron-pair acceptor. A base increases the concentration of OH^- ions when it is dissolved in water, accepts a proton in a chemical reaction, or is an electron-pair donor. Therefore, only Choice *C* is correct.

21. A: A synthesis reaction occurs when two or more elements or compounds are joined together to form a single product. Choice *A* shows the chemical equation for the synthesis of nitrogen dioxide (NO_2) from nitric oxide (NO) and oxygen (O_2). Choice *B* is a decomposition reaction because a single reactant (carbonic acid, which is in soft drinks) is broken down into two or more products (in this case, water and carbon dioxide). Choices *C* and *D* are single displacement reactions, which occur when a single element or ion takes the place of another element in a compound.

22. B: The reaction between methane (CH_4) and oxygen is a combustion reaction, which is a special type of double displacement reaction. Double displacement reactions occur when two elements or ions exchange a single element to form two different compounds. This means that the final compounds have different combinations of cations and anions than the reactants did. Redox reactions and acid-base reactions are also special types of double replacement reactions. In combustion reactions, a hydrocarbon reacts with oxygen to form carbon dioxide and water.

23. B: The percent yield for a reaction is the actual yield is divided by the theoretical yield and then multiplied by 100. Since 65 grams of CaO were expected, this value is the theoretical yield. The actual yield is the 45 grams produced. Thus, the percent yield is:

$$\frac{45\text{ g}}{65\text{ g}} \times 100 = 69\%$$

24. B: An atom, ion, or molecule that loses electrons and becomes more positively charged has been oxidized. A substance is reduced when it gains electrons and becomes more negatively charged. Choices *C* and *D* are incorrect because when electrons (which carry a negative charge) are lost, the substance that lost them has less of a negative charge. Therefore, the charge of the substance that lost the electrons becomes more positive.

25. A: A conjugate base is the ion that is formed when the acid it is paired with loses a proton. HSO_4^- is the conjugate base of the acid H_2SO_4. Choice *B* is incorrect because it reverses the relationship. Remember that the acid donates a proton, so the conjugate base pair of an acid has the same molecular formula of the acid, except it has one less proton (H^+). Therefore, the conjugate base ion has lost a positive charge, so it should have a negative charge. Thus, Choice *C* is incorrect.

26. C: Crystalline solids do not become soft before they melt. Amorphous solids become soft and pliable before melting because some of the bonds between the nonidentical units break before others. In crystalline solids, the bonds all break at the same time, Choice D. This is because the bonds between the identical repeating units are all equal in strength. This also gives the crystalline solid an exact melting point, Choice *A*. Crystalline solids also display cleavage and break across a plane, Choice *B*.

27. D: The molecule is methanol. There are three hydrogen atoms attached to the carbon atom, giving CH_3, and one hydrogen atom attached to an oxygen atom, giving OH, which makes the formula CH_3OH, Choice *D*. Choices *A, B,* and *C* do not have the correct number of carbon, hydrogen, or oxygen atoms as depicted in the Lewis diagram.

28. D: Semiconductors are covalent network solids that are in between being good insulators and good conductors but are neither in entirety. Choice *D* is the correct answer. Covalent network solids are formed between nonmetals with strong covalent bonds. Metallic solids, Choice *A,* are good conductors because of the delocalized electrons that transfer electricity. The electrons in ionic solids, Choice *C,* are held tightly in place, so they cannot conduct electricity at all.

29. A: When fossil fuels react with oxygen gas, they are burning, which causes a combustion reaction. Combustion reactions create carbon dioxide and water vapor. Combination reactions, Choice *B,* take two smaller molecules and make one larger molecule. Choice *C,* vaporization, would indicate liquids becoming gases, and Choice *D,* solidification, would indicate liquids becoming solids, neither of which is occurring in this reaction.

30. D: To find the age of the animal bone, the following equations must be used:

$$t_{\frac{1}{2}} = \frac{0.693}{k} \text{ and } ln\frac{[A]_t}{[A]_0} = -kt$$

First, find the rate constant for carbon-14 which has a half-life of 5730 years:

$$k = \frac{0.693}{t_{\frac{1}{2}}} = \frac{0.693}{5730 \text{ years}} = 1.209 \times 10^{-4}/\text{years}$$

The initial concentration $[A]_0$ of carbon-14 corresponds the amount of this isotope found in present-day animals. Recall that carbon-14 is found in animals because they can ingest plants that consume carbon dioxide from the upper atmosphere. However, once the animal dies, the concentration of carbon-14 will gradually decrease over time and is represented by $[A]_t$. The latter is the concentration of carbon-14 at time *t,* or the age of the animal bone. Concentration in this problem is represented by the units dpm/(g carbon). $[A]_0$is equal to 15.0 dpm/(g Carbon) and $[A]_t$ is 5.0 dpm/(g Carbon). Notice that $[A]_t$should be less than the initial concentration. Solving for the age of the animal bone (t) using the calculated value of k gives:

$$t = -\frac{1}{k} ln \frac{[A]_t}{[A]_0} = -\frac{1}{1.209 \times 10^{-4}/\text{years}} \ln \frac{5.0 \text{ dpm/(g carbon)}}{15.0 \text{ dpm/(g carbon)}}$$

$$t = 9{,}087 \text{ years or } 9.0 \times 10^3 \text{ years}$$

The age of the animal bone is approximately 9,000 years.

Anatomy and Physiology

1. C: Eosinophils, like neutrophils, basophils, and mast cells, are a type of leukocyte in a class called granulocytes. They are found underneath mucous membranes in the body and they primarily secrete destructive enzymes and defend against multicellular parasites like worms. Choice *A* describes basophils and mast cells, and Choices *B* and *D* describe neutrophils. Unlike neutrophils, which are aggressive phagocytic cells, eosinophils have low phagocytic activity.

2. B: The innermost epidermal tissue is a single layer of cells called the stratum basale. The melanocytes in the stratum basale produce melanin, an important pigment that absorbs UV rays to protect the skin from sun damage. The outermost epidermal layer, called the stratum corneum, helps repel water; therefore, Choice *A* is incorrect. The stratum granulosum produces keratin, so Choice *C* is incorrect. The dermis, which is underneath the epidermis, contains the oil glands that produce and secrete oil.

3. C: Tendons connect muscle to bone. Ligaments connect bone to bone. Both are made of dense, fibrous connective tissue (primarily type I collagen) to give strength. However, tendons are more organized, especially in the long axis direction like muscle fibers themselves, and they have more collagen. This arrangement makes sense because muscles have specific orientations of their fibers, so they contract in somewhat predictable directions. Ligaments are less organized and have more of a woven pattern because bone connections are not as organized as bundles of muscle fibers, so ligaments must have strength in multiple directions to protect against injury.

4. D: Cartilage is avascular, which is one reason why it is limited in its ability to repair itself following an injury. It receives materials such as nutrients via diffusion.

5. D: The smallest functional unit of the body is the cell. Groups of similar cells are arranged into *tissues,* such as nervous tissue, epithelial tissue, and adipose tissue. From there, different tissues are arranged into *organs,* and organs that work together form entire *organ systems.*

6. C: Oil glands, like sweat glands, are exocrine glands of the skin. Oil glands, which are attached to hair follicles, secrete sebum. Sebum is an oily substance that moisturizes the skin, protects it from water loss, helps keep the skin elastic, and provides a chemical defense against bacterial and fungal infections due to its slight acidity. Evaporative cooling, which is when the hottest water particles on the skin evaporate and leave behind the coolest ones to help cool the body, is not a function of sebum. In hot conditions, the hypothalamus will initiate a pathway that vasodilates blood vessels near the surface of the skin to increase heat loss and stimulate sweating.

7. A: Skeletal muscle fibers are made of myofibrils, which interact when a muscle contracts in a model called the sliding filament theory. The myofibrils are arranged in each muscle fiber in functional units called sarcomeres. The thicker filaments, called myosin, are in between the thinner actin filaments, which are anchored to Z lines. One sarcomere is defined as the region between two adjacent Z lines. Myosin filaments are attached to a central M line. When a muscle is at rest, there is a gap between the Z line and the myosin filaments; in fact, it is the arrangement of filaments that gives skeletal muscle its striated appearance. When the muscle contracts, the heads of the myosin filaments attach to the actin and form cross-bridges, which are used to pull the actin filaments closer to the M line.

8. D: Epithelial tissue covers the external surfaces of organs and lines many of the body's cavities. It can be arranged into four patterns. Transitional epithelium is noted for its ability to expand and contract. Choice *A* is incorrect because it describes simple epithelial tissue. Choice *B* is incorrect because it describes pseudostratified epithelial tissue. Choice *C* is incorrect because although transitional epithelial tissue does help protect the body from invading microbes, this ability is not unique to transitional epithelium. Instead, it is a characteristic of all epithelial tissue.

9. A: Antibiotics, Choice *B*, fight bacteria, but the body does not make them naturally. White blood cells, not red blood cells, Choice *D*, are the blood cells produced that fight the bacteria. Vaccines, Choice *C*, are given to create antibodies and prevent future illness.

10. B: Red blood cells are the chief transport vehicle for oxygen. Red blood cells contain hemoglobin, a protein that helps transport oxygen throughout the circulatory system.

11. C: The axial skeleton includes the bones of the skull and face (so the mandible, or jaw bone, is included), the ribs, the vertebral column (so the atlas, which is the name of the first cervical bone, is included), the sternum, and the hyoid. The bones of the shoulder girdle, clavicles, pelvis, and limbs are considered the bones that comprise the appendicular skeleton. Therefore, the ilium, a bone of the pelvis, is not part of the axial skeleton.

12. C: The epididymis stores sperm and is a coiled tube located near the testes. The immature sperm that enters the epididymis from the testes migrates through the 20-foot long epididymis tube in about two weeks, where viable sperm are concentrated at the end. The vas deferens is a tube that transports mature sperm from the epididymis to the urethra. Seminal vesicles are pouches attached that add fructose to the ejaculate to provide energy for sperm. The prostate gland excretes fluid that makes up about a third of semen released during ejaculation. The fluid reduces semen viscosity and contains enzymes that aid in sperm functioning; both effects increase sperm motility and ultimate success.

13. C: In the female reproductive system, many different hormones work together to propagate the species. The function of each one is listed below.

Hormone	Source	Action
GnRH	Hypothalamus	Stimulates anterior pituitary to secrete FSH and LH
FSH	Anterior pituitary	Stimulates ovaries to develop mature follicles (with ova); follicles produce increasingly high levels of estrogen
LH	Anterior pituitary	Stimulates the release of the ovum by the follicle; the follicle is then converted into a corpus luteum that secretes progesterone
Estrogen	Ovary (follicle); placenta	Stimulates repair of endometrium of uterus; negative feedback effect inhibits hypothalamus production of GnRH
Progesterone	Ovary (corpus luteum); placenta	Stimulates thickening of, and maintains, endometrium; negative feedback inhibits pituitary production of LH
Prolactin	Anterior pituitary	Stimulates milk production after childbirth
Oxytocin	Posterior pituitary	Stimulates milk "letdown"
Androgens	Adrenal glands	Stimulates sexual drive
hCG	Embryo (if pregnant)	Stimulates production of progesterone

14. A: Epithelial cells line the cavities and surfaces of the body's organs and glands, and the three main shapes are squamous, columnar, and cuboidal. Epithelial cells contain no blood vessels, and their functions involve absorption, protection, transport, secretion, and sensing. Simple squamous epithelium is made of flat cells; it is present in lungs and lines the heart and vessels. Their flat shape aids in their function, which is diffusion of materials. The tunica intima, the inner layer of blood vessels, is lined with simple squamous epithelial tissue that sits on the basement membrane. Simple cuboidal epithelium is found in ducts, and simple columnar epithelium is found in tubes with projections (uterus, villi, bronchi). Any of these types of epithelial cells can be stacked, and then they are called stratified, not simple.

15. B: Anatomical directions are referenced to the midline (medial and lateral), to the center (proximal and distal), to the front and rear (anterior and posterior), toward the head and tail (cephalic and caudal), and to the head and feet (superior and inferior). In anatomical position, the body stands erect with palms facing forward. The clavicle would be medial and superior to the humerus, as it is closer to the midline and head.

16. A: This node is the primary stimulator of electrical activity in the heart. The other structures listed play a role in blood flow, but do not deal with electrical stimulation.

17. C: Generally, all sensory pathways that extend from the sensory receptor to the brain are composed of three long neurons called the primary, secondary, and tertiary neurons. The primary one stretches from the sensory receptor to the dorsal root ganglion of the spinal nerve, and the secondary one stretches from the cell body of the primary neuron to the spinal cord or the brain stem. The tertiary one stretches from the cell body of the secondary one into the thalamus. Each type of sense, such as touch, hearing, and vision, has a different pathway designed specifically for that sensation.

18. C: Visual processing begins in the retina. When an individual sees an image, it is taken in through the cornea and lens and then transmitted upside down onto the retina. The cells in the retina process what is being seen and then send signals to the ganglion cells, whose axons make up the optic nerve. The optic nerve cells connect the retina to the brain, which is where the processing of the visual information is completed and the images are returned to their proper orientation.

19. D: Receptors in the dermis help the body maintain homeostasis, for example, in terms of regulating body temperature. Signals travel to the hypothalamus, which then secretes hormones that activate effectors to keep the internal temperature at a set point of 98.6 °F (37 °C). For example, if the environment is too cold, the hypothalamus will initiate a pathway that will cause the muscles to shiver because shivering helps heat the body.

20. B: The radius and ulna are the bones from the elbow to the wrist, and the humerus is the bone between the elbow and the shoulder. The tibia and fibula are the bones from the knee to the ankle, and the femur is the bone from the knee to the hip. The other choices are bones in the body as well, just not limb bones. The mandible is the jaw, the scapula is the shoulder blade, and the carpal bones are in the wrist.

21. D: The primary function of the endocrine system is to maintain homeostasis, which means it makes constant adjustments to the body's systemic physiology to maintain a stable internal environment. Homeostasis requires an adequate heart rate, respirations, and water and electrolyte balance, as well as many other physiological processes; therefore, Choice *D* is the correct answer. The other answers are false because they represent only one aspect of homeostasis.

22. D: Thyroid hormone is responsible for regulating metabolism, so Choice *D* is the correct answer. Insulin is involved in glucose uptake into tissues, testosterone is for sperm production and secondary male sexual characteristics, and adrenaline is responsible for mechanisms in the flight-or-fight response, making Choices *A*, *B*, and *C* incorrect.

23. B: Smooth, skeletal, and cardiac muscle have defining characteristics, due to their vastly different functions. All have actin and myosin microfilaments that slide past each other to contract.

Skeletal muscles have long fibers made of clearly defined sarcomeres, which make them appear striated. Sarcomeres consist of alternating dark A bands (thick myosin) and light I bands (thin actin). Upon muscle contraction, fibers slide past each other. Skeletal muscles are attached to bone via tendons and are responsible for voluntary movement; their contraction brings bones together. They contain multiple nuclei due to their bundling into fibers.

Cardiac muscles also contain sarcomeres and appear striated, but they are branched cells with a single nucleus. Branching allows each cell to connect with several others, forming a huge network that has more strength (the whole is greater than the sum of its parts).

Smooth muscles are non-striated and are responsible for involuntary movement (such as digestion). They do not form cylindrical fibers like skeletal muscles. Their lack of striations is because they have no sarcomeres, and the filaments are randomly arranged.

24. B: The reflex arc is the simplest nerve pathway. The stimulus bypasses the brain, going from sensory receptors through an afferent (incoming) neuron to the spinal cord. It synapses with an efferent (outgoing) neuron in the spinal cord and is transmitted directly to muscle. There is no interneuron involved in a reflex arc. The classic example of a reflex arc is the knee-jerk response. Tapping on the patellar tendon of the knee stretches the quadriceps muscle of the thigh, resulting in contraction of the muscle and extension of the knee.

25. A: The sternum is medial to the deltoid because it is much closer to (typically right on) the midline of the body, while the deltoid is lateral at the shoulder cap. Superficial means that a structure is closer to the body surface and posterior means that it falls behind something else. For example, skin is superficial to bone and the kidneys are posterior to the rectus abdominis.

26. C: The relative density of eccrine sweat glands varies in different areas of the body. The palms and soles of the feet have the highest density, reaching values of approximately 400 sweat glands per square centimeter of epidermis. The head also has a high density of sweat glands, though significantly less than on the palms and soles. Areas such as the upper arms and thighs have only around 80 eccrine sweat glands per square inch of skin.

27. C: The cerebellum is important for balance and motor coordination. Aside from the brainstem and cerebellum, the outside portion of the brain is the cerebrum, which is the advanced operating system of the brain that is responsible for learning, emotion, memory, perception, and voluntary movement. The amygdala (associated with emotions), language areas, and corpus callosum all exist within the cerebrum.

28. A: Choice *B* might be an attractive answer choice, but neutrophils are part of the innate immune system and are not considered part of the primary immune response. The first event that happens in a primary immune response is that macrophages ingest pathogens and display their antigens. Then, they secrete interleukin 1 to recruit helper T cells. Once helper T cells are activated, they secrete interleukin 2 to simulate plasma B cell and killer T cell production. Only then can plasma B cells make the pathogen specific antibodies.

29. D: Cartilage and synovial fluid are the primary sources of cushioning for joints during impact. The proprioceptive system is responsible for body awareness, coordinating reflexes for balance, and modifying movements based on neural feedback.

30. A: When a muscle is stretched, the embedded spindles are also stretched, activating sensory neurons in the spindles. This activation sends an impulse to the spinal cord, where the sensory neurons synapse with motor neurons. These motor neurons exit the spinal cord and travel back towards the limb, where they innervate the extrafusal fibers, which receive the message to relax.

Physics

1. D: Circular motion occurs around an invisible line around which an object can rotate. This invisible line is called an axis. Choice *A,* center of mass, is the average location of an object's mass. Choice *B,* the center of matter, is not a real term. Choice *C,* elliptical, describes an elongated circle and is not a viable selection.

2. D: An object at rest has forces acting upon it, including gravitational, normal, and frictional forces. All of these forces are in balance with each other and cause no movement in the object's position. This is equilibrium. An object in constant motion is also considered to be in equilibrium or a state of balanced forces.

3. B: For charges, like charges repel each other and opposite charges attract each other. Negatives and positives will attract, while two positive charges or two negative charges will repel each other. Charges have an effect on each other, so Choices *C* and *D* are incorrect.

4. D: Mass refers to the amount or quantity there is of an object. Light, sound, and heat are all forms of energy that can travel in waves.

5. C: Motion with one dimension or measurement is known as a scalar quantity, and includes things such as length, speed, or time. Motion with two dimensions is known as a vector quantity. This would be speed with a direction, or velocity. Choices *A, B,* and *C* (mass, length, speed) are all measurements of magnitudes—one-dimensional scalar quantities.

6. B: It appears to bend because of the refraction of light traveling from air to water. When light travels from one material to another it can reflect, refract, and go through different materials. Choice *A* is incorrect, as the pencil does not actually become warped but only appears to be warped. Choice *C* is incorrect; although the pencil appears to bend because of its immersion into separate mediums where speed is different, the pencil does not become temporarily warped—it only appears to be warped. Choice *D* is incorrect; it is the refraction of light, not reflection. The latter happens within the same medium, which makes the answer choice incorrect.

7. A: According to Ohm's Law, $V = IR$, so using the given variables:

$$3.0 \text{ V} = I \times 6.0 \ \Omega$$

Solving for I:

$$I = \frac{3.0 \text{ V}}{6.0 \ \Omega} = 0.5 \text{ A}$$

Choice *B* incorporates a miscalculation in the equation by multiplying 3.0 V by 6.0 Ω, rather than dividing these values. Choices *C* and *D* are labeled with the wrong units; Joules measure energy, not current.

8. C: This is a fundamental law of thermodynamics. Energy can only transfer, transform, or travel. The amount of energy in a system is always the same.

9. D: When electricity is run through a wire, it is carrying a current. This current has a charge. Therefore, there is a charge running down the wire, which creates a magnetic field that can attract and repel just like any magnet.

10. B: In broad terms, energy is divided into kinetic and potential energy. Kinetic energy refers to an object in motion. It is the product of mass and velocity ($KE = \frac{1}{2}mv^2$). Potential energy refers to the capacity for doing work. Its gravitational configuration is the product of mass, acceleration due to gravity, and height ($PE = mgh$). Examples of kinetic energy include heat (which is the thermal energy from atoms and molecules moving around), waves like light, and physical motion. Potential energy examples include gravitational energy and chemical energy stored in bonds.

11. C: The answer is 1,800 seconds:

$$45 \text{ km} \times \frac{1{,}000 \text{ m}}{1 \text{ km}} \times \frac{1 \text{ s}}{25 \text{ m}} = 1{,}800 \text{ seconds}$$

12. D: The ship is traveling faster than the current, so it will be east of the starting location. Its net forward velocity is 0.5 m/s which is 1.8 km/hr, or 3.6 kilometers in two hours.

13. B: First, find the change in speed.

$$132 \text{ km/hr} - 60 \text{ km/hr} = 72 \text{ km/hr}$$

Then, convert this value to meters per second.

$$\frac{72 \text{ km}}{1 \text{ hr}} \times \frac{1{,}000 \text{ m}}{1 \text{ km}} \times \frac{1 \text{ hr}}{3{,}600 \text{ s}} = 20 \text{ m/s}$$

Average acceleration is found by dividing the change in velocity (or speed with a given direction) by the change in time.

$$a = \frac{\Delta}{\Delta t} = \frac{20 \text{ m/s}}{10 \text{ s}} = 2 \text{ m/s}^2$$

Therefore, the average acceleration after the engine is floored is 2 m/s^2.

14. C: The equation $F = ma$ should be memorized. All of the values are given in the correct units, so plug them into the equation:

$$F = 100{,}000\text{ kg} \times 0.5\text{ m/s}^2 = 50{,}000\text{ N}$$

15. B: This is actually a trick question. The mass of the astronaut is the same everywhere (it is the weight that varies from planet to planet). The astronaut's mass in kilograms is calculated by dividing his weight on Earth by the acceleration of gravity on Earth:

$$\frac{1{,}962\text{ N}}{9.81\text{ m/s}^2} = 200\text{ kg}$$

16. C: This question relies on Newton's second law of motion, typically expressed as $Force = Mass \times Acceleration$. However, in this problem, we are given the force and the mass and are tasked with finding the acceleration. This requires shifting the equation to $Acceleration = \frac{Force}{Mass}$. Plugging in the car's mass and Jerome's force gives us $\frac{1{,}500}{1{,}000} = 1.5$. With both speed and direction, acceleration is a vector quantity, so the answer will be expressed in meters per second squared, making Choice *C* the correct answer. Choices *A*, *B*, and *D* are incorrect because the values and/or units do not match the result of the force calculation.

17. C: The answer is her angular velocity increases from (a) to (b) as she pulls her arms in close to her body and reduces her moment of inertia.

18. C: As long as there is a closed path for electrons and a voltage, current will flow. Voltage, which is essentially the electromotive potential, causes current. However, if there is a suitable path for electrons but no voltage, or voltage in the absence of a viable path, current will cease.

19. B: The answer is at Point C, the bottom of the arc. The bottom of the arc must have the greatest kinetic energy because it is the point with the least potential energy, since the total energy is equivalent to the sum of both potential and kinetic energy.

20. C: This question must be read carefully. Choice *A* is incorrect. Even though the total energy is at a maximum at Points A and E, it isn't equal at only those points. The total energy is the same at all points. Choice *B* is incorrect. The kinetic energy is at a maximum at C, but not the total energy. The correct answer is Choice *C*. The total energy is conserved, so it's the same at all points on the arc. Choice *D* is incorrect. The motion of a pendulum is independent of the mass. Just like how all objects fall at the same rate, all pendulum bobs swing at the same rate, dependent on the length of the cord.

21. C: Many factors can impact the trajectory and speed of a projectile in motion, and a slight change in one of these variables can result in a major change in flight path or length. For example, the initial angle at which a baseball comes off a bat can be the difference between a pop fly that goes high but doesn't leave the infield and a homerun that lands in the upper deck. Choice *A* is therefore incorrect. Similarly, a golf ball hit by a professional golfer likely has a much higher velocity than one hit by a young child teeing off for their first time, and the former likely travels much faster and further. Choice *B* is therefore incorrect. Both initial angle and velocity can majorly impact the amount of time the projectile spends in the air, as well as whether it sails through the air or quickly skips along the ground. Choice *D* is therefore incorrect. Under all these scenarios, however, one factor remains constant: the acceleration experienced by these projectiles as they are released. In every case, the acceleration these objects experience is equal to the acceleration of gravity, which is constant everywhere on Earth. Two projectiles would only experience different accelerations after being released if they were released on different planets. Therefore, the correct answer is Choice *C*.

22. D: Valence electrons are the electrons contained with the outermost shell of an atom. The number of valence electrons a particular atom has determines how reactive that atom is. Generally speaking, atoms will lose or gain electrons in order to have the maximum number of electrons in their outermost shells. For most energy levels (another way to describe the "shells" of an atom), the maximum number of valence electrons is eight. Atoms with eight valence electrons do not readily react with other atoms and are considered chemically inert. The noble gases are a series of elements which have eight valence electrons in their natural state (except for helium, which only has two valence electrons) and are chemically inert with other atoms and molecules. Therefore, Choice *D* is correct. The other choices represent atoms with incomplete valence shells, and such atoms would likely readily react with other atoms or molecules.

23. C: Velocity is a quantity used to measure both the magnitude and direction of an object's motion. The magnitude of an object's velocity can be equal to that object's speed, but velocity and speed are distinct because velocity contains the direction of the speed as well. Therefore, Choice *C* is correct. Choice *A* is incorrect because the announcer did not report a direction for the velocity, so he did not accurately report the velocity. Choices *B* and *D* are incorrect because velocity can be calculated both for a specific moment in time (its instantaneous velocity) and over a stretch of time (its average velocity).

24. B: In physics, physical quantities are defined as any property of a material that can be measured and quantified, such as the length, area, or acceleration. Physical quantities can be further defined as either being a scalar quantity or a vector quantity. Scalar quantities have only a measurement for magnitude, whereas vector quantities have measurements for both magnitude and direction. This means Choice *B* is correct, as force is the only choice for which both the magnitude and direction of the physical quantity is necessary. Choices *A*, *C*, and *D* are all physical quantities for which only the magnitude must be known. It is nonsensical to ask what physical direction a pressure, temperature, or mass is directed at.

25. B: Objects are classified as negatively or positively charged bodies based on the relative level of negatively charged electrons present in the objects. If one object has more electrons than another, that object is considered negatively charged, and the other object is considered positively charged. When connected by a conductor, which allows for the electrons in both bodies to flow around the system, the electrons in the negatively charged body begin to flow towards the positively charged body, since electrons naturally repel each other and there are fewer electrons present in the positively charged body. The correct answer is Choice *B*. Choice *A* is incorrect because all electrons repel each other, not just electrons from oppositely charged bodies. Choice *C* is incorrect because the negatively charged body has a higher number of electrons than the positively charged body. Choice *D* is incorrect because electrons from the two opposing systems would not connect with each other but would repel each other.

26. D: In physics, torque can be defined as the turning effectiveness of a force. The magnitude of torque can be calculated with the equation $\tau = rFsin(\theta)$, where τ is torque, r is the length of the lever arm, F is the magnitude of the linear force, and θ is the angle between the lever arm and the force. Since sin is at its maximum at $90°$, torque is at its maximum when the angle between the lever arm and the force is $90°$. Therefore, Choice *D* is correct. All other choices would result in less than the maximum amount of torque.

27. A: When classifying the reflection of light off various surfaces and under various conditions, physicists divide the reflection of light into two categories. The first is specular reflection, which occurs when light reflects off a smooth surface. Due to the smoothness of the reflective surface, all the light rays are reflected back at the same angle at which they hit the surface. The second category is diffuse reflections, which occur when light reflects off relatively rough surfaces. The roughness of the surface reflects the light back in multiple different directions. Therefore, Choice *A* is correct. Choices *B* and *C* are incorrect because both specular and diffuse reflections can occur with multiple light sources, as the defining factor is the quality of the reflective surface. Choice *D* is incorrect because the quality of a reflection does not depend on the number of reflective surfaces, but rather on the reflective quality of those surfaces.

28. C: The exact properties of light have long been a matter of scientific speculation, and some of the greatest scientific minds in history have posited radically different theories. Isaac Newton, for instance, believed light acted like a particle, and called these light particles *corpuscles*. Many of his contemporaries believed instead that light acted like a wave. In 1801, British scientist Thomas Young demonstrated that light has properties of both particles and waves through the famous double-slit experiment. Therefore, the correct answer is Choice *C*.

29. C: Using the kinetic friction equations provided, the magnitude of the kinetic friction acting on the brick is equal to the product of the coefficient of kinetic friction and the normal force, which is equal to the product of the mass of the object and g (gravity). Therefore, $F_N = (2)(10) = 20$, and $F_f = (0.70)(20) = 14$ N. The correct answer is Choice *C*. All other answer choices result from improperly setting up the equations provided for kinetic friction.

30. D: According to Newton's third law of motion, for every force exerted onto an object there is an equal and opposite force directed back at the entity applying that force. Consequently, the amount of force the curling stone imparts onto the steel hockey puck is the same as the amount of force the steel hockey puck imparts on the curling stone. Therefore, Choices *A* and *B* are incorrect. The force of the collision must be greater than the force of friction on either object, as the question itself states that the collision occurred, meaning the force of the stones was greater than the force of friction working in the opposite direction. Therefore, Choice *C* is incorrect, leaving Choice *D* as the correct answer.

HESI A2 Practice Test #2

Mathematics

1. Add $5{,}089 + 10{,}323$.
   a. 15,402
   b. 15,412
   c. 5,234
   d. 15,234

2. Add $103{,}678 + 487$.
   a. 103,191
   b. 103,550
   c. 104,265
   d. 104,165

3. Add $1.001 + 5.629$.
   a. 6.630
   b. 4.628
   c. 5.630
   d. 6.628

4. Add $143.77 + 5.2$.
   a. 138.57
   b. 148.97
   c. 138.97
   d. 148.57

5. Add and express in reduced form: $\frac{5}{12} + \frac{4}{9}$
   a. $\frac{9}{17}$
   b. $\frac{1}{3}$
   c. $\frac{31}{36}$
   d. $\frac{3}{5}$

6. Add and express in reduced form: $\frac{14}{33} + \frac{10}{11}$
   a. $\frac{2}{11}$
   b. $\frac{6}{11}$
   c. $\frac{4}{3}$
   d. $\frac{44}{33}$

7. Subtract $9{,}576 - 891$.
   a. 10,467
   b. 9,685
   c. 8,325
   d. 8,685

8. Subtract $112{,}076 - 1{,}243$.
   a. 110,833
   b. 113,319
   c. 113,833
   d. 110,319

9. Subtract $50.888 - 13.091$.
   a. 37.797
   b. 63.979
   c. 37.979
   d. 33,817

10. Subtract $701.1 - 52.33$.
   a. 753.43
   b. 648.77
   c. 652.77
   d. 638.43

11. Subtract and express in reduced form: $\frac{23}{24} - \frac{1}{6}$
   a. $\frac{22}{18}$
   b. $\frac{11}{9}$
   c. $\frac{19}{24}$
   d. $\frac{4}{5}$

12. Subtract and express in reduced form: $\frac{43}{45} - \frac{11}{15}$
   a. $\frac{10}{45}$
   b. $\frac{16}{15}$
   c. $\frac{32}{30}$
   d. $\frac{2}{9}$

13. Multiply 578×15.
   a. 8,770
   b. 8,760
   c. 8,660
   d. 8,670

14. Multiply $13,114 \times 191$.
   a. 2,504,774
   b. 250,477
   c. 150,474
   d. 2,514,774

15. Multiply 12.4×0.2.
   a. 12.6
   b. 2.48
   c. 12.48
   d. 2.6

16. Multiply $1,987 \times 0.05$.
   a. 9.935
   b. 99.35
   c. 993.5
   d. 999.35

17. Multiply and reduce $\frac{15}{23} \times \frac{54}{127}$.
   a. $\frac{810}{2,921}$
   b. $\frac{81}{292}$
   c. $\frac{69}{150}$
   d. $\frac{810}{2,929}$

18. Multiply and reduce $\frac{54}{55} \times \frac{5}{9}$.
   a. $\frac{59}{64}$
   b. $\frac{270}{495}$
   c. $\frac{6}{11}$
   d. $\frac{5}{9}$

19. Divide and express the result as a mixed number: $1,202 \div 44$.
   a. 27 and $\frac{2}{7}$
   b. 2 and $\frac{7}{22}$
   c. 7 and $\frac{2}{7}$
   d. 27 and $\frac{7}{22}$

20. Divide and express the result as a mixed number: $188 \div 16$
   a. 1 and $\frac{3}{4}$
   b. 111 and $\frac{3}{4}$
   c. 10 and $\frac{3}{4}$
   d. 11 and $\frac{3}{4}$

21. Divide $702 \div 2.6$.
   a. 27
   b. 207
   c. 2.7
   d. 270

22. Divide $1{,}015 \div 1.4$.
   a. 7,250
   b. 725
   c. 7.25
   d. 72.50

23. Divide and reduce $\frac{26}{55} \div \frac{26}{11}$.
   a. $\frac{52}{11}$
   b. $\frac{26}{11}$
   c. $\frac{1}{5}$
   d. $\frac{2}{5}$

24. Divide and reduce $\frac{4}{13} \div \frac{27}{169}$.
   a. $\frac{52}{27}$
   b. $\frac{51}{27}$
   c. $\frac{52}{29}$
   d. $\frac{51}{29}$

25. What number does the Roman numeral MCDXXXII represent?
   a. 142
   b. 1642
   c. 1632
   d. 1432

26. What number does the Roman numeral CCLI represent?
    a. 1111
    b. 1151
    c. 151
    d. 251

27. Express 111 in Roman numerals.
    a. CCI
    b. CXI
    c. DDI
    d. DXI

28. Express 515 in Roman numerals.
    a. CVI
    b. DCV
    c. DXV
    d. VDV

29. Convert 1300 hours into a 12-hour clock time.
    a. 1:00 p.m.
    b. 11:00 a.m.
    c. 1:00 a.m.
    d. 11:00 p.m.

30. Convert 0830 hours into a 12-hour clock time.
    a. 8:30 p.m.
    b. 8:30 a.m.
    c. 11:30 a.m.
    d. 11:30 p.m.

31. What time is 5:00 p.m. in military (24-hour clock) time?
    a. 1500 hours
    b. 1700 hours
    c. 0500 hours
    d. 0700 hours

32. What time is 11:00am in military (24-hour clock) time?
    a. 0100 hours
    b. 1100 hours
    c. 1200 hours
    d. 0200 hours

33. The hospital has a nurse-to-patient ratio of $1:25$. If a maximum of 325 patients may be admitted at a time, how many nurses are there?
    a. 13 nurses
    b. 25 nurses
    c. 325 nurses
    d. 12 nurses

34. A hospital has a bed-to-room ratio of $2:1$. If there are 145 rooms, how many beds are there?
   a. 145 beds
   b. 2 beds
   c. 90 beds
   d. 290 beds

35. Solve for x: $\frac{2x}{5} - 1 = 59$
   a. 60
   b. 145
   c. 150
   d. 115

36. A National Hockey League store in the state of Michigan advertises 50% off all items. Sales tax in Michigan is 6%. How much would a hat originally priced at $32.99 and a jersey originally priced at $64.99 cost during this sale? Round to the nearest penny.
   a. $97.98
   b. $103.86
   c. $51.93
   d. $48.99

37. Store-brand coffee beans cost $1.23 per pound. A local coffee bean roaster charges $1.98 per $1\frac{1}{2}$ pounds. How much more would 5 pounds from the local roaster cost than 5 pounds of the store brand?
   a. $0.55
   b. $1.55
   c. $1.45
   d. $0.45

38. Paint Inc. charges $2,000 for painting the first 1,800 feet of trim on a house and $1.00 per foot for each foot after. How much would it cost to paint a house with 3,125 feet of trim?
   a. $3,125
   b. $2,000
   c. $5,125
   d. $3,325

39. A bucket can hold 11.4 liters of water. A kiddie pool needs 35 gallons of water to be full. How many times will the bucket need to be filled to fill the kiddie pool? (Use the conversion 1 gallon = 3.8 liters.)
   a. 12
   b. 35
   c. 11
   d. 45

40. In Jim's school, there are a total of 650 boys and girls. There are 3 girls for every 2 boys. How many students are girls?
   a. 260
   b. 130
   c. 65
   d. 390

41. Convert 0.351 to a percentage.
   a. 3.51%
   b. 35.1%
   c. $\frac{351}{100}$
   d. 0.00351%

42. Convert $\frac{2}{9}$ to a percentage.
   a. 22.22%
   b. 4.5%
   c. 450%
   d. 0.22%

43. Convert 57% to a decimal.
   a. 570
   b. 5.70
   c. 0.06
   d. 0.57

44. What is 3 out of 8 expressed as a percent?
   a. 37.5%
   b. 37%
   c. 26.7%
   d. 2.67%

45. What is 39% of 164?
   a. 63.96
   b. 23.78
   c. 6,396
   d. 2.38

46. 32 is 25% of what number?
   a. 64
   b. 128
   c. 12.65
   d. 8

47. Convert $\frac{5}{8}$ to a decimal, rounding to the nearest hundredth.
   a. 0.62
   b. 1.05
   c. 0.63
   d. 1.60

48. Change $3\frac{3}{5}$ to a decimal.
   a. 3.6
   b. 4.67
   c. 5.3
   d. 0.28

49. Change 0.56 to a fraction.

a. $\frac{5.6}{100}$

b. $\frac{14}{25}$

c. $\frac{56}{1000}$

d. $\frac{56}{10}$

50. Change 9.3 to a fraction or a mixed number.

a. $9\frac{3}{7}$

b. $\frac{903}{1000}$

c. $\frac{9.03}{100}$

d. $9\frac{3}{10}$

51. A rectangle was formed out of pipe cleaner. Its length was $\frac{1}{2}$ foot and its width was $\frac{11}{2}$ inches. What is its area in square inches?

a. $\frac{11}{4}\text{ in}^2$

b. $\frac{11}{2}\text{ in}^2$

c. 22 in^2

d. 33 in^2

52. What is the perimeter of the figure below? Note that the solid outer line is the perimeter.

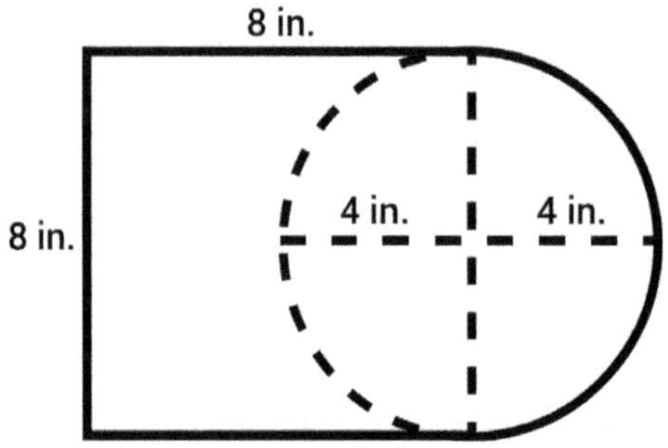

a. 48.565 in
b. 36.565 in
c. 39.78 in
d. 39.565 in

53. What is the slope of this line?

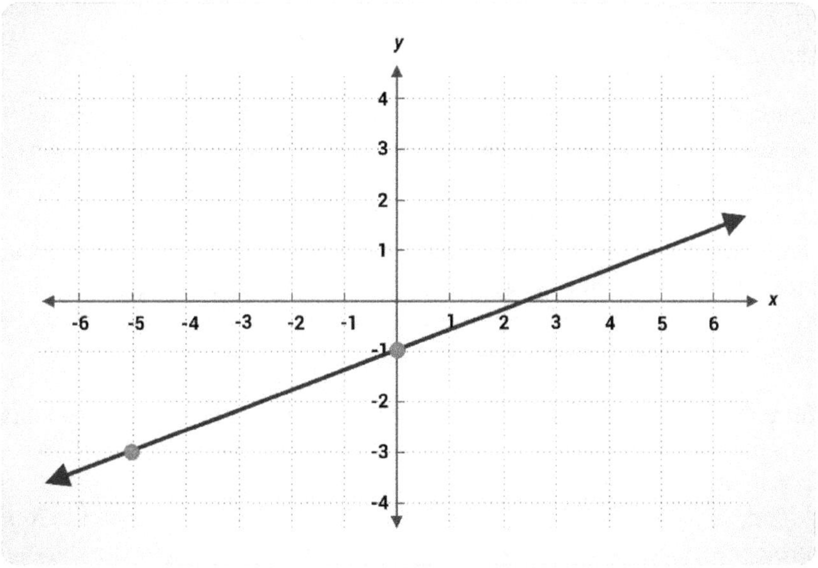

a. 2
b. $\frac{5}{2}$
c. $\frac{1}{2}$
d. $\frac{2}{5}$

54. Find the following sum, and round to the nearest hundredths place:

$$4.673 + 2.651$$

a. 73.24
b. 7.32
c. 7.33
d. 7.324

55. A shuffled deck of 52 cards contains 4 kings. One card is drawn, and is not put back in the deck. Then a second card is drawn. What's the probability that both cards are kings?

a. $\frac{1}{169}$
b. $\frac{1}{221}$
c. $\frac{1}{13}$
d. $\frac{4}{13}$

Reading Comprehension

Questions 1–6 are based on the following passage:

When researchers and engineers undertake a large-scale scientific project, they may end up making discoveries and developing technologies that have far wider uses than originally intended. This is especially true at NASA, one of the most influential and innovative scientific organizations in America. NASA *spinoff technology* refers to innovations originally developed for NASA space projects that are now used in a wide range of different commercial fields. Many consumers are unaware that products they are buying are based on NASA research! Spinoff technology proves that it is worthwhile to invest in scientific research because it could enrich people's lives in unexpected ways.

The first spinoff technology worth mentioning is baby food. In space, where astronauts have limited access to fresh food and fewer options about their daily meals, malnutrition is a serious concern. Consequently, NASA researchers were looking for ways to enhance the nutritional value of astronauts' food. Scientists found that a certain type of algae could be added to food to improve the food's neurological benefits. When experts in the commercial food industry learned of this algae's potential to boost brain health, they were quick to begin their own research. The nutritional substance from algae was then developed into a product called life's DHA, which can be found in over 90% of infant food sold in America.

Another intriguing example of a spinoff technology can be found in fashion. People who are always dropping their sunglasses may have invested in a pair of sunglasses with scratch-resistant lenses, which are made of glass that is impossible to scratch, even when dropped on an abrasive surface. This innovation is incredibly advantageous for people who are clumsy, but most shoppers don't know that this technology was originally developed by NASA. Scientists first created scratch-resistant glass to help protect costly and crucial equipment from getting scratched in space, especially the helmet visors in space suits. However, sunglasses companies later realized that this technology could be profitable for their products, and they licensed the technology from NASA.

1. What is the main purpose of this article?
   a. To advise consumers to do more research before making a purchase
   b. To persuade readers to support NASA's research
   c. To tell a narrative about the history of space technology
   d. To define and describe instances of spinoff technology

2. What is the organizational structure of this article?
   a. A general definition followed by more specific examples
   b. A general opinion followed by supporting evidence
   c. An important moment in history followed by chronological details
   d. A popular misconception followed by counterevidence

3. Why did NASA scientists research algae?
   a. They already knew algae was healthy for babies.
   b. They were interested in how to grow food in space.
   c. They were looking for ways to add health benefits to food.
   d. They hoped to use it to protect expensive research equipment.

4. What does the word *neurological* mean in the second paragraph?
    a. Related to the body
    b. Related to the brain
    c. Related to vitamins
    d. Related to technology

5. Why does the author mention space suit helmets?
    a. To give an example of astronaut fashion
    b. To explain where sunglasses got their shape
    c. To explain how astronauts protect their eyes
    d. To give an example of valuable space equipment

6. Which statement would the author probably NOT agree with?
    a. Consumers don't always know the history of the products they are buying.
    b. Sometimes new innovations have unexpected applications.
    c. It is difficult to make money from scientific research.
    d. Space equipment is often very expensive.

Questions 7–13 are based on the following passage:

People who argue that William Shakespeare is not responsible for the plays attributed to his name are known as anti-Stratfordians (from the name of Shakespeare's birthplace, Stratford-upon-Avon). The most common anti-Stratfordian claim is that William Shakespeare simply was not educated enough or from a high enough social class to have written plays overflowing with references to such a wide range of subjects like history, the classics, religion, and international culture. William Shakespeare was the son of a glove-maker, he only had a basic grade-school education, and he never set foot outside of England—so how could he have produced plays of such sophistication and imagination? How could he have written in such detail about historical figures and events, or about different cultures and locations around Europe? According to anti-Stratfordians, the depth of knowledge contained in Shakespeare's plays suggests a well-traveled writer from a wealthy background with a university education, not a countryside writer like Shakespeare. But in fact, there is not much substance to such speculation, and most anti-Stratfordian arguments can be refuted with a little background about Shakespeare's time and upbringing.

First of all, those who doubt Shakespeare's authorship often point to his common birth and brief education as stumbling blocks to his writerly genius. Although it is true that Shakespeare did not come from a noble class, his father was a very successful glove-maker and his mother was from a very wealthy landowning family—so while Shakespeare may have had a country upbringing, he was certainly from a well-off family and would have been educated accordingly. Also, even though he did not attend university, grade-school education in Shakespeare's time was actually quite rigorous and exposed students to classic drama through writers like Seneca and Ovid. It is not unreasonable to believe that Shakespeare received a very solid foundation in poetry and literature from his early schooling.

Next, anti-Stratfordians tend to question how Shakespeare could write so extensively about countries and cultures he had never visited before. For instance, several of his most famous works like Romeo and Juliet and The Merchant of Venice were set in Italy, which is located on the opposite side of Europe from England. But again, this criticism does not hold up under scrutiny. For one thing, Shakespeare was living in London, a bustling metropolis of international trade, the most populous city in England, and a political and cultural hub of Europe. In the daily crowds of people,

Shakespeare would certainly have been able to meet travelers from other countries and hear firsthand accounts of life in their home country. And, in addition to the influx of information from world travelers, this was also the age of the printing press. This jump in technology made it possible to print and circulate books much more easily than in the past. This also facilitated a freer flow of information across different countries, allowing people to read about life and ideas from all over Europe. One needn't travel the continent in order to learn and write about its culture.

7. What is the main purpose of this article?
   a. To explain two sides of an argument and allow readers to choose which side they agree with
   b. To encourage readers to be skeptical about the authorship of famous poems and plays
   c. To give historical background on an important literary figure
   d. To criticize a theory by presenting counterevidence

8. Which sentence contains the author's thesis?
   a. People who argue that William Shakespeare is not responsible for the plays attributed to his name are known as anti-Stratfordians.
   b. But in fact, there is not much substance to such speculation, and most anti-Stratfordian arguments can be refuted with a little background about Shakespeare's time and upbringing.
   c. It is not unreasonable to believe that Shakespeare received a very solid foundation in poetry and literature from his early schooling.
   d. Next, anti-Stratfordians tend to question how Shakespeare could write so extensively about countries and cultures he had never visited before.

9. How does the author respond to the claim that Shakespeare was not well-educated because he did not attend university?
   a. By insisting upon Shakespeare's natural genius
   b. By explaining grade-school curriculum in Shakespeare's time
   c. By comparing Shakespeare with other uneducated writers of his time
   d. By pointing out that Shakespeare's wealthy parents probably paid for private tutors

10. What does the word "bustling" in the third paragraph most nearly mean?
   a. Busy
   b. Foreign
   c. Expensive
   d. Undeveloped

11. What can be inferred from the article?
   a. Shakespeare's peers were jealous of his success and wanted to attack his reputation.
   b. Until recently, classic drama was only taught in universities.
   c. International travel was extremely rare in Shakespeare's time.
   d. In Shakespeare's time, glove-makers were not part of the upper class.

12. Why does the author mention *Romeo and Juliet*?
   a. It is Shakespeare's most famous play.
   b. It was inspired by Shakespeare's trip to Italy.
   c. It is an example of a play set outside of England.
   d. It was unpopular when Shakespeare first wrote it.

13. Which statement would the author probably agree with?
  a. It is possible to learn things from reading rather than from firsthand experience.
  b. If you want to be truly cultured, you need to travel the world
  c. People never become successful without a university education.
  d. All of the world's great art comes from Italy.

The next four questions are based on the following passage:

> Four score and seven years ago our fathers brought forth on this continent, a new nation, conceived in Liberty, and dedicated to the proposition that all men are created equal.
>
> Now we are engaged in a great civil war, testing whether that nation, or any nation so conceived and so dedicated, can long endure. We are met on a great battle-field of that war. We have come to dedicate a portion of that field, as a final resting place for those who here gave their lives that that nation might live. It is altogether fitting and proper that we should do this.
>
> But, in a larger sense, we cannot dedicate—we cannot consecrate—we cannot hallow—this ground. The brave men, living and dead, who struggled here, have consecrated it, far above our poor power to add or detract. The world will little note, nor long remember what we say here, but it can never forget what they did here. It is for us the living, rather, to be dedicated here to the unfinished work which they who fought here have thus far so nobly advanced. It is rather for us to be here dedicated to the great task remaining before us—that from these honored dead we take increased devotion to that cause for which they gave the last full measure of devotion—that we here highly resolve that these dead shall not have died in vain—that this nation, under God, shall have a new birth of freedom—and that government of the people, by the people, for the people, shall not perish from the earth.

Adapted from "Address Delivered at the Dedication of the Cemetery at Gettysburg" by Abraham Lincoln, November 19, 1863.

14. The best description for the phrase "Four score and seven years ago" is:
  a. A unit of measurement
  b. A period of time
  c. A literary movement
  d. A statement of political reform

15. Which war is Abraham Lincoln referring to in the following passage:

> Now we are engaged in a great civil war, testing whether that nation, or any nation so conceived and so dedicated, can long endure.

  a. World War I
  b. The War of Spanish Succession
  c. World War II
  d. The American Civil War

16. What message is the speaker trying to convey through this address?
  a. The audience should perpetuate the ideals of freedom that the soldiers died fighting for.
  b. The audience should honor the dead by establishing an annual memorial service.
  c. The audience should form a militia that would overturn the current political structure.
  d. The audience should forget the lives that were lost and discredit the soldiers.

17. What is the effect of Lincoln's statement in the following passage:

> But, in a larger sense, we cannot dedicate—we cannot consecrate—we cannot hallow—this ground. The brave men, living and dead, who struggled here, have consecrated it, far above our poor power to add or detract.

a. His comparison emphasizes the great sacrifice of the soldiers who fought in the war.
b. His comparison serves as a reminder of the inadequacies of his audience.
c. His comparison serves as a catalyst for guilt and shame among audience members.
d. His comparison suggests that the dedication ceremony was inappropriate.

The next three questions are based on the following passage:

> "Did you ever come across a protégé of his—one Hyde?" He asked.
>
> "Hyde?" repeated Lanyon. "No. Never heard of him. Since my time."
>
> That was the amount of information that the lawyer carried back with him to the great, dark bed on which he tossed to and fro until the small hours of the morning began to grow large. It was a night of little ease to his toiling mind, toiling in mere darkness and besieged by questions.
>
> Six o'clock struck on the bells of the church that was so conveniently near to Mr. Utterson's dwelling, and still he was digging at the problem. Hitherto it had touched him on the intellectual side alone; but now his imagination also was engaged, or rather enslaved; and as he lay and tossed in the gross darkness of the night in the curtained room, Mr. Enfield's tale went by before his mind in a scroll of lighted pictures. He would be aware of the great field of lamps in a nocturnal city; then of the figure of a man walking swiftly; then of a child running from the doctor's; and then these met, and that human Juggernaut trod the child down and passed on regardless of her screams. Or else he would see a room in a rich house, where his friend lay asleep, dreaming and smiling at his dreams; and then the door of that room would be opened, the curtains of the bed plucked apart, the sleeper recalled, and, lo! There would stand by his side a figure to whom power was given, and even at that dead hour he must rise and do its bidding. The figure in these two phases haunted the lawyer all night; and if at any time he dozed over, it was but to see it glide more stealthily through sleeping houses, or move the more swiftly, and still the more smoothly, even to dizziness, through wider labyrinths of lamplighted city, and at every street corner crush a child and leave her screaming. And still the figure had no face by which he might know it; even in his dreams it had no face, or one that baffled him and melted before his eyes; and thus it was that there sprung up and grew apace in the lawyer's mind a singularly strong, almost an inordinate, curiosity to behold the features of the real Mr. Hyde. If he could but once set eyes on him, he thought the mystery would lighten and perhaps roll altogether away, as was the habit of mysterious things when well examined. He might see a reason for his friend's strange preference or bondage, and even for the startling clauses of the will. And at least it would be a face worth seeing: the face of a man who was without bowels of mercy: a face which had but to show itself to raise up, in the mind of the unimpressionable Enfield, a spirit of enduring hatred.
>
> From that time forward, Mr. Utterson began to haunt the door in the by-street of shops. In the morning before office hours, at noon when business was plenty and time scarce, at night under the face of the fogged city moon, by all lights and at all hours of solitude or concourse, the lawyer was to be found on his chosen post.

"If he be Mr. Hyde," he had thought, "I should be Mr. Seek."

Excerpt from The Strange Case of Dr. Jekyll and Mr. Hyde by Robert Louis Stevenson.

18. What can one infer about the meaning of the word *Juggernaut* from the author's use of it in the passage?
   a. It is an apparition that appears at daybreak.
   b. It scares children.
   c. It is associated with space travel.
   d. Mr. Utterson finds it soothing.

19. What is the definition of the word *haunt* in the following passage?

   From that time forward, Mr. Utterson began to haunt the door in the by-street of shops. In the morning before office hours, at noon when business was plenty and time scarce, at night under the face of the fogged city moon, by all lights and at all hours of solitude or concourse, the lawyer was to be found on his chosen post.

   a. To levitate
   b. To constantly visit
   c. To terrorize
   d. To daunt

20. What can one reasonably conclude from the final comment of this passage:

   "If he be Mr. Hyde," he had thought, "I should be Mr. Seek."

   a. The speaker is considering a name change.
   b. The speaker is experiencing an identity crisis.
   c. The speaker has mistakenly been looking for the wrong person.
   d. One can conclude that the speaker intends to continue to look for Hyde.

Questions 21–25 are based on the following passage:

Dana Gioia argues in his article that poetry is dying, now little more than a limited art form confined to academic and college settings. Of course, poetry remains healthy in the academic setting, but the idea of poetry being limited to this academic subculture is a stretch. New technology and social networking alone have contributed to poets and other writers' work being shared across the world. YouTube has emerged to be a major asset to poets, allowing live performances to be streamed to billions of users. Even now, poetry continues to grow and voice topics that are relevant to the culture of our time. Poetry is not in the spotlight as it may have been in earlier times, but it's still a relevant art form that continues to expand in scope and appeal.

Furthermore, Gioia's argument does not account for live performances of poetry. Not everyone has taken a poetry class or enrolled in university—but most everyone is online. The Internet is a perfect launching point to get all creative work out there. An example of this was Buddy Wakefield's performance of his poem "Hurling Crowbirds at Mockingbars." Wakefield is a well-known poet who has published several collections of contemporary poetry. "Crowbirds" is one of my favorite works by Wakefield, especially because of his performance of it at New York University in 2009. Although his reading was a campus event, views of his performance online number in the thousands. His poetry attracted people outside of the university setting.

Naturally, the poem's popularity can be attributed to both Wakefield's performance and the quality of his writing. "Crowbirds" touches on themes of core human concepts such as faith, personal loss, and growth. These are not ideas that only poets or students of literature understand, but all human beings: "You acted like I was hurling crowbirds at mockingbars / and abandoned me for not making sense. / Evidently, I don't experience things as rationally as you do." Wakefield weaves together a complex description of the perplexed and hurt emotions of the speaker who is undergoing a separation from a romantic interest. The line "You acted like I was hurling crowbirds at mockingbars" conjures up an image of someone confused, seemingly out of their mind ... or in the case of the speaker, passionately trying to grasp at a relationship that is fading. The speaker is looking back and finding the words that described how he wasn't making sense. This poem is particularly human and gripping in its message, but the entire effect of the poem is enhanced through the physical performance.

At its core, poetry is about addressing issues and ideas in the world. Part of this is also addressing the perspectives that are exiguously considered. Although the platform may look different, poetry continues to have a steady audience due to the emotional connection the poet shares with the audience.

21. Which of the following best explains how the passage is organized?
   a. The author begins with a long definition of the main topic and then proceeds to prove how that definition has changed over the course of modernity.
   b. The author presents a puzzling phenomenon and uses the rest of the passage to showcase personal experiences in order to explain it.
   c. The author contrasts two different viewpoints and then builds a case showing preference for one over the other.
   d. The passage is an analysis of a theory that the author has no stake in.

22. The author of the passage would likely agree most with which of the following?
   a. Buddy Wakefield is a genius and is considered at the forefront of modern poetry.
   b. Poetry is not irrelevant; it is an art form that adapts to the changing times while retaining its core elements.
   c. Spoken word is the zenith of poetic forms and the premier style of poetry in this decade.
   d. Poetry is on the verge of vanishing from our cultural consciousness.

23. Which of the following words, if substituted for the word exiguously in the last paragraph, would least change the meaning of the sentence?
   a. Indolently
   b. Inaudibly
   c. Interminably
   d. Infrequently

24. Which of the following is most closely analogous to the author's opinion of Buddy Wakefield's performance in relation to modern poetry?
   a. Someone's refusal to accept that the Higgs boson particle will validate the Standard Model of physics
   b. An individual's belief that soccer will lose popularity within the next 50 years
   c. A professor's opinion that poetry contains the language of the heart, while fiction contains the language of the mind
   d. A student's insistence that psychoanalysis is a subset of modern psychology

25. What is the primary purpose of the passage?
   a. To educate readers on the development of poetry and describe the historical implications of poetry in media
   b. To disprove Dana Gioia's stance that poetry is becoming irrelevant and is only appreciated in academia
   c. To inform readers of the brilliance of Buddy Wakefield and to introduce them to other poets that have influenced contemporary poetry
   d. To prove that Gioia's article does have some truth to it and to shed light on its relevance to modern poetry

The next four questions are based on the following passage:

> Mineralogy is the science of minerals, which are the naturally occurring elements and compounds that make up the solid parts of the universe. Mineralogy is usually considered in terms of materials in the Earth, but meteorites provide samples of minerals from outside the Earth.
>
> A mineral may be defined as a naturally occurring, homogeneous solid, that is inorganically formed, with a definite chemical composition, and an ordered atomic arrangement. The qualification naturally occurring is essential because it is possible to reproduce most minerals in the laboratory. For example, evaporating a solution of sodium chloride produces crystal indistinguishable from those of the mineral halite, but such laboratory-produced crystals are not minerals.
>
> A homogeneous solid is one consisting of a single kind of material that cannot be separated into simpler compounds by any physical method. The requirement that a mineral be solid eliminates gases and liquids from consideration. Thus, ice is a mineral (a very common one, especially at high altitudes and latitudes) but water is not. Some mineralogists dispute this restriction and would consider both water and native mercury (also a liquid) as minerals.
>
> The restriction of minerals to inorganically formed substances eliminates those homogenous solids produced by animals and plants. Thus, the shell of an oyster and the pearl inside, though both consist of calcium carbonate indistinguishable chemically or physically from the mineral aragonite, are not usually considered minerals.
>
> The requirement of a definite chemical composition implies that a mineral is a chemical compound, and the composition of a chemical compound is readily expressed by a formula. Mineral formulas may be simple or complex, depending upon the number of elements present and the proportions in which they are combined.
>
> Minerals are crystalline solids, and the presence of an ordered atomic arrangement is the criterion of the crystalline state. Under favorable conditions of formation, the ordered atomic arrangement is expressed in the external crystal form. In fact, the presence of an ordered atomic arrangement and crystalline solids was deduced from the external regularity of crystals by a French mineralogist, Abbé R. Haüy, early in the 19th century.

Excerpt adapted from "Mineralogy," Encyclopedia International, by Grolier.

26. According to the text, an object or substance must have all of the following criteria to be considered a mineral except for which?
   a. It must be naturally occurring.
   b. It must be a homogeneous solid.
   c. It must be organically formed.
   d. It must have a definite chemical composition.

27. One can deduce that French mineralogist Abbé R. Haüy specialized in what field of study?
    a. Geology
    b. Psychology
    c. Biology
    d. Botany

28. What is the definition of the word *homogeneous* as it appears in the following passage?

    A homogeneous solid is one consisting of a single kind of material that cannot be separated into simpler compounds by any physical method.

    a. Made of a single substance
    b. Differing in some areas
    c. Having a higher atomic mass
    d. Lacking necessary properties

29. The suffix *-logy* refers to:
    a. The properties of
    b. The chemical makeup of
    c. The study of
    d. The classification of

The next four questions are based on the following passage:

> Three years ago, I think there were not many bird-lovers in the United States who believed it possible to prevent the total extinction of both egrets from our fauna. All the known rookeries accessible to plume-hunters had been totally destroyed. Two years ago, the secret discovery of several small, hidden colonies prompted William Dutcher, President of the National Association of Audubon Societies, and Mr. T. Gilbert Pearson, Secretary, to attempt the protection of those colonies. With a fund contributed for the purpose, wardens were hired and duly commissioned. As previously stated, one of those wardens was shot dead in cold blood by a plume hunter. The task of guarding swamp rookeries from the attacks of money-hungry desperadoes, to whom the accursed plumes were worth their weight in gold, is a very chancy proceeding. There is now one warden in Florida who says that "before they get my rookery they will first have to get me."
>
> Thus far, the protective work of the Audubon Association has been successful. Now there are 20 colonies, which contain all told, about 5,000 egrets and about 120,000 herons and ibises which are guarded by the Audubon wardens. One of the most important is on Bird Island, a mile out in Orange Lake, Central Florida, and it is ably defended by Oscar E. Baynard. To-day, the plume hunters who do not dare to raid the guarded rookeries are trying to study out the lines of flight of the birds, to and from their feeding-grounds, and shoot them in transit. Their motto is "Anything to beat the law, and get the plumes." It is there that the state of Florida should take part in the war.
>
> The success of this campaign is attested by the fact that last year a number of egrets were seen in eastern Massachusetts—for the first time in many years. And so to-day the question is, can the wardens continue to hold the plume-hunters at bay?

Excerpt from Our Vanishing Wildlife by William T. Hornaday.

30. What is the meaning of the word *rookeries* in the following text?

> To-day, the plume hunters who do not dare to raid the guarded rookeries are trying to study out the lines of flight of the birds, to and from their feeding-grounds, and shoot them in transit.

a. Houses in a slum area
b. A place where hunters gather to trade tools
c. A place where wardens go to trade stories
d. A colony of breeding birds

31. What is on Bird Island?
a. Hunters selling plumes
b. An important bird colony
c. Bird Island Battle between the hunters and the wardens
d. An important egret with unique plumes

32. What is the main purpose of the passage?
a. To persuade the audience to act in preservation of the bird colonies
b. To show the effect hunting egrets has had on the environment
c. To argue that the preservation of bird colonies has had a negative impact on the environment
d. To demonstrate the success of the protective work of the Audubon Association

33. Why are hunters trying to study the lines of flight of the birds?
a. To study ornithology, which requires knowing the lines of flight that birds take
b. To help wardens preserve the lives of the birds
c. To have a better opportunity to hunt the birds
d. To build their homes under the lines of flight because they believe it brings good luck

The next six questions are based on the following passage:

The Myth of Head Heat Loss

It has recently been brought to my attention that most people believe that 75% of your body heat is lost through your head. I had certainly heard this before, and I'm not going to attempt to say I didn't believe it when I first heard it. It is natural to be gullible to anything said with enough authority. But the "fact" that the majority of your body heat is lost through your head is a lie.

Let me explain. Heat loss is proportional to surface area exposed. An elephant loses a great deal more heat than an anteater because it has a much greater surface area than an anteater. Each cell has mitochondria that produce energy in the form of heat, and it takes a lot more energy to run an elephant than an anteater.

So, each part of your body loses its proportional amount of heat in accordance with its surface area. The human torso probably loses the most heat, though the legs lose a significant amount as well. Some people have asked, "Why does it feel so much warmer when you cover your head than when you don't?" Well, that's because your head loses a lot of heat when it is not clothed, while the clothing on the rest of your body provides insulation. If you went outside with a hat and pants but no shirt, not only would you look stupid, but your heat loss would be significantly greater because so much more of you would be exposed. So, if given the choice to cover your chest or your head in the cold, choose the chest. It could save your life.

34. What is the primary purpose of this passage?
   a. To provide evidence that disproves a myth
   b. To compare elephants and anteaters
   c. To explain why it is appropriate to wear clothes in winter
   d. To show how people are gullible

35. Which of the following best describes the main idea of the passage?
   a. It is better to wear a shirt than a hat.
   b. Heat loss is proportional to surface area exposed.
   c. It is natural to be gullible.
   d. The human chest loses the most heat.

36. Why does the author compare elephants and anteaters?
   a. To express an opinion
   b. To give an example that helps clarify the main point
   c. To show the differences between them
   d. To persuade why one is better than the other

37. The statement, "If you went outside with a hat and pants but no shirt, not only would you look stupid, but your heat loss would be significantly greater because so much more of you would be exposed" is which of the following?
   a. An opinion
   b. A fact
   c. An opinion within a fact
   d. Neither

38. Which of the following best describes the tone of the passage?
   a. Harsh
   b. Angry
   c. Casual
   d. Indifferent

39. Which of the following sentences provides the best evidence to support the main idea?
   a. "It is natural to be gullible to anything said with enough authority."
   b. "So, each part of your body loses its proportional amount of heat in accordance with its surface area."
   c. "So, if given the choice to cover your chest or your head in the cold, choose the chest."
   d. "But the 'fact' that the majority of your body heat is lost through your head is a lie."

The next eight questions are based on the following passage:

The Global Water Crisis

For decades, the world's water supply has been decreasing. At least 10% of the world's population, or over 780 million people, does not have access to potable water. They have to walk for miles, carrying heavy buckets in intense heat, in order to obtain the essential life source that comes freely from our faucets.

We are in a global water crisis. Only 2.5% of the water on Earth is suitable for drinking, and over 70% of this water is frozen in the polar ice caps or located deep underground. This leaves a very small percentage available for drinking. And yet, we see millions of gallons of water being wasted on watering huge lawns in deserts like Arizona, running dishwashers that are only half-full, or filling personal pools in Los Angeles. Meanwhile, people in Africa are dying of thirst.

In order to reduce water waste, Americans and citizens of other first world countries should adhere to the following guidelines: run the dishwasher only when it is full, do only full loads of laundry, wash the car with a bucket and not with a hose, take showers only when necessary, swim in public pools, and just be <u>cognizant</u> of how much water they are using in general. Our planet is getting thirstier by the year, and if we do not solve this problem, our species will surely perish.

40. Which of the following best supports the assertion that we need to limit our water usage?
    a. People are wasting water on superfluous things.
    b. There is very little water on Earth suitable for drinking.
    c. At least 10% of the world population does not have access to drinking water.
    d. There is plenty of drinking water in industrialized countries but not anywhere else.

41. How is the content in the selection organized?
    a. In chronological order
    b. Compare and contrast
    c. As a set of problems and solutions
    d. As a series of descriptions

42. Which of the following, if true, would challenge the assertion that we are in a global water crisis?
    a. There are abundant water stores on Earth that scientists are not reporting.
    b. Much of the water we drink comes from rain.
    c. People in Africa only have to walk less than a mile to get water.
    d. Most Americans only run the dishwasher when it is full.

43. The selection is written in which of the following styles?
    a. As a narrative
    b. In a persuasive manner
    c. As an informative piece
    d. As a series of descriptions

44. Which of the following is implicitly stated within the following sentence:
    "This leaves a very small percentage available for drinking. And yet, we see millions of gallons of water being wasted on watering huge lawns in deserts like Arizona, running dishwashers that are only half-full, or filling personal pools in Los Angeles. Meanwhile, people in Africa are dying of thirst."

    a. People run dishwashers that are not full.
    b. People in Africa are dying of thirst.
    c. People take water for granted.
    d. People should stop watering their lawns.

45. Why does the author mention that people have to walk for miles in intense heat to get water?
    a. To inform the reader on the hardships of living in a third-world country
    b. To inspire compassion in the reader
    c. To show that water is only available in industrialized countries
    d. To persuade the reader to reduce their water usage

46. What is meant by the word *cognizant*?
    a. To be interested
    b. To be amused
    c. To be mindful
    d. To be accepting

47. What is the main idea of the passage?
    a. People should reduce their water usage.
    b. There is very little drinking water on earth.
    c. People take their access to water for granted.
    d. People should swim in public pools.

Directions for questions 48–55: After reading the passage, choose the best answer to the question based on what is stated in the passage.

48. There are two major kinds of cameras on the market right now for amateur photographers. Camera enthusiasts can either purchase a digital single-lens reflex (DSLR) camera or a compact system camera (CSC). The main difference between a DSLR and a CSC is that the DSLR has a full-sized sensor, which means it fits in a much larger body. The CSC uses a mirrorless system, which makes for a lighter, smaller camera. While both take quality pictures, the DSLR generally has better picture quality due to the larger sensor. CSCs still take very good quality pictures and are more convenient to carry than a DSLR. This makes the CSC an ideal choice for the amateur photographer looking to step up from a point-and-shoot camera.
What is the main difference between the DSLR and CSC?
    a. The picture quality is better in the DSLR.
    b. The CSC is less expensive than the DSLR.
    c. The DSLR is a better choice for amateur photographers.
    d. The DSLR's larger sensor makes it a bigger camera than the CSC.

49. When selecting a career path, it's important to explore the various options available. Many students entering college may shy away from a major because they don't know much about it. For example, many students won't opt for a career as an actuary because they aren't exactly sure what it entails. They would be missing out on a career that is very lucrative and in high demand. Actuaries work in the insurance field and assess risks and premiums. The average salary of an actuary is $100,000 per year. Another career option students may avoid, due to lack of knowledge of the field, is a hospitalist. This is a physician that specializes in the care of patients in a hospital, as opposed to those seen in private practices. The average salary of a hospitalist is upwards of $200,000. It pays to do some digging and find out more about these lesser-known career fields.
What is an actuary?
    a. A doctor who works in a hospital
    b. The same as a hospitalist
    c. An insurance agent who works in a hospital
    d. A person who assesses insurance risks and premiums

50. Hard water occurs when rainwater mixes with minerals from rock and soil. Hard water has a high mineral count, including calcium and magnesium. The mineral deposits from hard water can stain hard surfaces in bathrooms and kitchens as well as clog pipes. Hard water can stain dishes, ruin clothes, and reduce the life of any appliances it touches, such as hot water heaters, washing machines, and humidifiers.
One solution is to install a water softener to reduce the mineral content of water, but this can be costly. Running vinegar through pipes and appliances and using vinegar to clean hard surfaces can also help with mineral deposits.
From this passage, what can be concluded?

a. Hard water can cause a lot of problems for homeowners.
b. Calcium is good for pipes and hard surfaces.
c. Water softeners are easy to install.
d. Vinegar is the only solution to hard water problems.

51. Coaches of kids' sports teams are increasingly concerned about the behavior of parents at games. Parents are screaming and cursing at coaches, officials, players, and other parents. Physical fights have even broken out at games. Parents need to be reminded that coaches are volunteers, giving up their time and energy to help kids develop in their chosen sport. The goal of kids' sports teams is to learn and develop skills, but it's also to have fun. When parents are out of control at games and practices, it takes the fun out of the sport.

From this passage, what can be concluded?

a. Coaches are modeling good behavior for kids.
b. Organized sports are not good for kids.
c. Parents' behavior at their kids' games needs to change.
d. Parents and coaches need to work together.

52. While scientists aren't entirely certain why tornadoes form, they have some clues into the process. Tornadoes are dangerous funnel clouds that occur during a large thunderstorm. When warm, humid air near the ground meets cold, dry air from above, a column of the warm air can be drawn up into the clouds. Winds at different altitudes blowing at different speeds make the column of air rotate. As the spinning column of air picks up speed, a funnel cloud is formed. This funnel cloud moves rapidly and haphazardly. Rain and hail inside the cloud cause it to touch down, creating a tornado. Tornadoes move in a rapid and unpredictable pattern, making them extremely destructive and dangerous. Scientists continue to study tornadoes to improve radar detection and warning times.
The main purpose of this passage is to do which of the following?

a. Show why tornadoes are dangerous
b. Explain how a tornado forms
c. Compare thunderstorms to tornadoes
d. Explain what to do in the event of a tornado

53. Many people are unsure of exactly how the digestive system works. Digestion begins in the mouth where teeth grind up food and saliva breaks it down, making it easier for the body to absorb. Next, the food moves to the esophagus, and it is pushed into the stomach. The stomach is where food is stored and broken down further by acids and digestive enzymes, preparing it for passage into the intestines. The small intestine is where the nutrients are taken from food and passed into the blood stream. Other essential organs like the liver, gall bladder, and pancreas aid the stomach in breaking down food and absorbing nutrients. Finally, food waste is passed into the large intestine where it is eliminated by the body.
The purpose of this passage is to do which of the following?

a. Explain how the liver works
b. Show why it is important to eat healthy foods
c. Explain how the digestive system works
d. Show how nutrients are absorbed by the small intestine

54. Osteoporosis is a medical condition that occurs when the body loses bone or makes too little bone. This can lead to brittle, fragile bones that easily break. Bones are already porous, and when osteoporosis sets in, the spaces in bones become much larger, causing them to weaken. Both men and women can contract osteoporosis, though it is most common in women over age 50. Loss of bone can be silent and progressive, so it is important to be proactive in prevention of the disease.
The main purpose of this passage is to do which of the following?
  a. Discuss some of the ways people contract osteoporosis.
  b. Describe different treatment options for those with osteoporosis.
  c. Explain how to prevent osteoporosis.
  d. Define osteoporosis.

55. Vacationers looking for a perfect experience should opt out of Disney parks and try a trip on Disney Cruise Lines. While a park offers rides, characters, and show experiences, it also includes long lines, often very hot weather, and enormous crowds. A Disney cruise, on the other hand, is a relaxing, luxurious vacation that includes many of the same experiences as the parks, minus the crowds and lines. The cruise has top-notch food, maid service, water slides, multiple pools, Broadway-quality shows, and daily character experiences for kids. There are also many activities, such as bingo, trivia contests, and dance parties that can entertain guests of all ages. The cruise even stops at Disney's private island for a beach barbecue with characters, waterslides, and water sports. Those looking for the Disney experience without the hassle should book a Disney cruise.
The main purpose of this passage is to do which of the following?
  a. Explain how to book a Disney cruise
  b. Show what Disney parks have to offer
  c. Show why Disney parks are expensive
  d. Compare Disney parks to a Disney cruise

Vocabulary

1. The medication side effects that the patient experienced were diaphoresis and dizziness. Diaphoresis means:
  a. Excessive sweating
  b. Dyspnea
  c. Wheezing
  d. Frequent urination

2. What is the best definition of the word *brevity*?
  a. Dullness
  b. Dangerous
  c. Brief
  d. Ancient

3. *Altitude* most nearly means
  a. Behavior
  b. Outlook
  c. Haughtiness
  d. Height

4. What is the best definition of the word *irate*?
  a. Angry
  b. Knowledgeable
  c. Tired
  d. Confused

5. Select the meaning of the underlined word in the following sentence:

The nurse noticed that Becky's abdomen had become more distended since her last vitals check.

a. Occluded
b. Suppressed
c. Bloated
d. Impaired

6. What does *ineffable* mean?
a. Insincere
b. Inefficient
c. Indescribable
d. Inexperienced

7. What does *gregarious* most nearly mean?
a. Monstrous
b. Meek
c. Sociable
d. Impressive

8. What word is a synonym for *caustic*?
a. Sarcastic
b. Luxurious
c. Expensive
d. Uncooperative

10. The patient is having trouble forming thoughts into sentences, and one side of his face appears to be drooping. What emergency condition is likely occurring in the patient?
a. Meningitis
b. Migraine
c. Seizure
d. Cerebrovascular accident

11. What is the best definition of the word *retort*?
a. Conversation
b. Jest
c. Counter
d. Flexible

12. What is a synonym for *obtuse*?
a. Slow-witted
b. Large
c. Gluttonous
d. Stretched

13. Which of the following words is most synonymous with the underlined word in the sentence below?

The toddler, who had just learned to speak, seemed rather loquacious.

a. Verbose
b. Humorous
c. Silent
d. Cranky

14. The nurse reported that the patient experienced dyspnea and dizziness. Dyspnea means:
a. Difficulty breathing
b. Difficulty sleeping
c. Rapid pulse
d. Nasal discharge

15. What word means *sordid*?
a. Semantic
b. Surly
c. Vile
d. Basic

16. ________ may present with vague signs which may mimic chest pain, depression, or other physical illnesses.
a. Bereavement
b. Stroke
c. Anorexia nervosa
d. Myocardial infarction

17. _______ have a side effect causing excessive thirst.
a. Antidepressants
b. Antibiotics
c. Antispasmodics
d. Anti-inflammatories

18. What does *solicit* mean?
a. Ask
b. Donate
c. Perturb
d. Solace

19. What kind of ulcer is most commonly found between the knees and ankles?
a. Arterial
b. Neuropathic
c. Venous
d. Stage IV

20. What type of strength exercise is performed against resistance without moving the joint?
a. Isometric
b. Isotonic
c. Isokinetic
d. Plyometric

21. Select the best meaning of the italicized word in the following sentence:

Given his rude comments, her reaction seemed *plausible*.

a. Conceivable
b. Skeptical
c. Diurnal
d. Erudite

22. *Discourse* most nearly means:
a. Praise
b. Disagreement
c. Speech
d. Path

23. Select the best meaning of the italicized word in the following sentence:

The young boy seemed to be capable of nothing, other than his uncanny ability to *exasperate* his babysitter.

a. Annoy
b. Breathe
c. Disappoint
d. Stifle

24. Which of the following is the best definition for *genicular?*
a. Relating to aging
b. Relating to the knee
c. Relating to sperm
d. Relating to the genitals

25. Based on the words *transfer*, *transact*, *translation*, and *transport*, what is the meaning of the prefix *trans*?
a. Separation
b. All or everywhere
c. Forward
d. Across, beyond, or over

26. The term *cubital* refers to what body region?
a. The skin
b. The fingertips
c. The elbow
d. The shoulder

27. What word meaning "to make less severe" best fits in the following sentence:

The doctor tried her best to ________ the patient's discomfort by prescribing pain medication.

a. Mitigate
b. Focus
c. Intensify
d. Aggravate

28. ____________ is a structural protein and the primary constituent of things like hair and nails.
   a. Keratin
   b. Antigens
   c. Channel proteins
   d. Actin

29. Which word best fits in the following sentence:

   The dermis is _________ relative to the epidermis.

   a. Superficial
   b. Deep
   c. Superior
   d. Inferior

30. Select the correct meaning of the underlined word in the following sentence:

   The student wanted to become a <u>phlebotomist</u>.

   a. A professional who takes x-rays
   b. A professional who makes artificial limbs
   c. A professional who draws blood
   d. A professional who counsels patients

31. What word meaning "to return to an earlier state" best fits in the following sentence:

   The child seemed to emotionally ___________ when he felt sick.

   a. Rescind
   b. Digress
   c. Regress
   d. Diverge

32. What is the best definition of the word *subliminal*?
   a. Subconscious
   b. Transportation
   c. Underground
   d. Substitute

33. Select the correct meaning of the underlined word in the following sentence:

   The patient's eyes appeared <u>glassy.</u>

   a. Sad
   b. Expressionless
   c. Emotional
   d. Blind

34. What word meaning "to be in alignment so that there is a continuous plane" best fits in the following sentence:

It is important that the brace remains __________ with the skin to avoid skin irritation.

a. Flush
b. Flesh
c. Articulated
d. Adjacent

35. What is the meaning of the word *innervate*?
a. To attach a muscle to a bone
b. To shorten a muscle
c. To supply nerves to
d. To conduct a nerve impulse

36. What is the best definition of the word *incite*?
a. Understanding
b. Illumination
c. Rally
d. Judgment

37. What word meaning "urgent" best fits in the following sentence:

The _________ demands of the supervising physician made it difficult to complete paperwork in a timely manner.

a. Lenient
b. Extol
c. Exigent
d. Lackadaisical

38. Select the correct meaning of the underlined word in the following sentence:

The patient had aphasia after his stroke.

a. Memory loss
b. Droopy face
c. Impairment in facial recognition
d. Language impairment

39. What is the best definition of the word *sustain*?
a. Strength
b. Invigorate
c. Embolden
d. Expedite

40. Select the correct meaning of the underlined word in the following sentence:

The professor was notorious for his jejune lectures.

a. Dull
b. Stimulating
c. Interactive
d. Expert

41. What word meaning "shortage" best fits in the following sentence:

The salary hike for all unionized workers increased the hospital's budgetary ______________.

a. Deficit
b. Diffident
c. Dearth
d. Defiant

42. What is the best definition of the word *paradox*?

a. Sensation
b. Hypothesis
c. Insinuation
d. Contradiction

43. What word meaning "agile" best fits in the following sentence:

The ______________ dancer was graceful and beautiful to watch.

a. Lithe
b. Ballerina
c. Unwieldly
d. Chivalrous

44. What word meaning "a bluish discoloration of the skin caused by lack of oxygen" best fits in the following sentence:

It is not uncommon for a choking or drowning child to exhibit ________________.

a. Flushing
b. Cyanosis
c. Listlessness
d. Rall

45. What is the best definition of the word *venerate*?

a. Respect
b. Reject
c. Expect
d. Deserve

46. What word meaning "a fungal infection or disease" best fits in the following sentence:

Ringworm is considered a type of __________.

a. Lichen
b. Mycosis
c. Virus
d. Pustule

47. What word meaning "blood in the urine" best fits in the following sentence:

A common sign of a kidney infection is __________________.

a. Anuria
b. Nocturia
c. Uremia
d. Polyurea

48. What is the best definition of the word *malevolent*?
a. Evil
b. Concerned
c. Maximum
d. Cautious

49. Select the correct meaning of the underlined word in the following sentence:

The patient had a difficulty with <u>proprioception.</u>

a. Spatial awareness of the body
b. Balance and agility
c. Pain detection
d. Sensory integration

50. The charge nurse used the word "archetype" in a handoff report. Which of the following words is closest in meaning to that word?
a. Ancestor
b. Literature
c. Policy
d. Model

Grammar

1. Which of the following sentences has an error in capitalization?
a. The East Coast has experienced very unpredictable weather this year.
b. My Uncle owns a home in Florida, where he lives in the winter.
c. I am taking English Composition II on campus this fall.
d. There are several nice beaches we can visit on our trip to the Jersey Shore this summer.

2. Julia Robinson, an avid photographer in her spare time, was able to capture stunning shots of the local wildlife on her last business trip to Australia.

Which of the following is an adjective in the preceding sentence?

a. Time
b. Capture
c. Avid
d. Photographer

3. Which of the following sentences uses correct punctuation?
a. Carole is not currently working; her focus is on her children at the moment.
b. Carole is not currently working and her focus is on her children at the moment.
c. Carole is not currently working, her focus is on her children at the moment.
d. Carole is not currently working her focus is on her children at the moment.

4. Which of these examples is a compound sentence?
a. Alex and Shane spent the morning coloring and later took a walk down to the park.
b. After coloring all morning, Alex and Shane spent the afternoon at the park.
c. Alex and Shane spent the morning coloring, and then they took a walk down to the park.
d. After coloring all morning and spending part of the day at the park, Alex and Shane took a nap.

5. Which of these examples shows INCORRECT use of subject-verb agreement?
a. Neither of the cars are parked on the street.
b. Both of my kids are going to camp this summer.
c. Any of your friends are welcome to join us on the trip in November.
d. Each of the clothing options is appropriate for the job interview.

6. When it gets warm in the spring, _______ and _______ like to go fishing at Cobbs Creek.

Which of the following word pairs should be used in the blanks above?

a. me, him
b. he, I
c. him, I
d. he, me

Directions for questions 7–14: Choose the best version of the underlined segment of the sentence. If you feel the original sentence is correct, then choose the first answer choice.

7. Since none of the furniture were delivered on time, we have to move in at a later date.
a. none of the furniture were delivered
b. none of the furniture was delivered
c. all of the furniture were delivered
d. all of the furniture was delivered

8. An important issues stemming from this meeting is that we won't have enough time to meet all of the objectives.
a. An important issues stemming from this meeting
b. Important issue stemming from this meeting
c. An important issue stemming from this meeting
d. Important issues stemming from this meeting

9. There were many questions about what causes the case to have gone cold, but the detective wasn't willing to discuss it with reporters.
   a. about what causes the case to have gone cold
   b. about why the case is cold
   c. about what causes the case to go cold
   d. about why the case went cold

10. The fact the train set only includes four cars and one small track was a big disappointment to my son.
   a. the train set only includes four cars and one small track was a big disappointment
   b. that the trains set only include four cars and one small track was a big disappointment
   c. that the train set only includes four cars and one small track was a big disappointment
   d. that the train set only includes four cars and one small track were a big disappointment

11. The rising popularity of the clean eating movement can be attributed to the fact that experts say added sugars and chemicals in our food are to blame for the obesity epidemic.
   a. to the fact that experts say added sugars and chemicals in our food are to blame for the obesity epidemic.
   b. in the facts that experts say added sugars and chemicals in our food are to blame for the obesity epidemic.
   c. to the fact that experts saying added sugars and chemicals in our food are to blame for the obesity epidemic.
   d. with the facts that experts say added sugars and chemicals in our food are to blame for the obesity epidemic.

12. She's looking for a suitcase that can fit all of her clothes, shoes, accessory, and makeup.
   a. clothes, shoes, accessory, and makeup.
   b. clothes, shoes, accessories, and makeup.
   c. clothes, shoes, accessories, and makeups.
   d. clothes, shoe, accessory, and makeup.

13. Shawn started taking guitar lessons if he wanted to become a better musician.
   a. while he wanted to become a better musician.
   b. so that he wanted to become a better musician.
   c. even though he wanted to become a better musician.
   d. because he wanted to become a better musician.

14. Considering the recent rains we have had, it's a wonder the plants haven't drowned.
   a. Considering the recent rains we have had, it's a wonder
   b. Consider the recent rains we have had, it's a wonder
   c. Considering for how much recent rain we have had, its a wonder
   d. Considering, the recent rains we have had, its a wonder

15. Which of the following is an imperative sentence?
   a. Pennsylvania's state flag includes two draft horses and an eagle.
   b. Go down to the basement and check the hot water heater for signs of a leak.
   c. You must be so excited to have a new baby on the way!
   d. How many countries speak Spanish?

16. Which of the following examples is a compound sentence?
    a. Shawn and Jerome played soccer in the backyard for two hours.
    b. Marissa last saw and spoke to Elena this morning.
    c. The baby was sick, so I decided to stay home from work.
    d. Denise, Kurt, and Eric went for a run after dinner.

17. Which of the following sentences uses correct subject-verb agreement?
    a. There is two constellations that can be seen from the back of the house.
    b. At least four of the sheep needs to be sheared before the end of summer.
    c. Lots of people were auditioning for the singing competition on Saturday.
    d. Everyone in the group have completed the assignment on time.

18. Philadelphia is home to some excellent walking tours where visitors can learn more about the culture and rich history of the city of brotherly love.

What are the adjectives in the preceding sentence?

a. Philadelphia, tours, visitors, culture, history, city, love
b. Excellent, walking, rich, brotherly
c. Is, can, learn
d. To, about, of

19. The realtor showed __________ and __________ a house on Wednesday afternoon.

Which of the following pronoun pairs should be used in the blanks above?

a. she, I
b. she, me
c. me, her
d. her, me

20. Which of the following examples uses correct punctuation?
    a. Recommended supplies for the hunting trip include the following: rain gear, a large backpack, hiking boots, a flashlight, and non-perishable foods.
    b. I left the store, because I forgot my wallet.
    c. As soon as the team checked into the hotel; they met in the lobby for a group photo.
    d. None of the furniture came in on time: so they weren't able to move into the new apartment.

21. Which of the following sentences shows correct word usage?
    a. Your going to have to put you're jacket over their.
    b. You're going to have to put your jacket over there.
    c. Your going to have to put you're jacket over they're.
    d. You're going to have to put your jacket over their.

22. A teacher notices that, when students are talking to each other between classes, they are using their own unique vocabulary words and expressions to talk about their daily lives. When the teacher hears these non-standard words that are specific to one age or cultural group, what type of language is she listening to?
    a. Slang
    b. Jargon
    c. Dialect
    d. Vernacular

23. A teacher wants to counsel a student about using the word *ain't* in a research paper for a high school English class. What advice should the teacher give?

a. *Ain't* is not in the dictionary, so it isn't a word.
b. Because the student isn't in college yet, *ain't* is an appropriate expression for a high school writer.
c. *Ain't* is incorrect English and should not be part of a serious student's vocabulary because it sounds uneducated.
d. *Ain't* is a colloquial expression, and while it may be appropriate in a conversational setting, it is not standard in academic writing.

24. What is the structure of the following sentence:

The restaurant is unconventional because it serves both Chicago style pizza and New York style pizza.

a. Simple
b. Compound
c. Complex
d. Compound-complex

25. The following sentence contains what kind of error:

This summer, I'm planning to travel to Italy, take a Mediterranean cruise, going to Pompeii, and eat a lot of Italian food.

a. Parallelism
b. Sentence fragment
c. Misplaced modifier
d. Subject-verb agreement

26. The following sentence contains what kind of error:

Forgetting that he was supposed to meet his girlfriend for dinner, Anita was mad when Fred showed up late.

a. Parallelism
b. Run-on sentence
c. Misplaced modifier
d. Subject-verb agreement

27. The following sentence contains what kind of error:

Some workers use all their sick leave, other workers cash out their leave.

a. Parallelism
b. Comma splice
c. Sentence fragment
d. Subject-verb agreement

28. A student writes the following in an essay:

Protestors filled the streets of the city. Because they were dissatisfied with the government's leadership.

Which of the following is an appropriately punctuated correction for this sentence?

a. Protestors filled the streets of the city, because they were dissatisfied with the government's leadership.
b. Protesters, filled the streets of the city, because they were dissatisfied with the government's leadership.
c. Because they were dissatisfied with the government's leadership protestors filled the streets of the city.
d. Protestors filled the streets of the city because they were dissatisfied with the government's leadership.

29. What is the part of speech of the underlined word in the sentence:

We need to come up with a fresh approach to this problem.

a. Noun
b. Verb
c. Adverb
d. Adjective

30. What is the part of speech of the underlined word in the sentence:

Investigators conducted an exhaustive inquiry into the accusations of corruption.

a. Noun
b. Verb
c. Adverb
d. Adjective

31. The underlined portion of the sentence is an example of which sentence component:

New students should report to the student center.

a. Dependent clause
b. Adverbial phrase
c. Adjective clause
d. Noun phrase

32. Which pair of words will correctly fill in the blanks?

Increasing the price of bus fares has had a greater ______ on ridership ______ expected.

a. affect; then
b. affect; than
c. effect; then
d. effect; than

33. The following is an example of what type of sentence:

Although I wished it were summer, I accepted the change of seasons, and I started to appreciate the fall.

a. Compound
b. Simple
c. Complex
d. Compound-Complex

34. A student reads the following sentence:

A hundred years ago, automobiles were rare, but now cars are ubiquitous.

However, she doesn't know what the word *ubiquitous* means. Which key context clue is essential to decipher the word's meaning?

a. Ago
b. Cars
c. Now
d. Rare

35. Which word in the following sentence is a proper noun:

People think the Statue of Liberty is an awesome sight.

a. People
b. Statue of Liberty
c. Awesome
d. Sight

36. Which word in the following sentence is a plural noun:

The black kitten was the girl's choice from the litter of kittens.

a. Kitten
b. Girl's
c. Choice
d. Kittens

37. Which pronoun makes the following sentence grammatically correct:

__________ ordered the flowers?

a. Whose
b. Whom
c. Who
d. Who've

38. Which pronoun makes the following sentence grammatically correct:

The giraffe nudged __________ baby.

a. it's
b. hers
c. them
d. its

39. What is the word *several* in the following sentence called:

Several are laughing loudly on the bus.

a. Singular indefinite pronoun
b. Plural indefinite pronoun
c. Singular objective pronoun
d. Indefinite adjective

40. Which word in the following sentence is an adjective:

The connoisseur slowly enjoyed the delectable meal.

a. Delectable
b. Connoisseur
c. Slowly
d. Enjoyed

41. Which choice identifies all of the prepositions in the following sentence:

We went down by the water, near the lake, before dawn, to see the pretty sunrise.

a. Went, to see, pretty
b. By, near, before
c. Water, lake, dawn, sunrise
d. We, down, the, pretty

42. Which sentence has an interjection?

a. The cookie was full of chocolaty goodness.
b. Well, Carrie didn't like the cookie.
c. Can't you see that cookie is broken?
d. That's too bad, but I'll still eat it!

43. Identify the complete subject in the following sentence:

The heaviest green bike is mine.

a. Bike
b. Green bike
c. The heaviest green bike
d. Is mine

44. Identify the complete predicate in the following sentence:

My house is the yellow one at the end of the street.

a. My house
b. Is the yellow one
c. At the end of the street.
d. Is the yellow one at the end of the street.

45. Which sentence shows incorrect subject/verb agreement?
a. All of the kittens in the litter show their courage.
b. The black kitten pounce on the ball of yarn.
c. The calico kitten eats voraciously.
d. My favorite kitten snuggles with its mother.

46. What is the indirect object in the following sentence:

Calysta brought her mother the beautiful stained-glass lamp.

a. Stained-glass lamp
b. Brought
c. Her mother
d. Beautiful

47. Which sentence is grammatically correct?
a. They're on their way to New Jersey but there not there yet.
b. Their on their way to New Jersey but they're not there yet.
c. They're on their way to New Jersey but they're not there yet.
d. They're on their way to New Jersey but there not their yet.

48. Identify the prepositional phrase in the following sentence:

For the longest time, I have wanted to learn to roller skate.

a. I have wanted
b. Wanted to learn
c. Learn to roller skate
d. For the longest time

49. Identify the sentence structure of the following sentence:

The weight of the world was on his shoulders, so he took a long walk.

a. Simple sentence
b. Compound sentence
c. Complex sentence
d. Compound-complex sentence

50. Identify the sentence structure of the following sentence:

The last thing she wanted to do was see the Eiffel Tower before the flight.

a. Simple sentence
b. Compound sentence
c. Complex sentence
d. Compound-complex sentence

Directions for questions 51–55: Choose the best version of the underlined segment of the sentence. If you feel the original sentence is correct, then choose the first answer choice.

51. Besides the novel's engaging writing style the story's central theme remains highly relevant in a world of constant discovery and moral dilemmas.

a. writing style the story's central theme
b. writing style the central theme of the story
c. writing style, the story's central theme
d. the story's central theme's writing style

52. Looking deeper into the myth of Prometheus sheds light not only on the character of Frankenstein but also poses a psychological dilemma to the audience.

a. but also poses a psychological dilemma to the audience
b. but also poses a psychological dilemma with the audience
c. but also poses a psychological dilemma for the audience
d. but also poses a psychological dilemma there before the audience

53. There are many things to consider when addressing this question but the chief factor is whether there is credible evidence.

a. this question but the chief factor
b. this question, but the chief factor
c. this question however the chief factor
d. this question; but the chief factor

54. For science to formally recognize that such a species exists, there needs to be physical proof.

a. For science to formally recognize that such a species exists, there needs to be physical proof.
b. Physical proof are needed in order for science to formally recognize that such a species exists.
c. For science to formally recognize that such a species exists there needs to be physical proof.
d. For science, to formally recognize that such a species exists, there needs to be physical proof.

55. Today, laws prohibit the use of unnecessary force in self-defense; these serve to eliminate beating someone to a pulp once they have been neutralized.

a. use of unnecessary force in self-defense; these serve to eliminate
b. use of unnecessary force in self-defense serving to eliminate
c. use of unnecessary force, in self-defense, these serve to eliminate
d. use of unnecessary force. In self-defense, these serve to eliminate

Biology

1. A scientist is trying to determine the amount of poison that will kill a rat the fastest. Which of the following statements is an example of an appropriate hypothesis?
   a. Rats that are given lots of poison seem to die quickly.
   b. Does the amount of poison affect how quickly the rat dies?
   c. The more poison a rat is given, the quicker it will die.
   d. Poison is fatal to rats.

2. Which of the following is NOT a property of water?
   a. High cohesion and adhesion
   b. High surface tension
   c. High density upon melting
   d. High freezing point

3. A metabolic reaction that releases energy is called:
   a. Catabolic
   b. Carbolic
   c. Anabolic
   d. Endothermic

4. What organic compounds facilitate chemical reactions by lowering activation energy?
   a. Carbohydrates
   b. Lipids
   c. Enzymes
   d. Nucleotides

5. Which structure is exclusively in eukaryotic cells?
   a. Cell wall
   b. Nucleus
   c. Cell membrane
   d. Vacuole

6. Which of these is NOT found in the cell nucleus?
   a. Golgi complex
   b. Chromosomes
   c. Nucleolus
   d. Chromatin

7. Which is the cellular organelle used for digestion to recycle materials?
   a. Golgi apparatus
   b. Lysosome
   c. Centriole
   d. Mitochondria

8. What are the energy-generating structures of the cell called?
   a. Nucleoplasm
   b. Mitochondria
   c. Golgi apparatus
   d. Ribosomes

9. Which is a component of plant cells NOT found in animal cells?
   a. Nucleus
   b. Plastid
   c. Cell membrane
   d. Lysosome

10. What is the last phase of mitosis?
   a. Prophase
   b. Telophase
   c. Anaphase
   d. Metaphase

11. The combination of alleles in an organism, when expressed, manifests as the organism's _______.
   a. genotype
   b. phenotype
   c. gender
   d. karyotype

12. Which of the choices below are the reproductive cells produced by meiosis?
   a. Zygotes
   b. Germ cells
   c. Blastocyst
   d. Gametes

13. What is the process of cell division in somatic (most body) cells called?
   a. Mitosis
   b. Meiosis
   c. Respiration
   d. Cytogenesis

14. Water has many unique properties due to its unique structure. Which of the following does NOT play a role in water's unique properties?
   a. Hydrogen bonding between molecules
   b. Polarity within one molecule
   c. Molecules held apart in solid state
   d. Equal sharing of electrons

15. Which statement is true about natural selection?
   a. Individuals are selected based on their genotype.
   b. An extreme phenotype is always selected.
   c. It only occurs after a drought.
   d. Individuals are selected based on phenotypes that are advantageous for survival and reproduction.

16. What is an alteration in the normal gene sequence called?
   a. Mutation
   b. Gene migration
   c. Polygenetic inheritance
   d. Incomplete dominance

17. Blood type is a trait determined by multiple alleles, and two of them are co-dominant: I^A codes for A blood and I^B codes for B blood. The i allele codes for O blood and is recessive to both. If an A heterozygous individual and an O individual have a child, what is the probability that the child will have A blood?
   a. 25%
   b. 50%
   c. 75%
   d. 100%

18. What are the building blocks of DNA called?
   a. Helices
   b. Proteins
   c. Genes
   d. Nucleotides

19. Which statement is NOT true about DNA?
   a. It has guanine.
   b. DNA enables living organisms to pass on their genetic information.
   c. It contains uracil.
   d. DNA replication happens in interphase.

20. Which of the following is true about an endergonic reaction?
   a. The reaction results in a negative delta G ($-\Delta G$).
   b. The reaction is considered spontaneous.
   c. The reaction absorbs energy.
   d. The reaction releases energy.

21. What is the term used for the set of metabolic reactions that convert chemical bonds to energy in the form of ATP?
   a. Photosynthesis
   b. Reproduction
   c. Active transport
   d. Cellular respiration

22. An enzymatic reaction requires free energy to proceed. Which term best describes this reaction?
   a. Exergonic
   b. Combustion
   c. Endergonic
   d. Redox

23. What is the broadest, or least specialized, classification of the Linnaean taxonomic system?
   a. Species
   b. Family
   c. Domain
   d. Phylum

24. Which of the following is NOT a function of lipids?
   a. They provide cellular instructions.
   b. They can be chemical messages.
   c. They provide energy.
   d. They compose cell membranes.

25. What is the cell structure responsible for protein synthesis called?
   a. DNA
   b. Golgi apparatus
   c. Nucleus
   d. Ribosome

Questions 26–30 pertain to the passage:

Scientists often use an assay called an enzyme-linked immunosorbent assay, or ELISA, to quantify specific substances within a larger sample. An ELISA works based on the specificity of an antibody to an antigen. One type of ELISA is called a sandwich ELISA. In this type of ELISA, a plate is coated with a capture antibody that adheres the antigen in the sample when it is added. Then the primary antibody (or "detection" antibody) is added and sticks to any antigen bound to the capture antibody. Next, a secondary antibody is added. Once it attaches to the primary antibody, it releases a colored tag that can be detected by a piece of laboratory equipment. If more color is released, it is indicative of more antigen having been present in the sample.

Figure 1 below describes how a sandwich ELISA works.

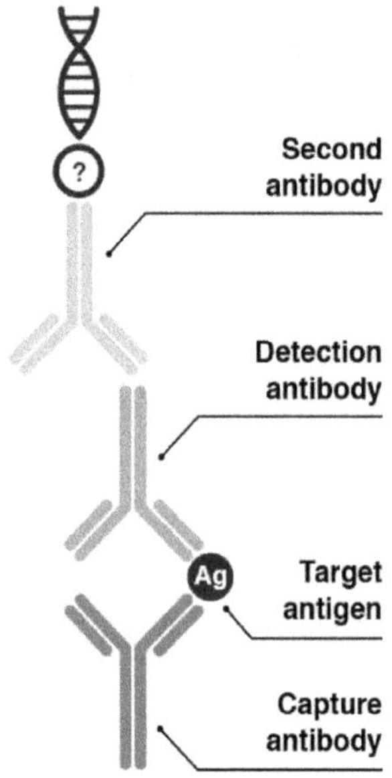

The cytokine protein IL-1β is a marker of inflammation in the body. Scientist A took samples from different locations within the body to find out where there was elevated inflammation in a patient.

Figure 2 below is a picture of the ELISA plate from Scientist A's experiment.

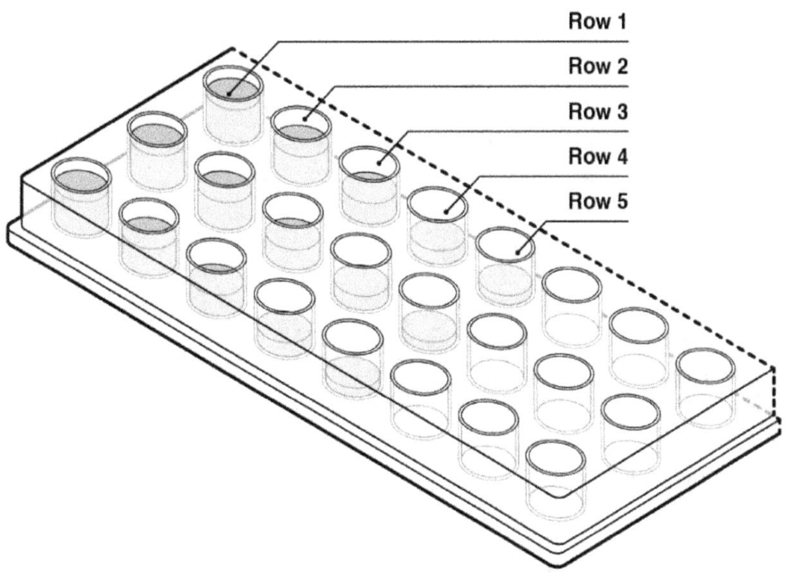

Figure 3 below is a graph of the results of Scientist A's experiment.

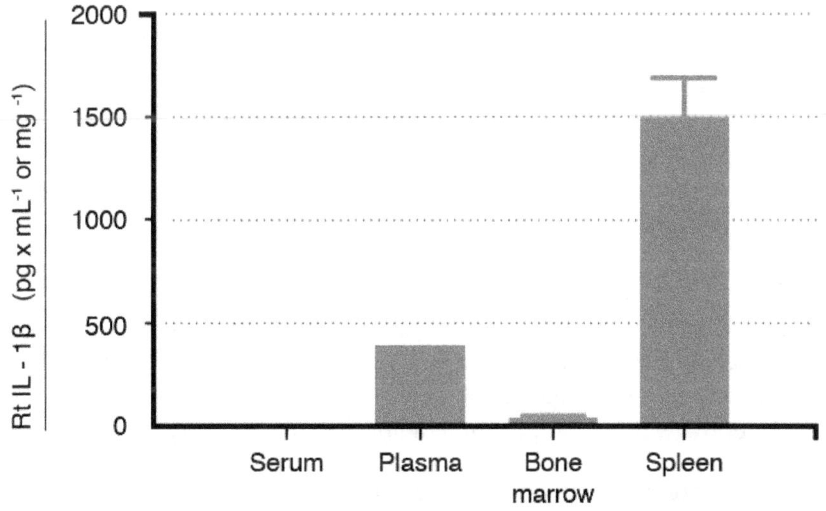

26. Which step of the ELISA allows for the color to be released for detection of the antigen?
    a. Addition of the antigen
    b. Addition of the primary antibody
    c. The presence of the capture antibody
    d. Addition of the secondary antibody

27. According to Figure 2, which row had the largest amount of antigen in the sample?
   a. Row 2
   b. Row 1
   c. Row 5
   d. Row 3

28. According to the ELISA results in Figure 3, which area of the body had the most inflammation?
   a. Serum
   b. Plasma
   c. Spleen
   d. Bone marrow

29. Which two antibodies sandwich the antigen in a sandwich ELISA?
   a. Capture antibody and secondary antibody
   b. Capture antibody and primary antibody
   c. Primary antibody and secondary antibody
   d. Two units of the secondary antibody

30. What is the purpose of an ELISA?
   a. To quantify specific substances within a larger sample
   b. To quantify all substances within a larger sample
   c. To create a colorful pattern with the samples
   d. To develop different antibodies

Chemistry

1. What is 45 °C converted to °F?
   a. 113 °F
   b. 135 °F
   c. 57 °F
   d. 88 °F

2. What is the electrical charge of the nucleus?
   a. A nucleus always has a positive charge.
   b. A stable nucleus has a positive charge, but a radioactive nucleus may be neutral with no charge.
   c. A nucleus is always neutral with no charge.
   d. A stable nucleus is neutral with no charge, but a radioactive nucleus may have a charge.

3. What is the temperature in Fahrenheit when it is 35 °C outside?
   a. 67 °F
   b. 95 °F
   c. 63 °F
   d. 75 °F

4. How are a sodium atom and a sodium isotope different?
   a. The isotope has a different number of protons.
   b. The isotope has a different number of neutrons.
   c. The isotope has a different number of electrons.
   d. The isotope has a different atomic number.

5. Which statement is true about nonmetals?
   a. They form cations.
   b. They form covalent bonds.
   c. They are mostly absent from organic compounds.
   d. They are all diatomic.

6. What is the basic unit of matter?
   a. Elementary particle
   b. Atom
   c. Molecule
   d. Photon

7. Which particle is responsible for all chemical reactions?
   a. Electrons
   b. Neutrons
   c. Protons
   d. Orbitals

8. Which of these give atoms a negative charge?
   a. Electrons
   b. Neutrons
   c. Protons
   d. Orbital

9. How are similar chemical properties of elements grouped on the periodic table?
   a. In rows according to their total configuration of electrons
   b. In columns according to the electron configuration in their outer shells
   c. In rows according to the electron configuration in their outer shells
   d. In columns according to their total configurations of electrons

10. In a chemical equation, the reactants are on which side of the arrow?
   a. Right
   b. Left
   c. Neither right nor left
   d. Both right and left

11. What does the law of conservation of mass state?
   a. All matter is equally created.
   b. Matter changes but is not created.
   c. Matter can be changed, and new matter can be created.
   d. Matter can be created, but not changed.

12. Which factor decreases the solubility of solids?
   a. Heating
   b. Agitation
   c. Large Surface area
   d. Decreasing solvent

13. What information is used to calculate the quantity of solute in a solution?
   a. Molarity of the solution
   b. Equivalence point
   c. Limiting reactant
   d. Theoretical yield

14. How does adding salt to water affect its boiling point?
   a. It increases it.
   b. It has no effect.
   c. It decreases it.
   d. It prevents it from boiling.

15. What is the effect of pressure on a liquid solution?
   a. It decreases solubility.
   b. It increases solubility.
   c. It has little effect on solubility.
   d. It has the same effect as with a gaseous solution.

16. Nonpolar molecules must have what kind of regions?
   a. Hydrophilic
   b. Hydrophobic
   c. Hydrolytic
   d. Hydrochloric

17. Which of these is a substance that increases the rate of a chemical reaction?
   a. Catalyst
   b. Brine
   c. Solvent
   d. Inhibitor

18. Which of the following are composed of chains of amino acids?
   a. Lipids
   b. Nucleic acids
   c. Proteins
   d. Carbohydrates

19. What is the balance of the following chemical equation?

$$\_F_2 + \_H_2O \rightarrow \_HF + \_O_2$$

   a. 1:5:5:2
   b. 1:9:5:2
   c. 2:9:10:4
   d. 2:5:10:4

20. Which type of bonding results from transferring electrons between atoms?
   a. Ionic bonding
   b. Covalent bonding
   c. Hydrogen bonding
   d. Dipole interactions

21. Which substance is oxidized in the following reaction?

$$4\ Fe + 3\ O_2 \rightarrow 2\ Fe_2O_3$$

a. Fe
b. O
c. O_2
d. Fe_2O_3

22. Which statements are true regarding nuclear fission?

I. It splits heavy nuclei.
II. It is utilized in power plants.
III. It occurs on the sun.

a. I only
b. II and III only
c. I and II only
d. III only

23. Which type of nuclear decay is occurring in the equation below?

$$U_{92}^{236} \rightarrow He_2^4 + Th_{90}^{232}$$

a. Alpha
b. Beta
c. Gamma
d. Delta

24. Which statement is true about the pH of a solution?
a. A solution cannot have a pH less than 1.
b. The more hydroxide ions there are in the solution, the higher the pH will be.
c. If an acid has a pH of greater than -2, it is considered a weak acid.
d. A solution with a pH of 2 has ten times more hydrogen ions than a solution with a pH of 1.

25. Which radioactive particle is the most penetrating and damaging and is used to treat cancer in radiation therapy?
a. Alpha
b. Beta
c. Gamma
d. Delta

Questions 26–30 pertain to the passage:

In chemistry, a titration is a method that is used to determine the concentration of an unknown solution. Generally, a known volume of a solution of known concentration is mixed with the unknown solution. Once the reaction of the two solutions has been completed, the concentration of the unknown solution can be calculated. When acids and bases are titrated, the progress of the reaction is monitored by changes in the pH of the known solution. The equivalence point is when just enough of the unknown solution has been added to neutralize the known solution. A color reaction may also occur so that with the drop of solution that causes complete neutralization; for example, the solution may turn bright pink. For acids that only have one proton, usually a hydrogen atom, the halfway point between the beginning of the curve and the equivalence point is where the amount of acid and base are equal in the solution. At this point, the pH is equal to the pK_a, or the acid dissociation constant.

Figure 1 below shows a general titration curve of a strong acid with a strong base.

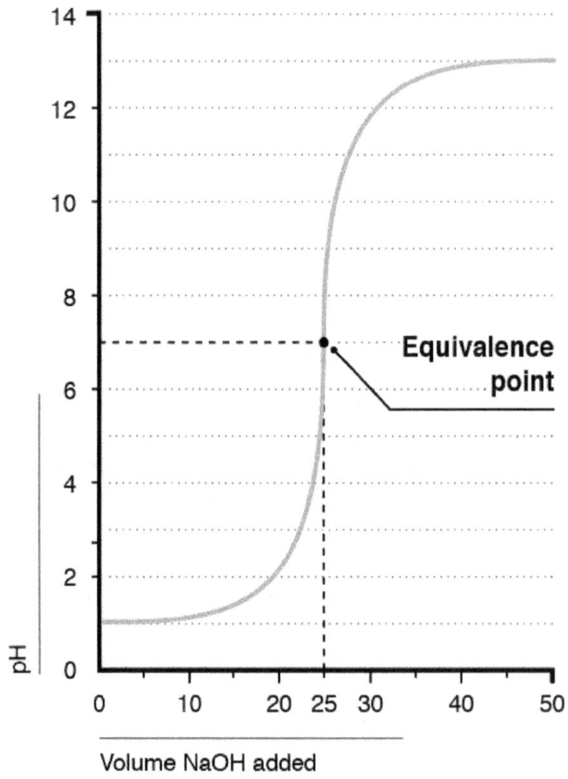

Figure 2 below shows the chemical reaction of a strong acid with a strong base.

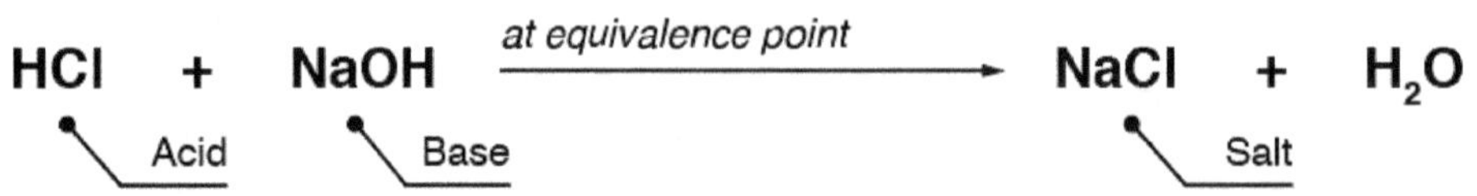

Figure 3 shows the titration curve for acetic acid.

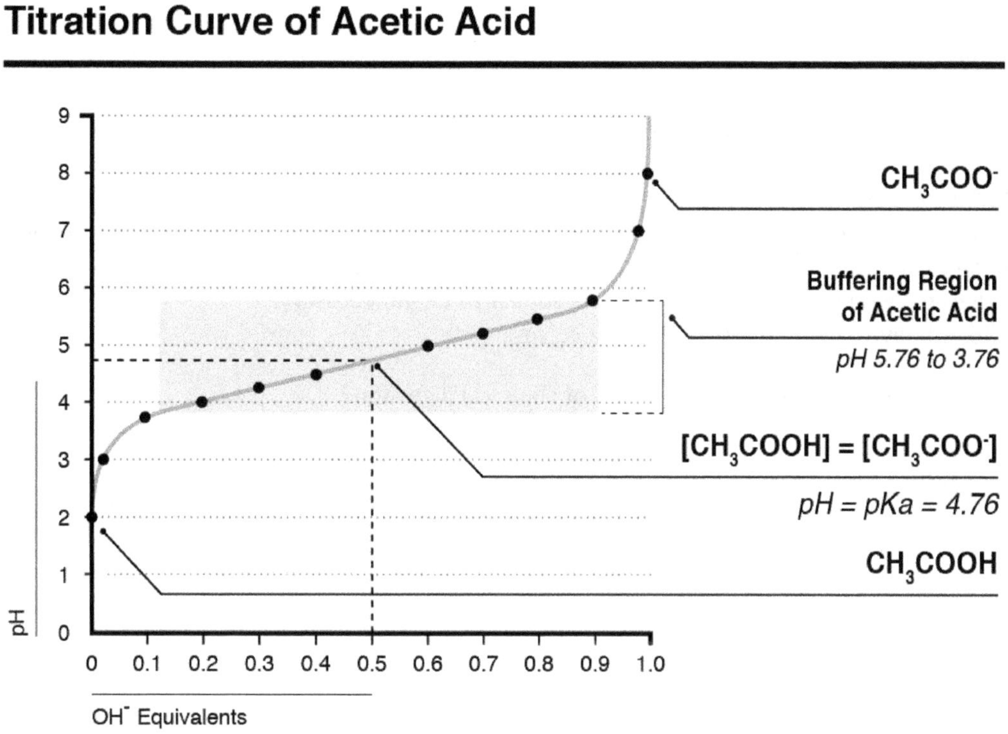

26. How much NaOH is added to the HCl solution to reach the equivalence point in Figure 1?
   a. 10
   b. 40
   c. 50
   d. 25

27. What is the acid dissociation constant of the titration curve in the Figure 3?
   a. 4.21
   b. 3.50
   c. 4.76
   d. 6.52

28. What is the pH of the acetic acid before the titration has started in Figure 3?
   a. 2
   b. 4.76
   c. 7
   d. 6

29. What is one of the products of the chemical equation in Figure 2?
   a. HCl
   b. NaCl
   c. NaOH
   d. Cl^-

30. How would you describe the solution at the equivalence point in Figure 1?
   a. Neutral
   b. Acidic
   c. Basic
   d. Unknown

Anatomy and Physiology

1. Why do arteries have valves?
   a. They have valves to maintain high blood pressure so that capillaries diffuse nutrients properly.
   b. Their valves are designed to prevent backflow due to their low blood pressure.
   c. The valves have no known purpose and thus appear to be unnecessary.
   d. They do not have valves, but veins do have valves.

2. Which locations in the digestive system are sites of chemical digestion?

   I. Mouth
   II. Stomach
   III. Small Intestine

   a. II only
   b. III only
   c. II and III only
   d. I, II, and III

3. Which of the following are functions of the urinary system?

   I. Synthesizing calcitriol and secreting erythropoietin
   II. Regulating the concentrations of sodium, potassium, chloride, calcium, and other ions
   III. Reabsorbing or secreting hydrogen ions and bicarbonate
   IV. Detecting reductions in blood volume and pressure

   a. I, II, and III
   b. II and III
   c. II, III, and IV
   d. All of the above

4. If the pressure in the pulmonary artery is increased above normal, which chamber of the heart will be affected first?
   a. The right atrium
   b. The left atrium
   c. The right ventricle
   d. The left ventricle

5. What is the purpose of sodium bicarbonate when released into the lumen of the small intestine?
   a. It works to chemically digest fats in the chyme.
   b. It decreases the pH of the chyme so as to prevent harm to the intestine.
   c. It works to chemically digest proteins in the chyme.
   d. It increases the pH of the chyme so as to prevent harm to the intestine.

6. Which of the following describes a reflex arc?
   a. The storage and recall of memory
   b. The maintenance of visual and auditory acuity
   c. The autoregulation of heart rate and blood pressure
   d. A stimulus and response controlled by the spinal cord

7. Ligaments connect what?
   a. Muscle to muscle
   b. Bone to bone
   c. Bone to muscle
   d. Muscle to tendon

8. Identify the correct sequence of the 3 primary body planes as numbered 1, 2, and 3 in the following image.

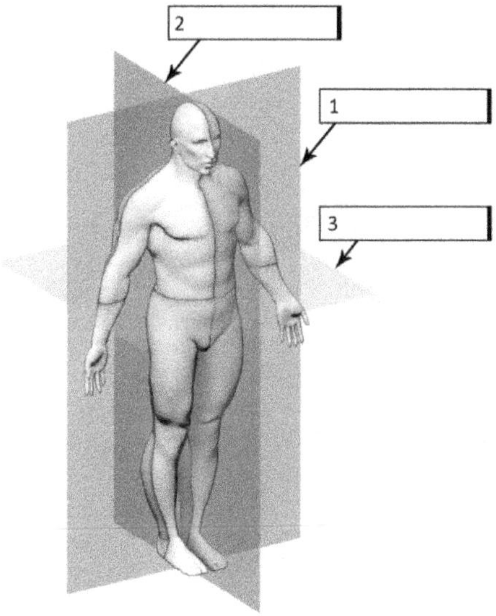

   a. Plane 1 is coronal, plane 2 is sagittal, and plane 3 is transverse.
   b. Plane 1 is sagittal, plane 2 is coronal, and plane 3 is medial.
   c. Plane 1 is coronal, plane 2 is sagittal, and plane 3 is medial.
   d. Plane 1 is sagittal, plane 2 is coronal, and plane 3 is transverse.

9. Which of the following is NOT a major function of the respiratory system in humans?
   a. It provides a large surface area for gas exchange of oxygen and carbon dioxide.
   b. It helps regulate the blood's pH.
   c. It helps cushion the heart against jarring motions.
   d. It is responsible for vocalization.

10. Which of the following is NOT a function of the forebrain?
   a. To regulate blood pressure and heart rate
   b. To perceive and interpret emotional responses like fear and anger
   c. To perceive and interpret visual input from the eyes
   d. To integrate voluntary movement

11. A patient's body is not properly filtering blood. Which of the following body parts is most likely malfunctioning?
   a. Medulla
   b. Heart
   c. Nephrons
   d. Renal cortex

12. A pediatrician notes that an infant's cartilage is disappearing and being replaced by bone. What process has the doctor observed?
   a. Mineralization
   b. Ossification
   c. Osteoporosis
   d. Calcification

13. Which of the following creates sperm?
   a. Prostate gland
   b. Seminal vesicles
   c. Scrotum
   d. Seminiferous tubules

14. Which of the following functions corresponds to the parasympathetic nervous system?
   a. It stimulates the fight-or-flight response.
   b. It increases heart rate.
   c. It stimulates digestion.
   d. It increases bronchiole dilation.

15. Which of the following is the gland that helps regulate calcium levels?
   a. Osteoid gland
   b. Pineal gland
   c. Parathyroid glands
   d. Thymus gland

16. What makes bone resistant to shattering?
   a. The calcium salts deposited in the bone
   b. The collagen fibers
   c. The bone marrow and network of blood vessels
   d. The intricate balance of minerals and collagen fibers

17. What type of vessel carries oxygen-rich blood from the heart to other tissues of the body?
   a. Veins
   b. Intestines
   c. Bronchioles
   d. Arteries

18. The somatic nervous system is responsible for which of the following?
   a. Breathing
   b. Thought
   c. Movement
   d. Fear

19. Which blood component is chiefly responsible for clotting?
    a. Platelets
    b. Red blood cells
    c. Antigens
    d. Plasma cells

20. What is the function of the sinuses?
    a. To trap the many airborne pathogens
    b. To direct air down the trachea rather than the esophagus
    c. To warm, humidify, and filter air
    d. To sweep away pathogens and direct them toward the top of the trachea

21. During which step of digestion do the teeth tear up food that has entered the mouth?
    a. Secretion
    b. Absorption
    c. Excretion
    d. Mechanical processing

22. A cluster of capillaries that functions as the main filter of the blood entering the kidney is known as which of the following?
    a. The Bowman's capsule
    b. The loop of Henle
    c. The glomerulus
    d. The nephron

23. What is the name for the sac-shaped structures that facilitate the exchanging of carbon dioxide and oxygen?
    a. Kidneys
    b. Medulla oblongata
    c. Alveoli
    d. Bronchioles

24. The muscular tube that connects the outer surface to the cervix in a woman's birth canal is referred to as which of the following?
    a. The uterus
    b. The cervix
    c. The vagina
    d. The ovaries

25. Which of the following organs functions as both an endocrine and exocrine gland?
    a. The kidney
    b. The spleen
    c. The pancreas
    d. The stomach

26. Which of the following correctly identifies a difference between the primary and secondary immune responses?
    a. In the secondary response, macrophages migrate to the lymph nodes to present the foreign microorganism to helper T lymphocytes
    b. The humoral immunity that characterizes the primary response is coordinated by T lymphocytes.
    c. The primary response is quicker and more powerful than the secondary response.
    d. Suppressor T cells activate in the secondary response to prevent an overactive immune response.

27. High blood sugar stimulates the kidneys to do which of the following?
   a. Produce less urine
   b. Concentrate the urine
   c. Retain more sodium
   d. Produce more urine

28. A patient experiencing itching related to an allergic reaction likely has the substance histamine being secreted by which type of white blood cell?
   a. Lymphocytes
   b. Basophils
   c. Neutrophils
   d. Monocytes

29. Which structure of the brain is responsible for producing cerebrospinal fluid?
   a. Pons
   b. Ventricles
   c. Thalamus
   d. Corpus callosum

30. Which of the following statements is true?
   a. As fluid levels decrease, electrolyte levels increase.
   b. As fluid levels increase, electrolyte levels increase.
   c. As fluid levels osmose, electrolyte levels diffuse.
   d. As fluid levels homogenize, electrolyte levels dissipate.

Physics

1. A snowboarder begins at the top of a mountain and rides down the slope to the bottom; at which point is their potential energy the greatest?
   a. Standing still on top of the mountain
   b. Halfway down the slope
   c. At maximum speed reaching the bottom of the slope
   d. Just after starting down the slope at the top of the mountain

2. What is the definition of acceleration?
   a. The rate at which an object moves
   b. The rate of change in velocity
   c. Speed in a given direction
   d. The velocity of an object multiplied by its mass

3. Which of the following is NOT one of Newton's three laws of motion?
   a. An object a rest tends to stay at rest, and an object in motion tends to stay in motion
   b. $\mathrm{E} = \mathrm{mc}^2$
   c. For every action, there is an equal and opposite reaction
   d. $\mathrm{F} = \mathrm{ma}$

4. For circular motion, what is the name of the actual force pulling toward the axis of rotation?
    a. Centrifugal force
    b. Gravity
    c. Centripetal force
    d. No force is acting

5. The energy of motion is also referred to as what?
    a. Potential energy
    b. Kinetic energy
    c. Electric energy
    d. Electromagnetic energy

6. What is the purpose of a wave?
    a. To carry matter
    b. To transfer energy
    c. To do work
    d. To slow down matter

7. What is the term for when a wave bends?
    a. Refraction
    b. Diffraction
    c. Reflection
    d. Solarization

8. A spinning ice skater who extends their arms horizontally to slow down is demonstrating which of the following?
    a. Conservation of angular momentum
    b. Conservation of mechanical energy
    c. Conservation of matter
    d. Conservation of mass

9. How does electrical energy flow?
    a. From objects with lesser potential energy to objects with greater potential energy
    b. Equally between objects with equal potential energy
    c. From objects with greater potential energy to objects with lesser potential energy
    d. From objects with greater magnetic energy to objects with greater electrical energy

10. Which of the following is true regarding electromagnetism?
    a. Opposite charges attract.
    b. Like charges attract.
    c. Opposite charge are neutral towards one another.
    d. Like charges are neutral towards one another.

11. A 150-kilogram mass is placed on the left side of the lever as shown. What force must be exerted on the right side (in the location shown by the arrow) to balance the weight of this mass?

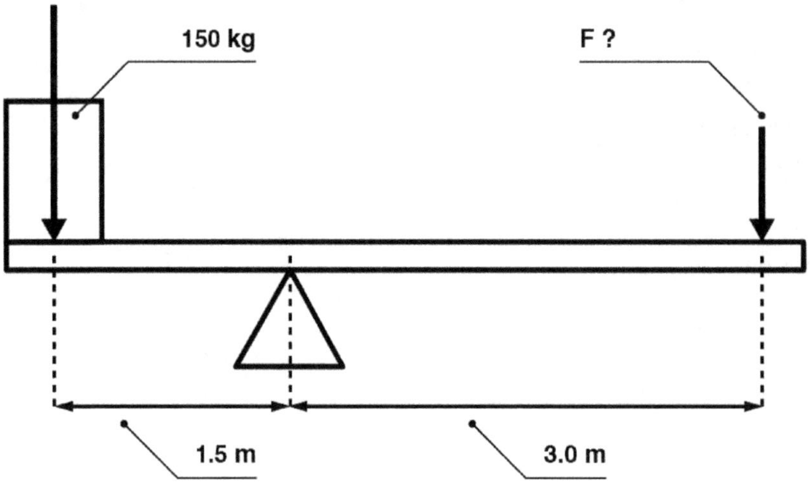

a. $675 \text{ kg} \cdot \text{m}$
b. 735.75 N
c. $1{,}471.5 \text{ N}$
d. $2{,}207.25 \text{ N} \cdot \text{m}$

12. For the wheel and axle assembly shown, the shaft radius is 20 millimeters and the wheel radius is 300 millimeters. What's the required effort to lift a 600 N load?

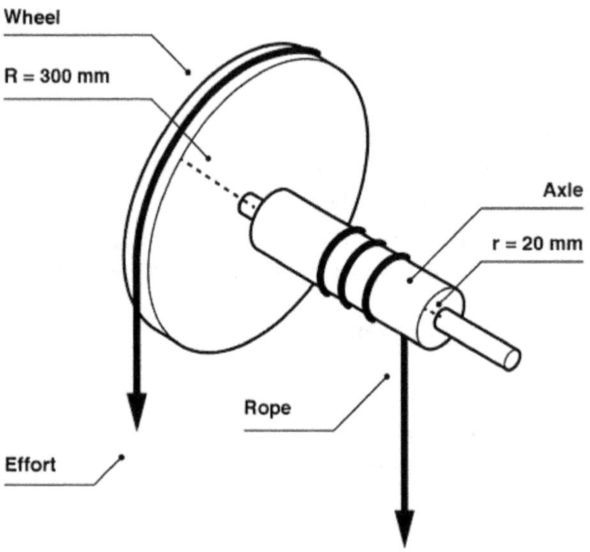

a. 10 N
b. 20 N
c. 30 N
d. 40 N

13. The driver gear (Gear A) turns clockwise at a rate of 60 RPM. What direction and rotational speed does Gear B turn at?

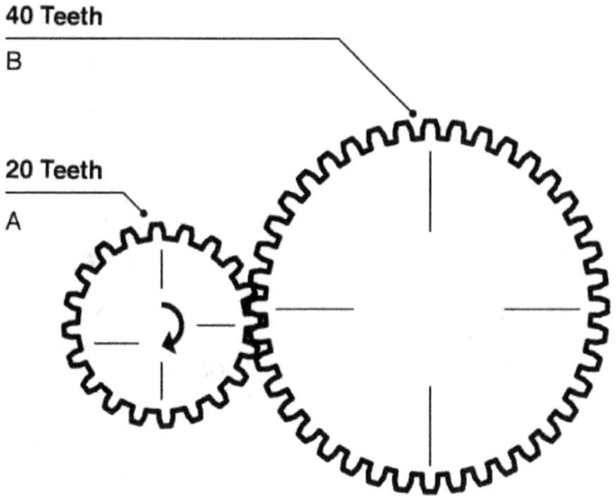

a. Clockwise at 120 RPM
b. Counterclockwise at 120 RPM
c. Clockwise at 30 RPM
d. Counterclockwise at 30 RPM

14. The three steel wheels shown are connected by rubber belts. The two wheels at the top have the same diameter, while the wheel below is twice their diameter. If the driver wheel at the upper left is turning clockwise at 60 RPM, at what speed and in which direction is the large bottom wheel turning?

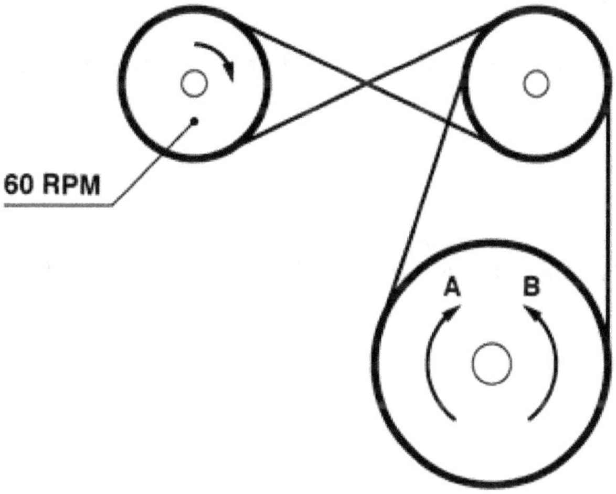

a. 30 RPM, clockwise (A)
b. 30 RPM, counterclockwise (B)
c. 120 RPM, clockwise (A)
d. 120 RPM, counterclockwise (B)

15. In case (a), both blocks are fixed. In case (b), the load is hung from a moveable block. Ignoring friction, what is the required force to move the blocks in both cases?

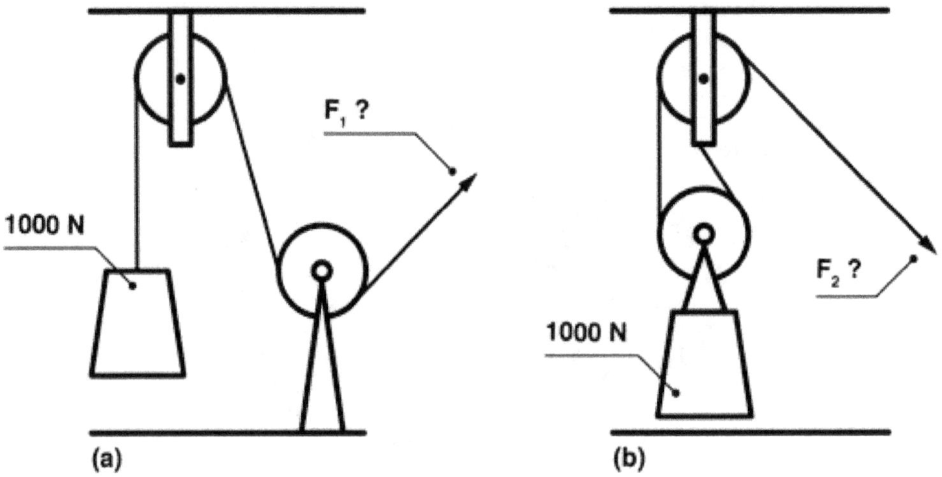

a. $F_1 = 500\text{ N}; F_2 = 500\text{ N}$
b. $F_1 = 500\text{ N}; F_2 = 1{,}000\text{ N}$
c. $F_1 = 1{,}000\text{ N}; F_2 = 500\text{ N}$
d. $F_1 = 1{,}000\text{ N}; F_2 = 1{,}000\text{ N}$

16. What is the total mechanical energy of a system?
a. The total potential energy
b. The total kinetic energy
c. Kinetic energy plus potential energy
d. Kinetic energy minus potential energy

17. What is the name of the scale used in sound level meters to measure the intensity of sound waves?
a. Doppler
b. Electron
c. Watt
d. Decibel

18. What effect changes the oscillations of a wave and can alter the appearance of light waves?
a. Reflection
b. Refraction
c. Dispersion
d. Polarization

19. What is the primary difference between an elastic and inelastic collision?
   a. In an elastic collision, the objects collide and then travel in different directions; in an inelastic collision, the objects collide and then stick together in their final direction of travel.
   b. In an elastic collision, the objects collide and then stick together in their final direction of travel; in an inelastic collision, the objects collide and then travel in different directions.
   c. An elastic collision adheres to the principle of the conservation of linear momentum while an inelastic collision does not.
   d. An inelastic collision adheres to the principle of the conservation of linear momentum while an elastic collision does not.

20. How is mechanical advantage calculated?
   a. The force input divided by the force output
   b. The force input multiplied by the force output
   c. The force output divided by 100
   d. The force output divided by the force input

21. Which of the following statements accurately explains how the speed and linear velocity of an object in uniform circular motion changes over time?
   a. Both the speed and the linear velocity of the object increase the longer the object is in uniform circular motion.
   b. Speed continues to increase as long as the object is held in uniform circular motion, but the linear velocity of the object remains constant.
   c. Linear velocity remains constant as long as the object is held in uniform circular motion, but the speed of the object constantly changes as the object is held in uniform circular motion.
   d. Speed remains constant as long as the object is held in uniform circular motion, but the linear velocity of the object constantly changes as the object is held in uniform circular motion.

22. A barbell at the gym undergoes a force of 5,000 N for the 3 seconds it takes the body builder to complete the bench press. What is the impulse experienced by the barbell, given that $\Delta p = F\Delta t$?
   a. $0.0006 \text{ N} \cdot \text{s}$
   b. $1{,}666 \text{ N} \cdot \text{s}$
   c. $15{,}000 \text{ N} \cdot \text{s}$
   d. $555 \text{ N} \cdot \text{s}$

23. Which of the following measurements can be multiplied by the square of the speed of light to calculate the binding energy of a nucleus?
   a. Change in electrical charge
   b. Change in mass
   c. Change in velocity
   d. Change in polarity

24. A biologist records the mating call of a reclusive species of bird. Using the recording, they are able to conclude that the call moved at $300 \ \frac{\text{m}}{\text{s}}$ with a frequency of 50 s^{-1}. What is wavelength of the bird's call, given that $v = \lambda f$?
   a. 0.16 m
   b. 6 m
   c. 60 m
   d. 15,000 m

25. An Olympic sprinter weighing 75 kg reaches a maximum speed of $12\ \frac{\text{m}}{\text{s}}$ during the 100-meter dash. How much kinetic energy did the sprinter have at their maximum speed, given that $K = \frac{1}{2}mv^2$?

a. 450 J
b. 900 J
c. 5,400 J
d. 10,800 J

26. A quarterback needs to throw the football as far as he can for a hail Mary play at the end of the game. Assuming he can throw equally hard in all scenarios, what angle should the quarterback aim to release the ball at to maximize the distance it will travel?

a. 30°
b. 45°
c. 60°
d. 75°

27. To successfully calculate the gravitational force between the moon and the sun, which of the following measurements are NOT required?

a. The mass of both the moon and the sun
b. The velocity of both the moon and the sun
c. The distance between the centers of masses for the moon and the sun
d. The gravitational constant

28. Which of the following statements accurately describes how the electrostatic force between charged objects changes as those two objects are moved further and further apart?

a. The magnitude of the electrostatic force between charged objects will decrease at a constant rate as the objects are moved further apart.
b. The magnitude of the electrostatic force between charged objects will decrease at an increasing rate as the objects are moved further apart.
c. The magnitude of the electrostatic force between charged objects will increase at an increasing rate as the objects are moved further apart.
d. The magnitude of the electrostatic force between charged objects will increase at a decreasing rate as the objects are moved further apart.

29. Snell's law is a formula used to describe the relationship between which two concepts?

a. Newton's first and second laws of motion
b. Kinetic energy and potential energy
c. Sound wave frequency and wavelength
d. Angles of incidence and refraction

30. A crash test dummy is placed into a new amusement park ride that quickly spins riders around on a rotating metal arm. The radius of the metal arm is measured at 5 meters, and the dummy is recorded to have undergone maximum centripetal acceleration of $20\ \frac{\text{m}}{\text{s}^2}$. What was the velocity of the crash test dummy at the moment of maximum acceleration, given that $a_c = \frac{v^2}{r}$?

a. $4\ \frac{\text{m}}{\text{s}}$
b. $10\ \frac{\text{m}}{\text{s}}$
c. $20\ \frac{\text{m}}{\text{s}}$
d. $100\ \frac{\text{m}}{\text{s}}$

Answer Explanations #2

Mathematics

1. B: Set up the problem and add each column, starting on the far right (ones). Add, carrying anything over 9 into the next column to the left. Solve from right to left.

2. D: Set up the problem and add each column, starting on the far right (ones). Add, carrying anything over 9 into the next column to the left. Solve from right to left.

3. A: Set up the problem, with the larger number on top and numbers lined up at the decimal point. Add, carrying anything over 9 into the next column to the left. Solve from right to left.

4. B: Set up the problem, with the larger number on top and numbers lined up at the decimal point. Insert 0 in any blank spots to the right of the decimal as placeholders. Add, carrying anything over 9 into the next column to the left.

5. C: To find a common denominator, look for a number that has both denominators (12 and 9) as factors. 36 works. Multiply the top and bottom of each fraction by whatever number will make the denominator 36:

$$\frac{5}{12} \times \frac{3}{3} = \frac{15}{36} \text{ and } \frac{4}{9} \times \frac{4}{4} = \frac{16}{36}$$

Now that we have a common denominator, add the numerators.

$$\frac{15}{36} + \frac{16}{36} = \frac{15 + 16}{36} = \frac{31}{36}$$

Since 31 and 36 have no common factors except 1, this fraction can't be reduced.

6. C: To find a common denominator, look for a number that has both denominators (33 and 11) as factors. 33 works. Multiply the top and bottom of each fraction by whatever number will make the denominator 33.

$$\frac{14}{33} \times \frac{1}{1} = \frac{14}{33} \text{ and } \frac{10}{11} \times \frac{3}{3} = \frac{30}{33}$$

Now that we have a common denominator, add the numerators.

$$\frac{14}{33} + \frac{30}{33} = \frac{14 + 30}{33} = \frac{44}{33}$$

Since 31 and 36 have no common factors except 1, this fraction can't be reduced. Reduce by dividing both the numerator and denominator by 11.

$$\frac{44 \div 11}{33 \div 11} = \frac{4}{3}$$

7. D: Set up the problem, with the larger number on top. Begin subtracting with the far-right column (ones). Borrow 10 from the column to the left when necessary.

8. A: Set up the problem, with the larger number on top. Begin subtracting with the far-right column (ones). Borrow 10 from the column to the left when necessary.

9. A: Set up the problem, larger number on top and numbers lined up at the decimal point. Begin subtracting with the far-right column. Borrow 10 from the column to the left when necessary.

10. B: Set up the problem, with the larger number on top and numbers lined up at the decimal point. Insert 0 in any blank spots to the right of the decimal point as placeholders. Begin subtracting with the far-right column. Borrow 10 from the column to the left when necessary.

11. C: To find a common denominator, look for a number that has both denominators (24 and 6) as factors. 24 works. Multiply the top and bottom of each fraction by whatever number will make the denominator 24:

$$\frac{23}{24} \times \frac{1}{1} = \frac{23}{24} \text{ and } \frac{1}{6} \times \frac{4}{4} = \frac{4}{24}$$

Now that we have a common denominator, subtract the numerators:

$$\frac{23}{24} - \frac{4}{24} = \frac{23 - 4}{24} = \frac{19}{24}$$

Since 19 and 24 have no common factors except 1, this fraction can't be reduced.

12. D: Set up the problem and find a common denominator for both fractions.

$$\frac{43}{45} - \frac{11}{15}$$

Multiply each fraction across by 1 to convert to a common denominator.

$$\frac{43}{45} \times \frac{1}{1} - \frac{11}{15} \times \frac{3}{3}$$

Once over the same denominator, subtract across the top.

$$\frac{43 - 33}{45} = \frac{10}{45}$$

Reduce:

$$\frac{10 \div 5}{45 \div 5} = \frac{2}{9}$$

13. D: Begin with the far-right digit on top and the far-right digit on the bottom (8×5).

Move one column left on top and multiply by the far-right column on the bottom. Remember to add the carry over after you multiply.

Starting on the far-right column, on top, repeat this pattern for the next digit left on the bottom. Write the answers below the first line of answers. Remember to begin with a zero placeholder.

Continue the pattern.

Add the answer rows together, making sure they are still lined up correctly.

14. A: Line up the numbers (the number with the most digits on top) to multiply. Begin with the right column on top and the right column on bottom.

Move one column left on top and multiply by the far-right column on the bottom. Remember to add the carry over after you multiply. Continue that pattern for each of the numbers on the top row.

Starting on the far-right column on top, repeat this pattern for the next digit left on the bottom. Write the answers below the first line of answers; remember to begin with a zero placeholder. Continue for each number in the top row.

Starting on the far-right column on top, repeat this pattern for the next digit left on the bottom. Write the answers below the previous line of answers. Remember to begin with two zero placeholders this time.

Once this is completed, ensure the answer rows are lined up correctly, then add.

15. B: This problem can be multiplied as 124×2, except at the end, the decimal point needs to be moved two places to the left (because in the problem, we have a total of two digits after decimal points: 4 and 2). Performing the multiplication will give 248, and moving the decimal point over two places results in 2.48.

16. B: This problem can be multiplied as $1{,}987 \times 5$, except at the end, the decimal point needs to be moved two places to the left (because in the problem, we have a total of two digits after decimal points: 0 and 5). Performing the multiplication will give 9,935, and moving the decimal point over two places results in 99.35.

17. A: Multiply across the top and across the bottom.

$$\frac{15 \times 54}{23 \times 127} = \frac{810}{2{,}921}$$

This matches Choice *A*, but we must decide whether it can be reduced. Because the numbers are so large, it may be difficult to tell, so the easiest method may be to look at each of the other answer choices. With Choice *B*, we can tell that the denominator, 292, is not a factor of 2,921 because $292 \times 10 = 2{,}920$, not 2,921, so that doesn't work. With Choice *C*, again, we can see that the denominator, 150, is not a factor of 2,921, because 150 is a multiple of 10 and 2,921 isn't. Finally, in Choice *D*, the numerator is the same as in our original fraction, but the denominator isn't, so this can't have the same value. The other choices are eliminated, so the answer must be Choice *A*.

18. C: Line up the fractions.

$$\frac{54}{55} \times \frac{5}{9}$$

Reduce fractions through cross-canceling.

$$\frac{6}{11} \times \frac{1}{1}$$

Multiply across the top and across the bottom.

$$\frac{6 \times 1}{11 \times 1} = \frac{6}{11}$$

19. D: Set up the division problem.

```
44|1202
```

44 does not go into 1 or 12 but does go into 120, so start there.

```
     27
44|1202
  - 88
    322
  - 308
     14
```

The answer is $27\frac{14}{44}$. Reduce the fraction for the final answer: $27\frac{7}{22}$.

20. D: Set up the division problem.

```
16|188
```

16 does not go into 1, but it does go into 18, so start there.

```
     11
16|188
 - 16
    28
  - 16
    12
```

The result is $11\frac{12}{16}$. Reduce the fraction for the final answer: $11\frac{3}{4}$.

21. D: Set up the division problem.

```
2.6|702
```

Move the decimal point over one place to the right in both numbers.

```
26|7020
```

26 does not go into 7, but it does go into 70, so start there.

```
     270
26|7020
 - 52
   182
 - 182
     0
```

The result is 270.

22. B: Set up the division problem.

$$1.4\overline{)1015}$$

Move the decimal point over one place to the right in both numbers.

$$14\overline{)10150}$$

14 does not go into 1 or 10 but does go into 101, so start there.

$$\begin{array}{r} 725 \\ 14\overline{)10150} \\ -98 \\ \hline 35 \\ -28 \\ \hline 70 \\ -70 \\ \hline 0 \end{array}$$

The result is 725.

23. C: Set up the division problem.

$$\frac{26}{55} \div \frac{26}{11}$$

Flip the second fraction and multiply.

$$\frac{26}{55} \times \frac{11}{26}$$

Reduce fractions through cross-canceling.

$$\frac{1}{5} \times \frac{1}{1}$$

Multiply across the top and across the bottom.

$$\frac{1 \times 1}{5 \times 1} = \frac{1}{5}$$

24. A: Flip the second fraction and multiply.

$$\frac{4}{13} \times \frac{169}{27}$$

Simplify the fractions before multiplying to make the numbers simpler to work with.

$$\frac{4}{1} \times \frac{13}{27}$$

Multiply across the top and across the bottom.

$$\frac{4 \times 13}{1 \times 27} = \frac{52}{27}$$

The numerator and denominator do not have any factors in common, so this fraction cannot be reduced.

25. D: Break down the Roman numeral MCDXXXII into parts.

M is equal to 1000.

C is before D and is smaller than D, so it means $\mathrm{D} - \mathrm{C}$.

$$\mathrm{CD} = 500 - 100 = 400$$

Add the following:

$$\mathrm{XXX} = 10 + 10 + 10 = 30$$

$$\mathrm{II} = 1 + 1 = 2$$

Add all parts:

$$1{,}000 + 400 + 30 + 2 = 1432$$

26. D: Break down the Roman numeral CCLI into parts.

Add the following:

$$\mathrm{CC} = 100 + 100 = 200$$

$$\mathrm{L} = 50$$

$$\mathrm{I} = 1$$

Add all parts:

$$200 + 50 + 1 = 251$$

27. B: Break down the number into parts.

$$111 = 100 + 10 + 1$$

100 is represented by C or $100 = \text{C}$.

10 is represented by X or $10 = \text{X}$.

1 is represented by 1 or $1 = \text{I}$.

Combine the Roman numerals.

CXI

28. C: Break down the number into parts.

$$515 = 500 + 10 + 5$$

500 is represented by D or $500 = \text{D}$.

10 is represented by X or $10 = \text{X}$.

5 is represented by V or $5 = \text{V}$.

Combine the Roman numerals.

DXV

29. A: Since military time starts with 0100 at 1:00 a.m., add 12 to get to 1300 hours, or 1:00 p.m.

30. B: Anything before 1200 would be in the a.m. hours of a 12-hour clock, so 0830 hours is 8:30 a.m.

31. B: To convert 5:00 p.m. into 24-hour time, add 12 to 5.

32. B: Anything before noon converts into its a.m. value.

33. A: Using the given information of 1 nurse to 25 patients and 325 total patients, set up an equation to solve for the number of nurses (N):

$$\frac{N}{325} = \frac{1}{25}$$

Multiply both sides by 325 to get N by itself on one side.

$$\frac{N}{1} = \frac{325}{25} = 13 \text{ nurses}$$

34. D: Using the given information of 2 beds to 1 room and 145 rooms, set up an equation to solve for the number of beds, set up an equation to solve for number of beds (B):

$$\frac{B}{145} = \frac{2}{1}$$

Multiply both sides by 145 to get B by itself on one side.

$$\frac{B}{1} = \frac{290}{1} = 290 \text{ beds}$$

35. C: Set up the initial equation:

$$\frac{2x}{5} - 1 = 59$$

Add 1 to both sides:

$$\frac{2x}{5} - 1 + 1 = 59 + 1$$

Multiply both sides by $\frac{5}{2}$:

$$\frac{2x}{5} \times \frac{5}{2} = 60 \times \frac{5}{2} = 150$$

$$x = 150$$

36. C: We can first find the total cost of the hat and jersey, then multiply by 0.5 to apply the 50% off:

$$(32.99 + 64.99) \times 0.5 = 48.99$$

Finally, we calculate the sales tax of 6% (that is, 0.06) and add it to the total:

$$48.99 + (48.99 \times 0.06) = 51.93$$

37. D: 5 pounds of store-brand coffee would cost $\frac{\$1.23}{1\ lbs} \times 5\ lbs = \$6.15$. For 5 pounds of local coffee, the cost would be $\frac{\$1.98}{1.5\ lbs} \times 5\ lbs = \$6.60$. Calculate the price difference: $\$6.60 - \$6.15 = \$0.45$.

38. D: Find how many feet are left after the first 1,800 ft:

$$3{,}125 \text{ ft} - 1{,}800 \text{ ft} = 1{,}325 \text{ ft}$$

At $1 per foot, this part will cost $1,325. Add this to the $2,000 for the first 1,800 ft to get the total cost:

$$\$2{,}000 + \$1{,}325 = \$3{,}325$$

39. A: Calculate how many gallons the bucket holds.

$$11.4 \text{ L} \times \frac{1 \text{ gal}}{3.8 \text{ L}} = 3 \text{ gal}$$

Next, calculate how many buckets are needed to fill the 35-gallon pool.

$$\frac{35}{3} = 11.67$$

Since the amount is more than 11 but less than 12, we must fill the bucket 12 times.

40. D: Three girls for every two boys can be expressed as a ratio: 3: 2. This can be visualized as splitting the school into 5 groups: 3 girl groups and 2 boy groups. The number of students that are in each group can be found by dividing the total number of students by 5:

$$\frac{650 \text{ students}}{5 \text{ groups}} = \frac{130 \text{ students}}{\text{group}}$$

To find the total number of girls, multiply the number of students per group (130) by the number of girl groups in the school (3). This equals 390, Choice *D*.

41. B: To convert from a decimal to a percentage, the decimal needs to be moved two places to the right. In this case, that makes 0.351 become 35.1%.

42. A: Converting a fraction to a percentage takes two steps. First, divide the numerator by the denominator to turn the fraction into a decimal:

$$\frac{2}{9} = 0.2222\ldots$$

The "..." indicates a repeating decimal with an infinite number of 2's.

Now, to convert to a percentage, move the decimal point two places to the right:

22.22%

43. D: To convert from a percentage to a decimal, or vice versa, you always need to move the decimal point two places. A percentage like 57% has an invisible decimal point after the 7, like this:

$$57.\%$$

That decimal point needs to be moved two places to the left to get:

$$0.57$$

44. A: Converting a fraction to a percentage takes two steps. First, divide the numerator by the denominator to turn the fraction into a decimal:

$$\frac{3}{8} = 0.375$$

Now, to convert to a percentage, move the decimal point two places to the right:

37.5%

45. A: This question involves the percent formula. Since we're beginning with a percent, also known as a number divided by 100, we'll put 39 on the right side of the equation:

$$\frac{x}{164} = \frac{39}{100}$$

Cross-multiply to get $100x = 164 \times 39 = 6{,}396$. We can solve for x by calculating $x = 6{,}396 \div 100 = 63.96$.

46. B: This question involves the percent formula:

$$\frac{32}{x} = \frac{25}{100}$$

Cross-multiply to get $25x = 32 \times 100 = 3{,}200$. We can solve for x by calculating $x = 3{,}200 \div 25 = 128$.

As an alternative, we could recall that 25% is $\frac{1}{4}$ and simply multiply 32 by 4 to get 128.

47. C: Divide 5 by 8, which results in 0.625. This rounds up to 0.63.

48. A: Divide 3 by 5 to get 0.6, and add that to the whole number, 3, to get 3.6. An alternative is to convert $3\frac{3}{5}$ to an improper fraction: $\frac{18}{5}$. Then divide 18 by 5 to get 3.6.

49. B: Since 0.56 goes to the hundredths place, it can be placed over 100:

$$\frac{56}{100}$$

Essentially, the way we got there is by multiplying the numerator and denominator by 100:

$$\frac{0.56}{1} \times \frac{100}{100} = \frac{56}{100}$$

Then, the fraction can be simplified down to $\frac{14}{25}$:

$$\frac{56}{100} \div \frac{4}{4} = \frac{14}{25}$$

50. D: To convert a decimal to a fraction, remember that any number to the left of the decimal point will be a whole number. Then, since 0.3 goes to the tenths place, the 3 can be placed over 10.

51. D: Recall the formula for area of a rectangle, area $=$ length $\times$ width. The answer must be in square inches, so all values must be converted to inches. Half of a foot is equal to 6 inches. Therefore, the area of the rectangle is equal to:

$$6 \text{ in} \times \frac{11}{2} \text{in} = \frac{66}{2} \text{in}^2 = 33 \text{ in}^2$$

52. B: The figure is composed of three sides of a square and a semicircle. The sides of the square are simply added: $8 + 8 + 8 = 24$ inches. The circumference of a circle is found by the equation $C = 2\pi r$. The radius is 4 in, so the circumference of the circle is approximately 25.13 in. Only half of the circle makes up the outer border of the figure (part of the perimeter) so half of 25.13 in is 12.565 in. Therefore, the total perimeter is: $24 \text{ in} + 12.565 \text{ in} = 36.565 \text{ in}$. The other answer choices use the incorrect formula or fail to include all of the necessary sides.

53. D: The slope is given by the change in y divided by the change in x. Specifically, it's:

$$slope = \frac{y_2 - y_1}{x_2 - x_1}$$

The first point is $(-5, -3)$, and the second point is $(0, -1)$. Work from left to right when identifying coordinates. Thus, the point on the left is point 1 $(-5, -3)$ and the point on the right is point 2 $(0, -1)$.

Now we just need to plug those numbers into the equation:

$$slope = \frac{-1 - (-3)}{0 - (-5)}$$

It can be simplified to:

$$slope = \frac{-1 + 3}{0 + 5}$$

$$slope = \frac{2}{5}$$

54. B: To add decimals, add them vertically, making sure to align the decimals. First, add the thousandths place: $3 + 1 = 4$. Next, add the hundredths place: $7 + 5 = 12$. The 1 gets carried to the tenths place, so adding the digits in the tenths place results in $1 + 6 + 6 = 13$. The 1 here gets carried to the ones place as well, so the sum of the ones are: $1 + 4 + 2 = 7$. Putting this together results in 7.324. The 2 is in the hundredths place, and the value to the right is 4, which is less than 5. Therefore, this value rounds to 7.32.

55. B: For the first card drawn, the probability of a king being pulled is $\frac{4}{52}$. Since this card isn't replaced, if a king is drawn first, the probability of a king being drawn second is $\frac{3}{51}$. The probability of a king being drawn in both the first and second draw is the product of the two probabilities:

$$\frac{4}{52} \times \frac{3}{51} = \frac{12}{2{,}652}$$

To reduce this fraction, divide the top and bottom by 12 to get $\frac{1}{221}$.

Reading Comprehension

1. D: This is an example of a purpose question—why did the author write this? The article contains facts, definitions, and other objective information without telling a story or arguing an opinion. In this case, the purpose of the article is to inform the reader. Choice *A* and *B* are incorrect because they argue for an opinion or present a position. Choice *C* is incorrect because the focus of the article is spinoff technology, not the history of space technology.

2. B: This organization question asks readers to analyze the structure of the essay. The topic of the essay is about spinoff technology, and the thesis statement at the end of the first paragraph offers the opinion, "Spinoff technology proves that it is worthwhile to invest in scientific research because it could enrich people's lives in unexpected ways." The next two paragraphs provide evidence to support this opinion. Choice *A* is the second-best option because the first paragraph gives a general definition of spinoff technology, while the following two paragraphs offer more detailed examples to help illustrate this idea. However, it is not the best answer because the main idea of the essay is that spinoff technology enriches people's lives in unexpected ways. Choice *C* is incorrect because the essay does not provide details of any specific moment in history. Choice *D* is incorrect because the essay does not discuss a popular misconception.

3. C: This reading comprehension question can be answered based on the second paragraph, which describes how scientists were concerned about astronauts' nutrition and began researching useful nutritional supplements. Choice *A* in particular is not true because it reverses the order of discovery. First NASA identified the algae for astronauts to use and then it was further developed for use in baby food, not the other way around. Choices *B* and *D* are not uses of algae discussed in the article.

4. B: Even for readers who have never encountered the word neurological before, the passage does provide context clues. The sentence following the statement about neurological benefits says algae has "potential to boost brain health." From this context, readers should be able to infer that neurological is related to the brain.

5. D: This purpose question requires readers to understand the relevance of the given detail. In this case, the author mentions "costly and crucial equipment" before mentioning space suit visors, which are given as an example of something that is very valuable. Choice *A* is not correct because fashion is only related to sunglasses, not to NASA equipment. Choice *B* can be eliminated because it is simply not mentioned in the passage. While Choice *C* seems like it could be a true statement, it is also not relevant to what is being explained by the author.

6. C: The article gives several examples of how businesses have been able to capitalize on NASA research, so it is unlikely that the author would agree with this statement. Evidence for the other answer choices can be found in the article. In Choice *A,* the author mentions that "many consumers are unaware that products they are buying are based on NASA research." Choice *B* is a general definition of spinoff technology. Choice *D* is mentioned in the final paragraph.

7. D: The author mentions anti-Stratfordian arguments in the first paragraph, but then goes on to debunk these theories with more facts about Shakespeare's life in the second and third paragraphs. Choice *A* is not correct because, while the author does present arguments from both sides, the author is far from unbiased; in fact, the author clearly disagrees with anti-Stratfordians. Choice *B* is also not correct because it is more closely aligned to the beliefs of anti-Stratfordians, with whom the author disagrees. Choice *C* can be eliminated because, while it is true that the author gives historical background, the main purpose of the article is using that information to disprove a theory.

8. B: The thesis is a statement that contains the author's topic and main idea. As seen in question 7, the main purpose of this article is to use historical evidence to provide counterarguments to anti-Stratfordians. *A* is simply a definition; *C* is a supporting detail, not a main idea; and *D* represents an idea of anti-Stratfordians, not the author's opinion.

9. B: This question asks readers to refer to the organizational structure of the article and demonstrate understanding of how the author provides details to support their argument. This particular detail can be found in the second paragraph where the author says, "even though he did not attend university, grade-school education in Shakespeare's time was actually quite rigorous."

10. A: This is a vocabulary question that can be answered using context clues. Other sentences in the paragraph describe London as "the most populous city in England" filled with "crowds of people," giving an image of a busy city full of people. *B* is not correct because London was in Shakespeare's home country, not a foreign one. *C* is not mentioned in the passage. *D* is not a good answer choice because the passage describes how London was a popular and important city, not an undeveloped one.

11. D: Anti-Stratfordians doubt Shakespeare's ability because he was not from the upper class. His father was a glove-maker. Therefore, in at least this instance, glove-makers were not included in the upper class (this is an example of inductive reasoning, or using two specific pieces of information to draw a more general conclusion).

12. C: This detail comes from the third paragraph, where the author responds to skeptics who claim that Shakespeare wrote too much about places he never visited, so Romeo and Juliet is mentioned as a famous example of a play with a foreign setting. In order to answer this question, readers need to understand the author's main purpose in the third paragraph and how the author uses details to support this purpose. *A* and *D* are not mentioned in the passage, and *B* is clearly not true because the passage mentions more than once that Shakespeare never left England.

13. A: This inference can be made from the final paragraph, where the author refutes anti-Stratfordian skepticism by pointing out that books about life in Europe could easily circulate throughout London. From this statement, readers can conclude that the author believes it is possible that Shakespeare learned about European culture from books, rather than visiting the continent on his own. Choice *B* is not true because the author believes that Shakespeare contributed to English literature without traveling extensively. Similarly, Choice *C* is not a good answer because the author explains how Shakespeare got his education without university. Choice *D* can also be eliminated because the author describes Shakespeare's genius and clearly Shakespeare is not from Italy.

14. B: "Four score and seven years ago" is the equivalent of eighty-seven years, because the word "score" means "twenty." Choices *A* and *C* are incorrect because the context for describing a unit of measurement or a literary movement is lacking. Choice *D* is incorrect because although Lincoln's speech is a cornerstone in political rhetoric, the phrase "four score and seven years ago" is better narrowed to a period of time.

15. D: Though the US was involved in World War I and II, Choices *A* and *C* are incorrect because they occurred long after the Gettysburg address. Choice *B* is incorrect, as the War of Spanish Succession involved Spain, Italy, Germany, and the Netherlands, and not the United States.

16. A: The speech calls on the audience to perpetuate the ideals of freedom, so that the soldiers' deaths on the battlefield would not be in vain. Choice *B* is incorrect because, although they are there to "dedicate a portion of that field," there is no mention in the text of an annual memorial service. Choice *C* is incorrect because there is no aggressive language in the text, only reverence for the dead. Choice *D* is incorrect because forgetting the lives that were lost is the opposite of what Lincoln is suggesting.

17. A: Choice *A* is correct because Lincoln's intention was to memorialize the soldiers who had fallen as a result of war as well as celebrate those who had put their lives in danger for the sake of their country. Choices *B, C,* and *D* are incorrect because Lincoln's speech was supposed to foster a sense of pride among the members of the audience while connecting them to the soldiers' experiences, not to alienate or discourage them.

18. B: The passage states that the Juggernaut causes the children to scream. Choices *A* and *D* don't apply because the text doesn't mention either of these instances specifically. Choice *C* is incorrect because there is nothing in the text that mentions space travel.

19. B: The mention of *morning*, *noon*, and *night* make it clear that the word *haunt* refers to frequent appearances at various times. Choice *A* doesn't work because the text makes no mention of levitating. Choices *C* and *D* are not correct because the text makes mention of Mr. Utterson's anguish and disheartenment because of his failure to find Hyde but does not make mention of Mr. Utterson's feelings negatively affecting anyone else.

20. D: The speaker invokes the game of hide and seek to indicate they will continue their search for Hyde. Choices *A* and *B* are not possible answers because the text doesn't refer to any name changes or an identity crisis, despite Mr. Utterson's extreme obsession with finding Hyde. The text also makes no mention of a mistaken identity when referring to Hyde, so Choice *C* is also incorrect.

21. C: The passage is organized such that the author contrasts two different viewpoints in the opening paragraphs, then builds a case showing preference for one over the other. Choice *A* is incorrect because the introduction does not contain an impartial definition, but rather, an opinion. Choice *B* is incorrect. There is no puzzling phenomenon given, as the author doesn't mention any peculiar cause or effect that is in question regarding poetry. While Choice *D* is correct that the passage does contain another's viewpoint at the beginning of the passage; however, to say that the author has no stake in this argument is incorrect, as the author uses personal experiences to build their case.

22. B: Choice *B* accurately describes the author's argument in the text: that poetry is not irrelevant. While the author does praise, and even value, Buddy Wakefield as a poet, the author never heralds him as a genius. Eliminate Choice *A,* as it is an exaggeration. Not only is Choice *C* an exaggerated statement, but the author never mentions spoken word poetry in the text. Choice *D* is incorrect because this statement contradicts the writer's argument.

23. D: *Exiguously* means not occurring often, or occurring rarely, so Choice D would least change the meaning of the sentence. Choice *A, indolently*, means unhurriedly, or slow, and does not fit the context of the sentence. Choice *B, inaudibly*, means quietly or silently. Choice *C, interminably*, means endlessly, or all the time, and is the opposite of the word *exiguously*.

24. D: A student's insistence that psychoanalysis is a subset of modern psychology is the most analogous option. The author of the passage tries to insist that performance poetry is a subset of modern poetry, and therefore, tries to prove that modern poetry is not "dying," but thriving on social media for the masses. Choice *A* is incorrect, as the author is not refusing any kind of validation. Choice *B* is incorrect; the author's insistence is that poetry will not lose popularity. Choice *C* mimics the topic but compares two different genres, making it incorrect as the author makes no comparison in this passage.

25. B: The author's purpose is to disprove Gioia's article, which claims that poetry is a dying art form that only survives in academic settings. In order to prove this argument, the author educates the reader about new developments in poetry, Choice *A*, and describes the brilliance of a specific modern poet, Choice *C*, but these serve as examples of a growing poetry trend that counters Gioia's argument. Choice *D* is incorrect because it contradicts the author's argument.

26. C: The text mentions all of the listed properties of minerals except the instance of minerals being organically formed. Objects or substances must be naturally occurring, must be a homogeneous solid, and must have a definite chemical composition in order to be considered a mineral.

27. A: Choice *A* is the correct answer because geology is the study of earth-related science. Choice *B* is incorrect because psychology is the study of the mind and behavior. Choice *C* is incorrect because biology is the study of life and living organisms. Choice *D* is incorrect because botany is the study of plants.

28. A: Choice *A* is the correct answer because the prefix *homo-* means same. Choice *B* is incorrect because "differing in some areas" would be linked to the prefix *hetero-*, meaning "different" or "other." Choices *C* and *D* are incorrect because the sentence does not mention anything about atomic masses or the properties of homogenous solids.

29: C: Choice *C* is the correct answer because *-logy* refers to the study of a particular subject matter.

30. D: A *rookery* is a colony of breeding birds. Although *rookery* could mean Choice *A,* houses in a slum area, it does not make sense in this context. Choices *B* and *C* are both incorrect, as this is not a place for hunters to trade tools or for wardens to trade stories.

31. B: The previous sentence is describing "twenty colonies" of birds, so what follows should be a bird colony. Choice *A* may be true, but we have no evidence of this in the text. Choice *C* does touch on the tension between the hunters and wardens, but there is no official "Bird Island Battle" mentioned in the text. Choice *D* does not exist in the text.

32. D: The text mentions several different times how and why the Audubon Association has been successful and gives examples to back this fact. Choice *A* is incorrect because the passage doesn't mention the need for people to take action. Likewise, Choices *B* and *C* are not mentioned in the text.

33. C: Choice *A* might be true in a general sense, but it is not relevant to the context of the text. Choice *B* is incorrect because the hunters are not studying lines of flight to help wardens, but to hunt birds. Choice *D* is incorrect because nothing in the text mentions that hunters are trying to build homes underneath lines of flight of birds for good luck.

34. A: Not only does the article provide examples to disprove a myth, the title also suggests that the article is trying to disprove a myth. Further, the sentence, "But the 'fact' that the majority of your body heat is lost through your head is a lie," and then the subsequent "let me explain," demonstrates the author's intention in disproving a myth. Choice *B* is incorrect because although the selection does compare elephants and anteaters, it does so in order to prove a point, and is not the primary reason that the selection was written. Choice *C* is incorrect because even though the article mentions somebody wearing clothes in the winter, and that doing so could save your life, wearing clothes in the winter is not the primary reason this article was written. Choice *D* is incorrect because the article only mentions that people are gullible once, and makes no further comment on the matter, so this cannot be the primary purpose.

35. B: If the myth is that most of one's body heat is lost through their head, then the fact that heat loss is proportional to surface area exposed is the best evidence that disproves it, since one's head has a great deal less surface area than the rest of the body, making *B* the correct choice. "It is better to wear a shirt than a hat" does not provide evidence that disproves the fact that the head loses more heat than the rest of the body. Thus, Choice *A* is incorrect. Choice *C* is incorrect because gullibility is mentioned only once in this passage and the rest of the article ignores this statement, so clearly it is not the main idea. Finally, Choice *D* is incorrect because though the article mentions that the human chest probably loses the most heat, it is to provide an example of the evidence that heat loss is proportional to surface area exposed, so this is not the main idea of the passage.

36. B: Choice *B* is correct because the author is trying to demonstrate the main idea, which is that heat loss is proportional to surface area, so they compare two animals with different surface areas to clarify the main point. Choice *A* is incorrect because the author uses elephants and anteaters to prove a point, that heat loss is proportional to surface area, not to express an opinion. Choice *C* is incorrect because though the author does use them to show differences, they do so in order to give examples that prove the above points. Choice *D* is incorrect because there is no language to indicate favoritism between the two animals.

37. C: Since there is an opinion presented along with a fact, Choice *C* is the correct answer. Choice *A* is incorrect. "Not only would you look stupid," is an opinion because there is no way to prove that somebody would look stupid by not wearing a shirt in the cold, even if that may be a popular opinion. However, this opinion is sandwiched inside a factual statement. Choice *B* is incorrect because again, this is a factual statement, but it has been editorialized by interjecting an opinion. Because of the presence of both a fact and an opinion, Choice *D* is the opposite of the correct answer.

38. C: Because of the way the author addresses the reader and the colloquial language the author uses (e.g., "let me explain," "so," "well," "didn't," "you would look stupid"), Choice *C* is the best answer because it has a much more casual tone than the usual informative article. Choice *A* may be a tempting choice because the author says the "fact" that most of one's heat is lost through their head is a "lie" and that someone who does not wear a shirt in the cold looks stupid. However, this only happens twice within the passage, and the passage does not give an overall tone of harshness. Choice *B* is incorrect because again, while not necessarily nice, the language does not carry an angry charge. The author is clearly not indifferent to the subject because of the passionate language that they use, so Choice *D* is incorrect.

39. B: The primary purpose of the article is to provide evidence to disprove the myth that most of a person's heat is lost through their head. The fact that each part of the body loses heat in proportion to its surface area is the best evidence to disprove this myth. *A* is incorrect because again, gullibility is not a main contributor to this article, but it may be common to see questions on the test that give the same wrong answer in order to try and trick the test taker. Choice *C* only suggests what you should do with this information; it is not the primary evidence itself. Choice *D,* while tempting, is actually not evidence. It does not give any reason for why it is a lie; it simply states that it is. Evidence is factual information that supports a claim.

40. B: Choice *B* is correct because having very little drinking water on Earth is a very good reason that one should limit their water usage so that the human population does not run out of drinking water and die out. People wasting water on superfluous things does not support the fact that we need to limit our water usage. It merely states that people are wasteful. Therefore, Choice *A* is incorrect. Answer Choice *C* may be tempting, but it is not the correct one, as this article is not about reducing water usage in order to help those who don't have easy access to water. It is about the fact that the planet is running out of drinking water. Choice *D* is incorrect because nowhere in the article does it state that only industrialized countries have access to drinking water.

41. C: The primary purpose is to present a problem (the planet is running out of water) with a solution (to reduce water waste), therefore the correct answer is *C.* Choice *A* is incorrect because the passage does not have a sequential timeline of events and is therefore not in chronological order. It may be tempting to think the author compares and contrasts people who do not have access to drinking water to those who do, but that does not fit with the primary purpose of the article, which is to convince people to reduce their water usage. Thus, Choice *B* is incorrect. Choice *D* is incorrect because descriptions are not the primary content of this article. Remember that a descriptive writing style describes people, settings, or situations in great detail with many adjectives. While a descriptive writing voice may be used alongside a persuasive writing style, it is generally not the primary voice when trying to convince a reader to take a certain stance.

42. A: If the assertion is that the Earth does not have enough drinking water, then having abundant water stores that are not being reported would certainly challenge this assertion. Choice *B* is incorrect because even if much of the water we drink does come from rain, that means the human population would be dependent on rain in order to survive, which would support the assertion rather than challenge it. Because the primary purpose of the passage is not to help those who cannot get water, Choice *C* is not the correct answer. Even if Choice *D* were true, it does not dismiss the other ways in which people are wasteful with water and is also not the point.

43. B: Choice *B* is correct because the article uses a lot of emotionally charged language and also suggests what needs to be done with the information provided. The article does not contain elements of a narrative, which include plot, setting, characters, and themes. Not only does the article lack these things, but it does not follow a timeline, which is a key element of a narrative voice. Thus, Choice *A* is incorrect. Choice *C* is incorrect because the article uses information in order to be persuasive, but the purpose is not solely to inform on the issue. Choice *D* is incorrect because the article is not written in primarily descriptive language.

44. C: Choice *C* is correct because people who waste water on lawns, half-full dishwashers, or personal pools are not taking into account how much water they are using because they get an unlimited supply; therefore, they are taking it for granted. Choices *A* and *B* are incorrect because they are both explicitly stated within the given sentence. While Choice *D* is implicitly stated within the whole article, it is not implicitly stated within the sentence.

45. B: Choice *B* is correct because the author uses this example in order to show people, through emotional appeal, that they take water for granted because they get water freely from their faucets, while millions of people have to endure great hardships to get drinking water. Choice *A* does not pertain directly to the main idea of the article, nor does it pertain to the author's purpose. The main idea is that people should reduce their water usage, and the author's purpose is to persuade the reader to do so. Choice *C* is incorrect because the selection never mentions that water is only available in industrialized countries. Choice *D* is the author's purpose for the entire passage but not the purpose for mentioning the difficulty in getting water for some of the population.

46. C: To be mindful means to be aware, so *C* is the best answer. Choice *A* may be a tempting answer, because if people are interested in the water they are using, they may be more aware of it, but this is not the best answer of the choices. Being amused by water does not make sense in this context, so Choice *B* is incorrect. Being accepting of the amounts of water they use is the opposite of what the author is trying to get the reader to do. Thus, Choice *D* is incorrect.

47. A: Choice *B* is a reason that people should reduce their water usage, but it is not the main idea. Choice *C* is an explanation for water waste but, again, not the main idea. Choice *D* is a suggestion for reducing water usage but still not the main idea.

48. D: The passage directly states that the larger sensor is the main difference between the two cameras. Choices *A* and *B* may be true, but these answers do not identify the major difference between the two cameras. Choice *C* states the opposite of what the paragraph suggests is the best option for amateur photographers, so it is incorrect.

49. D: An actuary assesses risks and sets insurance premiums. While an actuary does work in insurance, the passage does not suggest that actuaries have any affiliation with hospitalists or working in a hospital, so all other choices are incorrect.

50. A: The passage focuses mainly on the problems of hard water. Choice *B* is incorrect because calcium is not good for pipes and hard surfaces. The passage does not say anything about whether water softeners are easy to install, so Choice *C* is incorrect. Choice *D* is also incorrect because the passage does offer other solutions besides vinegar.

51. C: The main point of this paragraph is that parents need to change their poor behavior at their kids' sporting events. Choice *A* is incorrect because the coaches' behavior is not mentioned in the paragraph. Choice *B* suggests that sports are bad for kids, but the paragraph is about parents' behavior, so it is incorrect. While Choice *D* may be true, it offers a specific solution to the problem, which the paragraph does not discuss.

52. B: The main point of this passage is to show how a tornado forms. Choice *A* is off base because while the passage does mention that tornadoes are dangerous, it is not the main focus of the passage. While thunderstorms are mentioned, they are not compared to tornadoes, so Choice *C* is incorrect. Choice *D* is incorrect because the passage does not discuss what to do in the event of a tornado.

53. C: The purpose of this passage is to explain how the digestive system works. Choice *A* focuses only on the liver, which is a small part of the process and not the focus of the paragraph. Choice *B* is off-track because the passage does not mention healthy foods. Choices *D* and *E* each only focus on one part of the digestive system.

54. D: The main point of this passage is to define osteoporosis. Choice *A* is incorrect because the passage does not list ways that people contract osteoporosis. Choice *B* is incorrect because the passage does not mention any treatment options. While the passage does briefly mention prevention, it does not explain how, so Choice *C* is incorrect.

55. D: The passage compares Disney cruises with Disney parks. It does not discuss how to book a cruise, so Choice *A* is incorrect. Choice *B* is incorrect because though the passage does mention some of the park attractions, it is not the main point. The passage does not mention the cost of either option, so Choice *C* is incorrect.

Vocabulary

1. A: Excessive sweating. Causes of diaphoresis are varied and can include anxiety, medication side effects, malaria, and diabetes.

2. C: *Brevity* literally means brief or concise. Note the similar beginnings of *brevity* and *brief*—from the Latin "brevis," meaning brief.

3. D: The other choices refer to *attitude*, a word spelled and pronounced similarly to altitude. Someone's attitude can reflect haughtiness, influence their outlook, and reflect their behavior. None of these terms describe *altitude*, which is the measure of height. *Height* is directly related to altitude.

4. A: *Irate* means being in a state of anger. Clearly this is a negative word that can be paired with another negative word. The closest word to match this is obviously *angry*. Research would also reveal that irate comes from the Latin "ira," which means anger.

5. C: Distended means bloated. Choice *A* is incorrect because occluded means blocked, which the nurse would not be able to see without an ultrasound. Choice *B* is incorrect because suppressed means to stop or hold back, which does not make sense in this context. Choice *D* is incorrect because impaired means damaged, which the nurse would not be able to know without further tests.

6. C: Something *ineffable* cannot be described with words. It often is used in connection to something so impressive, emotional, or great. The heartwarming feelings of a family reuniting after a parent has been deployed may be said to be *ineffable.*

7. C: Someone that is described as *gregarious* is social and talkative. *Meek* is more of an antonym because it means quiet and submissive.

8. A: *Caustic* is an adjective that is often used in the chemical context to describe a substance that is corrosive or able to burn tissues. In this way, it is typically an acidic and abrasive chemical. However, it can also be used to describe a person's demeanor, which is bitterly *sarcastic* or scathing.

9. C: This type of seizure with muscle rigidity, convulsions, and unconsciousness is called a *grand mal* seizure. A *myoclonic* seizure only involves one part of the body making jerking movements. An *absence* seizure involves a brief loss of consciousness where the patient may stare off into space. A *tonic* seizure is characterized by rigidity and stiffness of the muscles.

10. D: The patient is most likely experiencing a stroke, as evidenced by his difficulty with speech and facial drooping. *Meningitis* is an inflammation of the meninges and does not fit the description of symptoms here. A *migraine* is a severe headache that can sometimes mimic stroke symptoms but is less severe. A stroke should be suspected until it is proven otherwise in order to get the patient timely and effective treatment. A *seizure* is characterized by muscle rigidity, convulsions, and loss of consciousness.

11. C: *Retort* is a verb that means "to answer back," usually in a sharp manner. This term embodies the idea of a response, emphasized by the "re-" prefix meaning "back, again." While a *retort* can be used in a conversation or as a jest, neither term embodies the idea of addressing someone again. *Counter*, however, means to respond in opposition when used as a verb.

12. A: Someone that is *obtuse* is unintelligent or *slow-witted*. They might be described as ignorant or dense. In geometry, it refers to an angle greater than 90 degrees and less than 180 degrees, but this is a different usage of the word.

13. A: *Loquacious* reflects the tendency to talk a lot. While someone can be humorous and loquacious, *humorous* describes the kind of talk, not the fact that someone talks a lot. *Cranky* has nothing to do with the word, and *silent* is a clear opposite. This leaves *verbose*, meaning using an abundance of words; loquacious is a synonym.

14. A: *Dyspnea* means difficulty breathing. The prefix *dys-* means dysfunctional or abnormal. The suffix *-pnea* in a medical context refers to respiration and breathing. Sleep apnea is a breathing disorder that can occur during sleep.

15. C: *Sordid* means filthy, *vile*, or squalid. *Semantic* means referring to the meaning of words or language. *Surly* can mean either threatening in appearance or crabby (in terms of mood).

16. A: *Bereavement* may present as many different physical conditions and can be diagnosed by completing a thorough history. *Stroke* often presents as deficits on one side of the body. *Anorexia nervosa* presents with decreased appetite along with signs of malnutrition. M*yocardial infarction (MI)* often presents with tingling or pain in the left arm or jaw and chest pressure or pain.

17. C: Alternative medications are often ordered in place of *antispasmodics* for treatment of urinary incontinence due to side effects of excessive thirst.

18. A: To *solicit* is to *ask* for something, often with the goal of obtaining something from someone else. *Solicitation* is the noun that is derived from the term; it refers to the act of asking for something. Sometimes, homes or businesses will post a notice that "no solicitation is allowed," meaning no one is to knock on the door trying to sell something, asking for signatures in support of a cause, etc.

19. C: *Venous* ulcers are commonly found between the knees and ankles. *Arterial* ulcers are located at the end of the toe on pressure points or in non-healing wounds. *Neuropathic* ulcers are found on the toes and sides of the feet. *Staging* applies to all types of ulcers and is dependent upon size, tunneling, and other factors.

20. A: *Isometric* exercises are done against resistance without moving a joint. *Isotonic* exercise moves the joint, *isokinetic* exercise uses a machine, and *plyometric* exercise uses a combination of stretching followed by contraction.

21. A: *Plausible* means likely to be possible or accepted, the opposite of *skeptical. Diurnal* relates to daytime, so it is unrelated. *Erudite* means clever or intelligent, but not necessarily possible or correct. *Conceivable* means that something is able to be thought of or able to be done. Conceivable is the best match for plausible.

22. C: *Discourse* refers to spoken and written communication, or debate. *Path* doesn't have anything to do with discourse, unless used figuratively. While discourse may consist of *praise* or *disagreement*, all discourse—written or verbal—is a form of speech. Therefore, *speech* is the best term that encompasses the same meaning as discourse.

23. A: The Latin root, *asper*, means rough. *Exasperate*, then, means to make relations with someone rough or to rub them the wrong way. *Disappointment* can be the result of an exasperating situation, but it is not the same as exasperation itself. *Annoy* is a synonym, meaning to irritate and make someone slightly angry.

24. B: In a medical context, *genicular* or *geniculate* refer to something pertaining the knee. The term *geniculate* itself can be used in a more general context to refer to something bent sharply like the knee.

25. D: The prefix *trans* can mean *across*, *beyond*, or *over*. Choices *A*, *B*, and *C* are incorrect because they are the meanings of other prefixes. Choice *A* is a meaning of the prefix *de*. Choice *B* is the meaning of the prefix *omni*.

Choice *C* is one of the meanings of the prefix *pro*. The example words are helpful in determining the meaning of *trans*. All of the example words—*transfer, transact, translation*, and *transport*—indicate something being *across, beyond*, or *over* something else. For example, *translation* refers to text going across languages. If no example words were given, you could think of words starting with *trans* and then compare their meanings to try to determine a common definition.

26. C: *Cubital,* in terms of body regions, refers to *the elbow*. For example, the inner elbow area where blood draws are often collected is called the antecubital space. The shoulder region is referred to as the *acromial* area.

27. A: *Mitigate* refers to easing tension or making something less severe. Pain medication would help to mitigate, or alleviate, a patient's pain level. Choices *B, C*, and *D* are incorrect. *Focus* doesn't relate to this context. *Intensify* and *aggravate* are synonyms that mean to make something worse, the opposite of mitigate.

28. A: *Keratin* is a structural protein, and it is the primary constituent of things like hair and nails. Choice *B* is incorrect because *antigens* are immune proteins that help fight disease. Choice *C* is incorrect because *channel proteins* are transport proteins that help move molecules into and out of a cell. Lastly, Choice *D* is incorrect because *actin*, like myosin, is a motor protein because it is involved in the process of muscle contraction.

29. B: *Deep* is the term that best completes the sentence. The dermis is the deeper layer of skin under the more superficial epidermis.

30. C: A *phlebotomist* is a professional who draws blood. An x-ray technician takes x-rays, a prosthetist makes artificial limbs, and a psychologist, social worker, or therapist counsels patients.

31. C: *Regress* means to return to an earlier state. *Rescind* means to revoke or repeal. It often is used in relation to an agreement or law. *Digress* means to temporarily deviate from the main topic when speaking or writing (for example, telling a story that is just somewhat related to the main point). *Diverge* is to fork or separate from the main path or road.

32. A: *Subliminal* and *subconscious* share the Latin prefix "sub-," meaning under or below, or more commonly used when talking about messages the sender doesn't want the receiver to consciously take note of. The word *subliminal* means beneath the consciousness. Thus, *subconscious* is the perfect match.

33. B: Glassy eyes, like a doll's, are shiny and empty; they are expressionless. Someone with glassy eyes may have a fixed stare. Different conditions, such as severe dehydration and cholera, can cause glassy eyes.

34. A: Though *flush* has several definitions, in the context of the provided sentence, it means to align in a smooth, consistent way, forming an unbroken surface. It's important for braces, for example AFOs (ankle foot orthoses), to be flush with the skin. Otherwise, friction will occur between the skin and the brace where it contacts a prominence and cause blistering or skin breakdown.

35. C: *Innervate* means to supply nerves to. For example, the radial nerve innervates the extensors in the upper arm, such as the triceps.

36. C: Although *incite* usually has negative connotations, leaders can incite their followers to benevolent actions as well. In both cases, people rally to support a cause.

37. C: *Exigent* means urgent. *Lenient* means permissive and easy-going, to *extoll* is to praise, and *lackadaisical* means apathetic or lazy.

38. D: *Aphasia* is a loss in the ability to express or understand speech, so it is language impairment. It is often caused by brain damage, whether due to a stroke, TBI, or other cause. An inability to recognize things is *agnosia.*

39. B: *Sustain* is to revitalize, or to give strength. *Strength* would be a good choice, but strength alone does not describe the re-strengthening that sustain embodies. The best choice is *invigorate*, which is a verb like sustain, meaning to strengthen. This makes invigorate the better choice. *Expedite* is unrelated. While *embolden* means to give someone courage, which is a form of strength, invigorate and sustain speak more toward physical circumstances.

40. A: Something that is *jejune* is dull, simplistic, naïve, or unoriginal.

41. A: *Deficit* best completes the sentence. *Diffident* means shy or lacking in confidence. *Dearth* means scarcity, so it might be an attractive choice, but *deficit* is a better word in the context of the sentence. *Defiant* means obstinate or uncooperative.

42. D: A paradox can best be described as a *contradiction*. A paradox often seems self-contradictory, meaning that it is a true statement that doesn't follow what's expected or logical.

43. A: *Lithe* best completes the sentence. While Choice *B, ballerina,* may be described as agile and graceful, the correct choice is the adjective that describes the movement, *lithe.*

44. B: *Cyanosis* often results from an occlusion or circulation impairment, which causes an insufficient amount of oxygen to perfuse the tissues.

45. A: *Venerate* means respect. Someone who is venerated is respected and revered.

46. B: Ringworm is a type of *mycosis*. The prefix *myco-* means something related to fungus.

47. C: *Uremia* means blood in the urine. *Anuria* is no urine production, *nocturia* is nighttime urination, and *polyurea* refers to abnormally large volumes of urine.

48. A: *Malevolent* literally means bad or evil-minded. The clue is also in the Latin root "mal-," which translates to bad.

49. A: *Proprioception* is spatial awareness of the body. The body has sensory receptors, called proprioceptors, which help the body sense and respond to position and movement.

50. D: An *archetype* is an example of a person or thing, a recurrent symbol. An *ancestor* may be a good model of ideal behavior, but the term refers to someone who is related. Archetypes appear in literature, but these are different terms. *Policy* is unrelated. A *model* is a standard or representative, which is synonymous with archetype.

Grammar

1. B: In Choice *B* the word *Uncle* should not be capitalized because it is not functioning as a proper noun. If the word named a specific uncle, such as *Uncle Jerry*, then it would be considered a proper noun and should be capitalized. Choice *A* correctly capitalizes the proper noun *East Coast*. Choice *C* correctly capitalizes the name of a specific college course, which is considered a proper noun. Choice *D* correctly capitalizes the proper noun *Jersey Shore*.

2. C: In Choice *C, avid* is functioning as an adjective that modifies the word photographer. *Avid* describes the photographer Julia Robinson's style. The words *time* and *photographer* are functioning as nouns, and the word *capture* is functioning as a verb in the sentence. Other words functioning as adjectives in the sentence include *local*, *business*, and *spare*, as they all describe the nouns they precede.

3. A: Choice *A* is correct because it uses a semicolon to join the two independent clauses (clauses that could function as independent sentences). Choice *B* is incorrect because the conjunction is not preceded by a comma. A comma and conjunction should be used together to join independent clauses. Choice *C* is incorrect because a comma should only be used to join independent sentences when it also includes a coordinating conjunction such as *and* or *so*. Choice *D* does not use punctuation to join the independent clauses, so it is considered a fused (same as a run-on) sentence.

4. C: Choice *C* is a compound sentence because it joins two independent clauses with a comma and the coordinating conjunction *and*. The sentences in Choices *B* and *D* include one independent clause and one dependent clause, so they are complex sentences, not compound sentences. The sentence in Choice *A* has both a compound subject, *Alex and Shane*, and a compound verb, *spent and took*, but the entire sentence itself is one independent clause.

5. A: Choice *A* uses incorrect subject-verb agreement because the indefinite pronoun *neither* is singular and must use the singular verb form *is*. In Choice *B*, the pronoun both is plural and uses the plural verb form of *are*. The pronoun any can be either singular or plural. In Choice *C*, it is plural, so the plural verb form *are* is used. The pronoun *each* is singular and uses the singular verb form *is*, as seen in Choice *D*.

6. B: Choice *B* is correct because the pronouns *he* and *I* are in the subjective case. *He* and *I* are the subjects of the verb *like* in the independent clause of the sentence. Choices *A, C*, and *D* are incorrect because they all contain at least one objective pronoun (*me* and *him*). Objective pronouns should not be used as the subject of the sentence, but rather, they should come as an object of a verb. To test for correct pronoun usage, try reading the pronouns as if they were the only pronoun in the sentence. For example, *he* and *me* may appear to be the correct answer choices, but try reading them as the only pronoun.

> He like[s] to go fishing...
>
> Me like to go fishing...

When looked at that way, *me* is an obviously incorrect choice.

7. B: Choice *A* uses the plural form of the verb, when the subject is the pronoun *none*, which needs a singular verb. *C* also uses the wrong verb form and uses the word *all* in place of *none*, which doesn't make sense in the context of the sentence. *D* uses *all* again, and is missing the comma, which is necessary to set the dependent clause off from the independent clause.

8. C: In this answer, the article and subject agree, and the subject and predicate agree. Answer Choice *A* is incorrect because the article *an* and *issues* do not agree in number. *B* is incorrect because an article is needed before *important issue*. *D* is incorrect because the plural subject *issues* does not agree with the singular verb *is*.

9. D: Choices *A* and *C* use additional words and phrases that aren't necessary. *B* is more concise, but uses the present tense of *is*. This does not agree with the rest of the sentence, which uses past tense. The best choice is *D*, which uses the most concise sentence structure and is grammatically correct.

10. C: Choice *A* is missing the word *that*. Choice *B* uses the plural verb *include*, which does not agree with the word *set*. Choice *D* changes *was* to *were*, which is in plural form and does not agree with the singular subject, *fact*.

11. A: Choices *B* and *D* both use the expression *attributed to the fact* incorrectly. It can only be attributed *to* the fact, not *with* or *in* the fact. Choice *C* incorrectly uses a gerund, *saying,* when it should use the present tense of the verb *say*.

12. B: Choice *B* is correct because it uses correct parallel structure of plural nouns. Choice *A* is incorrect because the word *accessory* is in singular form. Choice *C* is incorrect because it pluralizes *makeup*, which is already in plural form. Choice *D* is incorrect because it again uses the singular *accessory*, and it uses the singular *shoe*.

13. D: Because shows the cause/effect relationship between what Shawn did and why he did it.

14. A: In answer Choice *B,* the present tense form of the verb *consider* creates an independent clause joined to another independent clause with only a comma, which is a comma splice and grammatically incorrect. Choices *C* and *D* use the possessive form of *its*, when it should be the contraction *it's* for *it is*. Choice *D* also includes incorrect comma placement.

15. B: Choice *B* is an imperative sentence because it issues a command. In addition, it ends with a period, and an imperative sentence must end in a period or exclamation mark. Choice *A* is a declarative sentence that states a fact and ends with a period. Choice *C* is an exclamatory sentence that shows strong emotion and ends with an exclamation point. Choice *D* is an interrogative sentence that asks a question and ends with a question mark.

16. C: Choice *C* is a compound sentence because it joins two independent clauses—*The baby was sick* and *I decided to stay home from work*—with a comma and the coordinating conjunction *so*. Choices *A, B*, and *D* are all simple sentences, each containing one independent clause with a complete subject and predicate. Choices *A* and *D* each contain a compound subject, or more than one subject, but they are still simple sentences that only contain one independent clause. Choice *B* contains a compound verb (more than one verb), but it's still a simple sentence.

17. C: The simple subject of this sentence, the word *lots*, is plural. It agrees with the plural verb form *were*. Choice *A* is incorrect, because the simple subject *there*, referring to the two constellations, is considered plural. It does not agree with the singular verb form *is*. In Choice *B*, the plural subject *four* does not agree with the singular verb form *needs*. In Choice *D*, the singular subject *everyone* does not agree with the third person plural verb form *have*.

18. B: *Excellent* and *walking* are adjectives modifying the noun *tours*. *Rich* is an adjective modifying the noun *history*, and *brotherly* is an adjective modifying the noun *love*. Choice *A* is incorrect because all of these words are functioning as nouns in the sentence. Choice *C* is incorrect because all of these words are functioning as verbs in the sentence. Choice *D* is incorrect because all of these words are considered prepositions, not adjectives.

19. D: The object pronouns *her* and *me* act as the indirect objects of the sentence. If *me* is in a series of object pronouns, it should always come last in the series. Choice *A* is incorrect because it uses subject pronouns *she* and *I*. Choice *B* is incorrect because it uses the subject pronoun *she*. Choice *C* uses the correct object pronouns, but they are in the wrong order.

20. A: In this example, a colon is correctly used to introduce a series of items. Choice *B* places an unnecessary comma before the word *because*. A comma is not needed before the word *because* when it introduces a dependent clause at the end of a sentence and provides necessary information to understand the sentence. Choice *C* is incorrect because it uses a semi-colon instead of a comma to join a dependent clause and an independent clause. Choice *D* is incorrect because it uses a colon in place of a comma and coordinating conjunction to join two independent clauses.

21. B: Choice *B* correctly uses the contraction for *you are* as the subject of the sentence, and it correctly uses the possessive pronoun *your* to indicate ownership of the jacket. It also correctly uses the adverb *there*, indicating place. Choice *A* is incorrect because it reverses the possessive pronoun *your* and the contraction for *you are*. It also uses the possessive pronoun *their* instead of the adverb *there*. Choice *C* is incorrect because it reverses *your* and *you're* and uses the contraction for *they are* in place of the adverb *there*. Choice *D* incorrectly uses the possessive pronoun *their* instead of the adverb *there*.

22. A: *Slang* refers to non-standard expressions that are not used in elevated speech and writing. *Slang* tends to be specific to one group or time period and is commonly used within groups of young people during their conversations with each other. *Jargon* refers to the language used in a specialized field. The *vernacular* is the native language of a local area, and a *dialect* is one form of a language in a certain region. Thus, Choices *B*, *C*, and *D* are incorrect.

23. D: Colloquial language is that which is used conversationally or informally, in contrast to professional or academic language. While *ain't* is common in conversational English, it is a non-standard expression in academic writing. For college-bound students, high school should introduce them to the expectations of a college classroom, so Choice *B* is not the best answer. Teachers should also avoid placing moral or social value on certain patterns of speech. Rather than teaching students that their familiar speech patterns are bad, teachers should help students learn when and how to use appropriate forms of expression, so Choice *C* is wrong. *Ain't* is in the dictionary, so Choice *A* is incorrect, both in the reason for counseling and in the factual sense.

24. C: A complex sentence joins an independent or main clause with a dependent or subordinate clause. In this case, the main clause is "The restaurant is unconventional." This is a clause with one subject-verb combination that can stand alone as a grammatically-complete sentence. The dependent clause is "because it serves both Chicago style pizza and New York style pizza." This clause begins with the subordinating conjunction *because* and also consists of only one subject-verb combination. Choice *A* is incorrect because a simple sentence consists of only one verb-subject combination—one independent clause. Choice *B* is incorrect because a compound sentence contains two independent clauses connected by a conjunction. Choice *D* is incorrect because a compound-complex sentence consists of two or more independent clauses and one or more dependent clauses.

25. A: Parallelism refers to consistent use of sentence structure or word form. In this case, the list within the sentence does not utilize parallelism; three of the verbs appear in their base form—*travel*, *take*, and *eat*—but one appears as a gerund—*going*. A parallel version of this sentence would be "This summer, I'm planning to travel to Italy, take a Mediterranean cruise, go to Pompeii, and eat a lot of Italian food." Choice *B* is incorrect because this description is a complete sentence. Choice *C* is incorrect, as a misplaced modifier is a modifier that is not located appropriately in relation to the word or words they modify. Choice *D* is incorrect because subject-verb agreement refers to the appropriate conjugation of a verb in relation to its subject.

26. C: In this sentence, the modifier is the phrase "Forgetting that he was supposed to meet his girlfriend for dinner." This phrase offers information about Fred's actions, but the noun that immediately follows it is Anita, creating some confusion about the "do-er" of the phrase. A more appropriate sentence arrangement would be "Forgetting that he was supposed to meet his girlfriend for dinner, Fred made Anita mad when he showed up late." Choice *A* is incorrect, as parallelism refers to the consistent use of sentence structure and verb tense, and this sentence is appropriately consistent. Choice *B* is incorrect as this sentence contains appropriate punctuation for the number of independent clauses presented; it is not a run-on sentence. Choice *D* is incorrect because subject-verb agreement refers to the appropriate conjugation of a verb relative to the subject, and all verbs have been properly conjugated.

27. B: A comma splice occurs when a comma is used to join two independent clauses together without the additional use of an appropriate conjunction. One way to remedy this problem is to replace the comma with a semicolon. Another solution is to add a conjunction: "Some workers use all their sick leave, but other workers cash out their leave." Choice *A* is incorrect, as parallelism refers to the consistent use of sentence structure and verb tense; all tenses and structures in this sentence are consistent. Choice *C* is incorrect because a sentence fragment is a phrase or clause that cannot stand alone—this sentence contains two independent clauses. Choice *D* is incorrect because subject-verb agreement refers to the proper conjugation of a verb relative to the subject, and all verbs have been properly conjugated.

28. D: The problem in the original passage is that the second sentence is a dependent clause that cannot stand alone as a sentence; it must be attached to the main clause found in the first sentence. Because the main clause comes first, it does not need to be separated by a comma. However, if the dependent clause came first, then a comma would be necessary, which is why Choice *C* is incorrect. Choices *A* and *B* also insert unnecessary commas into the sentence.

29. A: A noun refers to a person, place, thing, or idea. Although the word *approach* can also be used as a verb, in the sentence it functions as a noun within the noun phrase "a fresh approach," so Choice *B* is incorrect. An adverb is a word or phrase that provides additional information of the verb, but because the verb is *need* and not *approach*, then Choice *C* is false. An adjective is a word that describes a noun, used here as the word *fresh*, but it is not the noun itself. Thus, Choice *D* is also incorrect.

30. D: An adjective modifies a noun, answering questions like "which one?" or "what kind?" In this sentence, the word *exhaustive* is an adjective that modifies the noun *investigation*. Another clue that this word is an adjective is the suffix *–ive*, which means "having the quality of." The nouns in this sentence are *investigators, inquiry, accusations,* and *corruption*; therefore, Choice *A* is incorrect. The verb in this sentence is *conducted* because this was the action taken by the subject *the investigators*; therefore, Choice *B* is incorrect. Choice *C* is incorrect because an adverb is a word or phrase that provides additional information about the verb, expressing how, when, where, or in what manner.

31. B: In this case, the phrase functions as an adverb modifying the verb *report*, so Choice *B* is the correct answer. "To the student center" does not consist of a subject-verb combination, so it is not a clause; thus, Choices *A* and *C* can be eliminated. This group of words is a phrase. Phrases are classified by either the controlling word in the phrase or its function in the sentence. Choice *D* is incorrect because a noun phrase is a series of words that describe or modify a noun.

32. D: In this sentence, the first answer choice requires a noun meaning *impact* or *influence*, so *effect* is the correct answer. For the second answer choice, the sentence is drawing a comparison. *Than* shows a comparative relationship whereas *then* shows sequence or consequence. Choices *A* and *C* can be eliminated because they contain the choice *then*. Choice *B* is incorrect because *affect* is a verb while this sentence requires a noun.

33. D: Since the sentence contains two independent clauses and a dependent clause, the sentence is categorized as compound-complex:

Independent clause: *I accepted the change of seasons*

Independent clause: *I started to appreciate the fall*

Dependent clause: *Although I wished it were summer*

34. D: Students can use context clues to make a careful guess about the meaning of unfamiliar words. Although all of the words in a sentence can help contribute to the overall meaning, in this case, the adjective that pairs with *ubiquitous* gives the most important hint to the student: cars were first *rare*, but now they are *ubiquitous.* The inversion of *rare* is what gives meaning to the rest of the sentence and *ubiquitous* means "existing everywhere" or "not rare." Choice *A* is incorrect because *ago* only indicates a time frame. Choice *B* is incorrect because *cars* does not indicate a contrasting relationship to the word *ubiquitous* to provide a good context clue. Choice *C* is incorrect because it also only indicates a time frame, but used together with *rare*, it provides the contrasting relationship needed to identify the meaning of the unknown word.

35. B: Proper nouns are specific. *Statue of Liberty* is a proper noun and specifies exactly which statue is being discussed. Choice *A* is incorrect because the word *people* is a common noun and it is only capitalized because it is at the beginning of the sentence. Choice *C* is incorrect. The word *awesome* is an adjective describing the sight. Choice *D* is incorrect. The word *sight* is a common noun. A clue to eliminate answer Choices *C* and *D* is that they were not capitalized. Proper nouns are always capitalized.

36. D: The word *kittens* is plural, meaning more than one kitten. Choice *A* is incorrect. The word *kitten* is singular. Choice *B* is incorrect. The word *girl's* is a singular possessive form. The girl is making the choice. There is only one girl involved. Choice *C* is incorrect. The word *choice* is a singular noun. The girl has only one choice to make. The word *litter* in this sentence is a collective plural noun meaning a group of kittens.

37. C: The word *who* in the sentence is a subjective interrogative pronoun; the sentence needed a subject that begins a question. Choice *A* is incorrect. The word *whose* is a possessive pronoun and it is not being asked who owns the flowers. Choice *B* is incorrect. The word *whom* is always an objective pronoun—never a subjective one; a subjective pronoun is needed in this sentence. Choice *D* is incorrect. The word *who've* is a contraction of the words *who* and *have*. We would not say, *"Who have ordered the flowers?"*

38. D: The word *its* in the sentence is the singular possessive form of the pronoun that stands in place for the word *giraffe's.* There is one baby that belongs to one giraffe. Choice *A* is incorrect. It is a contraction of the words *it* and *is.* You would not say, *"The giraffe nudged it is baby."* Choice *B* is incorrect. We do not know the gender of the giraffe; even if it was female, the proper word would be *her baby*, not *hers baby.* Choice *C* is incorrect. The word *them* is a plural objective pronoun and we need a singular possessive pronoun because there is only one giraffe doing the nudging.

39. B: The word *several* stands in for a plural noun at the beginning of the sentence, such as the noun *people*. It is also an indefinite pronoun because the number of people, for example, is not defined. Choice *A* is incorrect. The pronoun is plural, not singular. It indicates more than one person. We can tell because the sentence works with the plural word *are* for the verb; substituting the singular word *is* would not make sense. We wouldn't say, *"Several is laughing loudly on the bus."* Choice *C* is incorrect. *Several* is the subject of the sentence. Therefore, it is a subjective pronoun not an objective one. Choice *D* is incorrect. The word *several* does not modify a noun in the sentence. If the sentence said, *"Several people are laughing loudly on the bus,"* then the word *several* would be an indefinite adjective modifying the word *people.*

40. A: The word *delectable* is an adjective modifying the noun *meal* in the sentence. It answers the question: *"What kind of meal?"* Choice *B* is incorrect. The word *connoisseur* is a noun that is the subject of the sentence. Choice *C* is incorrect. The word *slowly* is an adverb telling how the subject enjoyed the meal. Choice *D* is incorrect. The word *enjoyed* is the past-tense verb in the sentence telling us what action the subject had taken.

41. B: The word *by* is a positional preposition telling where we are in relation to the water. The word *near* is also a positional preposition telling where *we* are in relation to the lake. The word *before* is a time preposition telling when in relation to the time of day, dawn. Choice *A* is incorrect because *went* and *to see* are both verbs and *pretty* is an adjective modifying the word *sunrise*. Choice *C* is incorrect because *water, lake, dawn,* and *sunrise* are all nouns in the sentence. Choice *D* is incorrect because the word *we* is a pronoun, the word *down* is an adverb modifying the verb *went*, the word *the* is an article, and the word *pretty* is an adjective modifying *sunrise*.

42. B: The word *well* at the beginning of the sentence is set apart from the rest of the sentence with a comma and is a mild interjection. Choice *A* is incorrect. The word *goodness* at the end of the sentence is a noun. It is the idea/state of being for the cookie. Choice *C* is incorrect. It is an interrogative sentence and all of the words in the sentence can be identified as other parts of speech. *Can't* is a contraction of the word cannot and it works with the word *see* as the verb in the sentence. The word *you* is a pronoun; the word *that* is an adjective modifying the word *cookie*; *cookie* is a noun; *is* is another verb; and *broken* is an adjective modifying the word *cookie*. Choice *D* is incorrect because the exclamation mark at the end of the sentence is not there to set apart an interjection. Rather, it is there to punctuate the exclamatory sentence.

43. C: The simple subject is *bike* and its modifiers *the heaviest* and *green* are included to form the complete subject. Choice *A* is incorrect because *bike* is the simple subject. Choice *B* is incorrect because it includes only one of the modifiers (*green*) of the word *bike*. Choice *D* is incorrect because *is mine* is the predicate of the sentence, not the subject.

44. D: The subject of the sentence is *my house;* therefore, the rest of the sentence is the predicate. Choice *A* is incorrect because *my house* is the subject, not the predicate. Choice *B* is incorrect because *is the yellow one* is only part of the predicate, but the sentence does not end there. Choice *C* is incorrect because *at the end of the street* is only a portion of the predicate.

45. B: The *kitten* is a singular subject and so the singular verb *pounces* should be used instead of *pounce*. Choice *A* is incorrect because the plural subject *kittens* agrees with the plural verb *show.* Choice *C* is incorrect because the singular subject *kitten* agrees with the singular verb *eats*. Choice *D* is incorrect because the singular subject *kitten* agrees with the singular verb *snuggles*.

46. C: *Her mother* is to whom Calysta brought the lamp. Choice *A* is incorrect because *stained-glass lamp* is the direct object of the sentence. Choice *B* is incorrect because *brought* is the verb. Choice *D* is incorrect because *beautiful* is an adjective modifying the noun *lamp*.

47. C: *They're* (they are) on *their* (possessive) way to New Jersey but *they're* (they are) not *there* (location) yet. This sentence makes sense. Choice *A* is incorrect because after the word *but* should be the word *they're* (they are). Choice *B* is incorrect because the sentence should begin with *they're* (they are) instead of *their* (possessive). Choice *D* is incorrect because after the word *not* should be *there* (location) instead of *their* (possessive).

48. D: *For the longest time* is an introductory prepositional phrase beginning with the preposition *for* and all the modifiers for the word *time*. Choice *A* is incorrect because it includes the past-tense verb *have wanted*, creating a clause. Choice *B* is incorrect because it includes the verb *wanted* and the infinitive *to learn*. Choice *C* is incorrect because it includes the verb *learn* and the infinitive *to skate*.

49. B: *The weight of the world was on his shoulders* and *he took a long walk* are both independent clauses connected with a comma and a coordinating conjunction. Choice *A* is incorrect because there are two independent clauses and a simple sentence has only one independent clause. Choice *C* is incorrect because the sentence has no dependent clauses and a complex sentence needs at least one dependent clause. Choice *D* is incorrect because, although there are two independent clauses, there are no dependent clauses and a compound-complex sentence will have at least two independent clauses and at least one dependent clause.

50. A: *The last thing she wanted to do was see the Eiffel Tower before the flight* has only one independent clause and no dependent clauses; therefore, it is a simple sentence. Choice *B* is incorrect because the sentence has only one independent clause. *The last thing she wanted to do* is a gerund phrase serving as the noun subject of the sentence, therefore it is not an independent clause. Choice *C* is incorrect because the sentence has no dependent clauses; therefore, it cannot be a complex sentence. Choice *D* is incorrect because the sentence has only one independent clause and no dependent clauses. A compound-complex sentence needs at least two independent clauses and at least one dependent clause.

51. C: Choice *C* correctly adds a comma after *style*, successfully joining the introductory phrase and independent clause as a single sentence. Choice *A* is incorrect because the introductory phrase and independent clause remain unsuccessfully combined without the comma. Choices *B* and *D* do nothing to fix this.

52. A: Choice *A* is correct, as *not only* and *but also* are correlative pairs. In this sentence, *but* successfully transitions the first part into the second half, making punctuation unnecessary. Additionally, the use of *to* indicates that an idea or challenge is being presented to the reader. Choice *B*'s *with*, *C*'s *for*, and *D*'s *there before* are not as active, meaning these revisions weaken the sentence.

53. B: Choice *B* correctly joins the two independent clauses with a comma before *but*. Choice *A* is incorrect because, without the comma, it is a run-on sentence. Choice *C* also lacks punctuation and uses *however*, which should be reserved for starting a new sentence or perhaps after a semicolon. Choice *D* works grammatically but makes the sentence awkward and too formal compared to the rest of the passage.

54. A: Choice *A* is correct because the sentence does not require modification. Choice *B* is incorrect because it uses the faulty subject/verb agreement "Physical proof are." Choice *C* is incorrect because a comma would need to follow *exists*. Choice *D* is incorrect because the comma after *science* is unnecessary.

55. A: Choice *A* is the best answer for several reasons. To begin, the section is grammatically correct in using a semicolon to connect the two independent clauses. This allows the different two ideas to be connected without separating them. In this context, the semicolon makes more sense for the overall sentence structure and passage as a whole. Choice *B* is incorrect because it forms a run-on. Choice *C* applies a comma incorrectly.

Biology

1. C: A hypothesis is a statement that makes a prediction between two variables. The two variables here are the amount of poison and how quickly the rat dies. Choice *C* states that the more poison a rat is given, the more quickly it will die, which is a prediction. Choice *A* is incorrect because it's simply an observation. Choice *B* is incorrect because it's a question posed by the observation but makes no predictions. Choice *D* is incorrect because it's simply a fact.

2. D: Water's unusual properties are due to intermolecular hydrogen bonding. These forces make water molecules "stick" to one another, which explains why water has unusually high cohesion and adhesion (molecules sticking to each other and sticking to other surfaces). Cohesion can be seen in beads of dew. Adhesion can be seen when water sticks to the sides of a graduated cylinder to form a meniscus. The stickiness to neighboring molecules also increases surface tension, providing a very thin film that light things cannot penetrate, which is observed when leaves float in swimming pools. Water has a low freezing point, not a high freezing point, because molecules must have a very low kinetic energy to arrange themselves in the lattice-like structure found in ice, its solid form.

3. A: Catabolic reactions release energy and are exothermic. Catabolism breaks down complex molecules into simpler molecules. Anabolic reactions are just the opposite—they absorb energy in order to form complex molecules from simpler ones. Proteins, carbohydrates (polysaccharides), lipids, and nucleic acids are complex organic molecules synthesized by anabolic metabolism. The monomers of these organic compounds are amino acids, monosaccharides, triglycerides, and nucleotides.

4. C: Metabolic reactions utilize enzymes to decrease their activation energy. Enzymes that drive these reactions are protein catalysts. Their mechanism is sometimes referred to as the "lock-and-key" model. "Lock and key" references the fact that enzymes have exact specificity with their substrate (reactant) like a lock does to a key. The substrate binds to the enzyme snugly, the enzyme facilitates the reaction, and then the product is formed while the enzyme is unchanged and ready to be reused.

5. B: The structure exclusively found in eukaryotic cells is the nucleus. Animal, plant, fungi, and protist cells are all eukaryotic. DNA is contained within the nucleus of eukaryotic cells, and they also have membrane-bound organelles that perform complex intracellular metabolic activities. Prokaryotic cells (archaea and bacteria) do not have a nucleus or other membrane-bound organelles and are less complex than eukaryotic cells.

6. A: The Golgi complex, also known as the Golgi apparatus, is not found in the nucleus. Chromosomes, the nucleolus, and chromatin are all found within the nucleus of the cell. The Golgi apparatus is found in the cytoplasm and is responsible for protein maturation, which is the process of proteins folding into their secondary, tertiary, and quaternary configurations. The structure appears folded in membranous layers and is easily visible with microscopy. The Golgi apparatus packages proteins in vesicles for export out of the cell or to their cellular destination.

7. B: The cell structure responsible for cellular storage, digestion, and waste removal is the lysosome. Lysosomes are like recycle bins. They are filled with digestive enzymes that facilitate catabolic reactions to regenerate monomers.

8. B: The mitochondria are cellular energy generators and the "powerhouses" of the cell. They provide cellular energy in the form of adenosine triphosphate (ATP). This process, called aerobic respiration, uses oxygen plus sugars, proteins, and fats to produce ATP, carbon dioxide, and water. Mitochondria contain their own DNA and ribosomes, which is significant because according to endosymbiotic theory, these structures provide evidence that they used to be independently functioning prokaryotes.

9. B: Plastids are the photosynthesizing organelles of plants, which are not found in animal cells. Plants have the ability to generate their own sugars through photosynthesis, a process where they use pigments to capture the sun's light energy. Chloroplasts are the most prevalent plastid, and chlorophyll is the light-absorbing pigment that absorbs all energy carried in photons except that of green light. This explains why the photosynthesizing parts of plants, predominantly leaves, appear green.

10. B: During telophase, two nuclei form at each end of the cell and nuclear envelopes begin to form around each nucleus. The nucleoli reappear, and the chromosomes become less compact. The microtubules are broken down by the cell, and mitosis is complete. The process begins with prophase as the mitotic spindles begin to form from centrosomes. Prometaphase follows, with the breakdown of the nuclear envelope and the further condensing of the chromosomes. Next, metaphase occurs when the microtubules are stretched across the cell and the chromosomes align at the metaphase plate. Finally, in the last step before telophase, anaphase occurs as the sister chromatids break apart and form chromosomes.

11. B: Phenotypes are observable traits, such as eye color, hair color, blood type, etc. They can also be biochemical or have physiological or behavioral traits. A genotype is the collective gene representation of an individual, whether the genes are expressed or not. Alleles are different forms of the same gene that code for specific traits, like blue eyes or brown eyes. In simple genetics, there are two forms of a gene: dominant and recessive. More complex genetics involves co-dominance, multiple alleles, and sex-linked genes. The other answer choices are incorrect because gender is determined by the presence of an entire chromosome, the Y chromosome, and a karyotype is an image of all of an individual's chromosomes.

12. D: Reproductive cells are referred to as gametes: egg (female) and sperm (male). These cells have only one set of 23 chromosomes and are haploid so that when they combine during fertilization, the zygote has the correct diploid number, 46. Reproductive cell division is called meiosis, which is different from mitosis, the type of division process for body (somatic) cells.

13. A: The process of cell division in somatic cells is called mitosis. In interphase, which precedes mitosis, cells prepare for division by copying their DNA. Once mitotic machinery has been assembled in interphase, mitosis occurs, which has five distinct phases: prophase, prometaphase, metaphase, anaphase, and telophase, followed by cytokinesis, which is the final splitting of the cytoplasm. The two diploid daughter cells are genetically identical to the parent cell.

14. D: In water, the electronegative oxygen sucks in the electrons of the two hydrogen atoms, making the oxygen slightly negatively-charged and the hydrogen atoms slightly positively-charged. This unequal sharing is called "polarity." This polarity is responsible for the slightly positive hydrogen atoms from one molecule being attracted to a slightly negative oxygen in a different molecule, creating a weak intermolecular force called a hydrogen bond, so *A* and *B* are true. *C* is also true, because this unique hydrogen bonding creates intermolecular forces that allow molecules with low enough kinetic energy (at low temperatures) to be held apart at "arm's length" (really, the length of the hydrogen bonds). This makes ice less dense than liquid water, which explains why ice floats, an unusual property of water. *D* is the only statement that is false, so it is the correct answer.

15. D: Natural selection is the idea that individuals are selected to survive and reproduce based on their ability to adapt to the environment. Their phenotypes are advantageous for survival and reproduction over those of other individuals. It is solely based on the phenotype of the individual, not the genotype, Choice *A*. Extreme phenotypes, Choice *B*, may be selected but are not always the most advantageous. It occurs all time, not just in extreme weather conditions, such as a drought, Choice *C*.

16. A: An alteration in the normal gene sequence is called a DNA point mutation. Mutations can be harmful, neutral, or even beneficial. Sometimes, as seen in natural selection, a genetic mutation can improve fitness, providing an adaptation that will aid in survival. DNA mutations can happen as a result of environmental damage, for example, from radiation or chemicals. Mutations can also happen during cell replication, as a result of incorrect pairing of complementary nucleotides by DNA polymerase. There are also chromosomal mutations as well, where entire segments of chromosomes can be deleted, inverted, duplicated, or sent or received from a different chromosome.

17. B: According to the Punnett square, the child has a 2 out of 4 chance of having A-type blood, since the dominant allele I^A is present in two of the four possible offspring. The type O blood allele is masked by the type A blood allele since it is recessive. Note that had the A-type individual been homozygous for IA, the chance of A-type offspring would instead be 100%.

	I^A	i
i	$I^A i$	ii
i	$I^A i$	ii

18. D: A nucleotide is a five-carbon sugar with a phosphate group and a nitrogenous base (adenine, guanine, cytosine, and thymine). DNA is a double helix and looks like a spiral ladder. Each side has a sugar/phosphate backbone, and the rungs of the ladder that connect the sides are the nitrogenous bases. Adenine always pairs with thymine via two hydrogen bonds, and cytosine always pairs with guanine via three hydrogen bonds. The weak hydrogen bonds are important because they allow DNA to easily be opened for replication and transcription.

19. C: DNA contains chemical bases that form chemical bonds with each other. The four bases in DNA are adenine, cytosine, thymine, and guanine. Uracil is a chemical base found in RNA, not DNA, so Choice *C* is the correct answer.

20. C: Endergonic reactions absorb free energy from their surroundings. Answer Choices *A*, *B*, and *D* are all qualities of exergonic reactions.

21. D: All respiration starts with glycolysis in the cytoplasm, and in the presence of oxygen, the process will continue to the mitochondria. In a series of oxidation/reduction reactions, primarily glucose will be broken down so that the energy contained within its bonds can be transferred to the smaller ATP molecules. It's like having a $100 bill (glucose) as opposed to having 100 $1 bills. This is beneficial to the organism because it allows energy to be distributed throughout the cell very easily in smaller packets of energy.

When glucose is broken down, its electrons and hydrogen atoms are involved in oxidative phosphorylation in order to make ATP, while its carbon and oxygen atoms are released as carbon dioxide. Anaerobic respiration does not occur frequently in humans, but during rigorous exercise, lack of available oxygen in the muscles can lead to anaerobic ATP production in a process called lactic acid fermentation. Alcohol fermentation, which occurs in yeast, is another type of anaerobic respiration. Anaerobic respiration is extremely less efficient than aerobic respiration, as it has a net yield of 2 ATP, while aerobic respiration's net yield exceeds 30 ATP.

22. C: Endergonic reactions are nonspontaneous, meaning that they need a positive standard change in free energy to occur. Exergonic reactions are the opposite of endergonic. They are spontaneous reactions that require no energy input to occur and result in energy flowing from the system into the surrounding environment. Combustion reactions are specific chemical reactions where an oxidant and a fuel release heat and result in water and carbon dioxide. Oxidation-reduction reactions, also known as redox reactions, involve the transfer of electrons from one molecule to another. Redox reactions result in one molecule being oxidized while the other is reduced.

23. C: In the Linnaean system, organisms are classified as follows, moving from few and general similarities to comprehensive and specific similarities: domain, kingdom, phylum, class, order, family, genus, and species. A popular mnemonic device to remember the Linnaean system is "Dear King Philip Came Over For Good Soup."

24. A: Choice *B* is true because steroid hormones are lipid based. Long-term energy is one of the most important functions of lipids, so *C* is true. *D* is also true because the cell membrane is not only composed of a lipid bilayer, but it also has cholesterol (another lipid) embedded within it to regulate membrane fluidity.

25. D: Ribosomes are the structures responsible for protein synthesis using amino acids delivered by tRNA molecules. They are numerous within the cell and can take up as much as 25% of the cell. Ribosomes are found free-floating in the cytoplasm and also attached to the rough endoplasmic reticulum, which resides alongside the nucleus. Ribosomes translate messenger RNA into chains of amino acids that become proteins. Ribosomes themselves are made of protein as well as rRNA. Choice *B* might be an attractive choice, since the Golgi is the site of protein maturation; however, it is not where proteins are synthesized. Choice *A* might be an attractive choice as well because DNA provides the instructions for proteins to be made, but DNA does not make the protein itself.

26. D: The color reagent is attached to the secondary antibody. It is released only when the secondary antibody attaches to the activated primary antibody. The antigen, primary antibody, and capture antibody, Choices *A, B,* and *C,* do not have any color reagent attached to them, so only the secondary antibody can cause the color reaction.

27. B: The color reagent is attached to the secondary antibody. If more antigen is present, more primary and secondary antibody will be attached to it and more color reagent will be released. Row 1 has the greatest depth of dark-colored antigen of all the samples tested in the plate in Figure 2.

28. C: Looking at the graph in Figure 3, the highest amount of IL-1β is found in the spleen. IL-1β is a marker of inflammation and indicates that the spleen had the most inflammation of the areas tested. Serum, Choice *A,* had no IL-1β in the sample. Plasma, Choice *B,* had the second highest amount of IL-1β in the sample, and bone marrow, Choice *D,* had the second lowest amount of IL-1β.

29. B: Looking at the diagram in Figure 1, the antigen is located between the capture antibody and the primary antibody (labeled as the detection antibody). The capture antibody keeps the antigen attached to the surface of the plate. The primary antibody recognizes the specific antigen. The secondary antibody generally recognizes the primary antibody is not specific to the antigen.

30. A: ELISAs are used to analyze specific substances within a larger sample. The antibodies used in an ELISA are designed specifically for a particular antigen. Sandwich ELISAs are generally used to quantify one antigen and not all substances in a larger sample, making Choice *B* incorrect. When used to quantify an antigen, the antibodies need to already be developed and able to detect the antigen, making Choice *D* incorrect.

Chemistry

1. A: Review the following conversion:

$$°F = \frac{9}{5}(°C) + 32$$

$$°F = \frac{9}{5}(45) + 32$$

$$°F = 113\ °F$$

Choices *B*, *C*, and *D* all incorporate a mistake in the order of operations necessary for converting degrees Celsius to degrees Fahrenheit: divide by 5, multiply by 9, and then add 32.

2. A: The neutrons and protons make up the nucleus of the atom. The nucleus is positively charged due to the presence of the protons. The negatively charged electrons are attracted to the positively charged nucleus by the electrostatic or Coulomb force; however, the electrons are not contained in the nucleus. The positively charged protons create the positive charge in the nucleus, and the neutrons are electrically neutral, so they have no effect. Radioactivity does not directly have a bearing on the charge of the nucleus.

3. B: The conversion from Celsius to Fahrenheit is:

$$°F = \frac{9}{5}(°C) + 32$$

Substituting the value for °C gives $°F = \frac{9}{5}(35) + 32$ which yields 95 °F. The other choices do not apply the formula correctly and completely.

4. B: Choices *A* and *D* both suggest a different number of protons, which would make a different element. It would no longer be a sodium atom if the proton number or atomic number were different, so those are both incorrect. An atom that has a different number of electrons is called an ion, so Choice *C* is incorrect as well.

5. B: If nonmetals form ionic bonds, they will fill their electron orbital (and become an anion) rather than lose electrons (and become a cation), due to their smaller atomic radius and higher electronegativity than metals. Choice *A* is, therefore, incorrect. There are some nonmetals that are diatomic (hydrogen, oxygen, nitrogen, and halogens), but that is not applied for all of them; thus, Choice *D* is incorrect. Organic compounds are carbon-based due to carbon's ability to form four covalent bonds. In addition to carbon, organic compounds are also rich in hydrogen, phosphorus, nitrogen, oxygen, and sulfur, so Choice *C* is incorrect as well.

6. B: The basic unit of matter is the atom. Each element is identified by a letter symbol for that element and an atomic number, which indicates the number of protons in that element. Atoms are the building block of each element and are comprised of a nucleus that contains protons (positive charge) and neutrons (no charge). Orbiting around the nucleus at varying distances are negatively charged electrons. An electrically neutral atom contains equal numbers of protons and electrons. Atomic mass is the combined mass of protons and neutrons in the nucleus. Electrons have such negligible mass that they are not considered in the atomic mass. Although the nucleus is compact, the electrons orbit in energy levels at great relative distances to it, making an atom mostly empty space.

7. A: Nuclear reactions involve the nucleus, and chemical reactions involve electron behavior alone. If electrons are transferred between atoms, they form ionic bonds. If they are shared between atoms, they form covalent bonds. Unequal sharing within a covalent bond results in intermolecular attractions, including hydrogen bonding. Metallic bonding involves a "sea of electrons," where they float around non-specifically, resulting in metal ductility and malleability, due to their glue-like effect of sticking neighboring atoms together. Their metallic bonding also contributes to electrical conductivity and low specific heats, due to electrons' quick response to charge and heat, given to their mobility. Their floating also results in metals' property of luster as light reflects off the mobile electrons. Electron movement in any type of bond is enhanced by photon and heat energy investments, increasing their likelihood to jump energy levels. Valence electron status is the ultimate contributor to electron behavior as it determines their likelihood to be transferred or shared.

8. A: Electrons give atoms their negative charge. Electron behavior determines their bonding, and bonding can either be covalent (electrons are shared) or ionic (electrons are transferred). The charge of an atom is determined by the electrons in its orbitals. Electrons give atoms their chemical and electromagnetic properties. Unequal numbers of protons and electrons lend either a positive or negative charge to the atom. Ions are atoms with a charge, either positive or negative.

9. B: On the periodic table, the elements are grouped in columns according to the configuration of electrons in their outer orbitals. The groupings on the periodic table give a broad view of trends in chemical properties for the elements. The outer electron shell (or orbital) is most important in determining the chemical properties of the element. The electrons in this orbital determine charge and bonding compatibility. The number of electron shells increases by row from top to bottom. The periodic table is organized with elements that have similar chemical behavior in the columns (groups or families).

10. B: In chemical equations, the reactants are on the left side of the arrow. The direction of the reaction is in the direction of the arrow, although sometimes reactions will be shown with arrows in both directions, meaning the reaction is reversible. The reactants are on the left, and the products of the reaction are on the right side of the arrow. Chemical equations indicate atomic and molecular bond formations, rearrangements, and dissolutions. The numbers in front of the elements are called coefficients, and they designate the number of moles of that element accounted for in the reaction. The subscript numbers tell how many atoms of that element are in the molecule, with the number "1" being understood. In H_2O, for example, there are two atoms of hydrogen bound to one atom of oxygen. The ionic charge of the element is shown in superscripts and can be either positive or negative.

11. B: The law of conservation of mass states that matter cannot be created or destroyed, but that it can change forms. This is important in balancing chemical equations on both sides of the arrow. Unbalanced equations will have an unequal number of atoms of each element on either side of the equation and violate the law.

12. D: Solids all increase solubility with Choices *A*, *B*, and *C*. Powdered hot chocolate is an example to consider. Heating, Choice *A*, and stirring, Choice *B*, make it dissolve faster. Regarding Choice *C*, powder is in chunks that collectively result in a very large surface area, as opposed to a chocolate bar that has a very small relative surface area. The small surface area to volume ratio dramatically increases solubility. Decreasing the solvent (most of the time, water) will decrease solubility.

13. A: The quantity of a solute in a solution can be calculated by multiplying the molarity of the solution by the volume. The equivalence point is the point at which an unknown solute has completely reacted with a known solute concentration. The limiting reactant is the reactant completely consumed by a reaction. The theoretical yield is the quantity of product produced by a reaction.

14. A: When salt is added to water, it increases its boiling point. This is an example of a colligative property, which is any property that changes the physical property of a substance. This particular colligative property of boiling point elevation occurs because the extra solute dissolved in water reduces the surface area of the water, impeding it from vaporizing. If heat is applied, though, it gives water particles enough kinetic energy to vaporize. This additional heat results in an increased boiling point. Other colligative properties of solutions include the following: their melting points decrease with the addition of solute, and their osmotic pressure increases (because it creates a concentration gradient that was otherwise not there).

15. C: Pressure has little effect on the solubility of a liquid solution because liquid is not easily compressible; therefore, increased pressure won't result in increased kinetic energy. Pressure increases solubility in gaseous solutions, since it causes them to move faster.

16. B: Nonpolar molecules have hydrophobic regions that do not dissolve in water. Oils are nonpolar molecules that repel water. Polar molecules combine readily with water, which is, itself, a polar solvent. Polar molecules are hydrophilic or "water-loving" because their polar regions have intermolecular bonding with water via hydrogen bonds. Some structures and molecules are both polar and nonpolar, like the phospholipid bilayer. The phospholipid bilayer has polar heads that are the external "water-loving portions" and hydrophobic tails that are immiscible in water. Polar solvents dissolve polar solutes, and nonpolar solvents dissolve nonpolar solutes. One way to remember these is "Like dissolves like."

17. A: A catalyst increases the rate of a chemical reaction by lowering the activation energy. Enzymes are biological protein catalysts that are utilized by organisms to facilitate anabolic and catabolic reactions. They speed up the rate of reaction by making the reaction easier (perhaps by orienting a molecule more favorably upon induced fit, for example). Catalysts are not used up by the reaction and can be used over and over again.

18. C: Proteins are made up of chains of amino acids. Lipids are usually nonpolar, hydrophobic molecules. Nucleic acids are made of nucleotides. Carbohydrates are ring-like molecules built using carbon, oxygen, and hydrogen.

19. C: These are the coefficients that follow the law of conservation of matter. The coefficient times the subscript of each element should be the same on both sides of the equation.

20. A: Ionic bonding is the result of electrons transferred between atoms. When an atom loses one or more electrons, a cation, or positively-charged ion, is formed. An anion, or negatively-charged ion, is formed when an atom gains one or more electrons. Ionic bonds are formed from the attraction between a positively-charged cation and a negatively-charged anion. The bond between sodium and chlorine in table salt, or sodium chloride ($NaCl$), is an example of an ionic bond.

21. A: Oxidation is when a substance loses electrons in a chemical reaction, and reduction is when a substance gains electrons. Any element by itself has a charge of 0, as iron and oxygen do on the reactant side. In the ionic compound formed, iron has a +3 charge, and oxygen has a -2 charge. Because iron had a zero charge that then changed to +3, it means that it lost three electrons and was oxidized. Oxygen that gained two electrons was reduced.

22. C: Fission occurs when heavy nuclei are split, and it is currently an energy source that fuels power plants. Fusion, on the other hand, is the combining of small nuclei and produces far more energy, and it is the nuclear reaction that powers stars like the sun. Harnessing the extreme energy released by fusion has proven impossible so far, which is unfortunate since its waste products are not radioactive, while waste produced by fission typically is.

23. A: Alpha decay involves a helium particle emission (with two neutrons). Beta decay involves emission of an electron or positron, and gamma is just high-energy light emissions.

24. B: Choice *A* is false because it is possible to have a very strong acid with a pH between 0 and 1. *C* is false because the pH scale is from 0 to 14, and -2 is outside the boundaries. *D* is false because a solution with a pH of 2 has ten times fewer hydronium ions than a pH of 1 solution.

25. C: Gamma is the lightest radioactive decay with the most energy, and this high energy is toxic to cells. Due to its weightlessness, gamma rays are extremely penetrating. Alpha particles are heavy and can be easily shielded by skin.

Beta particles are electrons and can penetrate more than an alpha particle because they are lighter. Beta particles can be shielded by plastic.

26. D: The equivalence point occurs when just enough of the unknown solution is added to completely neutralize the known solution. The equivalence point in Figure 1 is at the halfway point of the curve, when 25 volumes of NaOH have been applied to the solution. The pH is 7 at this point, which is a neutralization of the strong acid, HCl.

27. C: The acid dissociation constant is the pK_a of the solution. It is found at the halfway point between the beginning of the curve and the equivalence point, where the solution would have a pH of 7 and be completely neutralized. In Figure 3, it is marked as 4.76.

28. A: Looking at Figure 3, the vertical axis on the left side has information about the pH of the solution. The horizontal axis at the bottom has information about how much basic solution containing OH^- is being added to the acetic acid. When the OH^- is at 0, and none has been added yet, the pH of the acetic acid is marked as 2.

29. B: Looking at the chemical equation in Figure 2, the reactants are on the left side and the products are on the right side. HCl and NaOH, Choices *A* and *C,* are the reactants of the equation. NaCl is the salt that is formed as one of the products of the reaction. The chloride ion, Choice *D,* is not formed in this reaction.

30. A: The equivalence point occurs in all titration reactions when the solution is neutralized. If an acid and base are being titrated and reach the equivalence point, the solution is no longer acidic or basic, Choices *B* and *C*. It reaches a pH of 7 and is considered neutral.

Anatomy and Physiology

1. D: Veins have valves, but arteries do not. Valves in veins are designed to prevent backflow since they are the furthest blood vessels from the pumping action of the heart and steadily increase in volume (which decreases the available pressure). Capillaries diffuse nutrients properly because of their thin walls and high surface area and are not particularly dependent on positive pressure.

2. **D:** Mechanical digestion is physical digestion of food and tearing it into smaller pieces using force. This occurs in the stomach and mouth. Chemical digestion involves chemically changing the food and breaking it down into small organic compounds that can be utilized by the cell to build molecules. The salivary glands in the mouth secrete amylase that breaks down starch, which begins chemical digestion. The stomach contains enzymes such as pepsinogen/pepsin and gastric lipase which chemically digest protein and fats, respectively. The small intestine continues to digest protein using the enzymes trypsin and chymotrypsin. It also digests fats with the help of bile from the liver and lipase from the pancreas. These organs act as exocrine glands because they secrete substances through a duct. Carbohydrates are digested in the small intestine with the help of pancreatic amylase, gut bacterial flora and fauna, and brush border enzymes like lactose. Brush border enzymes are contained in the towel-like microvilli in the small intestine that soak up nutrients.

3. D: The urinary system has many functions, the primary of which is removing waste products and balancing water and electrolyte concentrations in the blood. It also plays a key role in regulating ion concentrations, such as sodium, potassium, chloride, and calcium, in the filtrate. The urinary system helps maintain blood pH by reabsorbing or secreting hydrogen ions and bicarbonate as necessary. Certain kidney cells can detect reductions in blood volume and pressure and then can secrete renin to activate a hormone that causes increased reabsorption of sodium ions and water. This serves to raise blood volume and pressure. Kidney cells secrete erythropoietin under hypoxic conditions to stimulate red blood cell production. They also synthesize calcitriol, a hormone derivative of vitamin D3, which aids in calcium ion absorption by the intestinal epithelium.

4. C: The blood leaves the right ventricle through a semi-lunar valve and goes through the pulmonary artery to the lungs. Any increase in pressure in the artery will eventually affect the contractibility of the right ventricle. Blood enters the right atrium from the superior and inferior venae cavae veins, and blood leaves the right atrium through the tricuspid valve to the right ventricle. Blood enters the left atrium from the pulmonary veins carrying oxygenated blood from the lungs. Blood flows from the left atrium to the left ventricle through the mitral valve and leaves the left ventricle through a semi-lunar valve to enter the aorta.

5. D: Sodium bicarbonate, a very effective base, functions chiefly to increase the pH of the chyme. Chyme leaving the stomach has a very low pH due to the high amounts of acid that are used to digest and break down food. If this is not neutralized, the walls of the small intestine will be damaged and may form ulcers. Sodium bicarbonate is produced by the pancreas and released in response to pyloric stimulation so that it can neutralize the acid. It has little to no digestive effect.

6. D: A reflex arc is a simple nerve pathway involving a stimulus, a synapse, and a response that is controlled by the spinal cord—not the brain. The knee-jerk reflex is an example of a reflex arc. The stimulus is the hammer hitting the tendon, reaching the synapse in the spinal cord by an afferent pathway. The response is the resulting muscle contraction reaching the muscle by an efferent pathway. None of the remaining processes is a simple reflex. Memories are processed and stored in the hippocampus in the limbic system. The visual center is located in the occipital lobe, while auditory processing occurs in the temporal lobe. The sympathetic and parasympathetic divisions of the autonomic nervous system control heart rate and blood pressure.

7. B: Ligaments connect bone to bone. Tendons connect muscle to bone. Both are made of dense, fibrous connective tissue (primarily Type 1 collagen) to give strength. However, tendons are more organized, especially in the long axis direction like muscle fibers themselves, and they have more collagen. This arrangement makes more sense because muscles have specific orientations of their fibers, so they contract in somewhat predictable directions. Ligaments are less organized and have more of a woven pattern because bone connections are not as organized as bundles of muscle fibers, so ligaments must have strength in multiple directions to protect against injury.

8. A: The three primary body planes are coronal, sagittal, and transverse. The coronal or frontal plane, named for the plane in which a corona or halo might appear in old paintings, divides the body vertically into front and back sections. The sagittal plane, named for the path an arrow might take when shot at the body, divides the body vertically into right and left sections. The transverse plane divides the body horizontally into upper or superior and lower or inferior sections. There is no medial plane, per se. The anatomical direction medial simply references a location close or closer to the center of the body than another location.

9. C: Although the lungs may provide some cushioning for the heart when the body is violently struck, this is not a major function of the respiratory system. Its most notable function is that of gas exchange for oxygen and carbon dioxide, but it also plays a vital role in the regulation of blood pH. The aqueous form of carbon dioxide, carbonic acid, is a major pH buffer of the blood, and the respiratory system directly controls how much carbon dioxide stays and is released from the blood through respiration. The respiratory system also enables vocalization and forms the basis for the mode of speech and language used by most humans.

10. A: The forebrain contains the cerebrum, the thalamus, the hypothalamus, and the limbic system. The limbic system is chiefly responsible for the perception of emotions through the amygdala, while the cerebrum interprets sensory input and generates movement. Specifically, the occipital lobe receives visual input, and the primary motor cortex in the frontal lobe is the controller of voluntary movement. The hindbrain, specifically the medulla oblongata and brain stem, control and regulate blood pressure and heart rate.

11. C: Nephrons are responsible for filtering blood. When functioning properly they allow blood cells and nutrients to go back into the bloodstream while sending waste to the bladder. However, nephrons can fail at doing this, particularly when blood flood to the kidneys is limited. The medulla (also called the renal medulla) (*A*) and the renal cortex (*D*) are both parts of the kidney but are not specifically responsible for filtering blood. The medulla is in the inner part of the kidney and contains the nephrons. The renal cortex is the outer part of the kidney. The heart (*B*) is responsible for pumping blood throughout the body rather than filtering it.

12. B: Ossification is the process by which cartilage, a soft, flexible substance is replaced by bone throughout the body. All humans regardless of age have cartilage, but cartilage in some areas is replaced by bones as a person grows.

13. D: The seminiferous tubules are responsible for sperm production. Had *testicles* been an answer choice, it would also have been correct since it houses the seminiferous tubules. The prostate gland (*A*) secretes enzymes that help nourish sperm after creation. The seminal vesicles (*B*) secrete some of the components of semen. The scrotum (*C*) is the pouch holding the testicles.

14. C: The parasympathetic nervous system is related to calm, peaceful times without stress that require no immediate decisions. It relaxes the fight-or-flight response, slows heart rate to a comfortable pace, and decreases bronchiole dilation to a normal size. On the other hand, the sympathetic nervous system is in charge of the fight-or-flight response and works to increase blood pressure and oxygen absorption.

15. C: The parathyroid gland impacts calcium levels by secreting parathyroid hormone (PTH). The osteoid gland is not a real gland. The pineal gland regulates sleep by secreting melatonin, and the thymus gland focuses on immunity. *Thyroid* would also be a correct answer choice as it influences the levels of circulating calcium.

16. D: Bone matrix is an intricate lattice of collagen fibers and mineral salts, particularly calcium and phosphorus. The mineral salts are strong but brittle, and the collagen fibers are weak but flexible, so the combination of the two makes bone resistant to shattering and able to withstand the normal forces applied to it.

17. D: Veins carry oxygen-poor blood back to the heart. Intestines carry digested food through the body. Bronchioles are passageways that carry air from the nose and mouth to the lungs.

18. C: The somatic nervous system is the voluntary nervous system, which is responsible for voluntary movement. It includes nerves that transmit signals from the brain to the muscles of the body. Breathing is controlled by the autonomic nervous system. Thought and fear are complex processes that occur in the brain, which is part of the central nervous system.

19. A: Platelets are the blood components responsible for clotting. There are between 150,000 and 450,000 platelets in healthy blood. When a clot forms, platelets adhere to the injured area of the vessel and promote a molecular cascade that results in adherence of more platelets. Ultimately, the platelet aggregation results in recruitment of a protein called fibrin, which adds structure to the clot. Too many platelets can cause clotting disorders. Too few platelets leads to bleeding disorders.

20. C: The sinuses function to warm, filter, and humidify air that is inhaled. Choice *A* is incorrect because mucus traps airborne pathogens. Choice *B* is incorrect because the epiglottis is the structure in the pharynx that covers the trachea during swallowing to prevent food from entering it. Lastly, Choice *D,* sweeping away pathogens and directing them toward the top of the trachea, is the function of cilia. Respiratory structures, such as the nasal passages and trachea, are lined with mucus and cilia.

21. D: In mechanical processing, the teeth tear up large chunks of food into smaller pieces. In secretion, Choice *A,* buffers, enzymes, and acids are secreted to help break complex molecules into simpler ones. In absorption, Choice

B, nutrients are absorbed through the digestive epithelium. In excretion, Choice *C,* waste products are removed from the body.

22. C: A cluster of capillaries that functions as the main filter of the blood entering the kidney is known as the glomerulus, so Choice *C* is correct. The Bowman's capsule surrounds the glomerulus and receives fluid and solutes from it; therefore, Choice *A* is incorrect. The loop of Henle is a part of the kidney tubule where water and nutrients are reabsorbed, so *B* is false. The nephron is the unit containing all of these anatomical features, making Choice *D* incorrect as well.

23. C: The alveoli are small sac-shaped structures at the end of the bronchioles where gas exchange takes place. The bronchioles are tubes through which air travels. The kidneys and medulla oblongata do not directly affect oxygen and carbon dioxide exchange.

24. C: The uterus and ovaries aren't part of the birth canal, so Choices *A* and *D* are false. The cervix is the uppermost portion of the birth canal, so Choice *B* is incorrect, making Choice *C* the correct answer. The vagina is the muscular tube on the lowermost portion of the birth canal that connects the exterior environment to the cervix.

25. C: The pancreas functions as an exocrine gland because it secretes enzymes that break down food components. It also functions as an endocrine gland because it secretes hormones that regulate blood sugar levels. The kidney isn't a gland; it is an organ located directly below the adrenal glands. The stomach is an organ that contains exocrine glands that secrete hydrochloric acid. Like the kidney and the stomach, the spleen is an organ, not a gland. Therefore, the only correct answer is *C.*

26. D: In the secondary immune response, suppressor T lymphocytes are activated to negate the potential risk of damage to healthy cells brought on by an unchecked, overactive immune response. Choice *A* is incorrect because this activity is characteristic of the primary response, not the secondary response. Choice *B* is incorrect because humoral immunity is mediated by antibodies produced by B, not T, lymphocytes. Choice *C* is wrong because the secondary response is faster than the primary response because the primary response entails the time-consuming process of macrophage activation.

27. D: Massive urine production, or polyuria, is the result of a hyperglycemic state in the body and a hallmark sign of any diabetic condition. Urine is not concentrated, but rather diluted. Sodium, potassium, and other electrolyte imbalances may occur as a result of polyuria but are not a direct effect of hyperglycemia.

28. B: Basophils are the white blood cells that secrete histamine, the substance that causes itching in allergic reactions. Lymphocytes are responsible for antibody creation. Neutrophils take out bacterial and fungal organisms and are quite numerous. Monocytes assist in breaking down bacterial organisms.

29. B: The ventricles of the brain are responsible for the production of cerebrospinal fluid. The pons are located at the end of the brain stem and are responsible for regulating breathing. The thalamus acts as a message exchange center for the cerebrum and limbic system and is located just above the brain stem. The corpus callosum is the fibrous tissue of white matter that connects the left and right brain.

30. A: Since electrolytes need to be suspended in a certain amount of liquid to move optimally and carry out their intended function, fluid level in the body is important. As fluid levels increase beyond a state of fluid-electrolyte balance, electrolyte levels will decrease, since there is too much fluid present. If fluid levels are too low, such as in a state of dehydration, there will be too many electrolytes per unit of fluid, which also prevents the electrolytes from carrying out their intended function.

Physics

1. A: This question focuses on the principles of potential and kinetic energy. The potential energy of the snowboarder is equal to the work that's required to lift them from the base of the mountain to their current position, while their kinetic energy is related to their mass and velocity. Standing still on top of the mountain, the snowboarder has no kinetic energy and the greatest amount of potential energy, making Choice *A* the correct answer. Choices *B*, *C*, and *D* are incorrect because the snowboarder at these points has less potential energy than in Choice *A*.

2. B: Acceleration is the rate of change in velocity. Speed is the rate at which an object moves, velocity is speed in a given direction, and momentum is the velocity of an object multiplied by its mass.

3. B: $\mathrm{E} = \mathrm{mc}^2$ is Einstein's theory of general relativity. It is not one of Newton's original three laws of motion. Newton's three laws describe how a force is defined as how much a mass is accelerated, how an object resists changes in inertia, and how all forces act with an equal and opposite reaction.

4. C: Centripetal force is the actual force recognized in a rotational situation. The reactive force acting opposite of the centripetal force is named the centrifugal force, but it is not an actual force on its own. A common mistake is to interchange the two terms. The real force acting in a rotational situation is pulling in toward the axis of rotation and is called the centripetal force. Gravity technically only acts between all mass, so it is not specific enough for the question.

5. B: Kinetic energy is energy an object has while moving; potential energy is energy an object has based on its position or height. Electric and electromagnetic energies are other descriptions of generally potential energy contained in waves or fields, but neither has anything directly to do with movement.

6. B: Waves are periodic disturbances in a gas, liquid, or solid as energy is transmitted. Waves don't carry or slow down matter but instead transfer energy.

7. A: The definition of refraction is when a wave bends (such as when the medium it is traveling through changes). Diffraction is when a wave bends around an object (such as when the medium it is traveling through runs into a barrier), so it is too specific an answer for the question. Reflection is when a wave bounces off a surface without losing energy or becoming distorted, and convection is the thermal energy transferred through gases and liquids by convection currents.

8. A: An object moving in a circular motion also has momentum; it is called *angular momentum* and it is determined by the amount of rotational inertia, rotational velocity, and the distance of the mass from the axis of rotation. Objects exhibiting circular motion also demonstrate the conservation of angular momentum. This means that the angular momentum of a system is always constant, regardless of the placement of the mass. Rotational inertia can be affected by the distance of the mass of the object from the center of rotation (axis of rotation). The farther the mass is from the center of rotation, the slower the rotational velocity. While mechanical energy, matter, and mass are all conserved, Choices *B*, *C*, and *D*, none of them deal directly with circular motion, so they would not apply to the question.

9. C: Electricity moves from objects with greater potential energy to objects with less potential energy. Similar to how warm air spreads towards colder environments or how gasses and liquids move from areas of high concentration to areas of low concentration, electric currents are generated by the electric field moving electrons from areas of high voltage potential to areas of low voltage potential.

10. A: The recurring theme in electricity and magnetism is that like, similar, or identical charges repel one another (whether it is two negative charges or two positive charges) while unlike, dissimilar, or different charges attract one another. This is exemplified by Coulomb's law, which states that charges of the same sign produce a positive force (which repels the particles) and that charges of opposite signs produce a negative force (which attracts the particles).

11. B: This is a simple calculation:

$$9.81 \text{ m/s}^2 \times 150 \text{ kg} \times 1.5 \text{ m} = 3 \text{ m} \times F$$

$$F = \frac{2{,}207.25 \text{ N} \cdot \text{m}}{3 \text{ m}} = 735.75 \text{ N}$$

12. D: Use the equation $F = L \times \frac{r}{R}$, where F is the force exerted, L is the load, r is the radius of the axle, and R is the radius of the wheel. Note that for an axle with a given, set radius, the larger the radius of the wheel, the greater the mechanical advantage:

$$F = 600 \text{ N} \times \frac{20 \text{ mm}}{300 \text{ mm}} = 40 \text{ N}$$

13. D: The driver gear is turning clockwise, and the gear meshed with it turns counter to it. Because of the 2 :1 gear ratio, every revolution of the driver gear causes half a revolution of the follower. Therefore, Gear B turns 30 RPM counterclockwise.

14. B: While meshed gears rotate in different directions, wheels linked by a belt turn in the same direction. This is applied unless the belt is twisted, in which case they rotate in opposite directions. So, the twisted link between the upper two wheels causes the right-hand wheel to turn counterclockwise, and the bigger wheel at the bottom also rotates counterclockwise. Since it's twice as large as the upper wheel, it rotates with half the RPMs. So, the bottom wheel rotates at 30 RPM counterclockwise.

15. C: In case (a), the fixed wheels only serve to change direction. They offer no mechanical advantage because the lever arm on each side of the axle is the same. Therefore, $F_1 = 1{,}000N$. In case (b), the lower moveable block provides a $2:1$ mechanical advantage. A quick method for calculating the mechanical advantage is to count the number of lines supporting the moving block (there are two in this question). Therefore, $F_2 = 500\ N$. Note that there are no moving blocks in case (a).

16. C: In any system, the total mechanical energy is the sum of the potential energy and the kinetic energy. Either value could be zero, but it still must be included in the total. Choices *A* and *B* only give the total potential or kinetic energy, respectively.

17. D: The decibel scale is a ratio of a particular sound's intensity to a standard value. It is a logarithmic scale; in other words, as decibels increase linearly, sound intensity goes up by factors of 10. Choice *A* is an effect experienced by an observer who is moving relative to the source of a wave; Choice *B* is a particle in an atom; Choice *C* is a unit for measuring power.

18. D: Polarization changes the oscillations of a wave and can alter the appearance in light waves. For example, polarized sunglasses remove the "glare" from sunlight by altering the oscillation pattern observed by the wearer. Choice *A,* reflection, is the bouncing back of a wave, such as in a mirror; Choice *B* is the bending of a wave as it travels from one medium to another, such as going from air to water; and Choice *C,* dispersion, is the spreading of a wave through a barrier or a prism.

19. A: In an elastic collision, the objects collide and then travel in different directions; in an inelastic collision, the objects collide and then stick together in their final direction of travel. Both types of collisions adhere to the principle of the conservation of linear momentum. As such, the total momentum for the objects in either an elastic or inelastic collision will be the same before and after a collision.

20. D: The mechanical advantage is calculated by comparing the force input by the user to the simple machine with the force output from the use of the machine. This calculation is performed through a ratio:

$$\text{Mechanical Advantage} = \frac{\text{output force}}{\text{input force}}$$

$$MA = \frac{F_{\text{out}}}{F_{\text{in}}}$$

Choice *A,* the force input divided by the force output, is the reciprocal of the mechanical advantage. Choice *B* is an incorrect equation and would result in a force, not a ratio. Choice *C* is not used for any calculation.

21. D: In physics, uniform circular motion refers to a specific type of motion in which an object travels around a circular path at a constant speed. Although speed remains constant, the linear velocity of an object held in uniform constant motion is constantly changing, since the direction that object is travelling changes as the object travels along the circular path. Therefore, the correct answer is Choice *D.*

22. C: Using the provided kinematic equation, the impulse experienced by the barbell is equal to the product of the force applied and elapsed time for which that force is applied. Therefore, $\Delta p = (5{,}000\ N)(3\ s) = 15{,}000\ N \cdot s$. Therefore, the correct answer is Choice *C.* All other choices incorrectly use the numbers provided to calculate impulse. Choice *A* would be the answer for if impulse was found by dividing elapsed time by force applied. Choice *B* is the result of dividing the force applied by the time elapsed rather than multiplying them together, and Choice *D* is the result of dividing the force applied by the square of the time elapsed.

23. B: In nuclear physics, binding energy is what holds a nucleus together. Einstein's famous mass-energy equivalence equation ($E = mc^2$) can be used to calculate the binding energy of a particular nucleus. Specifically, the binding energy is equal to the product of the square of the speed of light and a quantity known as the mass defect of the nucleus. The equation is commonly rewritten as $\Delta E = \Delta mc^2$. The mass defect of a nucleus is the difference between the mass of the nucleus itself and the sum of the masses of all its constituent elements (i.e., protons and neutrons). Therefore, the correct answer is Choice *C.*

24. B: In physics, the wavelength of a sound wave is the spatial distance between adjacent identical parts of the wave and can be calculated using the provided kinematic equation v=λf, where v is the velocity of the soundwave, λ is the wavelength, and f is the frequency (which can be understood as the number of times in a second a sound wave repeats itself). Using the information given in the question, the wavelength of the bird's call is $\lambda = \frac{v}{f} = \frac{300\frac{m}{s}}{50} s^{-1} = 6\ m$. Therefore, the correct answer is Choice *B.* None of the other choices use the equation provided to correctly solve for wavelength.

25. C: Kinetic energy refers to the energy a body possesses when in motion. Kinetic energy is commonly contrasted with potential energy, which is the energy a body possesses due to its physical position and other factors. Kinetic energy, commonly measured in joules (J), can be calculated using the provided kinematic equation. Filling in the information provided in the question, the kinetic energy of the Olympic sprinter at their maximum speed is $K = \frac{1}{2}(75\ kg)\left(12\frac{m}{s}\right)^2 = 5{,}400\ J$. Therefore, the correct answer is Choice *C.* All other answer choices do not use the information provided to accurately calculate the kinetic energy of the sprint. Choice *A* provides the product of the sprinter's weight, their maximum speed, and one-half, but neglects to square the velocity. Choice *B* provides the product of the sprinter's weight and their maximum speed, but neglects to multiple that product by one-half or to square the velocity first. Choice *D* provides the product of the sprinter's weight and the square of their maximum velocity but fails to further multiply that product by one-half.

26. B: In the stated scenario, the quarterback is looking to maximize the distance he can throw a projectile—in his case, a football. The kinematic equation for range of a projectile launched on flat ground (range here meaning the horizontal distance travelled) is $R = \frac{v^2}{g} \sin(2\theta)$, where R is the range, v is the velocity at which the projectile is launched, g is acceleration due to gravity, and θ is the angle at which the projectile is launched. Using this equation, it's clear that range is greatest where the $\sin(2\theta)$ part of the equation is greatest. Since $\sin$ is at its maximum at $90°$, a projectile's range is maximized when the launch angle is half of $90°$. Therefore, the correct answer is Choice *B.* All other choices result in suboptimal projectile ranges.

27. B: The gravitational force between any two bodies can be calculated using Newton's law of universal gravitation, which can be best understood using the equation $F = \frac{G(m_1 m_2)}{r^2}$. Using such an equation requires four measurements: m_1, which is equal to the mass of one of the bodies; m_2, which is equal to the mass of the other object; r, which is equal to the distance between the center of masses for the two bodies; and G, which is a number known as the gravitational constant. Therefore, the correct answer is Choice *B,* as all other choices are required to calculate the gravitational force between the moon and the sun.

28. B: The electrostatic force present between charged objects can be calculated using Coulomb's Law, which can be written as an equation in the form of $F = \frac{k(q_1 q_2)}{r^2}$. Like many scientific laws about physical properties, Coulomb's Law follows what is known as the inverse-square law. The inverse square law states that the magnitude of a physical quantity is inversely related to the square of the distance from that physical quantity. Therefore, not only does the electrostatic force between two separating charged bodies decrease, but it does so at an exponentially increasing rate. Therefore, the correct answer is Choice *B.* The other choices do not accurately reflect Coulomb's law or the basic nature of the inverse-square law.

29. D: Snell's law, which can be represented using the equation $n_1 \sin(\theta_1) = n_2 \sin(\theta_2)$, is used to describe the relationship between angles of incidence and refraction, which occur when light passes through media such as water, glass, and air. Therefore, the correct answer is Choice *D.* All the other choices refer to pairs of concepts that either have different names for the formulas relating them or have no formulas that relate them directly.

30. B: In physics, centripetal acceleration refers to the acceleration of a body in uniform circular motion. It is equal to quotient of the square of the body's velocity and the radius of the circle in which they are travelling. Such a relationship can be described with the provided equation of $a_c = \frac{v^2}{r}$, and this equation can be used to solve for the velocity of the body as well. Using the information from the question, $\left(20\frac{m}{s^2}\right) = \frac{v^2}{5\,m}$, so $v^2 = (20\frac{m}{s^2})(5m) = 100\ m/s$ and $v = 10\ m/s$. Therefore, the correct answer is Choice *B.* All the other answer choices do not use the information provided to accurately calculate the velocity of the crash test dummy at the moment of maximum acceleration.

HESI A2 Practice Tests #3, #4, #5, and #6

To keep the size of this book manageable, save paper, and provide a digital test-taking experience, the 3rd, 4th, 5th, and 6th practice tests can be found online. Scan the QR code or go to this link to access them:

testprepbooks.com/bonus/hesi

SCAN ME

The first time you access the tests, you will need to register as a "new user" and verify your email address.

If you have any issues, please email support@testprepbooks.com.

Index

Dear HESI Admission Assessment Test Taker,

Thank you for purchasing this study guide for your HESI exam. We hope that we exceeded your expectations.

Our goal in creating this study guide was to cover all of the topics that you will see on the test. We also strove to make our practice questions as similar as possible to what you will encounter on test day. With that being said, if you found something that you feel was not up to your standards, please send us an email and let us know.

We would also like to let you know about other books in our catalog that may interest you.

ATI TEAS 7

This can be found on Amazon: amazon.com/dp/1637759886

NCLEX-RN

amazon.com/dp/B0CJ49HKSF

We have study guides in a wide variety of fields. If the one you are looking for isn't listed above, then try searching for it on Amazon or send us an email.

Thanks Again and Happy Testing!
Product Development Team
info@studyguideteam.com

FREE Test Taking Tips Video/DVD Offer

To better serve you, we created videos covering test taking tips that we want to give you for FREE. **These videos cover world-class tips that will help you succeed on your test.**

We just ask that you send us feedback about this product. Please let us know what you thought about it—whether good, bad, or indifferent.

To get your **FREE videos**, you can use the QR code below or email freevideos@studyguideteam.com with "Free Videos" in the subject line and the following information in the body of the email:

a. The title of your product

b. Your product rating on a scale of 1-5, with 5 being the highest

c. Your feedback about the product

If you have any questions or concerns, please don't hesitate to contact us at info@studyguideteam.com.

Thank you!

SCAN HERE

Printed in the USA
CPSIA information can be obtained
at www.ICGtesting.com
LVHW081911120724
785355LV00006B/643

9 781637 753965